SOCIAL SECURITY
and Its
Discontents

SOCIAL SECURITY and Its Discontents: Perspectives on CHOICE

◆

EDITED BY

MICHAEL D. TANNER

CATO INSTITUTE
Washington, D.C.

Library of Congress Cataloging-in-Publication Data

Social security and its discontents : perspectives on choice /
edited by Michael D. Tanner.
 p. cm.
Includes bibliographical references and index.
ISBN 1-930865-55-4 (cloth : alk. paper)
1. Social security—United States. 2. Social security—United
States—Finance. 3. Social security—United States—Forecasting.
4. Economic forecasting—United States. 5. United States—Economic
conditions—2001– 6. United States. Social Security Administration.
I. Tanner, Michael, 1956– II. Cato Institute. III. Title.

HD7125.S5956 2004
368.4'3'00973—dc22

2004045199

Cover design by Parker Wallman.

Printed in the United States of America.

CATO INSTITUTE
1000 Massachusetts Ave., N.W.
Washington, D.C. 20001
www.cato.org

Contents

Acknowledgments

No book of this scope could have been put together without the advice, support, and assistance of a great many people. I would like thank Ed Crane, president of the Cato Institute, who has been a driving force behind the idea of Social Security reform since the institute was founded, and José Piñera and William Shipman, co-chairs of Cato's Project on Social Security Choice, who have helped guide and nurture this project throughout its existence. Others deserving special thanks include David Boaz, Cato's executive vice president, and Susan Chamberlin, Cato's director of government affairs. Berna Brannon, a policy analyst with the project, and Helen Mitchell, my research assistant, provided invaluable assistance. Mitchell in particular deserves to be singled out for the long hours and important contribution she made to this book. It would not have been possible without her help. And finally, as always, I must thank my wife, Ellen, who never stops reminding me that public policy is not an abstraction but something that affects real people.

Introduction

Michael Tanner

Social Security is America's largest and most popular government program. But it is also a deeply troubled one. In just 15 years, Social Security will begin to run a deficit, spending more on benefits than it takes in through taxes. Overall, the program faces nearly $26 trillion in unfunded liabilities. Without massive tax increases or benefit cuts, it quite simply cannot pay the benefits that it has promised. At the same time, payroll taxes are already so high that younger workers face a declining and below-market return on the taxes they pay.

This crisis has prompted the most far-reaching discussion of the purpose and structure of Social Security since the program was enacted in 1935. Not so very long ago, Social Security was rightly regarded as the "third rail" of American politics—touch it and your career dies. But no longer. Polls today show that the vast majority of Americans support proposals that would allow younger workers to privately invest at least part of their Social Security taxes through individual accounts.

The Cato Institute has been actively involved in the debate over Social Security reform since 1979 when Carolyn Weaver's article "Social Security: Has the Crisis Passed?" appeared in the very first issue of *Policy Report*. Peter Ferrara's classic book, *Social Security: The Inherent Contradiction*, was published in 1980. Throughout the 1980s and 1990s, while various commissions were "saving" Social Security, the Cato Institute continued to warn that Social Security's pay-as-you-go (PAYGO) structure was fundamentally unsound. In 1986 the Institute launched the Cato Project on Social Security Privatization, since renamed the Project on Social Security Choice, which has become perhaps the leading intellectual voice in favor of market-based Social Security reform.

Since the beginning of the project, we have published more than 30 studies and reports on the U.S. Social Security system, its many

problems, and proposals for reform. This book updates and repro-
duces some of the best of those papers.

In the first part of this book, we discuss the nature of the current
Social Security system and the problems it faces. Social Security as
it is currently structured is financially unsustainable. **Thomas Siems**,
a senior economist with the Federal Reserve Bank of Dallas, explores
the historical origins of Social Security, addresses some of the reasons
the current program is in trouble, and briefly discusses new proposals that warrant serious consideration. He explores the dimensions of
Social Security's financing problems and shows how the program's
PAYGO structure ultimately makes the program unsustainable. He
also shows that the same PAYGO structure has resulted in reduced
and below-market rates of return for young workers. He concludes
that the basic structure of today's Social Security system is fundamentally flawed and must be reengineered to take advantage of
savings and investment.

Siems's analysis is supported by **June O'Neill**, former director of
the Congressional Budget Office, who also demonstrates the irrele-
vancy of the Social Security Trust Fund. O'Neill shows that, in reality,
the Social Security Trust Fund is an accounting measure, not an
accumulation of real assets that can be used to pay future benefits.
That means current discussions of Social Security "lock boxes," or
whether the Social Security "surplus" is being "raided," are essentially irrelevant to the program's future. The federal government
lacks a mechanism that would allow it to save today against the
future demographic and financial pressures that will make Social
Security's current structure unsustainable over the long term. The
only real way to save Social Security surpluses is to take them out
of the hands of politicians and return them to individual workers.

But Social Security's problems are not just a question of financing.
Merely finding sufficient funding to preserve Social Security fails
to address the serious shortcomings of the current system. Therefore
I look at the question of whether our goal should be to simply "save"
Social Security or to develop the best possible retirement program
for American workers. I show how Social Security fails both as an
anti-poverty program and as a retirement program. I also begin to
explore the many inequities that are part of the current program
and the biases that penalize the poor, minorities, and working
women. Those issues will all be covered in greater depth later in

2

this book, but this discussion makes it clear that any true reform of Social Security will do more than simply pump more money into the existing program.

Suffolk University law professor **Charles Rounds** points out another flaw in traditional Social Security. Many workers assume that if they pay Social Security taxes into the system, they have some sort of legal guarantee to the system's benefits. The truth is exactly the opposite. It has long been settled law that there is no legal right to Social Security. In two important cases, *Helvering v. Davis* and *Flemming v. Nestor*, the U.S. Supreme Court has ruled that Social Security taxes are simply taxes and convey no property or contractual rights to Social Security benefits. As a result, a worker's retirement security is entirely dependent on political decisions by the president and Congress. Benefits may be reduced or even eliminated at any time. Given the program's looming financial crisis, such benefit cutbacks are increasingly likely. Therefore, the entirely political nature of Social Security places workers' retirement security at considerable risk. Indeed, some categories of workers have already had their Social Security benefits arbitrarily reduced. Moreover, because Social Security benefits are not a worker's property, they are not inheritable.

Martin Feldstein looks at Social Security in the context of larger economic issues. He concludes that our current Social Security system is acting as a drag on economic growth in two important ways. First, the payroll tax distorts the supply of labor and the type of compensation sought by workers. Those losses are inevitable because of the low return implied by the PAYGO character of the unfunded Social Security system. Second, the system reduces national savings and investment. He contrasts that with a system of individually owned, privately invested accounts, which would both increase capital investment and have a positive impact on labor productivity. A fully implemented system of individual accounts, according to Feldstein's calculations, would raise the well-being of future generations by an amount equal to 5 percent of gross domestic product each year as long as the system lasts. Although the transition to a funded system would involve economic as well as political costs, the net present value of the gain would be enormous—as much as $10 trillion to $20 trillion.

And, finally, **Daniel Shapiro**, professor of philosophy at the University of West Virginia, examines the moral issues involved in

Social Security reform. After all, Social Security reform would not be justifiable if it was economically beneficial but morally suspect. Shapiro looks at this question from a variety of philosophical perspectives including those of classical liberals that is based on individual liberty, as well as that of egalitarians, who frame their arguments in terms of fairness and are concerned with economic security, and of communitarians who seek to foster a greater sense of community. He concludes that regardless of the philosophical approach, a system of individual accounts would be morally preferable to today's Social Security system.

The book's second part looks at the impact of Social Security reform on vulnerable groups in society: the poor, women, and minorities. As mentioned above, the current Social Security system frequently works to the disadvantage of those groups. For example, **Leanne Abdnor**, a former member of President Bush's Commission to Strengthen Social Security, focuses on the clash between the current benefit structure and the socioeconomic changes that have occurred since 1935, such as the massive shift of women into the workforce, women marrying later or not at all, and a doubling of the divorce rate. By failing to keep pace with the changing nature of American families, Social Security's outdated benefit structure results in single women and dual-earner couples subsidizing the benefits of wealthier single-earner couples, creating a sharply regressive element to the current benefit structure.

Cato senior fellow **Jagadeesh Gokhale**, former chief economist with the Federal Reserve Bank of Cleveland, shows that, despite an ostensibly progressive benefit formula, Social Security does relatively little to help the poor. Moreover, because the poor are disproportionately dependent on Social Security for their retirement income, traditional reforms, such as raising taxes or cutting benefits, will leave low-income workers worse off. However, allowing workers to save and invest a portion of their Social Security taxes in individual accounts may avoid or offset potential benefit cuts, without increasing taxes.

Equally important, individual accounts may provide an opportunity to address some of the other problems with the current Social Security system, in particular its impact on wealth accumulation, the intergenerational transfer of wealth, and the inequality of wealth in America. Poor households currently save very little and therefore own almost no financial wealth at retirement. As a result, the distribution of bequeathable wealth among retirees in the United States is highly unequal. There is strong evidence that Social Security may be a factor contributing to this inequality. In contrast, a system of individual accounts would allow workers to accumulate real and bequeathable wealth, leading ultimately to a greater equality of wealth overall.

Finally, I look at how Social Security reform would affect African Americans. I show that Social Security benefits are inadequate to provide for African Americans' retirement needs, leaving nearly 30 percent of African-American seniors in poverty. Moreover, it is not simply inadequacy, but unfairness. Because African Americans generally have shorter life expectancies, they receive less total Social Security payments over the course of their lifetimes than do whites.

Building on Gokhale's work, I also warn that Social Security contributes to the growing wealth gap between blacks and whites. Because Social Security taxes squeeze out other forms of saving and investment, especially for low-income workers, many African Americans are unable to accumulate real wealth. Since Social Security benefits are not inheritable, this wealth inequity is compounded from generation to generation.

Having spelled out the problems with Social Security as we know it today, we next look at how Social Security can be reformed. In the first chapter of this part, I look at proposals for Social Security reform that do not involve individual accounts and find that most alternatives boil down to some very unpopular positions—raising taxes, cutting benefits, or government investment in the stock market. Not surprisingly, the alternative most frequently suggested by opponents of individual accounts is to increase taxes, either directly or indirectly. Suggested sources of revenue range from increases in payroll tax rates or the base income on which payroll taxes are collected to the use of general revenues, particularly repeal of income tax cuts that passed Congress in 2001. Other proposals include increasing capital gains taxes, taxing all stock transactions, increasing taxes on Social Security benefits, and requiring newly hired state and municipal workers to participate in Social Security.

Opponents of individual accounts are also willing to consider significant cuts in Social Security benefits. Many would increase the computation period used to calculate benefits—a proposal that would be particularly harmful to women and minorities—and raise the retirement age, which would particularly impact lower-income and minority workers with shorter life expectancies. Others would reduce spousal benefits or trim cost-of-living allowance increases. Finally, many opponents of individual accounts would allow the federal government to directly invest Social Security funds in private capital markets. But that approach risks politicizing the investment process and undermining our free-market economic system.

Given the problems inherent in these solutions, the only viable option is transforming Social Security from a PAYGO system to one based on savings and investment, allowing workers to privately invest all or part of their Social Security taxes through individual accounts.

One of the first and most successful examples of this type of reform took place in Chile in 1981. **José Piñera**, who as Chile's minister of labor and social security was responsible for the successful design and implementation of that country's reforms, explains how he accomplished them. In the years since the Chilean system was implemented, labor force participation, pension fund assets, and benefits have all grown. Today, more than 95 percent of Chilean workers have their own pension savings accounts; assets have grown to more than $34 billion, or about 42 percent of gross domestic product; and the average real rate of return has been approximately 11.3 percent per year, which has allowed workers to retire with better and more secure pensions.

The new system has allowed Chile and other Latin American countries that have followed the Chilean example to defuse the fiscal time bomb that is ticking for countries with PAYGO systems, as fewer and fewer workers have to pay for the retirement benefits of more and more retirees. More important, Chile has created a retirement system that, by giving workers clearly defined property rights in their pension contributions, offers proper work and investment incentives; acts as an engine of, not an impediment to, economic growth; and enhances personal freedom and dignity.

Chile's successful reforms have spread throughout the world, especially Latin America and Eastern Europe. They have also served as the basis for a renewed debate over reform here in the United States.

In May 2001 President Bush appointed a bipartisan commission to study Social Security reform. The President's Commission to

Strengthen Social Security unanimously recommended that younger workers be allowed to privately invest a portion of their Social Security taxes through individual accounts and provided three illustrative proposals for how this might be accomplished. **Andrew Biggs**, who served as a staff member for the commission as well as assistant director of Cato's project, examines the three proposals. The commission's three proposals address the creation of individual accounts in different ways, but all three would provide higher benefits than can be paid by the current Social Security system, and lower-income workers would receive higher benefits than are even promised by the current system. Moreover, all three plans would produce those benefits at a cost lower than that of maintaining the current system.

In the end, however, the commission's proposals would move only partway toward an investment-based Social Security system. Workers would be allowed to invest only a portion of their Social Security taxes, remaining dependent on the government-run system for a significant part of their retirement benefits. Therefore, I propose another alternative, a plan that would give workers still more control over their retirement funds. Workers would be allowed to privately invest 6.2 percentage points of the 12.4 percent payroll tax. Those choosing to do so would agree to forgo all future accrual of retirement benefits under the traditional Social Security system but would receive a "recognition bond" based on the accrued value of their past contributions to Social Security.

Of course there are serious questions that must be answered before any system of individual accounts can be established. Part IV looks at the most common and most difficult questions faced by supporters of individual accounts.

Milton Friedman, winner of the 1976 Nobel Prize in Economics, tackles the issue of transition costs. Critics of individual accounts have warned that making the transition to such a new system would impose substantial new costs on today's young workers. However, Friedman shows that given a proper understanding of Social Security's current unfunded liabilities, there are no real transition costs to privatizing Social Security, merely the explicit recognition of current implicit debt.

Critics of individual accounts also warn that such accounts would be too complex and costly to administer. However, **Robert Genetski** examines the administrative issues involved in individual accounts and shows that, while administrative issues should be carefully considered in designing a privatized system, individual accounts are both administrable and affordable.

The cost of administering existing retirement savings programs indicates that administrative and money management expenses for a system of individual accounts could amount to anywhere from roughly 1.15 percent to 1.83 percent of assets, or roughly $35–$55 per worker for the first year. After five years, as the size of the average account increases, the cost would be anywhere from roughly 30 to 45 basis points, or approximately $55–$115 per year. For the great majority of businesses with outside payroll services, the collection function would entail little, if any, additional cost. For those businesses that do payroll without the aid of technology, there would be some modest additional reporting requirements.

This cost is slightly higher than that of the current government-run Social Security program. However, in exchange for slightly greater administrative costs, workers in a privatized system would receive a greater rate of return on their investment and better and more secure retirement benefits.

Biggs looks at the question of risk, particularly in light of recent declines in the market. He shows that long-term market investment, while not risk free, is far safer than critics of individual accounts contend. In the real world, the combination of asset diversification between stocks and bonds and time diversification over long time horizons reduces the risk that a short-term market drop could substantially hurt workers' retirement income. In fact, even after the recent bear market, workers with individual accounts would retire with higher total retirement income than could be paid by the current Social Security system.

Last, Part V asks what the public thinks about the issue. **John Zogby**, one of America's foremost pollsters, shows that the American public is well ahead of its elected representatives in accepting both the need for reform and the advantages of individual accounts. Zogby conducts a careful examination of years of public opinion polling on this issue and shows that a substantial majority of the American public supports proposals to invest a portion of Social Security taxes through individual accounts. This public support is consistent over time and in a broad range of public opinion surveys taken by various organizations, including Gallup, Harris, ABC News/*Washington Post*, Princeton Research, Bloomberg, Public Opinion Strategies, and Zogby International, among others.

Zogby also concludes that support for individual accounts is based on fundamental values, particularly the idea that Americans should have control over their own money and retirement, rather than on such selling points as higher rates of return or higher benefits. As a result, support for individual accounts is less subject to erosion by outside events, such as fluctuations in the stock market. That is why there is no correlation between support for individual accounts and stock market performance. The growing support for individual accounts in the late 1990s was not a result of the bull market. Recent declines in stock prices have not significantly diminished support for individual accounts.

In Washington, the motto often seems to be "Why do today what you can put off until tomorrow?" That is particularly true if the issue is controversial or may offend some powerful interest group. But, when it comes to reforming Social Security, the president and Congress must realize that delay would be a serious mistake

Social Security is in need of fundamental reform, and that reform must come sooner rather than later. The system's financial problems are deep and coming much sooner than commonly believed. But even more important, young workers are already being denied the benefits of the much higher returns and benefits that a privately invested Social Security system would bring. Every day that passes without reforming Social Security robs those young workers of their future.

As Congress begins to wrestle with Social Security reform, we hope that the contributions in this volume will help provide a framework for the debate.

PART I

THE CRISIS

1. Reengineering Social Security for the 21st Century

Thomas F. Siems

One of our nation's most challenging public policy debates concerns Social Security reform. The program is in crisis and in need of reform as a result of maturation of the current pay-as-you-go (PAYGO) Social Security system coupled with an aging American population.

People who have participated in Social Security since its inception have received much higher average annual real rates of return on their contributions than have later participants. This is due, in part, to the basic design of the PAYGO program under which earlier participants received windfall gains as the necessary result of moving from the start-up phase to a mature phase, while later participants receive below-market returns. In contrast, real financial market returns increased over this time frame, widening the gap between market returns and Social Security returns.

With demographic changes, including the retirement of the baby-boom generation and increased life expectancy, looming on the horizon, action must soon be taken to ensure Social Security's future. Social Security gradually expanded from its inception through the early 1980s by increasing benefits and coverage for various groups. To pay for those modifications, payroll tax rates and the maximum earnings ceiling have been steadily raised. Now the Social Security trust funds are in long-term financial imbalance, and benefit cuts and more payroll tax rate increases seem inevitable if Americans are to retain the important social protections that Social Security currently offers.

Now is the time to consider more dramatic changes, including various proposals that allow for prefunding through individual

Originally published as Cato Institute Social Security Paper no. 22, January 23, 2001, and updated to reflect current information.

accounts. Several researchers have put forth proposals that aim to (1) give individuals greater choice among retirement options, (2) provide greater incentives for Americans to work and to save to bolster their economic security, (3) restore Social Security's solvency, and (4) preserve at least some of the current program's social protections. Although there will certainly be some transition costs in moving to a new system, continued delays in addressing Social Security's long-run financing needs will more than likely require even greater and costlier changes in the future.

The Rise of Social Security: Demographic Uncertainties

Like many industrialized countries, the United States has instituted programs to help individuals face the uncertainties brought on by disability and old age. The structure of these programs was initially shaped by important social, economic, and demographic changes that rendered traditional systems of economic security increasingly unworkable. To fully understand the reasons why the programs were structured as they were, let's review the circumstances and changes that led to their adoption.

The social insurance program in the United States, known as Social Security, was signed into law by President Franklin D. Roosevelt on August 14, 1935, and was designed primarily to pay eligible individuals aged 65 or older a continuing income after retirement. Three important social, demographic, and economic changes provided impetus for this legislation: (1) the Industrial Revolution, (2) increased life expectancies, and (3) the Great Depression.

As the American economy shifted from an agricultural to an industrial base during the last two decades of the 1800s and the early 1900s, the Industrial Revolution transformed the way people worked, where they worked, and with whom they worked. In the agricultural economy, most individuals were self-employed. People willing to work could generally provide at least a bare subsistence for themselves and their families. But, in the industrial economy, many individuals became wage earners who worked for industrial corporations. As a result of that transformation, factors outside individuals' control (e.g., recessions, business closures, and layoffs) threatened their economic security to a greater extent than before.

The Industrial Revolution also moved families from farms and small rural communities to cities that had industrial jobs. In 1890,

28 percent of the American population lived in cities; by 1930 that percentage had doubled to 56 percent. That movement of labor and the resulting trend toward urbanization also contributed to another significant demographic shift: the breakup of the extended family and the rise of the nuclear family.

In the agricultural economy, the extended family was available to provide support and assistance when needed. In the industrial economy, extended families became splintered as some family members moved to the cities and others stayed behind. As a result, individuals in need of assistance found it increasingly difficult to find support when their economic security was threatened.

Increased life expectancy also helped bring passage of the Social Security Act. Thanks to improved health care programs and facilities, from 1900 to 1930 Americans increased their average life span by 10 years, and the number of elderly Americans increased dramatically.

Furthermore, in the early 1930s America was in the midst of the worst economic crisis in its history. As the Great Depression unfolded, millions of people were unemployed, numerous banks and businesses failed, and billions of dollars of wealth were lost as domestic stock markets plunged. For millions of Americans, economic security vanished.

As a result of those social, economic, and demographic changes, political pressure grew for greater government involvement to restore confidence and provide for the economic security of citizens. To address those concerns, President Roosevelt conceived a social insurance program. Philosophically, social insurance relies on government institutions to provide citizens with economic security. Social insurance began in Europe in the 19th century, and several European and Latin American nations already had some form of social insurance by the time it was adopted in America.[1] While the details of social insurance programs can vary considerably, they generally combine an insurance element and a social element. That is, they provide insurance against some defined risk in a manner shaped by broader social objectives, rather than by the participants' self-interests.

The major provisions of the original Social Security Act of 1935 included old-age assistance, unemployment insurance, aid to dependent children, and grants to the states to provide various forms of

15

Table 1
PROVISIONS OF THE SOCIAL SECURITY ACT OF 1935

Title	Description
Title I	Grants to States for Old-Age Assistance
Title II	Federal Old-Age Benefits
Title III	Grants to States for Unemployment Compensation Administration
Title IV	Grants to States for Aid to Dependent Children
Title V	Grants to States for Maternal and Child Welfare
Title VI	Public Health Work
Title VII	Social Security Board
Title VIII	Taxes with Respect to Employment (for Old-Age Insurance)
Title IX	Tax on Employers of Eight or More (for Administration of Unemployment Compensation)
Title X	Grants to States for Aid to the Blind
Title XI	General Provisions

medical care (Table 1). Title II, Federal Old-Age Benefits, was the social insurance program most people think of as Social Security today. It sought to provide economic security for the elderly by requiring workers to contribute to their own future retirement benefits through taxes paid into a trust fund. As originally conceived, Title II differed from Title I (Grants to States for Old-Age Assistance) in that it was not meant to provide welfare benefits. Title I was a temporary relief program that would no longer be needed as more people obtained retirement income through the contributory system. Under the 1935 legislation, Title II benefits were to be paid only to the primary worker when he or she retired at age 65 and were to be based on lifetime payroll tax contributions. Taxes were to be collected first in 1937, with monthly benefits payable beginning in 1942. The delayed payment established a minimum participation period to qualify for benefits and allowed the trust fund to be built up.

Over time, a number of amendments have been made to the original Social Security Act. In 1939 benefit amounts were increased and the start date for the payment of monthly benefits was accelerated by two years, to 1940. As explained later, the 1939 legislation effectively transformed the system into a PAYGO program. Two new categories of benefits were also established: dependent benefits (for spouses and minor children of retired workers) and survivors' benefits (for survivors of covered workers who died prematurely).

By 1950 there were more welfare beneficiaries receiving greater average benefit checks under Title I of the act than there were Social Security retirees (Title II beneficiaries). To remedy that, amendments to the act were passed in 1950 to substantially increase benefits for existing and future Title II beneficiaries. In the mid-1950s amendments to the act initiated a disability insurance program to provide citizens with additional economic security. Amendments in the early 1960s lowered the eligibility age for old-age insurance to 62. In 1965 a new program—known as Medicare—was established to extend health coverage to most Americans aged 65 and older.

In the 1970s another new program, Supplemental Security Income, essentially replaced the already-established assistance programs for the aged, blind, and disabled. Automatic cost-of-living adjustments linked to the consumer price index were also provided under the 1972 amendments.

The 1983 amendments, based on recommendations made by a bipartisan commission chaired by Alan Greenspan, instituted the partial taxation of Social Security benefits for middle- and upper-income earners, made coverage compulsory for new federal civilian employees and employees of nonprofit enterprises, and provided for a gradual increase in the retirement age to 67. In 1993 new legislation increased the taxation of benefits at higher income levels.[2]

Those amendments have made Social Security the largest and most comprehensive public program in the United States. Social Security is part of nearly every American's life and an important source of income for most of today's older Americans. Social Security provides more than half of the total income of two-thirds of today's retirees. Social Security provides nearly all of the income of one-third of the elderly. The Social Security Administration estimates that, without Social Security benefits, 48 percent of individuals aged 65 and older would live in poverty, nearly five times as many as are in poverty today.[3]

The Fall of Social Security: Demographic Realities

For the most part, the mandatory contributions that are paid into Social Security are paid out immediately in benefits to retirees, disabled Americans, and their dependents and survivors. That is, Social

Security is not a funded plan under which contributions are accumulated and invested in financial assets and liquidated and converted into a pension at retirement. Rather, Social Security is essentially a PAYGO program, in which most Social Security taxes are used to immediately pay benefits for current retirees. However, since the 1983 reforms, contributions paid in have exceeded payments to retirees and have generated a relatively modest surplus, which is invested in government bonds. This partial advance funding has resulted in some accumulation of reserves, representing over 28 months of benefit payments, in the Social Security trust funds.

As an unfunded program, Social Security gives windfall returns to the first generations of participants, because they paid in little relative to the benefits they receive, and gives below-market returns to later generations. Paul Samuelson of the Massachusetts Institute of Technology found that an unfunded system with a constant tax rate provides a positive rate of return that, in equilibrium, is equal to the rate of growth of the payroll tax base.[4] As shown below, in a dynamically efficient economy, this rate of return is lower than the return on capital investment.[5] Now that the nation's Social Security system has matured (the tax rate has stabilized), it is inevitable that subsequent generations (including today's workers) will receive below-market rates of return on their contributions.

Even if there are many workers providing benefits for relatively few retirees and wage growth is strong, the PAYGO plan benefits the earliest generations at the expense of later generations. Consider a simple overlapping-generations model in which people are born in every time period, live for two periods (one as younger workers and the other as older retirees), and then die. As time passes, older generations are replaced by younger generations. In each period, two generations overlap, with younger workers coexisting with older retirees.[6]

A funded system is portrayed in Table 2 and a PAYGO Social Security system in Table 3. The columns represent successive periods (moving to the right) as time passes, and the rows represent successive generations (moving down). Each generation is labeled by the period of its birth, so that generation 1 is born in period 1 and so on. In each period there are two overlapping generations: the presently working generation and the previously working, but now retired, generation.

18

Table 2
A FUNDED SOCIAL SECURITY SYSTEM

Generation	Period 1	Period 2	Period 3	Period 4
0	Retired			
1	Working → **Contributions**	Retired **Benefits**		
2	Unborn	Working → **Contributions**	Retired **Benefits**	
3	Unborn	Unborn	Working → **Contributions**	Retired **Benefits**
4	Unborn	Unborn	Unborn	Working → **Contributions**

Table 3
AN UNFUNDED (PAY-AS-YOU-GO) SOCIAL SECURITY SYSTEM

Generation	Period 1	Period 2	Period 3	Period 4
0	Retired **Benefits**			
1	Working **Contributions**	Retired **Benefits**		
2	Unborn	Working **Contributions**	Retired **Benefits**	
3	Unborn	Unborn	Working **Contributions**	Retired **Benefits**
4	Unborn	Unborn	Unborn	Working **Contributions**

In the funded system (Table 2), each working generation contributes to an investment fund that accumulates as time passes. The proceeds from the fund, including interest earnings, are then used to pay that generation's benefits when it retires in the subsequent period. As shown, under a funded system, each generation contributes to its own retirement. For generation 0 (the currently retired population), nothing has been accumulated so that generation must rely on private savings and pensions.

In contrast, the PAYGO Social Security system provides a start-up bonus to generation 0 retirees by using the contributions of generation 1 workers to pay benefits to those already retired (Table 3).

This is an unfunded program because contributions never accumulate in a trust fund but are immediately paid out.[7] Contributions from each working generation are used to finance benefits for the older generation in the same period. Notice that the two programs differ in the number of periods in which benefits are paid. While both programs show four periods of contributions, the funded program provides three periods of benefits whereas the PAYGO plan provides four. This highlights the greatest differences between the two programs: the funded program has an accumulated fund and the PAYGO plan does not, and the PAYGO program has a start-up bonus and the funded system does not. It is interesting to note that the temptation of the start-up bonus is what led to the 1939 amendments that created today's PAYGO system.

This simple analysis demonstrates three important facts:

- First, the PAYGO program provides initial (generation 0) retirees a windfall equal to the benefits provided by generation 1 workers because generation 0 never paid taxes into the system.
- Second, subsequent generations earn a return from the PAYGO plan equal to the growth rate of aggregate wages.
- Third, generations 1 onward suffer combined losses exactly equal to the start-up bonus paid to generation 0 retirees.

In sum, below-market returns from a mature PAYGO scheme are inevitable as each generation is effectively forced to service the implicit "debt" issued to finance the windfall for earlier generations.

The effects of the maturation of the PAYGO plan are further exacerbated by the declining ratio of workers to beneficiaries due to demographic changes, which reduces the growth rate of the payroll tax base. In 1945, a decade after Social Security was established, the ratio of workers to beneficiaries was 41.9 to 1.[8] By 1950 that ratio had fallen to 16.5 to 1. And, as shown in Figure 1, the ratio of workers to beneficiaries has continued to decline, dropping to 5.1 to 1 by 1960 and to 3.2 to 1 by 1975.

Although this ratio has held fairly steady since the mid-1970s and currently stands at around 3.4 workers per beneficiary, the Social Security trustees project that it will steadily decline as the baby-boom generation retires and Americans live longer.[9] In 30 years the ratio of workers to beneficiaries is expected to be approximately 2 to 1 and still falling.

Figure 1
SOCIAL SECURITY WORKER-TO-BENEFICIARY RATIO

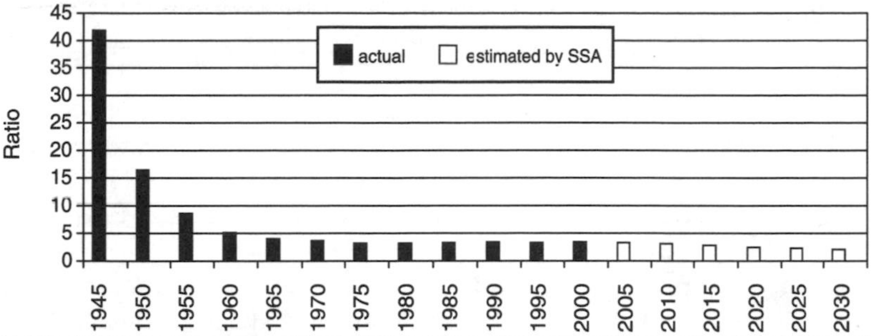

SOURCE: Board of Trustees, Federal Old-Age and Survivors Insurance and Disability Insurance Trust Funds, *2003 Annual Report* (Washington: Government Printing Office, 2003), p. 51.

The baby-boom generation consists of individuals born between 1946 and 1964, a period during which the return of World War II soldiers and postwar prosperity prompted many families to add dependents. By itself this would not be a problem, but the baby boom was followed by a baby bust with markedly lower birth rates.[10] The inevitable result is that fewer workers will be available to support a growing number of retirees. Aggravating this imbalance is a gradual increase in average life expectancy in the United States, even as the age for full Social Security benefits has remained unchanged from the program's inception until this year.[11]

Figure 2 shows that the number of Americans aged 65 and older increased from 9.5 million (6.8 percent of the population) in 1940 to 35.5 million (12.4 percent) in 2000. When the Social Security Act was signed into law in 1935, life expectancy at birth in the United States was 61 years, and those who reached age 65 were expected to live an additional 12 years. Today, average life expectancy at birth is 76.9 years, and those reaching age 65 are expected to live an additional 17.9 years.[12]

Consequently, the PAYGO financing structure has been under further stress as the worker-to-beneficiary ratio has declined. Greenspan has noted that the dramatic change in this projected ratio, as the baby boomers retire and enjoy greater longevity, makes the current PAYGO system unsustainable.[13]

21

Figure 2
NUMBER AND PERCENT OF AMERICANS AGED 65 AND OLDER

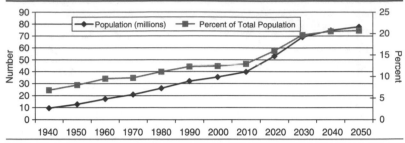

SOURCE: House Committee on Ways and Means, *2000 Green Book,* p. 992.

According to the Social Security trustees, Social Security tax revenues will exceed expenditures until 2018.[14] Although the interest earned on the trust fund will initially keep the fund in surplus, the fund will begin running annual deficits in 2027. By 2042 the assets in the trust fund will be fully exhausted, rendering the program insolvent. That will not mean a complete termination of benefits; roughly three-quarters of legislated benefits will still be paid from incoming taxes.

Previous attempts to shore up Social Security have focused mainly on increasing tax rates and cutting benefits.[15] As Figure 3 shows, the payroll tax rate and the maximum earnings level subject to Social Security taxes have increased nearly every year since the mid-1950s. The original Social Security tax was 2 percent (employer and employee combined rate) on the first $3,000 of earnings. In 2003 the payroll tax for Old-Age and Survivors Insurance (OASI), which excludes the disability program and Medicare, is 10.6 percent on the first $87,000 of earnings, and the maximum earnings level is adjusted each year on the basis of national average earnings. Thus, by 2001 the Social Security tax rate for OASI had increased by a factor of 5.3, and the maximum earnings level subject to the tax had increased by a factor of 2.3, after adjusting for inflation. In 1937 the maximum tax that any individual paid was $60; today it is $10,788. As noted by Martin Feldstein of Harvard University, another such increase in tax rates would be economically devastating and politically impossible.[16] The system has reached a mature phase in which returns are limited to the growth rate of the tax base.

Figure 3
CHANGES IN SOCIAL SECURITY TAX LEVELS

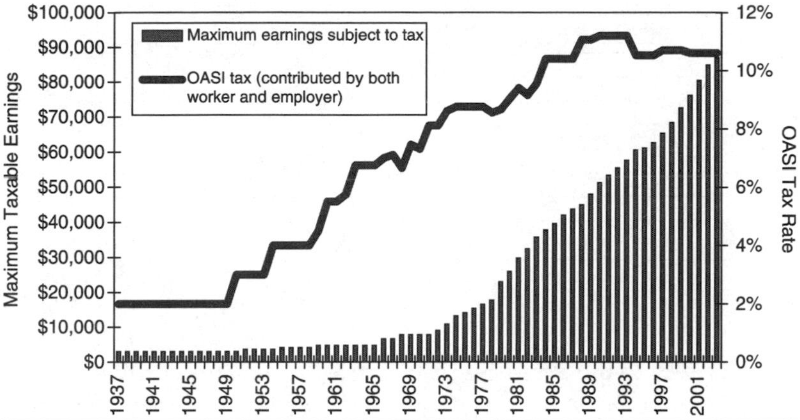

SOURCE: Board of Trustees, 2003, Table VI.A1.

Social Security is in trouble because of its basic structure and maturity as a PAYGO program. However, the aging of the huge baby-boom generation has come at the worst time as far as the maturity of the Social Security program is concerned. Attempting to fix this problem without considering more dramatic changes may only prolong the life of a flawed plan against the backdrop of demographic trends.

Facing the Facts: Social Security Is a Bad Investment

We can examine the return on contributions to Social Security through time and compare it with returns on several market-based portfolios, using three different earnings scenarios (low, medium, and high). In each case, workers are assumed to start their working careers at age 21, retire at the normal retirement age (age 65 prior to 2000), and then live the average life expectancy of a 65-year-old. During their careers, workers contribute a percentage of their earnings to Social Security each year.[17] At retirement, benefits are computed using the formula described in the accompanying box.

23

Calculating Social Security Benefits

The Social Security Administration calculates retiree benefits on the basis of a retiree's earnings history. First, yearly earnings totals from 1950 to the year in which the individual attains age 60 are adjusted for inflation using an average monthly wage calculated by the administration for this purpose. Using this range of earnings, an Average Indexed Monthly Earnings (AIME) amount is calculated on the basis of the 35 years with highest adjusted earnings. The AIME is then used to calculate the individual's benefit, or Primary Insurance Amount (PIA). The PIA is determined by segmenting the AIME into three parts; benefits are paid at 90 percent of the first segment, 32 percent of the second segment, and 15 percent of the highest segment. Two "bend points," dollar amounts that are updated yearly by the Social Security Administration, define the segments. The "bend point" structure replaces a higher percentage of the income of lower-wage workers. For example, in 2003 the bend points were $606 and $3,653. Individuals retiring in 2003 would have the first $606 of their monthly earnings replaced at 90 percent, any amount of their monthly earnings between $606 and $3,653 replaced at 32 percent, and any monthly earnings over $3,653 replaced at 15 percent.

After yearly contributions to Social Security and annual retirement benefits are determined, we can calculate the internal rate of return for each scenario.[18] The low-wage earnings scenario is based on eight-hour workdays at the federally mandated minimum wage (typically 2,088 hours per year). The medium-wage earnings scenario is based on the average wage per worker computed by the Social Security Administration. The high-wage earnings scenario is based on the maximum earnings subject to the Social Security tax.[19] For this analysis, no changes were made to the structure of the current program, although projections for future real wage growth and changes to the bend points increased by 1 percent annually and life expectancy increased each year by 0.08 years.[20]

Figure 4
INTERNAL RATES OF RETURN FOR SPECIFIED SOCIAL SECURITY
PAY-IN/BENEFIT FLOWS (ADJUSTED FOR INFLATION)

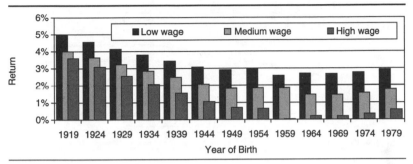

SOURCE: Author's calculations.

As shown in Figure 4, the average annual real (inflation-adjusted) rate of return has generally decreased since Social Security's inception for all three wage levels.[21] Low-wage earners born in 1919 receive a 4.96 percent average annual real return on their Social Security contributions. In contrast, low-wage earners born later, say, in 1959, receive a 2.57 percent annual real return on their contributions. For medium- and high-wage earners, the rates of return are even lower. Medium-wage earners born in 1919 receive a 4.00 percent annual real return and high-wage earners receive 3.59 percent. Medium-wage earners born in 1959 receive a 1.85 percent annual real return, and high-wage earners receive a paltry 0.03 percent. Following the overlapping-generations model, Feldstein, in his introduction to *Privatizing Social Security*, notes that the 2.6 percent average annual rate of growth of real wages and salaries since 1960 should approximate the yield of a PAYGO program. That is confirmed by my calculations.

These results highlight three important trends. First, consistent with the economic analysis of PAYGO plans, workers who contributed to the program near its inception have received higher average annual returns than workers who got started later in the program. And rates of return will probably decline further for future retirees. Second, on an annualized basis, low-wage workers consistently receive a higher average annual return than do medium-wage and high-wage workers.[22] Finally, although it appears that the average annual real rates of return on Social Security contributions have

Figure 5

RATES OF RETURN UNDER SOCIAL SECURITY AND THREE
INVESTMENT OPTIONS FOR LOW-WAGE INDIVIDUALS

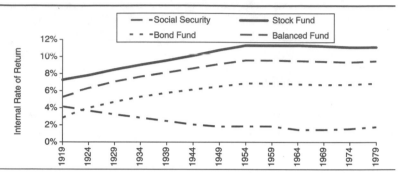

NOTE: Returns are adjusted for inflation. Low wages are defined by minimum wage guidelines.

stabilized (at about 2.9 percent for low-wage workers, 1.8 percent for medium-wage workers, and 0.5 percent for high-wage workers), recall that the Social Security program will run a payroll tax deficit by 2018 under current law. As the bonds in the trust fund are redeemed to pay benefits, the federal government will have to use other income to cover the Social Security obligations, which will indirectly lead to lower returns for future retirees.

How do these average annual rates of return compare with market-based rates? To answer that question, we can construct three market-based portfolios: a stock portfolio, a bond portfolio, and a balanced portfolio. The stock portfolio contains 90 percent large capitalization stocks and 10 percent small capitalization stocks. The bond portfolio contains 50 percent government bonds and 50 percent corporate bonds. The balanced portfolio contains 60 percent stocks and 40 percent bonds.

As shown in Figures 5–7, the market-based portfolios generally outperform the returns from Social Security contributions by a wide margin, except during the program's earliest years. Figures 5–7 show that, by investing in stocks and bonds, wage earners could have saved more for their retirement than Social Security provides. And the gap between the returns on Social Security contributions and those on stocks and bonds has increased as the Social Security program has matured. As the overlapping-generations model indicates,

Figure 6

RATES OF RETURN UNDER SOCIAL SECURITY AND THREE
INVESTMENT OPTIONS FOR MEDIUM-WAGE INDIVIDUALS

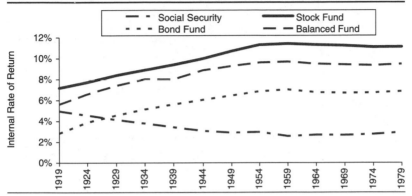

NOTE: Returns are adjusted for inflation. Medium wages are average total earnings per worker, taken from the 1997 annual supplement to the *Social Security Bulletin*.

Figure 7

RATES OF RETURN UNDER SOCIAL SECURITY AND THREE
INVESTMENT OPTIONS FOR HIGH-WAGE INDIVIDUALS

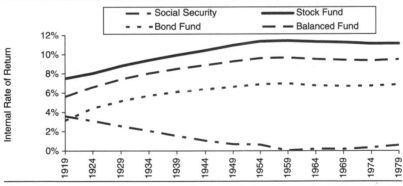

NOTE: Returns are adjusted for inflation. High wages are defined as the maximum taxable earnings set by the Social Security Act.

returns from Social Security have been good for only those individuals who contributed to the program in its earliest stages, when tax rates were being increased. As workers' start dates for making contributions to Social Security move forward to the period when the tax rate stabilizes, the returns decline. In contrast, average annual real returns from the market-based portfolios have mostly increased and have been favorable for nearly every time period examined, generally ranging between 5 and 10 percent per year.[23]

The Social Security program was never intended to serve as a pure investment because it contains important social insurance elements and inflation protection, but the fact remains that returns from Social Security are increasingly unattractive—a fact that hinders Social Security in its stated goal of preventing poverty. Somehow, Social Security must move away from a PAYGO system to one with greater prefunding of benefits. Prefunding would raise future output levels by building up the nation's capital stock and would provide higher rates of return. And reengineering Social Security should be pursued sooner rather than later. It is one of our nation's most pressing public policy issues, and the longer real reform is delayed, the costlier the fix will be.[24]

Reengineering Social Security: An Idea Whose Time Has Come

Reengineering Social Security must be guided by several overarching principles.[25] In keeping with the development of society and the economy, a system is needed that gives individuals greater control over and choice of their retirement options. Incentives should be established for citizens to work and save, so that returns are improved for future contributors. Moreover, the program's long-run solvency must be guaranteed. And, finally, the social protections currently provided under Social Security should be preserved.

Most Social Security reformers agree on these principles but disagree on ways to achieve them. Social Security is the federal government's largest and most popular spending program. It is viewed as an effective anti-poverty program and has provided financial protection to families of workers who die early or suffer work-related disabilities. Social Security also has been an effective hedge against inflation for the elderly. Its popularity has led to Social Security's being called the "third rail" of American politics—"touch it and you die." Proposed reforms range from minor modifications to major changes that would transform Social Security into a defined-contribution system of individually managed accounts.

Increasing Taxes

The standard method of dealing with Social Security's actuarial imbalances has been to raise taxes. Tax rates and the taxable ceiling for OASI contributions have increased steadily through the years. Further gradual increases in the tax rate and the taxable ceiling may prolong Social Security's solvency and preserve important social protections, but the cost to future generations may soon become politically intolerable.

For example, Jagadeesh Gokhale of the Federal Reserve Bank of Cleveland estimates that the OASI payroll tax rate would need to be increased by 4 percentage points (from 10.6 percent to 14.6 percent) to pay for projected benefits for the next 75 years and beyond.[26] Edward Gramlich of the Federal Reserve Board foresees a 3.3 percentage point immediate increase or a 5 to 6 percentage point future increase at a time when changes will be needed to maintain solvency.[27] Neil Howe and Richard Jackson of the Concord Coalition, however, argue that such "solutions" are seriously misleading because they count surpluses accumulated in the program's trust funds as genuine savings instead of as a stack of Treasury IOUs that will require additional taxes or borrowing from the public to redeem.[28]

Reducing Benefits

Reducing benefits to Social Security recipients by lowering the monthly amount received in retirement or by adjusting the formula used to compute average earnings and Social Security retirement benefits has not been undertaken.[29] Instead, reforms have been designed to keep workers in the workforce for longer periods by gradually increasing the "normal" retirement age at which unreduced retirement benefits are paid (as discussed earlier). Changes that have been considered include increasing the early retirement penalty, raising the initial entitlement age from 62, implementing a "means test" so that full Social Security benefits would be paid only when retiree incomes were below some specified threshold, and changing the indexing of benefits for inflation. Like raising taxes, reducing benefits, by itself, may help prolong Social Security's solvency but will eventually lead to lower rates of return for future retirees while failing to maintain all the protections currently provided to Social Security recipients. More important, these changes generally provide no or little prefunding; instead they prolong the PAYGO program without addressing the desire to increase workers' rates of return on their contributions.

New Proposals

As long as Social Security remains a PAYGO program, it is impossible to adhere to all the principles outlined earlier. Consequently, many reform proposals receiving attention today involve some degree of private investment. It is important to distinguish between funding and individual accounts when discussing reform. As defined by the National Academy of Social Insurance, funding involves building and maintaining greater total balances for Social Security, whether in individual accounts or the government's Social Security trust funds.[30] Establishing individual accounts involves replacing all or part of the current defined-benefit system with a defined-contribution system of accounts held in individual workers' names.

Proposals that increase advance funding (whether through the Social Security trust funds or individual accounts) would permit lower taxes or higher benefits, or both, in the future, since more assets would produce greater returns. However, increasing advance funding would require increased revenues in the short term. Thus, in general, improving the financial value of Social Security for future generations could come at the cost of worsening somewhat the financial value for current generations.[31]

This occurs because of the need for transition financing. The current Social Security system has, over the next 75 years, an unfunded liability of which the present value is $10.5 trillion. This is the value of benefits promised to retirees and workers for which no funds have been or will be accumulated under current tax provisions. It is tempting to suggest that government debt be issued to cover this cost. However, proposals that merely replace this unfunded liability with official debt would not change the debt burden on future generations, since they would have to service this debt just as they would have had to service the implicit debt of the PAYGO system.

Franco Modigliani, Maria Ceprini, and Arun Muralidhar of the Massachusetts Institute of Technology propose replacing the PAYGO plan with a new funded system.[32] Feldstein and Andrew Samwick of Dartmouth argue that the transition has a relatively low cost. They contend that shifting to a funded system would permit the existing 12.4 percent payroll tax (which includes the disability insurance contribution) to be replaced in the long run by a payroll tax of about 2 percent.[33] This is equivalent to a 5 percent permanent increase in real income. Michael Tanner of the Cato Institute argues that, instead of "saving" Social Security, we should begin the transition to a new and better retirement system based on individually owned, privately invested accounts.[34] He advocates funding the transition through reductions in other federal programs or the sale of federal assets, neither of which would significantly harm the average worker's well-being.

If advance funding is adopted, it is necessary to decide whether the assets will be invested by the government or by individual workers. The exceptional market-based returns experienced since the early 1940s and the demographic realities discussed earlier have prompted reform proposals that involve investing Social Security contributions in the equity and bond markets.[35] Since market-based returns are typically superior to those under the PAYGO structure, defenders of this view argue that allowing the government to invest Social Security funds in private capital markets will make future tax cuts or benefit increases, or both, less onerous.

While allowing the government to invest Social Security contributions in the stock market through a central fund may appear attractive on the surface, opponents of such plans warn of significant risks, including the effective socialization of a large portion of the U.S. economy.[36] As the potentially largest shareholder in nearly every company, the federal government would have a controlling interest in every sector of our economy.[37] And there is a danger that political pressures could influence investment practices.[38]

Proponents of individual accounts see several advantages. First, workers would have greater control over and choice of investment options.[39] Further, workers who see that they have clear ownership of new contributions and some control over investment choice are more likely to accept the increased savings necessary to prefund the system. Having a range of choices about how contributions are invested for retirement also gives workers the freedom to decide for themselves the level of risk they are willing to tolerate to maximize their expected well-being.

Proponents of reform also argue that individual accounts protect workers' retirement income from future legislative changes. This would reduce the risk that Congress and other government officials might exercise some control over future benefit payments.[40]

Conclusion

Policymakers, economists, and the public hotly debate the complex issue of Social Security reform. The time is right to seriously consider some new approaches to reforming Social Security. If we are to follow the principles outlined earlier, we need a reform that allows for prefunding with individual accounts.

Social Security emerged because of profound social, demographic, and economic changes. Now Social Security must be reengineered because of profound social, demographic, and economic changes. It appears that major improvements to the program are necessary. As was the case in the 1930s, the traditional system of economic security has become increasingly unworkable. But this time the traditional system is America's current Social Security program.

Notes

The author would like to thank Jason Saving and Alan Viard for comments and suggestions and Kory Killgo for research assistance.

1. For example, Chile's PAYGO system, the first in the Western Hemisphere, was instituted in 1924. In 1981 Chile was the first country to move away from PAYGO pensions to a system of funded personal retirement accounts.

2. The 1983 amendment required that up to 50 percent of benefits be made subject to income taxation for people whose incomes exceed certain thresholds—$25,000 for singles and $32,000 for married couples. The 1993 legislation taxed up to 85 percent of those benefits when incomes exceed $34,000 for singles and $44,000 for married couples. See C. Eugene Steuerle and Jon M. Bakija, *Retooling Social Security for the 21st Century: Right and Wrong Approaches to Reform* (Washington: Urban Institute Press, 1994).

3. These estimates assume no labor-leisure response from the elderly and no savings response by workers. In most cases, elderly Americans have made retirement plans that include Social Security benefits. Without the promised benefits and without mandatory taxation to fund them, many elderly Americans would have continued working to a later date or would have saved more during their working years. Anti-poverty claims, particularly of future workers, would be much reduced if it were assumed that payroll taxes were invested at market rates instead.

4. Paul Samuelson, "An Exact Consumption Loan Model of Interest with or without the Social Contrivance of Money," *Journal of Political Economy* 66 (1958): 467–82.

5. A dynamically efficient economy is one that is producing with a capital intensity lower than the so-called golden rule level (that is, the level at which the marginal product of capital is equal to the rate of aggregate economic growth). Because the U.S. economy is dynamically efficient, the return on capital must be greater than the aggregate economic growth rate, which, in the long run, is the PAYGO rate.

6. This is the canonical textbook analysis used to understand the differences between the PAYGO plan and a funded system. This analysis follows Neil Bruce, *Public Finance and the American Economy* (New York: Addison-Wesley, 1998).

7. While a trust fund may exist in name, it is simply a temporary repository for current contributions to be paid out in benefits. Moreover, the "assets" it does hold do not reduce the impact of future benefit obligations on future taxpayers. The Clinton administration's fiscal year 2000 budget made clear that trust fund "balances are available to finance future benefit payments . . . but only in a bookkeeping sense. . . . They do not consist of real economic assets that can be drawn down in the future to fund benefits. Instead, they are claims on the Treasury that when redeemed will have to be financed by raising taxes, borrowing from the public, or reducing benefits or other expenditures. The existence of large trust fund balances, therefore, does not, by itself, have any impact on the Government's ability to pay benefits." Office of Management and Budget, *Budget of the United States Government, Fiscal Year 2000* (Washington: Government Printing Office, 2000), Analytic Perspectives, p. 337.

8. This high ratio is not all demographics related. There was a low number of beneficiaries at first because many elderly Americans were not covered by the program.

9. Board of Trustees, Federal Old-Age and Survivors Insurance and Disability Insurance Trust Funds, *2003 Annual Report* (Washington: Government Printing Office, 2003).

10. The fertility rate in the United States fell from more than 3.5 children per woman in the 1950s to fewer than 1.9 children per woman in the 1980s, before recently rebounding to 2.0. Edward M. Gramlich, *Is It Time to Reform Social Security?* (Ann Arbor: University of Michigan Press, 1998), explains that, given normal patterns of sickness and mortality, if every woman had 2.1 children in her lifetime, the overall population of a country would stabilize. A fertility rate above 2.1 would lead to population growth; a rate less than 2.1 would result in an eventual decline in population.

11. The normal retirement age for Social Security benefits was 65 through 1999. In 2000 it is 65 years and 2 months, and it will increase by 2 months per year until it becomes 66 years in 2005. Following a 12-year hiatus, the normal retirement age advances again by 2 months per year from 2017 through 2022 and finally reaches 67 in 2022.

12. Life expectancies from Centers for Disease Control, National Center for Health Statistics, "United States Life Tables, 2000," *National Vital Statistics Reports* 51 (December 19, 2002): Tables 5-6, 8-9. Thomas F. Cooley and Jorge Soares, *Will Social Security Survive the Baby Boom?* Carnegie-Rochester Conference Series in Public Policy 45 (December 1996): 88–121, discuss the effect of demographic changes on the survival of Social Security.

13. Alan Greenspan, Testimony before the Senate Committee on the Budget, January 28, 1999, www.federalreserve.gov/boarddocs/testimony/1999/19990128.htm.

14. Board of Trustees, 2003.

15. The phasing in of benefit cuts raises the question of why younger workers are willing to take significant cuts in their implicit wealth while protecting the currently old. John McHale, "The Risk of Social Security Benefit Rule Changes: Some International Evidence," National Bureau of Economic Research Working Paper no. 7031, March 1999, uses a simple model to answer this question and concludes that those workers fear even larger cuts in their benefits if the tax burden on future workers rises too high.

16. Martin Feldstein, Introduction to *Privatizing Social Security*, ed. Martin Feldstein (Chicago: University of Chicago Press, 1998), pp. 1–29.

17. This percentage is equal to the combined employer and employee OASI payroll tax as shown in Figure 3.

18. Of course, it is helpful to remember that Social Security was intended to have both social (redistributive) and security (insurance) dimensions. Gramlich points out that if one agrees that such social protections have merit, then payroll taxes should be interpreted in part as a donation to the less fortunate and not only as a personal retirement investment. To separate some of the social effects, the disability and Medicare tax rates are removed from this analysis to focus only on the Old-Age and Survivors Insurance portion of the program.

19. As a point of reference, in 1996 the annual low-wage amount was $9,171, the annual medium-wage amount was $24,928, and the annual high-wage amount was $62,700.

20. These assumptions are slightly higher than the intermediate scenario assumptions made by the Social Security trustees. Board of Trustees, 2003, Table II.D2.

21. Rates of return computed here are consistent with those calculated by other researchers. See Steven Caldwell et al., "Social Security's Treatment of Postwar Americans," in *Tax Policy and the Economy*, ed. James Poterba, vol. 13 (Cambridge, Mass.: National Bureau of Economic Research, 1998); Dean R. Leimer, "Lifetime Redistribution under the Social Security Program: A Literature Synopsis," *Social Security Bulletin* 62, no. 2 (1999): 43–51; and Dean R. Leimer, "A Guide to Social Security Money's Worth Issues," *Social Security Bulletin* 58, no. 2 (1995): 3–20 for additional studies.

22. On a lifetime basis, however, Constantijn W. A. Panis and Lee A. Lillard, "Socioeconomic Differentials in the Returns to Social Security," RAND Corporation Working Paper (1996), show a net redistribution from poor to rich because income and life expectancy are correlated and higher-income workers collect for longer. Also, most citizens do not complain about these differing rates of return because of Social Security's inherent protections for the less fortunate. The greater concern is that returns for low-wage workers have fallen, along with those for medium-wage and high-wage workers, to very low levels.

23. Some opponents of Social Security privatization have argued that such rate-of-return comparisons are misleading because they fail to take into account transition costs. See, for example, John Geanakopolis, "Generation X: Does Bush Understand His Social Security Plan?" *New Republic*, October 23, 2000. They point out that the rate of return is the ratio of how much a person pays in to how much he actually gets out. Therefore, any measure of the return must take into account not just the amount paid into private investment but also anything paid to continue providing benefits to current beneficiaries. Remember the simple overlapping-generations model described earlier. Generation 1's benefits are paid by generation 2, generation 2's by generation 3, and so forth. Imagine that generation 3 wishes to privatize. To be able to invest its own payroll taxes in the market, generation 3 must also cover generation 2's benefits. Imagine that generation 3 does so at a 5 percent rate, while investing its own money at a 7 percent rate of return. The net gain is only 2 percent— the 7 percent gain from the investment minus the 5 percent interest the generation is paying on the money it is borrowing. And, in a properly functioning market, the 2 percent differential will be purely a function of risk. Therefore, there is no real gain to generation 3. Moreover, this debt would never end. The 5 percent interest rate cited is purely for servicing the debt, not for repaying it. Thus, it is arguable that no one ever receives a higher rate of return under privatization.

That argument is correct as far as it goes. Privatization is not simple arbitrage, and all costs must be taken into account. However, the critics are mistaken in assuming that all methods of paying those costs are the same. If, for example, the costs were paid purely through an increased payroll tax, the critics would be correct. Workers would see no increase in their rate of return. But if the transition is financed by cutting government spending, that is a different story. Most economists would agree that government makes far less productive use of capital than does the private sector. In many cases, government spending is actually harmful to the economy, producing, in a sense, a negative rate of return. Therefore, cutting government spending to fund the transition would not entail a loss in current welfare equivalent in present value terms to the gains in welfare in the future.

In short, the critics are correct to note that the transition to a privatized system ultimately requires an increase in national savings. If we wish to support a larger retiree population in the future, the only choices are to redistribute wealth to the old at the expense of the young or to increase economic output so that both groups can be made better off. Increasing savings is the most straightforward way to increase future economic output. All things being equal, therefore, the cost of the transition is simply the cost of increased savings. In order to increase savings, someone must forgo consumption today. The critics imply that someone must be the individual worker. However, under a properly structured privatization scenario, it would be the government that forwent consumption. Hence, workers would receive a higher rate of return and be better off.

Two other points should be made. First, if the transition were paid out of taxes rather than through reductions in government spending, it would far more likely be paid for out of income taxes than out of payroll taxes. Since the income tax system is highly progressive, low-wage workers would see the full rate of return from their individual accounts, there being little or no offsetting increase in their income taxes; high-income workers would bear most of the cost and see reduced rates of return. An income-tax-funded transition would be a large transfer from today's wealthy to both today's poor and workers of the future.

24. In 1997 the Federal Reserve Bank of Boston sponsored a conference on Social Security Reform. Conference participants agreed that Social Security does face a long-term fiscal problem that should be addressed now. The difficulty is in finding widespread agreement on specific reform proposals. See Steven A. Sass and Robert K. Triest, eds., *Social Security Reform Conference Proceedings*, Federal Reserve Bank of Boston Conference Series no. 41, June 1997.

25. See Harvey Rosenblum, "Why Social Security Should Be Privatized," Federal Reserve Bank of Dallas *Southwest Economy,* no. 3 (May–June 1997): 9–11, and Gramlich for discussions of similar goals.

26. Jagadeesh Gokhale, "Social Security's Treatment of Postwar Generations," Federal Reserve Bank of Cleveland *Economic Commentary,* November 1998.

27. Gramlich.

28. Neil Howe and Richard Jackson, "The Myth of the 2.2 Percent Solution," Cato Institute Social Security Paper no. 11, June 15, 1998.

29. Benefits have been taxed, however, which has the same effect as reducing them directly.

30. National Academy of Social Insurance, "Executive Summary: Evaluating Issues in Privatizing Social Security," *Social Security Bulletin* 62, no. 1 (1999): 65–74.

31. Ibid.

32. Franco Modigliani, Maria Ceprini, and Arun Muralidhar, "An MIT Solution to the Social Security Crisis," MIT Sloan School of Management Working Paper 4051, March 1999.

33. Martin Feldstein and Andrew Samwick, "The Transition Path in Privatizing Social Security," in *Privatizing Social Security*, pp. 215–60.

34. Michael Tanner, " 'Saving' Social Security Is Not Enough," Cato Institute Social Security Paper no. 20, May 25, 2000.

35. See Barry P. Bosworth, "Fund Accumulation: How Much? How Managed?" in *Social Security: What Role for the Future?* ed. Peter A. Diamond, David C. Lindeman, and Howard Young (Washington: National Academy of Social Insurance, 1996). Many proposals along these lines incorporate initial tax increases to help restore the long-run solvency of the Social Security trust funds. Without an increase in savings, there would be no prefunding of benefits.

36. Greenspan, in his testimony of January 28, 1999, said that investing a portion of the Social Security trust fund in equities would arguably put at risk the efficiency of our capital markets and, thus, our economy. See also Krysztof Ostaszewski, "Privatizing the Social Security Trust Fund? Don't Let the Government Invest," Cato Institute Social Security Paper no. 6, January 14, 1997.

37. A force for change and innovation in the American economy is the market for corporate control. Managers who fail to produce are overtaken by those willing to change, sometimes through hostile takeovers. If corporate control is in the hands of government bureaucrats because they are the largest shareholder, this force that ultimately leads to stable economic growth and higher living standards could be severely weakened.

38. Government ownership of the means of production and management of labor resources bring a host of serious problems that threaten the innovative and productivity-focused nature of competitive markets. For evidence, one need look no further than the conditions that led to the collapse of the former Soviet Bloc command economies over the past two decades.

39. According to Daniel Shapiro, "The Moral Case for Social Security Privatization," Cato Institute Social Security Paper no. 14, October 29, 1998, the most important arguments for a privatized Social Security system are moral, not economic. He concludes that a privatized system would give individuals more freedom to run their lives, be fairer, provide more security, and create less antagonism between generations, thus fostering a greater sense of community.

40. See Charles E. Rounds, "Property Rights: The Hidden Issue of Social Security Reform," Cato Institute Social Security Paper no. 19, April 19, 2000, who gives a legal account of the property rights issues and concludes that a privatized Social Security system, based on individual accounts, would provide workers with the benefits and the safeguards of true ownership.

2. The Trust Fund, the Surplus, and the Real Social Security Problem

June O'Neill

Yes, there are real problems with the Social Security system. No, the problem is not that we may raid the trust fund next year or that we have failed to provide a "lock box" to save the surplus. The real problem is very different. Social Security is essentially funded on a pay-as-you-go basis, meaning that the benefits of current retirees are paid by the taxes of current workers. As a result, the system is a potential "victim of demography."[1] Indeed, demography will turn against the system in the not-too-distant future when the baby boomers start to collect benefits. It will be tough to pay the bills because we have promised large and growing benefits but have not created any viable mechanism for prefunding those benefits.

Worrying about the size of the trust fund is misguided. It is a fund in name only; it holds no real assets. Consequently, it does not generate funds to pay future benefits. And there are other problems. Social Security discourages saving and distorts work incentives, negatively affecting income in old age and national income in general. Despite its huge expenditures, it has not eliminated poverty among the elderly.

The pundits tell us that Social Security is the third rail of politics. But it is difficult even to hold a dialogue on the subject because the operations of the program are so cloaked in complexity that the public is confused about the true nature of the program.

What Is the Trust Fund?

The phrase "Social Security Trust Fund" creates the illusion that it is an investment fund with tradable economic assets that can be held until needed to pay the benefits of future recipients. But in

Originally published as Cato Institute Social Security Paper no. 26, April 9, 2002, and updated to reflect current information.

reality the fund functions only as a mechanism for tracking Social Security revenues and outlays, each year recording the difference between Social Security tax collections and payments to current beneficiaries. In most years receipts have exceeded benefits, creating a "Social Security surplus." (In the years since 1937, when the Social Security program began to operate, it ran deficits in only 14 years— 8 of which occurred during the period 1975–1983.) The surpluses are credited as net additions to the trust fund. On paper, the reserves that accumulate in the trust fund are recorded as investments in special Treasury bonds and collect interest that is also recorded as an addition to the fund. However, those investments do not provide the government as a whole with additional resources, as is the case when a private individual pays taxes. The investments are merely records of transfers from one part of the government to another.

To understand the process, one must recognize that Social Security is not an entity separate from the government in any real sense. Rather, it is an intrinsic part of a unified federal budget. Operationally, payroll tax receipts for Social Security are intermingled with income taxes and other federal revenues. Social Security benefits are a part of total federal outlays. When the non–Social Security part of the budget is in deficit—meaning that revenues other than Social Security taxes fall short of non–Social Security outlays—budget surpluses in Social Security automatically cover the gap. Moreover, that situation has been the norm in most years.

Over the last 40 years the non–Social Security part of the budget was in deficit in every year except 2—1999 and 2000. In most years the Social Security surplus was not large enough to compensate for the deficit in the non–Social Security side of the budget. Thus, of the past 40 years, the unified federal budget was in deficit in all but 5 years: 1969 and 1998–2001.

At the end of fiscal year 2002, the accounts for the combined OASDI trust fund (containing both the Old-Age and Survivors Insurance and the Disability Insurance funds) recorded assets of more than $1.4 trillion. However, those so-called assets simply reflect the accumulated sum of funds transferred from Social Security over the years to finance other government operations.

What happens when Social Security taxes fall short of Social Security benefit payments? Because the trust fund does not hold assets that can be sold to pay current benefits, the federal government must acquire additional resources to make good on the commitment to pay benefits. The current pay-as-you-go system allows for acquiring these resources through a tax hike, a reduction in other government expenditures, or borrowing from the public. Social Security benefits can also be reduced in the short run, for example, by postponing a cost-of-living increase or in the longer run by modifying the formula for determining benefits or increasing the age of retirement. The condition of the economy and the total budget obviously would influence the decision. But so would the prevailing political winds. Pay-as-you-go is not risk free.

Current projections of the Social Security actuaries indicate that Social Security payments will begin to exceed Social Security taxes around 2018—a consequence of the surge in beneficiaries that is expected as baby boomers retire in large numbers. Although the actuaries do not expect the trust fund to be exhausted until 2042, the date of practical fiscal significance is clearly 2018. That is the year in which Social Security will become a current liability to the budget and the government will be compelled to take measures to find the extra funds needed to cover benefits. At that time, the trust fund is projected to hold about five trillion dollars in reserves. However, as noted, those reserves hold no assets that can simply be cashed to pay the bills. With or without the trust fund, the government must acquire additional resources from taxes, borrowing, and the like in order to cover a Social Security deficit. The existence of the trust fund in no way eases the real cash-flow problem.

And yet some argue that in a broad economic sense the Social Security trust fund should be viewed as a way to prefund Social Security benefits. For instance, four of the most prominent defenders of the current system—Henry Aaron, Alicia Munnell, Alan Blinder, and Peter Orszag—state, "The accumulation of trust fund reserves raises saving, reduces the public debt, and thereby reduces the annual cost of paying interest on that debt, and promotes economic growth."[2] Presumably such a favorable chain of events would make it easier to pay obligations in the future when Social Security payroll tax receipts are projected to fall short of benefit payments.

That argument, however, is based on assumptions about the behavior of policymakers and of the economy that are highly speculative. For one thing, in order for the Social Security surplus to have any chance of increasing saving, it must reduce the total (unified budget) deficit or increase the total surplus if a surplus already exists. But history has shown that Social Security surpluses have, if anything, led to more spending, not saving. As demonstrated by Kent Smetters, a leading economist and Treasury Department official, surpluses in the Social Security accounts have enabled the non–Social Security side of the budget to spend more and run larger deficits than otherwise would be the case.[3] Moreover, even if politicians were able to resist the siren song of a Social Security surplus and simply allow such a surplus to reduce the overall deficit, the effect on saving and economic growth would be uncertain. And beyond that there is no way to guarantee that any fruits of economic growth or reductions in the publicly held debt would be turned over to Social Security by future legislators. (See below for further discussion of this point.)

In sum, Social Security surpluses that accumulate as reserves in the trust fund do not build real assets that can be counted on to fund future shortfalls, either directly or indirectly. The surpluses, however, are a source of current revenue for the government to use for whatever purpose seems most pressing at the time. It would be difficult if not impossible to determine whether the use made by the government of the surpluses has made it easier or harder to pay the benefits of future beneficiaries.

Why then does the Social Security program have a trust fund? It was established by the 1939 amendments and, as John Cogan, an economist with the Hoover Institution and a member of the President's Commission to Strengthen Social Security, put it, it was "a labeling device designed to provide political protection against the charge that the funds were being misspent."[4] It is a misleading label, however, and gives workers the false sense of contributing to an account held for them in a fund, when in fact there is only a record of how much the government has borrowed from future recipients. The trust fund may help back up a promise that funds will be raised to pay benefits in the future when deficits occur. But depending on conditions of the day, keeping that promise may not be possible.

The Financial Outlook for the Current System

During the 1990s the Social Security accounts developed a sizable surplus partly due to a slowdown in the growth of new beneficiaries as the low-birth cohorts of the late 1920s and 1930s reached retirement age. A rise in the tax rate at the start of the decade, low unemployment, and rising wages also contributed, although the acceleration in wage growth eventually will put added strain on the fiscal balance of Social Security as higher earnings are translated into higher benefits.[5] By fiscal year 2000 the Social Security surplus had grown to $152 billion, or 1.5 percent of gross domestic product (GDP). The surplus increased to $159 billion in 2002, even as the surplus in the non–Social Security part of the budget faded. The Congressional Budget Office (CBO) projects the Social Security surplus will continue to increase over the next decade, reaching more than $300 billion in 2013.[6]

However, the demographic factors driving Social Security's financial status are expected to become increasingly unfavorable starting at the end of this decade, when the leading edge of the baby boomers, the huge cohort born between 1946 and 1964, first becomes eligible for benefits. Over the past 25 years when demographic factors were more advantageous, the number of beneficiaries increased at about the same rate as the number of covered workers. That situation is expected to change sharply as the number of beneficiaries mounts rapidly while growth in the number of workers slows. The coming surge in beneficiaries is tied both to the retiring baby boomers and to the lengthening life span of retirees. The expected slowdown in labor force growth is the result of the exit of the baby boomers from the labor force, which will leave a working-age population increasingly drawn from the smaller cohorts born after the baby boom.

Social Security's actuaries project that the worker-to-beneficiary ratio will fall from its current level of 3.4 covered workers per retiree to about 2 workers per retiree in 2030, with most of the change occurring after 2010. After 2030 the ratio is expected to continue to decline, albeit at a slower pace, dipping to 1.85 workers per beneficiary by 2075. Although all projections are uncertain, demographic projections such as these are likely to be less so because the sizes of the retired and working populations are reasonably well known for several decades. One uncertainty is the course of life expectancy.[7] Other uncertainties are changes in immigration and in work participation at older ages, both of which could influence the growth in the labor force. However, both immigration and work participation can be affected by policy, which is not easy to predict.

Long-run projections of the financial status of Social Security are directly related to the ratio of covered workers to beneficiaries. As noted, the Social Security surplus is expected to shrink rapidly after 2008, turning to a deficit in 2018 that will continue to grow in future decades. The existence of a trust fund of trillions of dollars recorded in the accounts will not pay the bills. At that point what will matter will be the ability of the government to make good on the promise implied by the fund. Under current policy, Social Security benefits alone will consume an increasing share of the nation's resources. The CBO estimates that benefits will increase from 4.4 percent of GDP this year to 6.6 percent in 2075.[8] Moreover, government expenditures on Medicare and Medicaid, two other large programs that serve the elderly, are likely to rise even faster than Social Security benefits because medical benefits are open-ended. CBO estimates that, taken together, Social Security, Medicare, and Medicaid will increase from close to 7 percent of GDP this year to almost 16 percent in 2075 if current policies are unchanged.[9]

Can a Near-Term Surplus Help Close the Post-2018 Deficits?

Although the future for Social Security finances looks bleak after 2018, the trustees project a large and growing Social Security surplus over the next decade, cumulating to $3.5 trillion from 2003 through 2012. Not surprisingly, a number of proposals suggest using that surplus to help pay the benefits of future retirees. Unfortunately, calling the tally of past Social Security surpluses a "trust fund" gives the impression that we have a direct mechanism—a "lock box," so to speak—for saving the current surplus to cover future shortfalls. But our current system affords no such mechanism because Social Security is funded on a pay-as-you-go basis.

Social Security surpluses do provide the government with a source of current revenue. Typically, the sole use for those revenues has been to help cover deficits in the non–Social Security side of the budget—a practice, as discussed earlier, that has likely encouraged the growth of non–Social Security spending. However, the shrinking of the non–Social Security deficit in 1998 and the emergence of a unified budget surplus gave rise to the idea that the Social Security surplus could be used to help fund the benefits of future retirees in an indirect way. That indirect way is to apply any unified-budget surplus that materializes toward retiring the publicly held debt.

Debt reduction might ease Social Security's future funding gap in two ways. First, reducing the debt reduces the annual interest charges the government pays on that debt, and doing so would presumably free up budgetary resources to be used for other purposes. However, there is no guarantee that those budget savings will be committed to paying Social Security benefits.

The second way is even more indirect. It relies on the presumption that retiring the debt would reduce interest rates and increase national savings, thereby enlarging the volume of funds available for investment and ultimately boosting the size of the economy and the incomes of future workers and taxpayers. However, it is debatable whether this favorable chain of events would occur with the strength needed to produce a significant increase in future national income.[10]

There are also other, simpler ways in which saving the surplus is not a reliable approach to solving the long-term problems of Social Security. First, for both economic and political reasons there may be no significant surplus to save. The budget projections made by CBO and the Office of Management and Budget at the start of 2001 showing large and growing surpluses came on the heels of several years of extraordinary growth that had converted total budget deficits into surpluses. Those projections have been scaled back in light of the slowdown in the economy in 2001 and the new defense and other demands placed on the budget after the attack on the World Trade Center on September 11, 2001. In addition, history suggests that if large surpluses return, they will not likely remain unclaimed for long.[11] That probability is not necessarily a bad thing because other uses for the surplus—funding the transition costs of individual Social Security accounts, for instance, or a well-designed tax reform—may be regarded as more beneficial than retiring the debt.

In the late 1990s, the prospect of a future of total budget surpluses inspired proposals to prefund future obligations by investing the surplus in private assets.[12] Proponents claim that investing the surplus in private assets is particularly attractive because if history is a guide, such investments would yield a high return. However, when a federal entity invests in private companies, numerous problems can easily arise. The size and composition of such government investments could destabilize markets. And at a time when the mere meeting of an economic group such as the World Trade Organization attracts legions of protestors, such public investment in private markets could be a source of ongoing political conflict.

Of course, as with any proposal that relies on using the surplus, federal investment in private assets depends on ensuring that the surplus is not diverted to other uses and that the earnings from the investment are dedicated to future Social Security liabilities. These types of investments are not the same as investments made by private individuals who own their own accounts. The only way to reliably prefund retirement benefits is through a system of individual accounts that are privately held and owned by the worker. Such an undertaking would require a more fundamental change in the system, as discussed below.

Can We Rely on Tax Increases Once Again?

In the past, as Social Security expanded, impending deficits were primarily resolved by raising the payroll tax rate and the ceiling on taxable covered earnings. From 1937 to 1949 the combined tax rate on workers and their employers was 2 percent. Today it is 12.4 percent in the OASDI programs and 15.3 percent when Hospital Insurance (HI) is added. The ceiling on taxable earnings was also increased, both absolutely and as a percent of the average wage. In 1951 it was $3,600, which was close to 150 percent of the average wage. By 1999 it had risen to $72,600, or 251 percent of the average wage. (In 2003 the maximum taxable earnings cap for OASDI is $87,000; the cap for the Medicare Hospital Insurance program was repealed altogether in 1993.)

Can taxes be raised again to resolve the coming crisis? Based on the actuaries' estimates, increasingly large tax hikes will be required simply to cover annual OASDI benefit costs after 2018. By 2035 taxes would have to increase by 4.6 percentage points of payroll to close the expected shortfall—about a 35 percent increase over the current tax level. The required tax increases would remain at that level until about 2050, when they would begin to mount still higher. Those estimates do not include the projected shortfall in the HI program, which is expected to grow even more rapidly than that in OASDI, almost doubling the size of the required tax increase by mid-century. In short, the cost of the combined OASDI and HI programs is projected to increase from its current level of 13.3 percent of taxable payroll to almost 25 percent by mid-century if current law is unchanged. Currently, legislated taxes are expected to cover costs until 2018 (2013 in HI). But taxes would have to rise by 50 percent (an 8.5 percentage point increase) to cover costs at mid-century. To rely on tax increases to fund the shortfall in Social Security and HI is to commit future workers to paying more than 18 percent of their wages to cover the benefits of retirees in another 18 years and 25 percent of wages to cover benefits at mid-century.

Fundamental Change

Social Security faces two different but related issues. One is the unsustainable financial situation of our current pay-as-you-go system, which will begin to run increasingly large deficits in about 15 years. That issue has been a major focus of this paper up to now. The other issue is the more fundamental one concerning the type of retirement system we want.

Over the past decade many analysts and at least two prominent government commissions have recommended major changes in Social Security.[13] A common goal of the proposed reforms is to shift Social Security partly or mainly to a system of individual accounts. Such a change would provide a mechanism for prefunding benefits and avoiding the drag of the pay-as-you-go system on the economy, and it would improve incentives to work and to save. Similar reforms have been adopted in various other countries.[14] Moreover, within the United States, private retirement plans have undergone analogous changes as participation has shifted from defined benefit to defined contribution plans. The shift to defined contribution plans more closely ties pension contributions to benefits, ensuring that they are prefunded, and usually gives workers more flexibility and control over their assets.

The growing interest in fundamental reform of Social Security stems from a growing recognition of the drawbacks of the current program. As it is now structured, Social Security is funded like most government programs in that the taxes of current workers pay the benefits of current recipients. In other government programs, however, either benefits are appropriated annually, and can therefore be adjusted to meet changing conditions, or the program is an entitlement, targeted on a relatively small proportion of the population defined as needy. Social Security, by contrast, is broadly targeted on the elderly and disabled, not on need, and is committed to paying large and growing benefits to a large and growing portion of the total population. The attempt to fund such a program on a pay-as-you-go basis when large swings in the birthrate and other factors cause major shifts in the ratio of beneficiaries to taxpayers is the source of the financing difficulty that we will soon face.

Is the existing program really what we want? Originally, the primary goal of Social Security, as stated in various government reports and presidential speeches, was to alleviate poverty among the elderly. In signing the Social Security Act on August 14, 1935, President Roosevelt said:

> We can never insure one hundred percent of the population against one hundred percent of the hazards and vicissitudes of life, but we have tried to frame a law which will give some measure of protection to the average citizen and to his family against the loss of a job and against poverty-ridden old age.

Social Security benefits, however, were never targeted to the poor. The political wisdom, as expressed by Wilbur J. Cohen, one of the major developers of the program, held that "a program that is only for the poor—one that has nothing in it for the middle income and upper income—is in the long run a program the public won't support."[15] Thus, from its early days, Social Security had a muddled mission. To support the program's welfare goals, the formula for calculating benefits at retirement was set to provide benefits that replaced a larger share of past earnings for low-wage workers than for high-wage workers. But to maintain the allegiance of the majority, the program was given the trappings of an earned right, funded by worker "contributions"—which is actually a payroll tax that is somewhat regressive. And despite the provision for declining replacement rates as earnings rise, those with higher earnings still get higher benefits.

How effective is Social Security as an anti-poverty program? It is true that the poverty rate of people age 65 and older has declined sharply over the years—from 35 percent in 1959 to 9.7 percent in 1999. Social Security undoubtedly played a significant role in that decline, although the general rise in income in the economy also contributed. However, only a minor portion of Social Security's huge expenditures actually serves to reduce poverty among the elderly. In 1999, in fact, only 20 percent of total Social Security expenditures would have been required to eliminate poverty altogether among those age 65 and over.[16] Thus the bulk of benefits is paid to those who would not be poor in any event, while a small portion goes to those whose incomes without any benefits would have been below poverty by varying amounts. Moreover, Social Security provides no benefits or very low benefits to those who neither earned enough themselves to qualify for benefits nor were married to someone who was so qualified. And such individuals are among the poorest elderly. That is why the current poverty rate of the elderly is 10.4 percent and not 0. Viewed simply as a transfer program, Social Security does not get high marks for cost-effectiveness.

Many analysts have also examined the way in which Social Security redistributes income both across and within cohorts when lifetime tax payments and benefits are taken into account. A general finding is that within a cohort, the effects of the progressive benefit structure that would tend to transfer income to those with lower earnings are partly or even fully offset by other factors such as the greater longevity of higher earners and the payment of spousal benefits.[17]

Many analysts also question the program's effects on saving and labor-force participation. In a pay-as-you-go system young workers are taxed to pay the benefits of current retirees. The introduction of Social Security has likely led individuals to reduce their own private savings, expecting to substitute Social Security benefits for those savings. Because the flow of funds each year is a straight transfer from young workers to retired workers, the system is a deterrent to net savings and capital formation. It is plausible that substituting a system of individual accounts in which individuals prefund their own retirement would increase national saving and contribute to economic growth.[18]

It also is likely that by promising a relatively generous benefit at a politically determined age of retirement, Social Security has distorted the decision about when to retire and has contributed to the sharp decline in work participation over time among men age 62 and older.[19] Work disincentives are greatest for low-wage workers who collect benefits that replace a high percentage of past earnings. Because Social Security provides only an annuity option, workers with shorter life expectancy, who are more likely to be low-wage workers, cannot receive a lump-sum withdrawal and therefore face a "use it or lose it" proposition. Moreover, because there is no asset accumulation, there is no possibility for bequests. The extent to which a move to individual accounts would improve incentives to spread work over older ages would depend on the particular design of the system. However, there is much more room for flexibility in such a system, which need not decree an arbitrarily set "age of retirement" and can allow for wealth accumulation with options for withdrawals and bequests.

Conclusion

Public discussion about the financial health of Social Security usually focuses on the long-run solvency of the system. Solvency is determined either by the year the actuaries estimate the trust fund will be exhausted (at present, 2042) or by the cumulated difference between Social Security receipts and benefit outlays over the next 70 years (at present, a shortfall of 27 percent of benefits).[20] However, focusing on trust fund balances misstates the problem. It can point out whether demographic trends are likely to be favorable or unfavorable. But by and large it does not raise the important issues relevant to system reform. It is time now to give serious thought to the question of the type of system we want to have.

Why do we need a government retirement program? As noted, from the start the main goal of Social Security was to prevent destitution among the elderly, who by dint of their age are assumed to be less able to fend for themselves. But that would call for a much smaller program focused only on the poor. The coverage of everyone else is usually said to be necessary because the young are myopic and would not perceive the need to accumulate assets for their old age in the absence of a government mandate. However, a mandate does not require a pay-as-you-go program. To the extent that compulsory saving is desired, it can be attained more directly with a system requiring individual accounts and the accumulation of privately held assets.

Most of the reform plans that have been proposed combine individual accounts with a pay-as-you-go component. That component varies in size from plan to plan but at least provides a safety net that can be designed to deal with redistributive goals. The most significant issue to be determined, however, is the overall size of the government program. We are now richer and better educated than our parents and grandparents; that trend is likely to continue with future generations. As a result, our ability to plan and direct our own lifetime savings should grow, particularly if changes are made in tax policy that eliminate saving disincentives. Thus in time we might plan for a reduced share of income going to a compulsory individual account system in the expectation that voluntary saving would grow. The generosity of the pay-as-you-go component is a particularly important consideration because the promise of a transfer that replaces a significant share of earnings is a very good reason not to save. Under the current system, benefits for new retirees have been growing much faster than has inflation because benefits are indexed to wage growth.

Serious thought should also be given to reducing the growth of benefits in the pay-as-you-go component in future years, particularly for those with average or higher earnings. This reduction could be attained by increasing the retirement age or, preferably in my view, by transitioning to a price-indexed system, a method suggested in the second of the three proposals of the President's Commission on Social Security.

Whatever the final shape of reform, it is time for Congress to stop playing verbal games over what are essentially accounting gimmicks and get down to serious work.

Notes

1. The apt phrase "victim of demography" is Jacob Mincer's.

2. See Henry Aaron, Alan Blinder, Alicia Munnell, and Peter Orszag, *Perspectives on the Interim Report of the President's Commission to Strengthen Social Security*, Center on Budget and Policy Priorities and the Century Foundation, July 23, 2001.

3. See Kent Smetters, "Has Mental Accounting Been Effective in 'Lock-Boxing' Social Security's Assets? Theory and Evidence," University of Pennsylvania and NBER, August 2001. Smetters' statistical analysis of the effect of increases in the Social Security surplus on non–Social Security spending covers the period 1979–2001 and includes controls for GDP growth, wages and salaries, and trend factors. His results indicate that the "leakage rate" could exceed 300 percent. That is, a one dollar increase in the Social Security surpluses is associated with a $3.39 decrease in non–Social Security surpluses (i.e., outlays and/or tax expenditures and other tax reductions), other things remaining the same.

4. See John F. Cogan, *The Congressional Response to Social Security Surpluses, 1935–1994* (Hoover Institution Essays in Public Policy, 1998).

5. Spurred by an imminent financial shortfall, the 1983 Amendment to the Social Security Act made a number of unprecedented changes. On the revenue side, the payroll tax rate was raised in the near term by moving forward the tax rate increases that had been scheduled for later years and extending coverage to workers in nonprofit

organizations and federal employees. Near-term benefits were effectively reduced for current retirees by postponing the scheduled cost-of-living adjustment for six months. Future benefits were reduced by raising the age at which full retirement benefits could be collected from 65 years to 67 years. The increase is phased in by two months a year starting with those attaining age 62 in 2000, and the full retirement age reaches 67 for those attaining age 62 in 2022. Social Security benefits were effectively further reduced by subjecting a varying portion of benefits to the federal income tax, depending on other income.

6. Congressional Budget Office (CBO), March 2002 projection.

7. Life expectancy at age 65 of the average 65-year-old has increased for men from 12.7 years in 1940 (the first year Social Security benefits were paid) to an estimated 16.3 years today, and for women from 14.7 years to 19.6 years (reported in CBO, *Social Security: A Primer*, September 2001). The projections to 2075 of the Social Security trustees assume that life expectancy at age 65 will continue to improve but at a slower rate. The trustees' assumptions have been questioned by demographers and others who believe that mortality is declining faster than the trustees expect. (See the discussion in Andrew G. Biggs, "Social Security, Is It 'A Crisis That Doesn't Exist?'" Cato Institute Social Security Paper no. 21, October 5, 2000.) If true, the financial imbalance would occur sooner than projected.

8. CBO, "The Future Growth of Social Security: It's Not Just Society's Aging," Long-Range Fiscal Policy Brief, no. 9, July 1, 2003.

9. CBO, "Comparing Budgetary and Trust Fund Measures of the Outlook for Social Security and Medicare," Long-Range Fiscal Policy Brief, no. 10, October 10, 2003.

10. Even assuming that a total budget surplus is realized over the next decade and that it is not used for any other purpose than paying down the debt, the extent to which national income would rise is uncertain. At issue is the response of private savers to the increase in government saving from running large surpluses. If private saving fully offset government saving, then there would be no net saving increase and no expected effect on investment and economic growth. (See the discussion in *Social Security: A Primer*). However, this is a difficult matter to resolve. Rudolph Penner, Sundeep Solanki, Eric Toder, and Michael Weisner estimate that economic growth would be positively affected by saving the surplus, but the effect would be small. Based on a projection that a total budget surplus would be realized every year from 2000 to 2021 and that all of it would be saved, they estimate that the growth of consumption per capita would be 0.1 percent higher per year over the 1999–2023 period. By 2023 the level of per capita consumption would be 2 percent higher. See *Saving the Surplus to Save Social Security: What Does It Mean?* Urban Institute, The Retirement Project, Brief Series, no. 7, October 1999.

11. See Cogan, and Smetters (2001).

12. See Henry Aaron and Robert Reischauer, *Countdown to Reform* (New York: Century Foundation Press, 1998). For a discussion and critique see Martin Feldstein and Jeffrey B. Liebman, "Social Security," NBER Working Paper 8451, September 2001, and CBO, *Social Security: A Primer*.

13. The 1994–1996 Advisory Council on Social Security, chaired by Edward M. Gramlich, produced three plans for reforming Social Security, two of which included a component of individual private accounts. The President's Commission on Social Security.

14. See James M. Poterba, S. P. Venti, and David Wise, "The Transition to Personal Accounts and Increasing Retirement Wealth: Macro and Micro Evidence," NBER Working Paper 8610, November 2001.

15. Quoted in C. Eugene Steuerle and Jon M. Bakija, *Social Security for the 21st Century, Right and Wrong Approaches* (Washington: Urban Institute Press, 2000), p. 26.

16. This is the author's estimate based on calculations from the 2000 CPS microdata file. Poverty is based on a measure of income that excludes Social Security and all other transfer payments. The calculation takes the difference between nontransfer income and the poverty threshold for each person age 65 and over and sums these differences. For unmarried persons the poverty threshold for a single individual is used even if they were living with others. Separate calculations were made for married couples.

17. See, for example, Jeffrey Liebman, "Redistribution in the Current U.S. Social Security Program," NBER Working Paper 8625, 2001; J. L. Coronado, D. Fullerton, and T. Glass, "Distributional Aspects of Proposed Changes to the Social Security System," in *Tax Policy and the Economy* 13, ed. James Poterba, NBER, 1999; Steuerle and Bakija, op. cit.; and the review and analysis in Feldstein and Liebman, 2001, op. cit.

18. James Poterba suggests that there is considerable support in the economics literature for the view that a shift from the current underfunded system to a fully funded system would raise national saving. He also reports on a survey of public finance economists conducted by himself, Victor Fuchs, and Alan Krueger in 1997 that asked what these economists thought was the effect of Social Security on the personal saving rate. The median respondent indicated that the personal saving rate would have been 3 percentage points higher in the absence of Social Security. But, not surprisingly, there was substantial dispersion in the estimated magnitude of the effect. See Poterba's concise discussion of this complex subject in Eric M. Engen and William Gale's *Effects of Social Security Reform on Private and National Saving*, published in *Social Security Reform, Links to Saving, Investment and Growth*, ed. Steven A. Sass and Robert K. Triest, Conference Proceedings, Series no. 41, June 1997, Federal Reserve Bank of Boston.

19. See *Social Security and Retirement around the World*, ed. Jonathan Gruber and David Wise (Chicago: University of Chicago Press, 1999). Also see the review and discussion of other research on the topic in Feldstein and Liebman, op. cit.

20. Both measures seriously understate the problem because they assume that the trust fund can accumulate assets that in turn bear interest. As discussed above, the trust fund has no mechanism for investing current surpluses to cover future shortfalls. In addition, by confining the long term to the next 75 years much of the unfunded liability of the system is uncounted, since the Social Security deficit is expected to continue to grow after the 75th year.

3. "Saving" Social Security Is Not Enough

Michael Tanner

The corridors of Washington are ringing with calls to "save" Social Security. And it is certainly easy to understand why the program needs "saving." Social Security is rapidly heading for financial insolvency. By 2018 the program will begin running a deficit, paying out more in benefits than it takes in through taxes. The resulting shortfall will necessitate at least a 50 percent increase in payroll taxes, a near one-third reduction in benefits, or some combination of benefit cuts and tax increases. Overall, Social Security faces a long-term funding shortfall of more than $25 trillion.[1]

As a result, there have been numerous proposals designed to shore up the program's shaky finances. Those proposals generally take one of two tracks: setting aside current Social Security surpluses in some form of "lock box" or injecting general revenue financing into the system.

There are serious flaws in both of those approaches. The lock-box proposals do not, in fact, do anything to change Social Security's financing. Currently, surplus Social Security taxes are used to purchase government bonds, which are held by the Social Security trust fund. Those bonds will eventually have to be repaid. To do so, the government will have to raise revenue. Thus the bonds represent nothing more than a claim against future tax revenues, in essence a form of IOU.[2] Revenue from the purchase of those bonds is credited to the unified federal budget and used to pay the general operating expenses of the federal government. Under lock-box proposals, the revenue from the purchase of the bonds could be used only to pay down the national debt. Paying down the national debt may or may not be a good thing, and it may make it easier for the federal

Originally published as Cato Institute Social Security Paper no. 20, May 25, 2000, and updated to reflect current information.

government to borrow money in the future, but it does nothing to change the date at which Social Security will begin to run a deficit. As the *Washington Post* has pointed out, "The same IOUs are put in the trust fund whether the surplus is used to finance other programs or pay down debt."[3]

Some proposals go beyond setting aside Social Security surpluses and would inject all or part of the current general revenue budget surpluses into the Social Security system. Aside from the fact that Social Security's liabilities far outstrip the amount of surplus available, it is impossible to prefund Social Security under the program's current structure. Any additional funds put into the system today would simply purchase more government bonds, which would have to be paid in the future from whatever tax monies were available then.

However, setting aside the important point that none of the current proposals to save Social Security actually does so, the current focus on "saving" Social Security is itself misguided. Merely finding sufficient funding to preserve Social Security fails to address the serious shortcomings of the current system. The question should be, not whether we can save Social Security, but whether we can provide the best possible retirement system for American workers. Such a system should keep seniors out of poverty as well as improve prospects for future generations. It should provide an adequate retirement income and the best possible return on an individual's money. It should be fair, treating similarly situated people equally. Certainly, it should not penalize the disadvantaged in society such as the poor and minorities. And it should allow people to own their benefits, freeing seniors from dependence on politicians and politics for retirement benefits.

On all those scores, Social Security is an abysmal failure. It fails both as an anti-poverty program and as a retirement program. It contains numerous inequities and leaves future retirement benefits to the whims of politicians. Why should the goal of public policy be to save such a program?

Instead of saving Social Security, we should begin the transition to a new and better retirement system based on individually owned, privately invested accounts. Such a system would allow workers to accumulate real wealth that would prevent their retiring to poverty. Because a system of individual accounts would provide a far higher rate of return, it would yield much higher retirement benefits. Because workers would own their accounts, money in them could be passed on to future generations. That would particularly benefit the poor and minorities. Finally, again because workers would own their retirement accounts, they would no longer be dependent on politicians for their retirement incomes.

Social Security as an Anti-Poverty Program

Social Security has elements of both an insurance and a welfare program. It is, in effect, both a retirement and an anti-poverty program.[4] Although people most often think of the retirement component of the program, the system's defenders often focus on its anti-poverty elements. For example, Rep. Bill Archer (R-Tex.), chairman of the House Ways and Means Committee and author of a proposal to save Social Security, calls the program "the country's greatest anti-poverty program."[5] But is it really?

There is no question that the poverty rate among the elderly has declined dramatically in the last half century. As recently as 1959, the poverty rate for seniors was 35.2 percent, more than double the 17 percent poverty rate for the general adult population.[6] Today, it has declined to approximately 10.4 percent.[7]

Clearly, Social Security has had a significant impact on that trend. A 1999 study by the Center on Budget and Policy Priorities found that in the absence of Social Security benefits approximately 47.6 percent of seniors would have incomes below the poverty level.[8] That suggests that receipt of Social Security benefits lifted more than 35 percent of seniors, approximately 11.4 million people, out of poverty. CBPP also points out that the percentage of elderly who would have been in poverty in the absence of Social Security has remained relatively constant over the last several decades, while the percentage of elderly in poverty after receiving Social Security benefits has been steadily declining, indicating the increased importance of Social Security as an anti-poverty remedy.[9]

The primary problem with this line of analysis is that it assumes that any loss of Social Security benefits would not be offset by income from other sources. In other words, it simply takes a retiree's current income and subtracts Social Security benefits to discover, no surprise, that total income is now lower and, indeed, frequently low enough to throw the retiree into poverty.

Social Security benefits are a substantial component of most retirees' income. Those benefits constitute more than 90 percent of retirement income for 29 percent of the elderly. Nearly six out of ten retirees receive at least half of their income from Social Security.[10] The question, therefore, is not whether the sudden elimination of Social Security income would leave retirees worse off—clearly it would—but whether in the absence of Social Security (or an alternative mandatory savings program) retirees would have changed their behavior to provide other sources of income for their own retirement.

For example, we could ask how many seniors, in the absence of Social Security, would still be working. If they were, they would have a source of income not considered by the CBPP study. Clearly, not all seniors are able to continue working. However, many can and would. Indeed, Congress recently repealed the Social Security earnings test precisely because there are many seniors who *want* to continue working.

A more important question is whether workers, without Social Security to depend on, would have changed their behavior and saved more for their retirement. The evidence is strong that Social Security discourages individual savings. For example, Martin Feldstein of Harvard University and Anthony Pellechio of the National Bureau for Economic Research have found that households reduce their private savings by nearly one dollar for every dollar of the present value of expected future Social Security benefits.[11] Other studies have put the amount of substitution somewhat lower but still indicate a substantial offset. Even two researchers for the Social Security Administration, Dean Leimer and David Richardson, have conceded that "a dollar of Social Security wealth substitutes for about three-fifths of a dollar of fungible assets."[12]

Therefore, given that many seniors would have replaced Social Security income with income from other sources, the impact of Social Security on reducing poverty among the elderly may be overstated.

However, even taking the arguments of Social Security's defenders on their own terms, the evidence suggests that Social Security fails as an anti-poverty tool. After all, despite receiving Social Security benefits, nearly one of ten seniors still lives in poverty.[13]

For some subgroups, the problem is far worse. For example, although the poverty rate for elderly married women is relatively low (5.4 percent), the poverty rate is far higher for elderly widowed women (16.8 percent) and for never married and divorced elderly women (24.7 percent).[14] African-American seniors are also disproportionately left in poverty. One out of four African Americans over the age of 65 has an income below the poverty level.[15]

Social Security's failure as an anti-poverty program is not surprising because Social Security benefits are actually quite low. A worker earning the minimum wage over his entire working life and retiring in 2002 would receive only $8,181 per year in Social Security benefits,[16] well below the 2002 poverty level of $8,628.[17] As mentioned above, nearly three out of ten elderly rely on Social Security for more than 90 percent of retirement income. Many have no other income at all. Social Security is insufficient to raise those seniors out of poverty.

This can be contrasted with what those people would have received had they been able to invest their payroll taxes in real capital assets. For example, if the minimum wage worker described above had been able to invest his payroll taxes, he would be receiving retirement benefits of more than $20,000 per year, nearly three times the poverty level.[18] Clearly, by forcing workers to invest in the current pay-as-you-go system, rather than in real capital assets, Social Security is actually contributing to poverty among the elderly.

Not only does Social Security contribute to poverty among current seniors, it also helps perpetuate poverty for future generations. Social Security benefits are not inheritable. A worker can pay Social Security taxes for 30 or 40 years, but, if that worker dies without children under the age of 18 or a spouse over the age of 65, none of the money paid into the system is passed on to his heirs.[19] As Jagadeesh Gokhale, an economist at the Federal Reserve Bank of Cleveland, and others have noted, Social Security essentially forces low-income workers to annuitize their wealth, preventing them from making a bequest of that wealth to their heirs.[20]

Moreover, because this forced annuitization applies to a larger portion of the wealth of low-income workers than of high-income workers, it turns inheritance into a "disequalizing force," leading to greater inequality of wealth in America. The wealthy are able to bequeath their wealth to their heirs, while the poor cannot. Indeed, Gokhale and Boston University economist Laurence Kotlikoff estimate that Social Security doubles the share of wealth owned by the richest 1 percent of Americans.[21]

57

Feldstein reaches a similar conclusion. He suggests that low-income workers substitute "Social Security wealth" in the form of promised future Social Security benefits for other forms of savings. As a result, a greater proportion of a high-income worker's wealth is in fungible assets. Since fungible wealth is inheritable, whereas Social Security wealth is not, a small proportion of the population holds a stable concentration of fungible wealth.[22] Feldstein's work suggests that the concentration of wealth in the United States would be reduced by as much as half if low-income workers were able to substitute real wealth for Social Security wealth. Individual accounts would allow them to do so.

Thus, far from being "the country's greatest anti-poverty program," Social Security appears to do a poor job of lifting seniors out of poverty and may in fact perpetuate their poverty while increasing inequality in this country.

Social Security as a Retirement Program

If Social Security is an inadequate anti-poverty program, does it at least meet its second goal as a retirement program? When Franklin Roosevelt proposed Social Security, he promised a program that would provide retirement benefits "at least as good as any American could buy from a private insurance company."[23] While that may have been true at one time, it certainly is no longer the case.

Social Security's rate of return has been steadily declining since the program's inception and is now far lower than the return from private capital investment. According to the Social Security Administration, workers born after 1973 will receive rates of return ranging from 5.05 percent for a low-wage, single-income couple to just 1.08 percent for a high-wage-earning single male.[24] The overall rate of return for all workers born in a given year was estimated at slightly below 3 percent for those born in 1940, 2 percent for those born in 1960, and below 1 percent for those who will be born this century.[25] Numerous private studies predict future rates of return for an average-wage earner ranging from 2 percent to a negative 3 percent.[26]

To make matters worse, the studies generally assume that Social Security will be able to pay all its promised benefits without increasing payroll taxes. However, the Social Security system is facing a long-term financial shortfall of more than $25 trillion. According to the system's own Board of Trustees, either taxes will have to be raised by at least 50 percent or benefits reduced by 27 percent. As a result, the rate of return will be even lower than the rates cited above. In many cases the return will actually be negative.[27]

By comparison, the average rate of return to the stock market since 1926 has been at least 7 percent.[28] That return has held despite a major depression, several recessions, World War II, two smaller wars, and the turbulent inflation-recession years of the 1970s. Of course, there have been ups and downs in the market, but there has been no 20-year period since 1926 during which the market was a net loser. Indeed, there has never been a 20-year period in which the market performed worse than projected future returns from Social Security.[29]

Even corporate bonds have consistently outperformed Social Security. Discounting the period 1941–51, when government price controls artificially reduced the return, corporate bonds have paid an average real annual return of more than 4 percent.[30]

Thus, because it deprives American workers of the ability to invest in private capital markets, the current Social Security system is costing American retirees hundreds of thousands of dollars. For example, a single-earner couple, whose wage earner was 30 years old in 2000 and earned $24,000 per year, can expect to pay more than $134,000 in Social Security taxes over their lifetimes and receive $292,320 in lifetime Social Security benefits (including spousal benefits), assuming that both husband and wife live to normally expected ages.[31] However, had they been able to invest privately, they would have received $875,280.[32] That means the current Social Security system is depriving them of more than half a million dollars.

A second way to consider Social Security's adequacy as a retirement program is to look at the replacement rate, that portion of preretirement income replaced by Social Security benefits. Most financial planners say that a person will need retirement benefits equal to between 60 and 85 percent of preretirement wages in order to maintain his or her standard of living.[33]

However, Social Security provides only 41.6 percent of preretirement income for average-income workers. Because Social Security has a progressive benefit formula, low-income workers do better with a replacement rate of 56.1 percent, still below what is needed. That is especially true since low-income workers lack other forms of retirement income. The replacement rate for maximum-income workers is only 29.8 percent.[34] In the future, the situation will grow even worse. Even under current law, replacement rates are scheduled to decline significantly. However, because Social Security cannot pay all promised future benefits, the Congressional Research Service estimates that the replacement rate for an average worker will decline to as low as 26 percent, a 40 percent decline from the current already inadequate levels.[35] Clearly, Social Security, both now and in the future, leaves many seniors without the income necessary to maintain their standard of living.

Again, compare this with the replacement rates provided under a system of private investment. Assuming that the worker described previously was able to invest the full nondisability portion of his Social Security taxes (10.6 percent of wages), his replacement rate would be an astounding 260 percent of preretirement income! If he invested just 4 percent of wages, he would still have a replacement rate equal to 100 percent of his preretirement income.

Social Security Is Unfair

As if it were not bad enough that Social Security fails in its stated mission as an anti-poverty and retirement program, the program also contains very serious inequities that make it fundamentally unfair.

The program's most obvious unfairness is *intergenerational*. Retirees currently receiving benefits paid a relatively low payroll tax over their working lifetimes and receive a fairly high rate of return. That high return is subsidized by much higher payroll taxes on today's young workers who, in turn, can expect much lower future benefits. As Daniel Shapiro, professor of philosophy at West Virginia University, has pointed out, one of the basic precepts of social justice is the minimization of *unchosen* inequalities.[36] However, the future generations forced to bear the burden of Social Security's unfunded liabilities must do so entirely because of the time of their birth and not through any fault or choice of their own.

The program's *intragenerational* inequities are less visible but just as unfair. As we have already noted, Social Security benefits are not inheritable. Therefore, lifetime Social Security benefits depend, in part, on longevity. As a result, people with identical earnings histories will receive different levels of benefits depending on how long they live. Individuals who live to be 100 receive far more in benefits than individuals who die at 66. Therefore, those groups in our society with shorter life expectancies, such as the poor and African Americans, are put at a severe disadvantage.

Of course, Social Security does have a progressive benefit formula, whereby low-income individuals receive proportionately higher benefits per dollar paid into the system than do high-income workers.[37] The question, therefore, is to what degree shorter life expectancies offset this progressivity.

The findings of studies that use income as the sole criterion are mixed. Some studies, such as those by Eugene Steuerle and Jan Bakja of the Urban Institute and Dean Leimer of the Social Security Administration, conclude that shorter life expectancies diminish but do not completely offset Social Security's progressivity.[38] However, there is a growing body of literature—including studies by Daniel Garrett of Stanford University, the RAND Corporation, and others—that shows that the progressive benefit formula is completely offset, resulting in redistribution of wealth from poor people to the already wealthy.[39]

The question of Social Security's unfairness to ethnic minorities appears more straightforward, particularly in the case of African Americans. African Americans of all income levels have shorter life expectancies than do whites. As a result, a black man or woman, earning exactly the same lifetime wages and paying exactly the same lifetime Social Security taxes as his or her white counterpart, will likely receive far less in lifetime Social Security benefits. For example, assume that a 30-year-old black man and a 30-year-old white man both earn an equivalent of $30,000 per year over their working lifetimes. By the time they retire, they will each have paid $136,740 in Social Security taxes over their lifetimes and will be entitled to monthly Social Security benefits of $1,162.[40] However, the white man can expect to live until age 81. If he does, he will receive $199,400 in total Social Security benefits. The black man, in contrast, can expect to live only to age 79.[41] He can expect to receive only $174,300, almost $25,000 less than his white counterpart. This may actually understate the unfairness of the current sysem, since it is based on life expectancies at age 65. However, if both men are age 30 today, the life expectancy for the white man is 76; for the black man it is only 71.[42] If those projections are accurate, the black man can expect to receive nearly $70,000 less in lifetime Social Security benefits than his white counterpart.

It seems amazing that this disparate impact, which would not be tolerated in any other government program, is so easily accepted within the current Social Security system.[43]

The current program is also unfair to women who work outside the home. Under the current system, a woman is automatically entitled to 50 percent of her husband's benefits, whether or not she has worked outside the home or paid Social Security taxes.[44] However, if a woman is able to claim benefits both as a spouse and in her own right, she may receive only the larger of the two. Because many women work only part-time, take years off from work to raise children, or earn lower wages than their husbands, 50 percent of the husband's benefits is frequently larger than the benefits a woman would be entitled to as a result of her own earnings. She will, therefore, receive only the benefits based on her husband's earnings. She will receive no additional benefits even though she may have worked and paid thousands of dollars in payroll taxes. Indeed, she would receive exactly the same benefits as if she had never worked a day outside the home or paid a dime in Social Security taxes. The taxes she paid earn her exactly *nothing*.[45]

Anyone concerned with fairness and equity in government programs must acknowledge that our current Social Security system falls far short of meeting those goals.

Social Security and the Dignity of Older Americans

Finally, it should be noted that the current Social Security system makes American seniors dependent on government and the political process for their retirement income. In essence, it reduces American seniors to supplicants, robbing them of their dignity and control over their own lives.

Americans, of course, do not get back the money that they individually paid into Social Security. Under our pay-as-you-go Social Security system, the money that workers pay in Social Security taxes is not saved or invested for their own retirement; it is instead used to pay for benefits for current retirees. Any overpayment is used by the federal government to pay its general operating expenses or, under various lock-box proposals, to pay down the national debt.

In exchange, workers receive a promise that the government will tax future workers in order to provide benefits to today's workers when they retire. However, that promise is not any sort of legally enforceable contract. It has long been settled law that there is no legal right to Social Security. In two important cases, *Helvering v. Davis* and *Flemming v. Nestor,* the U.S. Supreme Court has ruled that Social Security taxes are simply taxes and convey no property or contractual rights to Social Security benefits.[46]

As a result, a worker's retirement security is entirely dependent on political decisions made by the president and Congress. Benefits may be reduced or even eliminated at any time and are not directly related to Social Security taxes paid into the system.

Therefore, retirees are left totally dependent on the whims of politicians for their retirement income. A person can work hard, play by the rules, and pay thousands of dollars in Social Security taxes but at retirement his benefits depend entirely on the decisions of the president and Congress. Despite their best intentions, seniors have been turned into little more than wards of the state.

Conclusion

If Social Security didn't exist today, would we invent it? The current Social Security system is a failure by almost every criterion. It fails to lift many seniors out of poverty or to improve prospects for future generations. Indeed, it may actually redistribute money from the poor to the wealthy. Because it forces the poor to annuitize their savings, it prevents the accumulation of real wealth and prevents the poor from passing that wealth on to future generations. Social Security also fails as a retirement program. It does not provide an adequate retirement income or yield the best possible return on an individual's money. Nor is the program fair. It includes numerous inequities that unfairly discriminate against minorities, the poor, and working women. And, finally, because people do not have any legal ownership of their benefits, it leaves seniors dependent on politicians and politics for their retirement benefits.

Surely this cannot be what we seek from Social Security, especially when there are alternatives available. Workers should be allowed to take the money they are currently paying in Social Security taxes and redirect it to individually owned, privately invested accounts, similar to individual retirement accounts or 401(k) plans. The funds that accumulated in those accounts would be invested in real assets such as stocks and bonds, with safeguards against highly risky or speculative investments. The funds would be the account holders' personal property. At retirement, workers could convert all or part of their accumulated funds into an annuity or take a series of programmed withdrawals from the principal. If they choose the latter option, any funds remaining at their death would become part of their estate, fully inheritable by their heirs.

A retirement program based on individually owned, privately invested accounts would provide higher retirement benefits and a better rate of return than does Social Security. It would lift more seniors out of poverty and, because funds are inheritable, accumulated wealth could be passed on to future generations. It would not penalize groups with shorter life expectancies and would eliminate the penalty on working women. And workers would own their benefits and thus be free from political risk and dependence.[47]

When it comes to Social Security, policymakers should consider whether it is more important to save a system or to provide a better retirement for American seniors.

Notes

1. Board of Trustees, Federal Old-Age and Survivors Insurance and Disability Insurance Trust Funds, *2003 Annual Report* (Washington: Government Printing Office, March 17, 2003).

2. As President Clinton's own budget notes: "[Trust fund] balances are available to finance future benefit payments and other trust fund expenditures—but only in a bookkeeping sense. These funds are not set up to be pension funds like the funds of private pension plans. They do not consist of real economic assets that can be drawn down in the future to fund benefits. Instead, they are claims on the Treasury that, when redeemed, will have to be financed by raising taxes, borrowing from the public, or reducing benefits or other expenditures. The existence of large trust fund balances, therefore, does not, by itself, have any impact on the government's ability to pay benefits." Executive Office of the President of the United States, *Analytical Perspectives: Budget of the United States Government, Fiscal Year 2000* (Washington: Government Printing Office, 1999), p. 337.

3. "Ploys Will Be Ploys," Editorial, *Washington Post*, October 28, 1999.

4. W. Andrew Achenbaum, *Social Security: Visions and Revisions* (Cambridge: Cambridge University Press, 1986), pp. 54–55. See also Peter Ferrara, *Social Security: The Inherent Contradiction* (Washington: Cato Institute, 1980).

5. Bill Archer, Comments at Hearing on Social Security before the House Committee on Ways and Means, 106th Cong., 1st sess., June 9, 1999, transcript, p. 48, Federal News Service.

6. Daryl Jackson et al., "Understanding Social Security: The Issues and Alternatives," American Institute of Certified Public Accountants, Washington, November 1998, p. 17.

7. U.S. Census Bureau, Current Population Reports, Series P60-222, 2002, Table 2, p. 6.

8. Kathryn Porter, Kathy Larin, and Wendell Primus, "Social Security and Poverty among the Elderly: A National and State Perspective," Center on Budget and Policy Priorities, Washington, April 1999.

9. Ibid., p. 16.

10. "Income of the Population 55 or Older, 2000," Social Security Administration Office of Policy, February 2002, Table 6.A2, p. 107.

11. Martin Feldstein and Anthony Pellechio, "Social Security and Household Wealth Accumulation: New Microeconomic Evidence," *Review of Economics and Statistics* 61 (August 1979): 361–68.

12. Dean Leimer and David Richardson, "Social Security, Uncertainty, Adjustments, and the Consumption Decision," *Economica* 59 (August 1992): 29.

13. U.S. Census Bureau, Current Population Reports, Series P60-222, 2002, Table 2, p. 6.

14. U.S. House of Representatives, Committee on Ways and Means, 2000 *Green Book* (Washington: Government Printing Office, 2000), p. 999.

15. U.S. Census Bureau, Population Report P60-222, 2002, Table A-2, p. 30.

16. Board of Trustees, Federal Old-Age and Survivors Insurance and Disability Insurance Trust Funds, *2002 Annual Report* (Washington: Government Printing Office, March 26, 2002), Table VI.E.11.

17. U.S. Census Bureau, 2002 poverty threshold.

18. Assumes investment in stocks earning actual returns and that the individual was born in 1935, earned the minimum wage his entire working life, and retires in 2000.

19. Survivors' benefits may be extended to age 21 if the child is enrolled in college.

20. Jagadeesh Gokhale et al., "Simulating the Transmission of Wealth Inequality via Bequests," *Journal of Public Economics* 79 (2001).

21. Jagadeesh Gokhale and Laurence Kotlikoff, "The Impact of Social Security and Other Factors on the Distribution of Wealth," National Bureau of Economic Research, Cambridge, Mass., October 1999.

22. Martin Feldstein, "Social Security and the Distribution of Wealth," *Journal of the American Statistical Association* 71 (December 1976): 800–807.

23. Quoted in Warren Shore, *Social Security: The Fraud in Your Future* (New York: Macmillan, 1975), p. 2.

24. Orlo Nichols, Michael D. Clingman, and Milton Glanz, "Internal Real Rates of Return under the OASDI Program for Hypothetical Workers," Social Security Administration, Office of the Chief Actuary, Actuarial Note 144, June 2001, Table 4. Scaled earning patterns are for modified present law OASDI program.

25. Dean Leimer, "Cohort-Specific Measures of Lifetime Net Social Security Transfers," Social Security Administration, Office of Research and Statistics, Working Paper no. 59, February 1994.

26. For example, in our 1998 book, *A New Deal for Social Security*, Peter Ferrara and I updated a study that Ferrara conducted for the National Chamber Foundation in 1986. Using economic and demographic assumptions taken from the Social Security trustees' intermediate assumptions, adjusting for survivors' and disability benefits, and assuming that, somehow, Social Security would pay all promised benefits, we found that most workers who entered the workforce after 1985 would receive rates of return of 1.0 to 1.5 percent or less. Peter J. Ferrara and Michael Tanner, *A New Deal for Social Security* (Washington: Cato Institute, 1998), p. 69. Those results closely matched the results of a study that Ferrara conducted in 1985 with Professor John Lott, then at the Wharton School and now at Yale Law School. The 1985 study, which

looked at workers entering the workforce in 1983, also showed rates of return from Social Security for most workers in the range of 1.0 to 1.5 percent. Peter J. Ferrara and John Lott, "Social Security's Rates of Return for Young Workers," in *Social Security: Prospects for Real Reform,* ed. Peter Ferrara (Washington: Cato Institute, 1985), pp. 13–36. The Heritage Foundation concluded in 1998 that the rate of return to an average two-earner family (both 30 years old) was just 1.23 percent, while the return to African-American men was actually negative. William Beach and Gareth Davis, "Social Security's Rate of Return," Report no. 98-01 of the Heritage Center for Data Analysis, Washington, January 15, 1998. In a 1988 study for the National Bureau of Economic Research, John Geanakopolis, Olivia Mitchell, and Stephen Zeldes concluded that workers born after 1970 could expect a rate of return of less than 2 percent. John Geanakopolis, Olivia Mitchell, and Stephen Zeldes, "Social Security's Money Worth," National Bureau of Economic Research Working Paper no. 6722, Washington, September 1988. The U.S. General Accounting Office reports that a two-earner couple born in 1973 and making average wages would receive a rate of return from Social Security of approximately 2.1 percent. Bovbjerg, p. 13. The nonpartisan Tax Foundation suggests future rates of return as low as a negative 3 percent. Arthur Hall, "Forcing a Bad Investment on Retiring Americans," Tax Foundation Special Report no. 55, November 1995.

27. See, for example, Jagadeesh Gokhale and Laurence Kotlikoff, "Social Security's Treatment of Postwar Americans: How Bad Can It Get?" National Bureau of Economic Research Working Paper no. 7362, Cambridge, Mass., September 1999. See also Hall; Beach and Davis; and Geanakopolis, Mitchell, and Zeldes.

28. Michael Tanner, "The Better Deal: Estimating Rates of Return under a System of Individual Accounts," Cato Institute Social Security Paper no. 31, October 28, 2003.

29. Jeremy J. Siegel, *Stocks for the Long Run* (New York: McGraw-Hill, 1998), p. 26. Of course, critics of Social Security choice point out, correctly, that the past is no guarantee of future performance. But the critics' contention that the future performance of private capital markets will be significantly lower than past averages is unpersuasive. See, for example, Peter Ferrara, "Social Security Is Still a Hopelessly Bad Deal for Today's Workers," Cato Institute Social Security Paper no. 18, November 29, 1999.

The critics generally argue that, using the Social Security trustees' projections for future economic growth, economic growth will be too slow to sustain continued stock market gains. Dean Baker and Mark Weisbrot, for example, suggest that future returns will be below 3.5 percent. Dean Baker and Mark Weisbrot, *Social Security: The Phony Crisis* (Chicago: University of Chicago Press, 1999), pp. 88–104. However, the critics fail to acknowledge that the issue is not simply the return to capital markets but the spread between the return to capital markets and the return to Social Security. As Gokhale and Kotlikoff point out, Social Security tax payments and benefit receipts are closely linked to overall labor productivity growth, which is highly correlated with economic performance, which, in turn, is correlated with stock market performance. It is entirely reasonable to compare the real rate of return from stocks with the return from Social Security. Gokhale and Kotlikoff, "Social Security's Treatment of Postwar Americans," p. 15. In other words, if economic growth is so slow as to reduce the returns from private capital investment, it will also reduce the taxes collected by the Social Security system, exacerbating its fiscal imbalance, leading to lower benefits or higher taxes and a reduced Social Security rate of return. Thus, both Social Security's return and the return on capital could go up or they could go down, but private capital markets will always outperform Social Security. It is even possible to envision a scenario in which capital returns increase while Social Security tax receipts do not, for example, if wage growth takes place largely above the cap, or if economic growth translates to nonwage compensation rather than increased real wages. However, it is difficult to foresee a scenario under which real wages (and therefore Social Security revenues) rise while private capital markets do not.

Critics of Social Security choice also suggest that the return to private capital markets should be reduced to reflect administrative costs and the costs associated with the transition to a privatized system. Both arguments have been refuted extensively elsewhere. However, it is worth noting that the U.S. General Accounting Office suggests that administrative costs would range from a low of 10 basis points to a high of 300 basis points, with most estimates closer to the low end of the range. U.S. General Accounting Office, "Social Security Reform: Administrative Costs for Individual Accounts Depends on System Design," GAO/HEHS-99-131, June 1999. A study for the Cato Institute concluded that administrative costs would range between 30 and 65 basis points. Robert Genetski, "Administrative Costs and the Relative Efficiency of Public and Private Social Security Systems," Cato Institute Social Security Paper no. 15, March 9, 1999.

The question of transition costs is also highly misleading. First, it has been clearly demonstrated that it is possible to pay for the transition without additional taxes. See, for example, Ferrara and Tanner, pp. 175–204. Even more important, however, Milton Friedman and others have shown that, when Social Security's current unfunded liabilities are considered, there are no new costs associated with the transition. Milton Friedman, "Speaking the Truth about Social Security Reform," Cato Institute Briefing Paper no. 46, April 12, 1999. Indeed, as William Shipman has demonstrated, the cost of paying for the transition, regardless of the financing mechanism chosen, will always be less than the cost of preserving the current system. William Shipman, "Facts and Fantasies about Transition Costs," Cato Institute Social Security Paper no. 13, October 13, 1998.

30. Calculated from Moody's Investor Service, *Moody's Industrial Manual* and *Moody's Bond Survey*, 1920–96.

31. Assumes husband retires at age 67, husband collects full Social Security benefit, and wife collects spousal benefit until husband dies at age 75. Wife then collects widow's benefit until she dies at age 81.

32. Assuming historical rates of return.

33. A. Haeworth Robertson, *Social Security: What Every Taxpayer Should Know* (Washington: Retirement Policy Institute, 1992), p. 218.

34. Board of Trustees, Federal Old-Age and Survivors Insurance and Disability Insurance Trust Funds, *2003 Annual Report* (Washington: Government Printing Office, March 17, 2003), p. 189. Estimated annual scheduled benefit amounts for workers retiring at the normal retirement age in 2003 with various preretirement earnings patterns. Based on intermediate assumptions in the Trustees report.

35. David Koitz, "Social Security Reform: Assessing Changes to Future Retirement Benefits," Congressional Research Service Report for Congress RL-30380, December 14, 1999.

36. Daniel Shapiro, "The Moral Case for Social Security Privatization," Cato Institute Social Security Paper no. 14, October 29, 1998.

37. Social Security benefits are based on a formula that provides benefits equal to 90 percent of the first $606 of monthly income (adjusted according to a formula that

takes into account the growth in wages), 32 percent of the next $3,653, and 15 percent of remaining income up to the wage cap.

38. See C. Eugene Steuerle and John Bakija, *Retooling Social Security for the 21st Century: Right and Wrong Approaches to Reform* (Washington: Urban Institute, 1994), pp. 91–132; and Dean Leimer, "Lifetime Redistribution under the Social Security Program: A Literature Synopsis," *Social Security Bulletin* 62 (1999): 43–51.

39. Daniel Garrett, "The Effects of Differential Mortality Rates on the Progressivity of Social Security," *Economic Inquiry* 33 (July 1995): 457–75; W. Constantijn, A. Panis, and Lee Lillard, "Socioeconomic Differentials in the Return to Social Security," RAND Corporation Working Paper no. 96-05, February 1996; and Beach and Davis.

40. Counting only the OASI portion of the payroll tax. This figure does not include the disability portion.

41. Projected life expectancy at age 65. Centers for Disease Control, "United States Abridged Life Tables, 2000," *National Vital Statistics Report* 51, no. 3 (December 19, 2002): Table 5, 8. At 65, a white male can expect to live an additional 16.3 years, whereas a black male can expect to live for an additional 14.5 years.

42. Projected life expectancy at age 30. Ibid., Table 5, 8. At 30, a white male can expect to live an additional 46.4 years whereas a black male can expect to live an additional 41.1 years.

43. Supporters of the current system maintain that, overall, African Americans benefit from the current Social Security system because they earn lower incomes than whites and are more likely to have periods of unemployment. Therefore, they are more likely to benefit from the program's progressive benefit formula. However, as we have seen, the lifetime progressivity of Social Security is questionable. Supporters of the status quo also suggest that African Americans benefit disproportionately from the program's disability and survivors' benefits. However, there are no empirical studies to support that contention. Indeed, the Social Security Administration rejected a request from the 1996–98 Social Security Advisory Council to conduct such a study. Sylvester Schieber and John Shoven, *The Real Deal: The History and Future of Social Security* (New Haven, Conn.: Yale University Press, 1999), p. 227.

44. The provision is gender neutral, applying to both men and women. However, because of earning patterns in the United States, it affects women almost exclusively.

45. For a full discussion of the impact of the current Social Security system on women and the benefits of Social Security choice for women, see Darcy Ann Olsen, "Greater Financial Security for Women with Personal Retirement Accounts," Cato Institute Briefing Paper no. 38, July 20, 1998; and Ekaterina Shirley and Peter Spiegler, "The Benefits of Social Security Privatization for Women," Cato Institute Social Security Paper no. 12, July 20, 1998.

46. For a thorough discussion of this issue, see Charles Rounds, "Property Rights: The Hidden Issue of Social Security Reform," Cato Institute Social Security Paper no. 19, April 19, 2000.

47. For a full discussion of how a privatized Social Security system would work, see Ferrara and Tanner.

4. Property Rights: The Hidden Issue of Social Security Reform

Charles E. Rounds Jr.

One of the most enduring myths of Social Security is that there is a right to Social Security benefits. Many workers assume that, if they pay Social Security taxes "into the system," they have some sort of legal right to benefits "out of the system." That is not surprising. Much of the language surrounding the Social Security program is designed to convey that impression. For example, payroll taxes are called "insurance contributions" under the Federal Insurance Contribution Act. Social Security monies are placed in a "trust fund" to pay "Old-Age and Survivors Insurance" benefits.

In reality, however, all those terms are misleading to the point of dishonesty. The U.S. Supreme Court has ruled that payroll taxes are not "contributions" but are taxes like any others. Social Security has nothing to do with "insurance" contracts or any other type of contract, and nothing to do with segregated "accounts." Paying Social Security taxes does not give rise to any contractual right to Social Security benefits. In the Social Security Trust Fund, no property is held in trust for any worker or collection of workers.

In *Flemming v. Nestor*, decided in 1960, the Supreme Court ruled that Social Security is an umbrella term for two schemes that are legally unrelated.[1] One is a taxation scheme, the other a welfare scheme. Workers and their families have no legal claim on the tax payments that they make into the U.S. Treasury or that are made on their behalf. Those funds are gone, commingled with the general assets of the U.S. government. This decision rested on a previous case, *Helvering v. Davis*, in which the Court ruled that Social Security was *not* an insurance program.[2]

Originally published as Cato Institute Social Security Paper no. 19, April 19, 2000, and updated to reflect current information.

As a result, a worker's retirement security is entirely dependent on political decisions made by the president and Congress. Benefits may be reduced or even eliminated at any time. Indeed, Congress has already arbitrarily reduced the benefits of some groups of workers. In contrast, a Social Security system based on individual accounts would provide workers with the protections and the safeguards that go with true ownership. In addition, under the current system, because Social Security benefits are not the worker's property, they are not inheritable. But under a privately invested system, workers would be able to pass their benefits on to their heirs as they would any other property.

What Is Property?

When legal scholars discuss "property," they are, in fact, discussing not a physical object but a bundle of rights.[3] If there are no rights that are enforceable in some court, then, for all intents and purposes, there is no "property." The law generally puts property into one of three general categories: real property, tangible personal property, and intangible personal property. It is the last category that is at issue in Social Security.

An example of intangible personal property is the classic "nonvariable" private annuity "contract" issued by an insurance company. The insured pays a premium to the insurance company in exchange for a promise to make periodic payments. That enforceable promise is called "insurance." The premium belongs to the insurance company and is subject to the claims of its creditors. The premium does not exist as a separate entity, nor is it segregated. Instead, it is commingled with the general assets of the company. In return, the insured individual receives a contractual promise of benefits. Because that promise is enforceable in the courts, it is property.

Another example of intangible personal property is a bank account. That also is a contract. The deposited funds belong to the bank and are subject to the claims of its creditors. In return, the depositor possesses the bank's enforceable promise to pay interest and principal as agreed. In other words, the bank is a debtor and the depositor is a creditor. The bank's contractual promise (i.e., the "account") is property.

Private property is a bundle of rights. Accordingly, "the dichotomy between personal liberties and property rights is a false one.

Property does not have rights. People have rights."[4] Thus it is said, "The right of property is the guardian of every other right, and to deprive a people of this is in fact to deprive them of their liberty."[5] Were the U.S. government to own all the printing presses, the First Amendment would not be worth the paper it is printed on. We would be a citizenry of supplicants, constrained in our political expression by the whims and the predilections of politicians and state bureaucrats.

The bundle of private rights we call property is the guardian not only of our civil rights but also of our physical welfare. Thus, a public retirement benefit scheme under which the state, rather than its citizens, has untrammeled ownership of all the underlying property is a scheme that allows the state to reduce benefits or eliminate them altogether. Social Security, as currently structured, is such a scheme because under it "participants" have no legal right to any future benefits.

Social Security Involves No Property Rights

For some time, it has been law that workers have no property rights in Social Security. Two key Supreme Court decisions established that.

The first was the 1937 case of *Helvering v. Davis*, which began as an action by a shareholder of the Edison Electric Illuminating Company of Boston, Massachusetts, to restrain the corporation from making payments and deductions called for by the Social Security Act pending adjudication of the act's constitutionality. The federal district court declined to issue an injunction. Helvering, the Edison shareholder, appealed to the Circuit Court of Appeals for the First Circuit. The court of appeals held that the welfare component of Social Security was void as an invasion of powers reserved to the states or to the people by the Tenth Amendment. Accordingly, the taxation component of Social Security "collapsed" with the welfare component. The government appealed, and the Supreme Court agreed to hear the case.

One of the key issues facing the Court was whether Social Security was an insurance program or simply a welfare program. Although at the time the federal government's authority to operate a welfare

71

program was under debate (indeed, the plaintiffs in *Helvering* challenged that authority), it was generally agreed that a federal insurance program would be unconstitutional. As Edward Witte, executive director of the research staff of the Committee on Economic Security and one of the fathers of Social Security, warned supporters, "The only hope . . . is that the Court will find [that the Social Security Act] does not, in fact, establish an old-age insurance program."[6] In fact, the Social Security Administration was so concerned about that issue that it warned its employees to "play down the use of terms such as insurance and not allow, in any official reports or publicity, the coupling of the tax titles with the two insurance titles lest the Court take judicial notice when considering the constitutionality of the Act."[7]

On May 24, 1937, the Supreme Court sided with the federal government by upholding the constitutionality of the Social Security Act. In doing so, the Court essentially deferred to Congress on the question of which welfare schemes fall within the ambit of the Constitution's General Welfare Clause. However, the Court also explicitly concluded that Social Security was not an insurance program. The Court noted, "The proceeds of both employee and employer taxes are to be paid into the treasury like any other internal revenue generally, and are not earmarked in any way."[8]

The majority in *Helvering* did not provide a definitive answer about what legal relationship, if any, a worker has with the U.S. government with respect to his FICA payments. Social Security was not insurance. But what was it? Is the nexus between Social Security taxes and the welfare scheme so close that workers have constitutionally protected property rights in those payments? Something akin to an annuity purchased from a private insurance company? Or perhaps an individual retirement account?

That question would be decided in a second case, *Flemming v. Nestor*, which picked up where *Helvering* left off. Ephram Nestor was a one-time resident alien and, briefly, a member of the U.S. Communist Party. From December 1936 to January 1955, both Nestor and his employers had made FICA tax payments to the federal government. Classified as an undesirable alien because of his prior Communist Party affiliation, Nestor was deported to his native Bulgaria in July 1956.

In 1954, 15 years after Nestor had ceased being a communist and 18 years after he began paying his FICA taxes, Congress passed a law providing that any person who had been deported by reason of communist affiliation would have his Social Security benefits cut off. Accordingly, on his deportation, Nestor's old-age benefits were cut off.

Nestor sued, arguing that because he had paid Social Security taxes he had a right to Social Security benefits. Among other things, Nestor argued that he had a "property right" in his Social Security benefits and that, by cutting off those benefits, the government had made an unlawful "taking" of his property under the Fifth Amendment.

However, the Court disagreed. Standing on the shoulders of *Helvering*, Justice Harlan wrote:

> To engraft upon the Social Security system a concept of "accrued property rights" would deprive it of the flexibility and boldness in adjustment to ever-changing conditions which it demands.

The Court continued:

> It was doubtless out of an awareness of the need for such flexibility that Congress included in the original Act, and has since retained, a clause expressly reserving to it "[t]he right to alter, amend, or repeal any provision" of the Act. S 1104, 49 Stat. 648, 42 U.S.C. § 1304, 42 U.S.C.A. § 1304. That provision makes express what is implicit in the institutional needs of the program. . . . We must conclude that a person covered by the Act has not such a right in benefit payments as would make every defeasance of "accrued" interests violative of the Due Process Clause of the Fifth Amendment.[9]

The Court also rejected any comparison of Social Security with insurance or an annuity:

> It is apparent that the noncontractual interest of an employee covered by the Act cannot be soundly analogized to that of the holder of an annuity, whose right to benefits is bottomed on his contractual premium payments.[10]

In reaching those decisions, the Supreme Court was simply affirming the intent of Congress and the authors of Social Security, who, despite the rhetoric surrounding the program, always understood that workers would have no contractual rights to Social Security benefits.

In 1953, the House Committee on Ways and Means held hearings on that very issue. Among the witnesses was Arthur J. Altmeyer, who, having just retired as commissioner of the Social Security Administration, had been associated with the program since its inception. Altmeyer was a reluctant witness who ultimately had to be subpoenaed to appear. However, under questioning by Rep. John Dingell Sr. (D-Mich.), he admitted, "There is no individual contract between the beneficiary and the Government."[11]

That led to the following exchange between Altmeyer and Rep. Lawrence Winn (R-Kans.):

> *Congressman Winn:* Mr. Altmeyer, there being no contractual obligation between the Government and the worker, it follows, does it not, that the benefit payments under Title II of the Social Security Act are merely statutory benefits which Congress may withdraw or alter at any time?

> *Mr. Altmeyer:* I have answered your question, sir. If you will refer to section 1101, you will find, as you read into the record, that there are no vested rights.

> *Congressman Winn:* We have also established that there is no insurance contract between the Government and the worker within a covered wage whereby the rights and obligations of a party are set; that is correct, is it not?

> *Mr. Altmeyer:* No. You did not establish that. That has been self-evident since the law was passed in 1935.[12]

Even the Social Security Administration's official website notes that "entitlement to Social Security benefits is not [a] contractual right."[13] The SSA states, "There has been a temptation throughout the program's history for some people to suppose that their FICA payroll taxes entitle them to a benefit in a legal, contractual sense." However, SSA notes, "Congress clearly had no such limitation in mind when crafting the law." The SSA goes on to state, "This is the issue finally settled by *Flemming v. Nestor.*" There is no right to Social Security benefits.

To reiterate, Social Security as it is currently structured is a welfare program.[14] The government collects tax revenues through FICA and commingles them with its general assets. Congress then authorizes benefit payments out of general assets to those people it deems eligible. The citizen has no "property" interest in the scheme. There is no segregated "account." There is no "insurance contract." There is no "trust."

The bottom line is this: there is no legal nexus between what is taken in and what is disbursed. The government is free at any time to change the rules of the game or to close the game down altogether. When it comes to future Social Security payments, we are no more than supplicants.

Can We Trust the "Trust Fund"?

If individuals have no direct property right in Social Security, is there, perhaps, an indirect one through the Social Security Trust Fund? A "trust" is a fiduciary relationship with respect to "property."[15] The trustee takes title to the property for the benefit of the beneficiary. The trustee has a judicially enforceable duty of undivided loyalty—that is, a duty to act solely in the interest of the beneficiary. In other words, the trustee is accountable to the beneficiary. In another case, Justice Cardozo, writing for the majority, said:

> A trustee is held to something stricter than the morals of the marketplace. Not honesty alone, but the punctilio of an honor the most sensitive, is then the standard of behavior. As to this there has developed a tradition that is unbending and inveterate. Uncompromising rigidity has been the attitude of courts of equity when petitioned to undermine the rule of undivided loyalty by the "disintegrating erosion" of particular exceptions.[16]

Trust funds are segregated from the trustee's own assets and thus are insulated from the claims of the trustee's creditors and from diversion to purposes unrelated to the trust. The beneficiary's interest under a "trust" is said to be an equitable, or beneficial, interest. That beneficial, or equitable, interest is itself "property." A simple example of such a "property" interest is a mutual fund share. The trustees of the mutual fund have the title to the underlying assets. The investors, however, have the equitable, or beneficial, interest. Although the trustees have the legal title, the actual economic interest is with the investors.

The Social Security Trust Fund involves no "trust," as that term is commonly understood. The U.S. government is not a trustee of FICA receipts. The receipts are not segregated in the sense that that they are legally insulated from diversion to governmental purposes that are unrelated to paying old-age, survivors', or disability benefits. Social Security affords no equitable, or beneficial, property interest to anyone other than the federal government. In other words, under the current Social Security system, there is no judicially enforceable duty of undivided loyalty to workers and their families.[17]

Social Security, Property Rights, and Risk

The question of risk is extremely important to the debate over Social Security's future, because much of the opposition to individual accounts has been based on the faulty premise that the current Social Security system is less risky than private capital markets.

Of course, that argument overstates the risks of private markets. True, as Justice Putnam in the landmark trust case *Harvard College v. Amory* opined, "Do what you will, the capital is at hazard."[18] In other words, there is no investment that is risk free. However, over the long term, prudent, diversified private capital investments have proven remarkably safe and lucrative. That cannot be said for Social Security, which continues to place workers and their families at considerable economic risk. Why at risk? Because the scheme does not involve private property and the protections and the safeguards that go with it.

Social Security is facing a severe financial crisis. By 2018, the system will be running a deficit. Overall, Social Security is more than $25.3 trillion in debt.[19] One likely response to this shortfall will be a reduction in benefits. And, because workers have no property right to their benefits, Congress is free to cut them.

That would not be unprecedented. Social Security benefits have been cut in the past, both directly and indirectly. For example, the retirement age has been raised. Workers who entered the workforce in 1955 were told then that they would be able to retire at age 65 and receive full benefits. They paid taxes into the program under that expectation. However, in 1983, Congress changed the rules. Those workers must now work until age 65 years and two months to receive full benefits. For workers retiring in the future, the retirement age will continue to rise until it reaches age 67. Congress is already debating several future benefit cuts, including additional increases in the retirement age, reductions in the cost-of-living adjustment, and means testing. Indeed, if such cuts are to keep Social Security solvent, they will involve trillions of dollars in promised—

but lost—benefits. That makes the current Social Security system very risky indeed.

However, the risks posed by not having a legal property right to Social Security benefits go well beyond the program's future financial problems. Some Americans have already had their Social Security benefits arbitrarily reduced as the result of political decisions. For example, in an effort to combat "double dipping," Congress cut the benefits of retired federal workers. Many federal workers retire after 20 years of service and become eligible for a government pension. Because they are still quite young, many go back to work in the private sector in jobs at which they pay Social Security taxes. However, they do not receive full Social Security benefits in exchange for those taxes. Instead, those benefits will be reduced by an amount equal to two-thirds of their federal pension. Similar reductions apply to survivors' and spousal benefits. In essence, a large portion of those federal workers' Social Security benefits has been confiscated.

The government also confiscates a portion of the benefits of individuals who work after the age of 65. The Social Security earnings test reduces Social Security benefits by one dollar for every three dollars earned above a certain threshold. Earnings tests also apply to survivors' and disability benefits.[20]

Such unfairness is the inevitable result of a system in which benefits are determined solely by political decisions and are unrelated to any sort of property right.

Finally, it is important to note that, because there is no property right in Social Security, benefits do not become part of an individual's estate on death but, instead, revert to the government. As a result, Social Security benefits are not inheritable. A worker might pay Social Security taxes during his entire working life, but, if that person dies young, without a spouse or children under age 18, none of his benefits may be passed on to his heirs.

In contrast, workers would have a true property right in individual accounts. Not only would such accounts earn much higher rates of return, and therefore greater retirement benefits, through private investment, but also those benefits would be the worker's property. Because a worker would *own* his retirement nest egg, the government, under the Fifth Amendment of the U.S. Constitution, could not chip away at it or take it away altogether. Government could not arbitrarily reduce benefits for some categories of workers or impose earnings tests. Funds in an individual account would be fully inheritable, like any other property in an individual's estate. For instance, if the worker purchased an annuity with the proceeds of his account, he could go to court to enforce his rights should the insurance company not comply with its agreement. The same could not be said for a worker's so-called interest in the Social Security system.

Conclusion

Despite the widespread belief that workers have a right to their Social Security benefits, it has been settled law that workers have no legal right to Social Security benefits. In *Helvering* and *Flemming*, the Supreme Court ruled that Social Security taxes are simply taxes and convey no property or contractual rights to Social Security benefits.

Thus, in the current system, a worker's retirement security is dependent entirely on political decisions made by the president and Congress. Benefits may be reduced or even eliminated at any time. Given the program's looming financial crisis, such benefit cutbacks are increasingly likely, which places workers' retirement security at considerable risk.

In contrast, a Social Security system based on individual accounts would provide workers with true ownership of their retirement benefits and all the advantages—legal, economic, and otherwise—that go therewith.

Notes

1. *Flemming v. Nestor,* 363 U.S. 603 (1960).

2. *Helvering v. Davis,* 301 U.S. 619 (1937).

3. Tom Bethell, *The Noblest Triumph: Property and Prosperity through the Ages* (New York: St. Martin's, 1998), p. 19.

4. *Lynch v. Household Finance Corp.,* 405 U.S. 538, 552 (1972).

5. American revolutionary Arthur Lee, quoted in James W. Ely, *The Guardian of Every Other Right* (New York: Oxford University Press, 1992), p. 26. See also Bethell, p. 170.

6. Quoted in Carolyn Weaver, *The Crisis in Social Security: Economic and Political Origins* (Durham, N.C.: Duke University Press, 1982), p. 109.

7. Quoted in Charles McKinley and Robert Fraser, *Launching Social Security: 1935–1937* (Madison: University of Wisconsin Press, 1946), p. 453.

8. *Helvering* at 635.

9. *Flemming* at 610–11.

10. Ibid. at 610.

11. *Congressional Record* (83d Cong., 1st sess., November 27, 1953), p. 918.

12. Ibid., pp. 920–21.

13. http://www.ssa.gov/history/nestor.html.

14. *Helvering* at 640–45.

15. Charles E. Rounds Jr., *Loring: A Trustee's Handbook* (New York: Aspen Publishers, 2004), pp. 1–19.

16. *Meinhard v. Salmon,* 249 N.Y. 458, 464, 164 N.E. 545, 546 (1928).

17. While not relevant to the issue of the Social Security Trust Fund, which does not constitute a true trust fund, the U.S. government, under some circumstances, may act as a common law trustee. That was suggested by the Supreme Court in the 1982 case of *United States v. Mitchell,* which involved an action against the United States for alleged mismanagement of timberlands on an Indian reservation. The Court held that "[a]ll of the necessary elements of a common-law trust are present: a trustee (the United States), a beneficiary (the Indian allottees), and a trust corpus (Indian timber, lands and funds)." None of those elements applies to the Social Security Trust Fund.

It is interesting, however, to at least consider whether the U.S. government can ever be a *suitable* trustee of anything. Even its track record of looking after intangible personal property has been abysmal. Currently, there is a class action pending against the U.S. government for alleged mismanagement of funds to which it holds title as trustee for the benefit of individual Native Americans. On February 23, 1999, the *Wall Street Journal* editorialized that the dramatic events surrounding the litigation reveal a structural, even cultural, inability or unwillingness on the part of the government to act as a prudent common law trustee:

> The contempt orders against Interior Secretary Bruce Babbitt and Treasury Secretary Robert Rubin grew out of a class-action law suit over the government's mishandling of *300,000* trust fund accounts totaling $2.5 billion that it managed on behalf of American Indians. Last year, Senator John McCain said that if anyone in the private sector had operated the way the government had "they would be in jail today.". . . Indeed, the bottom line of U.S. District Court Judge Royce Lamberth's ruling is that Washington isn't exempt from the standards it sets for private trustees . . . that the government has a fiduciary obligation to properly manage accounts it controls (Social Security trustees take note). He noted that the Bureau of Indian Affairs lacked records for $2 billion of tribal account transactions over a 20-year period.

Why is the government chronically deficient in the stewardship department? I suggest that it is because there is no accountability. As a practical matter, the government is answerable to no one but itself. Accountability is the linchpin of the common law "trust." It is what keeps a private trustee honest. The trustee of a private "trust" is accountable to the beneficiaries. The private trustee of a charitable trust is accountable to the state's attorney general. Accordingly, the beneficiary or the state's attorney general, as the case may be, has standing to bring the matter of a private trustee's stewardship before a court for adjudication. Litigation over the stewardships of private trustees goes on all the time in the state courts. For the private trustee, a judicial sanction of fine or removal is a credible threat. The same, however, cannot be said for the government when it purports to act as a trustee.

18. *Harvard College v. Amory,* 26 Mass. (9 Pick.) 446, 461 (1830).

19. "The 2003 Annual Report of the Board of Trustees of the Federal Old-Age and Survivors Insurance and Disability Insurance Trust Funds," March 17, 2003, www.ssa.gov/OACT/TR/TR03/index.html.

20. The House of Representatives has voted to repeal the earnings test for retirement, though not for disability, benefits. However, the principle still holds.

5. Private Investment of Social Security: The $10 Trillion Opportunity

Martin Feldstein

Although reforming the Social Security retirement program is an issue of enormous importance, elected officials are still unwilling to confront this serious but politically dangerous problem. Eventually, however, the system's deteriorating financial condition will force major reforms.[1] Whether those reforms are good or bad, whether they deal with the basic economic problems of the system or merely protect the solvency of existing institutional arrangements, is the crucial policy issue. Simply protecting the solvency of the unfunded system by tampering with taxes and benefits will perpetuate existing adverse effects on labor markets and national saving. Shifting to a system of funded individual accounts can produce a major increase in national income and in the well-being of the population.

Central to the analysis of Social Security's impact on the economy is the concept of "Social Security wealth," defined as the present actuarial value of the Social Security benefits to which the current adult population will be entitled at age 65 (or are already entitled to if they are older than 65) minus the present actuarial value of the Social Security taxes that they will pay before reaching that age. Social Security wealth has now grown to about $10.5 trillion or roughly equal to the 2002 total value of GDP, which is equivalent to more than $48,000 for every adult in the country.[2] Its value substantially exceeds that of all other assets for the vast majority of American households.

Social Security wealth is of course not real wealth but only a claim on current and future taxpayers. Instead of labeling this key magnitude Social Security wealth, it could more accurately be called

Originally published as Cato Institute Social Security Paper no. 7, January 31, 1997, this essay was adapted from the author's Richard T. Ely lecture to the American Economics Association delivered in January 1996. It has been updated to reflect current information.

the nation's Social Security liability. Like ordinary government debt, Social Security wealth has the power to crowd out private capital accumulation. And it will continue to grow as long as our current system remains unchanged, displacing an ever larger stock of capital.

The $10.5 trillion Social Security liability is almost twice the official national debt ($6.2 trillion).[3] Even if the traditional deficit is eliminated someday, so that the traditional national debt is no longer increasing, the national debt in the form of the Social Security liability will continue to grow.

Looking further into the future, the aggregate Social Security liability will grow as the population expands, as it becomes relatively older, and as incomes rise. Government actuaries predict that, under existing law, the tax rate required to pay each year's Social Security benefit will rise over the next 50 years from the present level of slightly less than 12 percent to more than 18.[4]

The financial problems of the system are therefore serious indeed. This essay, however, will not discuss the financial insolvency of Social Security but will focus instead on the more fundamental economic effects of continuing with an unfunded system. Dealing appropriately with these economic effects will also solve the financial problems.

Labor Market Distortions

The Social Security payroll tax distorts the supply of labor and the form of compensation. These losses are inevitable because of the low return implied by the pay-as-you-go character of the unfunded Social Security system.

Unlike private pensions and individual retirement accounts, the Social Security system does not invest the money that it collects in stocks and bonds but pays those funds out as benefits in the same year that they are collected. (Although the system has been accumulating a fund since 1983 to smooth the path of tax rates, more than 90 percent of payroll tax receipts are still paid out immediately as benefits, and the assets in the Social Security trust fund are only about 5 percent of the Social Security liabilities.)

The rate of return that individuals earn on their mandatory Social Security contributions is therefore far less than they could earn in a private pension or in a funded Social Security system. An unfunded program with a constant tax rate provides a positive rate of return that is roughly equal to the rate of growth of the payroll tax base.

The average growth of real wages from 1960 to 1997—2.6 percent—can serve as a reasonable estimate of what an unfunded Social Security program can yield over the long-term future. In contrast, the real pretax return on nonfinancial corporate capital (i.e., profits before all taxes plus the net interest paid) averaged 9.3 percent over the same period.[5] Although individuals do not earn the full 9.3 percent pretax return even in individual retirement accounts (IRAs) and 401(k) accounts because of federal and state corporate taxes, a funded retirement system could deliver the full 9.3 percent pretax return to each individual saver if the government credited back the corporate tax collections.[6]

A simplified example will indicate the magnitude of the tax wedge implied by the Social Security program. Consider an employee who contributes $1,000 to Social Security at age 50 to buy benefits to be paid at age 75. With a 2.6 percent yield, the $1,000 grows to $1,900 after the 25 years. In contrast, a yield of 9.3 percent would allow the individual to buy the same $1,900 retirement income for only $206. Thus, forcing individuals to use the unfunded system dramatically increases their cost of buying retirement income. In the example, a funded plan would permit the individual to buy the same retirement income with a 2.5 percent contribution instead of the 12 percent payroll tax. The 9.5 percent difference is a pure real tax for which the individual gets nothing in return.

The distorting effect of this tax is much larger than one might at first think. The net Social Security tax rate is imposed on top of federal and state income taxes. The federal marginal tax rate is 25 percent (for single individuals with taxable incomes over $28,400 and married couples with combined incomes over $56,800),[7] and the typical state income tax rate is 5 percent. The Social Security tax therefore raises the total marginal tax rate to over 35 percent and substantially exacerbates the distortions and waste caused by the income tax.[8]

The combination of the income tax and the payroll tax distorts not only the number of hours that individuals work but also other dimensions of labor supply like occupational choice, location, and effort. It also distorts the form in which compensation is taken, shifting taxable cash into untaxed fringe benefits, nicer working conditions, etc. These distortions in the form of compensation are in effect distortions in the individual's pattern of consumption. They cause individuals to spend their potential income on things that they value less than those things that they could buy for cash. These distortions are dollar for dollar as important as the distortion in labor supply.[9]

In practice, these distortions are exacerbated by the haphazard relations between benefits and taxes that result from existing Social Security rules. For example, because benefits are based on the 35 years of highest earnings, most employees under age 25 receive no additional benefit for their payroll taxes. Because many married women and widows claim benefits based on their husbands' earnings, they also often receive no benefit in return for their payroll taxes. Because there is no extra reward for taxes paid at an early date, the effective tax rate for younger taxpayers can be a substantial multiple of the tax rate for older employees. The Social Security rules are so complex and so opaque that many individuals may simply disregard the benefits that they earn from additional work and act as if the entire payroll tax is a net tax no different in kind from the personal income tax.

The extra distortion that results from these very unequal links between incremental taxes and incremental benefits would automatically be eliminated in a funded system with individual retirement accounts. Although it could also be eliminated within the existing unfunded system by creating individual Social Security accounts for each taxpayer, the larger labor market distortions that result from the low rate of return in an unfunded system cannot be eliminated without shifting to either a funded public system or a system of individual retirement accounts.

Reduced National Saving

The loss that results from labor market distortions is not the only adverse effect of an unfunded Social Security system or even the largest one. Current and future generations lose by being forced to participate in a low-yielding, unfunded program (i.e., by being forced to accept a pay-as-you-go implicit return of 2.6 percent when the real marginal product of capital is 9.3 percent). Even though capital income taxes now prevent individuals from receiving that 9.3 percent on their personal savings, the public as a whole does receive that full return; what individuals do not receive directly, they receive in the form of reductions in other taxes or increases in government services.

The extent to which an unfunded Social Security system causes a decline in national capital income and economic welfare depends on how individual saving responds to Social Security taxes and benefits and on how the government acts to offset the reductions in private saving. Let's look at some facts.

An individual who has average earnings during his entire working life and who retires at age 65 with a "dependent spouse" now receives benefits equal to 63 percent of his earnings during the full year before retirement. Because the Social Security benefits of such an individual are not taxed, those benefits replace more than 80 percent of peak preretirement after-tax income. Common sense and casual observation suggest that individuals who can expect such a high replacement rate will do little saving for their retirement. Such saving as they do during their preretirement years is more likely to be done as a precautionary balance to deal with unexpected changes in income or consumption. Not surprisingly, the median financial assets of households with a head of household aged 45 to 54 were only $45,700 in 2001.[10] Even if we look beyond financial wealth, the median net worth (including the value of the home) of all households with a head of household aged 45 to 54 years was only $132,600.

To get a sense of the order of magnitude of the annual loss, it is helpful to begin with the simplest case in which each dollar of Social Security wealth reduces real private wealth by a dollar. The forgone private wealth would have earned about 9.3 percent, whereas the unfunded Social Security system provides a return equal to about 2.6 percent. The population incurs a loss equal to the difference between those two returns. The annual loss of real income would be 6.7 percent of the $10.5 trillion of Social Security wealth—an amount equal to $700 billion or 6.3 percent of total GDP.

Of course, each dollar of Social Security wealth does not necessarily replace exactly a dollar of real wealth. To the extent that Social Security induces earlier retirement, individuals will save more than they otherwise would. Social Security also affects private saving by providing a real annuity. And there are some individuals who, because they are irrational or myopic, do not respond at all to the provision of Social Security benefits. A number of research studies

SOCIAL SECURITY AND ITS DISCONTENTS

have been done on the extent to which Social Security wealth depresses saving and replaces real wealth.[11] Although none of these is a definitive study that establishes a precise measure of the substitution of Social Security wealth for other household wealth, taken together these studies do imply that the Social Security program causes each generation to reduce its savings substantially and thereby to incur a substantial loss of real investment income.

The Gain from Individual Accounts

Under the current Social Security system, each generation now and in the future loses the difference between the return to real capital that would be obtained in a funded system and the much lower return in the existing unfunded program. Shifting to a system of individual mandatory accounts that can be invested in a mix of stocks and bonds would permit individuals to obtain the full real pretax rate of return on capital. This would mean a larger capital stock and a higher national income.

In addition, eliminating the payroll tax would reduce the distortions in work effort and form of compensation that currently depress the productivity of the economy and the real standard of living. When the system of funded individual accounts is fully implemented, the mandatory contributions required to fund the current and projected levels of benefits would be only about 3 percent of payroll, far lower than the payroll tax, which is expected to rise from 12.4 percent now to at least 20 percent over the next 35 years.

Conservative assumptions imply that private investment of Social Security payroll taxes would increase the economic well-being of future generations by an amount equal to 5 percent of GDP each year as long as the system lasts. Although the transition to a funded system would involve economic as well as political costs, the net present value of the gain would be enormous—as much as $25 trillion.[12]

Conclusion

The rapidly deteriorating financial position of Social Security will eventually force politicians to deal with the problem of reform. The adverse impact of the current system on a wide variety of groups— including two-earner couples, the young, and the poor—may embolden some politicians to go beyond patching up the current system to proposing more fundamental reforms than have been considered in the past. Instead of the usual mix of tax increases and benefit cuts, we can move to a system based on mandatory, individually owned private savings accounts.

Such a private savings program would solve Social Security's long-run financial problems without the necessity for either huge tax increases or draconian benefit cuts. At the same time, it would yield enormous benefits to the economy. In short, individual accounts can increase real incomes for everyone while ensuring a dignified retirement for future retirees.

Notes

A longer and more technical version of this lecture appears in the Papers and Proceedings of the American Economics Association, *American Economic Review* 86, no. 2 (May 1996).

1. According to the most recent report of the Social Security system's Board of Trustees, Social Security will be insolvent by the year 2042. But Social Security's problems actually begin not in 2042 but as early as 2018, the year in which the system begins to run a deficit. *2003 Annual Report of the Board of Trustees of the Federal Old-Age and Survivors Insurance and Disability Insurance Trust Funds* (Washington: Government Printing Office, 2003).

2. This is a new estimate of Social Security wealth based on the detailed Social Security simulation model presented in Martin Feldstein and Andrew Samwick, "The Transition Path to Privatizing Social Security," National Bureau of Economic Research Working Paper no. 5761, September 1996, published in *Privatizing Social Security* (Chicago: Univesity of Chicago Press, 1998).

3. $6.2 trillion includes the bonds held by the Fed and the SS trust fund.

4. Derived from *2003 Annual Report of the Board of Trustees of the Federal Old-Age and Survivors Insurance and Disability Insurance Trust Funds*.

5. Martin Feldstein, Louis Dicks-Mireaux, and James Poterba, "The Effective Tax Rate and Pretax Rate of Return," *Journal of Public Economics* 21 (July 1993): 129–58, and Richard Rippe, "Further Gains in Corporate Profitability," *Economic Outlook Monthly*, August 1995.

6. Those taxes average 42 percent of pretax return. Ibid.

7. 2003 Tax Rate Schedules, Internal Revenue Service.

8. Economists measure this waste by the "deadweight loss" of the tax (i.e., the loss to the individual in excess of the revenue raised by the government). Economists can calculate that the incremental deadweight loss that results from the additional 9.5 percent net Social Security tax is equal to 4.7 percent of the product of the payroll tax base and the compensated elasticity of that tax base with respect to the net of tax share. That is about 10 times as large as the deadweight loss that would result if the Social Security tax were the only tax. For details of this calculation, see page 4 of the Ely lecture as published in the *American Economic Review*.

9. The deadweight loss due to the net Social Security tax is about 2.35 percent of the Social Security payroll tax base, a deadweight loss in 1995 of about $68 billion. This deadweight loss is about 1 percent of GDP and nearly one-fifth of total Social

Security payroll tax revenue. It increases the deadweight loss of the personal income tax by 50 percent. Details of this calculation are presented on pages 4 and 5 of the Ely Lecture.

10. Ana M. Aizcorbe, Arthur B. Kennickell, and Kevin B. Moore, "Recent Changes in U.S. Family Finances: Evidence from the 1998 and 2001 Survey of Consumer Finances," *Federal Reserve Bulletin*, January 2003.

11. See, for example, Martin Feldstein and Anthony Pellechio, "Social Security and Household Wealth Accumulation: New Microeconometric Evidence," *Review of Economics and Statistics* 61 (August 1979): 361–68; Peter Diamond and J. A. Hausman, "Individual Retirement and Savings Behavior," *Journal of Public Economics* 23 (February–March 1984): 81–114; Alan Blinder, R. Gordon, and David Wise, "Social Security, Bequests, and Life Cycle Theory of Savings: Cross-Sectional Tests," in *Inventory Theory and Consumer Behavior*, ed. Alan Blinder (Ann Arbor, Mich: University of Michigan Press, 1990), pp. 229–56; and Robert Barro, "The Impact of Social Security on National Savings," Washington, D.C., American Enterprise Institute, 1978.

12. The present value gain is the present value of annual gains of 5 percent of GDP. Since the current level of GDP is now $7.5 trillion, a gain of 5 percent of that would be $550 billion. The annual gain would increase in proportion to the GDP and would therefore grow at about 3 percent per year in real terms. Discounting this at a real rate of 5 percent (approximately the rate of return net of tax that an individual investor received on the Standard and Poors portfolio over the period since 1970) implies a present value of $27.5 trillion.

6. The Moral Case for a Market-Based Retirement System

Daniel Shapiro

The economic effects of changing Social Security to a market-based system are the subject of intense debate among public policy analysts. Will private investment boost national savings? Will it increase the rate of economic growth? What are the transition costs? These are all important questions. However, the primary concerns about changing Social Security to a system based on choice are moral, not economic. Social Security was accepted by most Americans on moral grounds. Ultimately, individual accounts will not be politically viable unless they are defensible on moral grounds. The morality of individual accounts is not, however, simply a strategic matter. Reform would not be justifiable if it were economically beneficial but morally suspect.

One might expect that a moral argument for a market-based retirement system choice would be framed in terms of classical liberal values, such as respect for individual rights and the liberty to manage one's own affairs. Indeed, such values are an important reason to give individuals the freedom to choose how to invest their pension contributions—but they are not the only reasons or the only values that direct us to a new retirement system based on individually owned, privately invested retirement accounts.

We live in a society that celebrates moral pluralism, where different values compete for the most politically significant award. While most Americans believe that individual rights and liberty are important, values such as fairness, community, and security are also considered important. When those values appear to be at odds, some people think liberty must be traded off for the other values. Thus, they do not consider arguments framed solely in terms of individual

Originally published as Cato Institute Social Security Paper no. 14, October 29, 1998, and updated to reflect current information.

rights to be compelling. Individual accounts, however, are defensible not only from the classical liberal or libertarian perspective but from virtually every perspective in political philosophy. Egalitarians who frame their arguments in terms of fairness, welfare theorists who frame their arguments in terms of economic security, communitarians who frame their arguments in terms of community, and anyone who frames an argument in terms of whether average citizens understand the institutions or programs that they are asked to support should all support individual accounts.

Liberty

The classical liberal view holds that individuals have the right to run their lives as they see fit, provided they do not interfere with the right of others to do the same. That, of course, is a very abstract concept that requires elaboration. Classical liberals or libertarians provide that elaboration via a set of rights to life, liberty, and property. These are negative rights, that is, the only duty they impose is to refrain from certain actions (murder, rape, assault, theft, and so on). Libertarians believe that positive rights, which require individuals to do something for someone, arise only through voluntary relations, for example, through contract or by assuming a responsibility such as being a parent.

Why is the liberty that is provided by protection of our basic rights so important? Four kinds of overlapping reasons are commonly invoked to answer that question. First, the fact that we don't know automatically what to do with our lives is a powerful reason for allowing people the freedom to discover what the best future might be. Humans don't come with a book of instructions. Though biology and culture give us various ends, we need to order these ends, figure out the best ways to pursue them, evaluate whether they are really worth pursuing, and—since we are all quite fallible— very likely revise some of them. Second, many of the plans, projects, and goals we pursue would have little value unless we chose them, endorsed them, or in some sense had a role in shaping them. Freedom from coercive interference is a necessary ingredient in this shaping, or molding, process. When we discover or decide what to do with our lives, we put our own stamp on the social matrix that helps shape our lives, so that our lives are not merely a social product but our own.

Third, liberty is essential—to paraphrase Immanuel Kant's often quoted dictum—we are to treat people as ends in themselves rather than merely as means. Coercion, using force or threats of serious harm to bend someone to one's own will, treats people as if they were mere resources for our consumption and pleasure. Voluntary interaction with others, on the other hand, demonstrates a respect for the kind of beings we are: human beings whose powers of rational thought and judgment enable us to live lives of our own and be responsible or accountable for what we make of them. That we view individuals as able to make something of themselves is (in part) what gives them dignity.

Fourth, liberty helps people flourish. The motto "be all you can be" is not just a slogan for the volunteer army but a reasonable description of how humans generally fare in a free society. A society that protects rights to life, liberty, and private property produces enormous prosperity and a flowering of voluntary organizations and associations. This in turn provides a wide range of opportunities for diverse individuals to find a way of life or career or project that is fulfilling. The more opportunities, the greater the possibility for finding fulfillment.

A purely voluntary pension system is most compatible with this classical liberal emphasis on liberty. From an economic standpoint, a pension system is an arrangement by which resources are made available (by investment and/or taxation) for retirement and old age. But from a classical liberal perspective, it is much more. Retirement decisions are part of major life decisions. Retirement decisions depend upon one's occupation, one's tradeoff between work and leisure, one's time preference, the extent to which concern for the future guides one's present plans and goals, and so forth—and all of these are intimately involved with one's self-definition, one's ambitions, and one's goals. Thus the freedom to decide what kind of retirement to have, when to cease working, how much to put aside for one's retirement at various points in one's life, and how to invest or utilize one's contributions to one's pension are all freedoms that go to the heart of the freedom and responsibility to shape one's life. A system that is most attuned to that freedom and responsibility will leave pensions solely to market arrangements and leave support for the elderly who have inadequate or no pensions to voluntary organizations and familial arrangements.

However, many people find the idea of a purely voluntary system scary: they think it will not adequately provide for those who do not or cannot plan for their future. Such worries are likely exaggerated. When people are treated as responsible, that is, accountable, for their lives, this tends to instill another type of responsibility, the type of responsibility we speak of when we commend or admire someone for being trustworthy, reliable, and dependable. When people are treated as accountable for what they have made of themselves, they tend to respond to life's challenges and opportunities. This response involves not only making something of their own lives, but assisting those who cannot or will not cope with the challenges life brings. Prior to the rise of the welfare state, a variety of charities and mutual aid societies flourished, and these groups attended to the needs of those who fared badly.[1] Even with today's oppressive level of taxation and regulation, Americans are quite generous and sensitive to the problems of the unfortunate and disadvantaged. Indeed, it is the welfare state that has decreased our sense of responsibility to others: if the state can provide, if we can get later generations to fund our pensions, our motivation to assist others is diminished.[2]

Having said all that, there is little doubt that a purely voluntary pension system is not a feasible alternative for the foreseeable future. The individual accounts proposals introduced in Congress, and suggested by leading think tanks, envision a system of mandatory savings. While those proposals take a variety of forms, one useful model is the system adopted first by Chile in 1981. In the Chilean system, the funding and management of pensions are left to the market: individuals own their own retirement account and choose, within limits,[3] how to invest their contributions, and at retirement, in what form to receive their pension (e.g., phased withdrawals or annuities). However, employees are required to contribute a certain minimum annual percentage of their salaries to their pension savings account, and the government provides a safety net for those whose pensions at retirement are inadequate or nonexistent.

A system of compulsory private pensions does arguably infringe on or interfere with one's liberty and property rights since it compels contributions without that compulsion being necessary for the protection of others' rights. But compared with Social Security, this is far more respectful of classical liberal values. There is no property right to a pension in Social Security[4]—not surprisingly—since the system is a pay-as-you-go system that funds pensions mainly by taxes on present workers, rather than prior investment of workers' contributions. Thus one has virtually no freedom to determine how one's contributions are to be utilized. Responsibility for one's retirement is shifted, to a significant extent, from workers and retirees to the government, particularly for those with limited income and little or no additional sources of retirement funds.

Equality and Fairness

It's no great surprise that a private pension system scores better on libertarian values than does the current Social Security system. But some people believe that a better score does not settle the question. For these people a just system is a fair one, and many academics understand fairness in an egalitarian sense.

Egalitarianism can be understood in two different ways.[5] Strictly speaking, egalitarians value equality as such, that is, they value equality not merely as a means to some other end but as an independent value. Understood this way, egalitarianism aims to minimize *relative* inequalities. On the other hand, sometimes egalitarianism is predicated on views that place a very high value on *absolute* improvements in the lives of the worst off or most disadvantaged and attach no independent value to the size of the gaps between the worst off and other groups.[6] Few egalitarians, it is important to emphasize, believe that inequalities per se or simply not being well off are injustices. Rather, most believe that justice requires minimizing *unchosen* inequalities or improving the condition of the worst off to the extent that their condition arises through no fault or choice of their own.[7]

By either definition egalitarians should favor private, individual accounts. To see why, compare the intergenerational effects (relations between generations) and the intragenerational effects (relations among members of the same generation) of the two alternative systems.

The intergenerational effects inherent in the evolution of a pay-as-you-go (PAYGO) system are well understood. Social Security was a great deal for earlier generations (roughly, those born prior to the end of World War II): payroll taxes were relatively low, and retirees (who did not pay into the system their whole lives) got a great "rate of return" on their taxes, far above a normal market investment. The support ratio—the ratio of workers to retirees—was high, thanks to vigorous population growth, which supplied a steady stream of new taxpayers, and the relatively low life expectancy of retirees, which moderated growth in the implicit public pension debt—that is, the liability for expected future benefits. Those days are gone. Today's retirees have paid Social Security taxes their whole lives, life expectancy has increased, and population growth has slowed. The maturation of the system and a decrease in the support ratio have left us with high payroll taxes, a poor "rate of return" for young workers, and a huge implicit public pension debt. (That debt has not been reduced by the so-called surplus in the Social Security trust fund because this "trust fund" is merely an accounting device that records the extent to which Social Security taxes are used to finance the general operations of the federal government.)[8] These burdens placed upon later generations—which result simply from their time of birth and thus are not their fault or choice—are absent in a private system that invests workers' contributions. A system that invests contributions doesn't burden later generations and yet still gives earlier ones a good rate of return.

The intragenerational effects of Social Security are somewhat more difficult to evaluate. Social Security may appear to have progressive redistribution because it has a progressive benefit formula: those with lower earning histories get a somewhat higher proportion of their past income in benefits than do higher-income recipients. However, upper-income people tend to enter the workforce later than the poor and to live longer after retirement. (Indeed, the poor have much higher death rates before age 65 than do the affluent.) This means upper-income people will pay into the system for fewer years and receive more in benefits than lower-income people over a lifetime. Furthermore, Social Security is funded in a regressive manner, by a flat payroll tax with a ceiling on the wages taxed. Studies of the intragenerational effects of Social Security have disagreed about whether the affluent's longer life expectancy, later entrance in the workforce, and Social Security's regressive funding make the system as a whole regressive in its intragenerational effects. Some have found that to be so, while others have found that the system is very slightly progressive.[9] However, the categories of "poor" and "affluent" are too simple for egalitarian purposes, as most egalitarians are interested in inequalities between the worst off or disadvantaged and the better off or advantaged; and being bad off or well off is not simply a matter of one's income. In this regard, Social Security has particularly pernicious effects among some groups that egalitarians are likely to consider among the most disadvantaged. For example, blacks do less well than whites,[10] and black males born in the early 1970s who earn about half the average wage will get a negative return from Social Security.[11] Thus, all in all, Social Security's intragenerational redistribution is pretty dismal by egalitarian standards.

Compulsory private pensions, in contrast, have more positive intragenerational effects. While market pensions do not redistribute wealth among persons or groups, the safety net provided by the Chilean system does create progressive redistribution, since it goes only to the elderly poor and is financed out of general revenues, not through regressive payroll taxes. Furthermore, the absolute position of the poor and disadvantaged will greatly improve under a private system. The rates of return in a private system are much greater than in Social Security,[12] and most of the poor's postretirement income at present comes from Social Security. Indeed, focusing on the rate of return may understate the benefits to the poor and disadvantaged of a market-based retirement system. Such a system enables the poor and the less affluent to enter and participate in a system of individual ownership and control, by making them all investors in their retirement, all owners of capital. Egalitarians ought to be wildly enthusiastic about this: the poor and less affluent would own a significant chunk of capital, they would have accumulated significant assets that they could pass on to their children, and the gap between those who own capital and those who don't would be eliminated. What could be better if one thinks justice requires minimizing unchosen inequalities or tilting toward aiding the worse off?

To summarize, egalitarians who are concerned with relative inequalities should favor a private system because it avoids the enormous intergenerational transfers from later to early generations and has more progressive intragenerational redistribution. Egalitarians who are concerned with the absolute position of the poor should also favor a private system because it will significantly raise their retirement income. Both kinds of egalitarians should also favor a private system because it will enable the less affluent to become investors and owners of capital.[13]

Economic Security

Welfare state programs are frequently justified by the claim that there are welfare rights—that is, positive rights to economic security or a minimal level of well-being. Classical liberals believe that there are no welfare rights; as noted earlier, they believe that positive rights arise only through voluntary relationships.[14] Clearly, not everyone agrees. Even so, it is odd to justify Social Security by appealing to welfare rights, since such rights are usually founded on need, and Social Security is not a need-based or means-tested program. True, there are some need-based aspects of Social Security, such as its progressive benefit formula and the reduction in benefits if one works after reaching the official retirement age. But the program as a whole is not run, and not considered by its recipients, as a welfare program. It is considered social insurance, with one's entitlements tied to one's earning history; and it is funded by a payroll tax, which is meant to suggest earmarked contributions, rather than by general revenues, which fund welfare programs. Thus, premises about welfare rights cannot be used to defend Social Security—even apart from the question of whether or not those premises are true.

However, political theorist J. Donald Moon has argued that social insurance programs can be defended as a politically viable way to enact welfare rights into law without undermining norms of self-respect.[15] Means-tested programs threaten the idea that self-respecting, able-bodied adults will support themselves through productive activity, because such programs base benefits upon need, thus enabling adults who can work to obtain benefits without work. They thus divide the community of able-bodied adults into two classes, those who are responsible moral agents who support themselves through work, and those who depend purely upon others for meeting their needs. That is why being "on welfare" is a pejorative phrase and why Congress in 1996 enacted welfare reform that was supposed to make welfare conditional upon work. Social insurance programs, in contrast, are universal, so no stigma is attached to being a beneficiary; and because one's benefits are tied to one's productivity, the right to receive benefits is compatible with being viewed as an independent person with self-respect, not someone purely dependent upon others for meeting one's needs. In this way, economic security is provided without being based upon need.

Moon's argument may show that Social Security is more compatible than means-tested programs with the idea that self-respecting, able-bodied adults should be productive and not purely dependent upon others for meeting their needs. However, if we use this standard of productiveness to compare a compulsory private pension system with Social Security, the former is a clear winner. Since Social Security is a PAYGO system, its link with individual productivity is extremely weak: while one's earning history does help determine, in part, one's benefits, one's pension is funded primarily by *others'* contributions or taxes. Normally, when we think of individuals as productive and supporting themselves through work, we mean that they receive income for *their own* contributions. That does not happen in Social Security. It does occur in a system of compulsory private pensions (except for the elderly poor who receive the minimum pension guarantee).[16]

Not only does a compulsory private system do a better job of maintaining the link between economic security and productiveness, it also provides more security, ironically, than Social Security. One's security is a function of (1) a guarantee or high probability of an income and (2) the amount of income guaranteed. In the early stage of a PAYGO system, retirees and workers who retire within 15 to 35 years after the founding of the system have more security than they have under any private alternative.[17] Social Security in this early stage performs better than a private system on (2), while it is no worse on (1), because, at this stage, benefit levels are being redefined to retirees' advantage and the large supply of workers and low life expectancy limit the disadvantage of an increase in workers' tax rates. However, in the later stages, retirees and workers have less of both (1) and (2) than in a private system. The rate of return is lower, and worries today about whether promises will be kept are widespread because, to maintain the benefit levels earlier generations received, taxes will have to rise sharply. Thus, Social Security *redistributes* security over time. Early generations are made more secure at the price of reducing security for later ones. In contrast, a private system keeps all generations at the same level of fairly high security, in the sense that over time one's rate of return in the capital market will provide one with a substantial pension, no matter to which generation one belongs.[18] The value of security seems to decrease if it is achieved at the expense of others. Thus, a private system is better than Social Security on this score.[19]

Community

Social Security is more coercive, less fair, and provides less economic security than a compulsory private system. Perhaps, though, Social Security can be defended on communitarian grounds. Communitarians are those who think our relationship to various communities is so important for our individual and social well-being that under today's circumstances some degree of individual liberty may need to be sacrificed to sustain that relationship.[20] Two ideas seem central to communitarians' analysis or definition of community. First, a community is an association of individuals who share some common values and interests—in particular a sense of what is public and private—or to put matters somewhat differently, a shared sense of the common good. Second, a community has a shared sense of solidarity, that is, a sense that one's identity is at least partially defined by one's membership in this association.[21] Since the United States, as a nation, does share some values and interests, and to some extent does constitute its citizens' identities, then communitarians will tend to favor the pension system that has a comparative advantage in sustaining common values, interests, and feelings of solidarity among Americans.

One way in which a pension system might sustain such values and interests is the way it expresses some idea of shared responsibility. Social Security might seem to have a comparative advantage for communitarians in this regard. A compulsory private system, which establishes a property right to a pension, is basically a system of individual responsibility plus a residual safety net for the indigent. Although Social Security has traces of a notion of individual responsibility (one's earning history helps determine one's benefit level), the absence of individual property rights to a pension and its PAYGO nature mean that it is primarily others—in one's own generation and previous generations—who assume responsibility for one's retirement (and vice versa.) As the Social Security Advisory Commission report put it, "Social Security is based on the premise that *we're all in this together*, with everyone sharing responsibility not only for contributing to their own and their family's security, but also the security of everyone else, present and future."[22] This communitarian defense of Social Security may have been plausible before current generations started getting a raw deal. But when a system produces severe intergenerational inequalities, and when public awareness of this unfairness comes to the surface, that system's mechanism for sharing responsibility no longer promotes a sense of solidarity among citizens or between generations. In fact, the opposite will more likely occur. Furthermore, as some communitarians have noted, a pension system cannot sustain a sense of solidarity if it does not keep its promises.[23] Social Security is rife with deceptive rhetoric and misleading terminology. Calling Social Security *social insurance*, payroll taxes *contributions,* and government IOUs *trust funds* all gives the distinct impression that Social Security is a funded pension plan rather than a PAYGO system.[24] Even if citizens believe they are not being promised a market rate of return and understand that Social Security cannot promise such a return,[25] PAYGO systems make it very difficult for them to understand the system and determine just what is being promised. The relationship between taxes paid and benefits received is opaque: frequent changes are made in the taxation and benefit rates and schedules, its actuarial status is heavily dependent upon population trends and growth in wages, and in general the system is subject to frequent political maneuvering. Not surprisingly, accurate information about the way the system is being run, its likely future performance, and so forth is hard to come by. The absence of individual property rights in a PAYGO system means there is no incentive to provide such information (and makes it harder to enforce any obligation to provide such information).[26]

A private investment system, on the other hand, is transparent compared with Social Security, and its promises are not difficult to keep. A private system, except for the minimum pension guarantee, is a defined contribution system: the value of one's pension at retirement depends upon market returns. Unless fraud is present, defined contribution systems generally deliver market rates of return, which is what they are designed to do.[27] The relationship between premiums and benefits is easy to understand. Private pension plans have both the incentive and the obligation to provide information about their actuarial status and their rate of return, so the investor or participant has a reasonable basis for understanding the system. In addition, participants have a genuine property right in the system, which adds further incentive to follow and monitor the progress of their investment or contribution. With the exception of the definition of the minimum contribution and minimum retirement pension, a private system is not inherently subject to political manipulation.

Thus, surface impressions to the contrary, communitarians should favor a private pension system. In its earlier stages, Social Security may indeed have helped sustain the kind of solidarity that communitarians prize. But the earlier stages have given way to the later stages, producing huge intergenerational inequalities and giving citizens a sense that solemn promises made to them will not be kept.[28] On the other hand, a private pension system avoids unfair intergenerational redistribution, keeps its promises, and still retains some sense of shared responsibility through its minimum pension guarantee. Thus it doesn't produce the same potential for setting citizen against citizen, generation against generation, that Social Security does in its later stages.[29]

The problem can be put a different way: communitarians should not applaud the sense in which "we are all in this together" in Social Security. In the later stages of Social Security, "we are all in this together" means, roughly, "we (later generations) are all stuck with this unfair pension system now and cannot easily escape its burdens." In a private investment system, "we are all in this together" is basically a reminder to help the elderly poor through the minimum pension guarantee. The latter, it is true, does not symbolize any intergenerational sharing of responsibility.[30] But since the system is fair and keeps its promises, it is more conducive to harmonious relations between generations.

It might be thought, however, that while communitarians should reject a PAYGO system because its intergenerational inequities and failure to keep its promises threaten to undermine solidarity between the generations, they nevertheless should not favor a market-based system, because the combination of individual accounts plus a safety net is too pallid a form of shared responsibility. Perhaps communitarians should favor neither Social Security nor a market-based system but a fully funded system that is managed by the government. Because such a system is fully funded, it avoids intergenerational inequities and keeps its promises. And if communitarians think of government investment as a sort of proximate stand-in for a kind of collective shared responsibility, then perhaps this system is better than a private system in meeting the communitarian criterion of shared responsibility.

The problem with this argument is that it completely ignores the political strife that would result from such a system. Communitarians presumably want to, above all, avoid the fierce and unresolvable political struggle that divides citizens, which is undermining a common set of interests and sense of solidarity. Yet, that is what almost certainly would occur if, in a democratic society, governments managed the investment of Social Security taxes, assuming, as I think is likely, that there will be pressures to invest at least some of these in the stock market to get a good rate of return. Disputes about the right way for the government to invest involve complex problems: we usually rely on experts for investment advice because sound investing involves skills and information most of us lack. When investment becomes collective and political, it's hard to see what commonly accepted principles would be used to solve disputes concerning how to invest payroll taxes. Not only will there be disagreements about investment strategies, these disagreements will be intertwined with fierce moral disagreements about the appropriateness of certain investments. (For example, should we invest in companies that do a substantial business in authoritarian or dictatorial regimes? In tobacco stocks? Liquor companies? Gun manufacturers? And so forth.) While there is perhaps a practical solution to these problems—a politically insulated agency that invests passively in index funds—the pot of money available is so great (trillions of dollars) that the temptation for meddling may well be irresistible, offering no alternative to fierce and endless disputes about investment decisions.

By contrast, the main source of politicization in a system of compulsory private pensions is likely to revolve around where to set the minimum pension guarantee. These disputes are likely to be less fierce and more resolvable. For one thing, the amount of money involved is much less, which tends to dampen political disputes. A more important point is that disputes about a safety net in a compulsory private system involve a relatively simple problem: at what level should the minimum pension guarantee be set? Certain commonly accepted principles could be used to solve the problem. One

101

solution is that the minimum pension guarantee should be set high enough to eliminate significant elderly poverty, but not so high as to create a moral hazard problem; that is, tempt people to engage in excessively risky investments, knowing that if they fail, the government will bail them out. This solution to the problem of where to set the minimum pension guarantee is not merely a theoretical point but a practical one. If the minimum pension guarantee is set at around today's average benefit of Social Security, then that eliminates any severe problem of elderly poverty. But the benefits from long-term investment are so much greater than today's average Social Security benefit that there is little risk of moral hazard.[31]

Thus, the claim that communitarianism should favor a fully funded government-managed system is unfounded. A private retirement system with a safety net for the elderly poor is far more consonant with communitarian values.

Public Justification

No one doubts that, until recently, social insurance programs like Social Security were quite popular.[32] Does this help justify Social Security, despite the arguments given above? No, because public *support* does not imply public *justification*. Public justification means that the public had good reasons for supporting the program. But the public could not have good reasons if it was seriously misled or misinformed about the program it endorsed, for then it could not understand what it endorsed. With regard to being misled, the rhetoric surrounding Social Security and the way it operates blocks the public's access to reasonably reliable or accurate information about the system. This is not true for a private system. With regard to being misinformed, there is considerable evidence that the illusion that Social Security is akin to funded pensions may very well have been crucial to obtaining the high level of support that it has enjoyed until very recently.[33]

A defender of Social Security may concede the above points but argue that a reformed Social Security system would be justified if it became more like market insurance and thus more comprehensible and less subject to misinformation. The following kind of reform may seem to help in this regard:

1. Place Social Security in a separate budget, and establish rules to prevent it from being influenced by the normal budgetary maneuvering.

2. Invest payroll taxes in whatever would lessen the implicit public pension debt with the least risk (e.g., some combination of private and government securities).
3. Allow individuals to partially opt out of Social Security, thus creating some direct competition between Social Security and market pensions.
4. Provide the equivalent of accurate quarterly or annual reports, and make widely available to all recipients of Social Security accurate information about its actuarial status, expected rates of return, and so on.

While reforms like these would make Social Security more like a private system, a Social Security system that merely imitates a private system is obviously inferior to the real thing. The reformed Social Security system would still remain PAYGO, and so determining one's rate of return, the actuarial status of the system, and so forth, would remain difficult compared with a private alternative.

There is an even deeper problem with arguments that Social Security can be reformed to make it easier to obtain accurate information about its functioning. Recall that this section began with the understanding that public *support* does not translate into public *justification* if the public has difficulty comprehending the institution it supports. However, making available accurate information about Social Security might well eliminate or drastically reduce public support for the system, so that the issue of the relationship between public support and justification wouldn't arise in the first place. Equating Social Security with fully funded market pensions (or viewing them as closely analogous) was and has been crucial to its support, suggesting that if the government advertised loudly, clearly, and persistently that the system is PAYGO (i.e., there are significant intergenerational transfers that harm later generations, one's taxes are not being invested in a genuine trust fund, and the system should not be confused with private pensions), then public support for Social Security would decline. On the other hand, since a compulsory private system is a market-based system, and not PAYGO, accurate information about its nature is no obstacle to its obtaining public support.

Conclusion

Social Security is one of the cornerstones of the welfare state. Until very recently, it was considered politically untouchable, morally sacrosanct, and a success story, one all welfare-state advocates could point to with pride. Those days are gone. Defenders of Social Security know that they have a fight on their hands. Individual accounts are now politically acceptable, and a significant number of Americans no longer see Social Security as a success story. The moral shroud that used to surround Social Security is an illusion: there is no moral argument for Social Security. Not only would a private system provide more freedom, as libertarians stress, not only would it provide economic benefits, as policy analysts stress, but it would be fairer and more comprehensible, provide greater security, and help blunt antagonisms between generations. In short, individual accounts are a win-win proposal that is justified regardless of which political values one thinks most important. This message should be trumpeted loudly and clearly. The retirement system we have been stuck with for so long is not just bad for our pocketbooks and our freedom—it's bad, period.[34]

Notes

1. For a history of mutual aid societies in the United States, see David Beito, *From Mutual to the Welfare State: Fraternal Societies and Social Services, 1890–1967* (Chapel Hill: University of North Carolina Press, 2000).

2. See, for example, David Schmidtz, "Taking Responsibility," in *Social Welfare and Individual Responsibility*, ed. David Schmidtz and Robert Goodin (Cambridge: Cambridge University Press, 1998), particularly chapters 1.1, 1.3, and 1.4, and Michael Tanner, *The Poverty of Welfare: Helping Others in Civil Society* (Washington: Cato Institute, 2003), particularly chapters 5 and 8.

3. In Chile, workers may invest only in specialized pension fund management companies. Only one fund per worker is allowed, and only one fund per management company. These restrictions are not necessary for the operation of a compulsory private pension system, nor an essential part of a defense of Social Security privatization. On Chile's system, see World Bank Policy Research Report, *Averting the Old-Age Crisis: Policies to Protect the Old and Promote Growth* (New York: Oxford University Press, 1994), ch. 6; L. Jacobo Rodriguez, "Chile's Private Pension at 18: Its Current State and Future Challenges," Cato Institute Social Security Paper no. 17 (July 30, 1999); Sebastian Edwards, "The Chilean Pension Reform: A Pioneering Program," in *Privatizing Social Security*, ed. Martin Feldstein (Chicago: University of Chicago Press, 1998), chapter 1; and H. Fred Mittelstaedt and John C. Olsen, "An Empirical Analysis of the Investment Performance of the Chilean Pension System," *Journal of Pension Economics and Finance* 2, no. 1 (2003): 7–24.

4. See *Flemming v. Nestor*, § 363 US 603 (1960).

5. See Larry S. Temkin, *Inequality* (New York: Oxford University Press, 1993), pp. 7–8.

6. In recent years, these views have been increasingly dubbed "prioritarian," or "the priority view," but since it will turn out a market-based retirement system that

should be supported by both egalitarianism and prioritarianism, it is not necessary here to use the latter term. For a discussion of the differences between egalitarianism, strictly speaking, and prioritarianism, or the priority view, see Derek Parfit, "Equality or Priority," in *Ideals of Equality*, ed. Andrew Mason (Oxford, England: Blackwell Publishers, 1998): 1–20, and, in particular, 12–13; and Richard J. Arneson, "Luck Egalitarianism and Prioritarianism," *Ethics* 110, no. 2 (January 2000): 340.

7. John Rawls' difference principle, which states that social and economic inequalities should be arranged so as to provide the greatest benefit to the least advantaged, is an important exception, since his conception of the "least advantaged" seems to ignore the question of responsibility for one's plight. See *A Theory of Justice* (Cambridge, Mass.: Harvard University Press, 1971), p. 302; and *Political Liberalism* (New York: Columbia University Press, 1993), p. 291. However, since *A Theory of Justice* was published, most egalitarians have endorsed a responsibility or choice condition in their egalitarian principles. For a good review of this literature, see G. A. Cohen, "On the Currency of Egalitarian Justice," *Ethics* 99, no. 4 (1989): 906–44; and Richard J. Arneson, "Equality," in *The Blackwell Guide to Social and Political Philosophy*, ed. Robert L. Simon (Malden, Mass.: Blackwell Publishing, 2002), pp. 85–105.

Two other complications about egalitarianism should be noted. First, some egalitarians answer the question "equality of what?" or "worse off in what respect?" in terms of resources such as income or wealth, while others focus on welfare, that is, some favorable psychological condition such as happiness or satisfaction. Second, egalitarians disagree about whether there are obligations of justice to future generations. Neither of these complications matters much for the purposes of this discussion. The first doesn't matter because when one system is much worse vis-à-vis resources, it will probably be worse vis-à-vis welfare. The second doesn't matter, because even those who reject obligations to future generations admit special obligations to their children and a concern for their descendants, even those not yet born; and so a pension system's effects on future generations are a matter of moral concern either way.

8. Here's how the "trust fund" really works. Excess payroll tax revenue not needed to meet current benefits is "invested" in new special-issue government bonds. The trust funds are credited with a bond—an IOU from one part of government to another—and the Treasury gets the cash. This cash is being used to finance the general operations of the federal government. Thus, the figures given for the surpluses supposedly in the trust fund are merely records of transfers from one part of government to another. When Social Security's cash outflow exceeds the cash inflow from taxes (probably around 2018), the government will not find any money to pay promised benefits, only Treasury obligations. When the government then calls in the IOUs, it will have to do what it would do were there no trust fund—raise taxes, and/or cut benefits, and/or borrow money, and/or monetize the debt (unless the system has been transformed into a market-based system by then). For an excellent account of why the U.S. trust fund is an utterly misleading term, see June O'Neill, "The Trust Fund, the Surplus, and the Real Social Security Problem," Cato Institute Social Security Paper no. 26, April 9, 2002, pp. 2–3. See also note 22.

Notice also that even if the trust fund monies had been invested, Social Security would not be fully funded and would remain a PAYGO system. Full funding would mean that the trust fund would be large enough that, if Social Security ended today and no future taxes were collected, the assets in the fund (the portion of the taxes on present workers that were not paid out immediately) plus interest could pay all the benefits to which existing workers and beneficiaries were entitled. This is not true and has never been true of Social Security.

9. See Julia Lynn Coronado, Don Fullerton, and Thomas Glass, "The Progressivity of Social Security," National Bureau of Economic Research Working Paper no. 7520, available at http://www.nber.org/papers/w7520; "Distributional Impacts of Proposed Changes to Social Security," in *Tax Policy and the Economy*, ed. J. Poterba (Boston: MIT Press, 1999), pp. 149–86; Jeffrey Liebman, "Redistribution in the Current U.S. Social Security System," in *The Distributional Aspects of Social Security and Social Security Reform*, ed. Martin Feldstein and Jeffrey B. Liebman (Chicago: University of Chicago Press, 2002), ch. 1.

10. Michael Tanner, "Disparate Impact: Social Security and African Americans," Cato Institute Briefing Paper no. 61, February 5, 2001, and General Accounting Office, "Social Security and Minorities," available at http://www.gao.gov/new.items/d03387.pdf. The GAO report found that black Americans receive lower net lifetime benefits than whites of the same income. Admittedly, it also found that, in the aggregate, blacks have higher disability rates and that this means that as a group they tend to receive greater benefits relative to taxes than whites. However, it is not clear whether disability benefits should be aggregated with the other Social Security benefits, and the study did not address whether whites of the same income level receive less or more disability benefits than blacks.

11. William W. Beach and Gareth E. Davis, *Social Security's Rate of Return* (Washington: Heritage Foundation, 1998), pp. 2 and 7.

12. One might deny this if one makes extremely pessimistic assumptions about future returns to equities and assumes that administrative costs of a market-based system will be quite high. For a thorough discussion and refutation of these assumptions, as well as other assumptions that some supporters of Social Security have used to deny that private accounts will have a significantly better rate of return than Social Security, see Michael Tanner, "The Better Deal: Estimating Rates of Return under a System of Individual Accounts," Cato Institute Social Security Paper no. 31, October 28, 2003.

13. The arguments given here also show that egalitarians should prefer a private system to a mixed system, that is a Social Security system that has added on or carved out private retirement accounts as a component of the system. (A number of European and Latin American countries have such systems.) Since mixed systems as a whole remain largely PAYGO, the same arguments against a PAYGO system apply to mixed systems.

14. David Kelley, *A Life of One's Own: Individual Rights and the Welfare State* (Washington: Cato Institute, 1998).

15. See "The Moral Basis of the Democratic Welfare State," in *Democracy and the Welfare State*, ed. Amy Gutmann (Princeton: Princeton University Press, 1988), pp. 30–36, 41–46, and "Introduction: Responsibility, Rights, and Welfare," in *Responsibility Rights and Welfare: The Theory of the Welfare State*, ed. J. Donald Moon (Boulder: Westview Press, 1988), pp. 4–8.

16. Income transfers to the elderly poor are not generally considered "welfare" in the pejorative sense. It is unlikely, then, that these transfers will cause the system to be perceived as a welfare system.

17. The benefits of Social Security in its earliest years were relatively modest, which is why those who retired somewhat after the system was first founded did better than the very first group of retirees.

18. One might argue that this is false because, when a compulsory private system begins, those with inadequate voluntary savings will have little security when they retire. But this only means that the safety net may have to be larger in the beginning of this system than in the later stages. It doesn't refute the point that a system of mandatory savings does not redistribute security through time.

19. The arguments in this section also show a private system is superior to mixed systems, since such systems still remain largely PAYGO, and it is the PAYGO feature of Social Security that undermines the link between productivity and benefits, and which causes a redistribution of security.

20. For guides to communitarian literature, see my "Liberalism and Communitarianism," *Philosophical Books* 36, no. 3 (July 1995): 145–55; Chandran Kukathas, "Liberalism, Communitarianism, and Political Community," *Social Philosophy and Policy* 13, no. 1 (Winter 1996): 80–90; and Daniel Bell, *Communitarianism and Its Critics* (Oxford: Oxford University Press, 1993).

21. A somewhat different way of explaining communitarianism is that certain kinds of communities partially constitute our identities and a commitment to the good of these constitutive communities is what we value most of all. See Bell, *Communitarianism and Its Critics,* pp. 93–94.

22. *Report of the 1994–1996 Advisory Council on Social Security Vol. 1: Findings and Recommendations* (Washington: Government Printing Office, 1997), p. 89, their emphasis.

23. Amitai Etzioni and Laura Brodbeck, *The Intergenerational Covenant: Rights and Responsibilities* (Washington: Communitarian Network, 1995), p. 3.

24. See note 8.

25. The recent availability of information from Cato's Web site, http://www.socialsecurity.org/calc/calculator.html, which compares one's Social Security return with normal stock market returns, makes it easier to grasp this point. However, for most of the history of Social Security, this Web site did not exist, and it's doubtful that many Americans have seen this Web site.

26. Not until 1990 was a law passed requiring the U.S. Social Security Administration to provide personal earnings statements and benefit estimates to everyone for whom a current address can be determined. This went into effect in October 1999. Statements to those under age 50 are not required to include estimates of monthly retirement benefits. Virginia P. Reno and Robert Friedland, "Strong Support but Low Confidence: What Explains the Contradiction?" in *Social Security in the 21st Century,* ed. Eric R. Kingson and James H. Schulz (New York: Oxford University Press, 1997), p. 194, note 8.

27. The Chilean system requires retirees to take out (indexed) annuities and/or periodic withdrawals at retirement. It prohibits lump-sum withdrawals. For information on the Chilean system, see World Bank, *Averting the Old-Age Crisis,* ch. 6.

28. For data on the lack of confidence in Social Security, see Reno and Friedland, "Strong Support but Low Confidence: What Explains the Contradiction?" in *Social Security in the 21st Century,* pp. 184–88.

29. The arguments I made about Social Security's intergenerational inequities and problems with keeping its promises also apply to mixed systems, since they still remain, fundamentally, PAYGO systems.

30. The living cannot share responsibility with the dead. Shared responsibility between completely removed generations—those whose lifetimes never overlap with that of present generations—exists only in a symbolic sense.

31. Ferrara and Tanner, *A New Deal for Social Security*, pp. 160–61, 211–12.

32. It is not entirely clear what Americans really believe about Social Security. On the one hand, Americans consistently express support for Social Security in the abstract, but majorities or near-majorities express low confidence in the program. Majorities support partial privatization and all candidates who ran on a platform of partial privatization won in the 2002 elections; furthermore, more people think that Social Security is riskier than partial privatization, because Social Security cannot pay all the benefits it has promised. For the data on Americans attitudes toward Social Security see John Zogby et al., "Public Opinion and Private Accounts: Measuring Risk and Confidence in Rethinking Social Security," Cato Institute Social Security Paper no. 29, January 6, 2003; and Fay Lomax Cook and Lawrence R. Jacobs, "Assessing Assumptions about Attitudes towards Social Security: Popular Claims Meet Hard Data," in *The Future of Social Insurance: Incremental Action or Fundamental Reform*, ed. Peter Edelman, Dallas L. Salisbury, and Pamela J. Larson (Washington: Brookings Institution, 2002), ch. 5. Cook and Jacobs and Zogby et al. disagree about majorities' support for partial privatization. Zogby affirms it, while Cook and Jacobs deny it, arguing that the support only exists in the abstract, but that when questions about the risks posed by private accounts are added to the question, support drops. However, Zogby points out that a question that just mentions risk of private accounts without mentioning risks of Social Security is biased in Social Security's favor; as I noted above, when questions are asked about which is a greater risk, Social Security failing to keep its promises, or people losing money in private accounts, more people choose the former.

33. See Carolyn L. Weaver, *The Crisis in Social Security* (Durham, N.C.: Duke University Press, 1982), pp. 80–86, 123–24; and Martha Derthick, *Policymaking for Social Security* (Washington, Brookings Institution, 1979), pp. 199–201, 204; and John Attarian, *Social Security: False Consciousness and Crisis* (New Brunswick, N.J.: Transaction Publishers, 2001), chs. 4–10.

34. For a longer and more philosophically complex version of the arguments given here, see my "Can Old-Age Social Insurance Be Justified?" *Social Philosophy and Policy* 14, no. 2 (Summer 1997): 116–44.

PART II

WOMEN, THE POOR, AND MINORITIES

7. Social Security Choices for the 21st-Century Woman

Leanne Abdnor

Since 1935 millions of senior citizens have relied on Social Security as the foundation for their retirement income. Women have often been the biggest beneficiaries of the program, because they have lower incomes and live longer than men and because Social Security grants generous benefits to spouses who do not work outside the home, most of whom have historically been women.

However, as our society has changed, with women achieving greater equality and becoming full participants in education, business, and politics, Social Security has failed to keep up. As a result, Social Security no longer meets the needs of today's families and today's women.

Although most women work today, Social Security's original benefit structure—designed for a time when the single-earner family was the norm—is largely unchanged. And although Social Security still provides partial protection against poverty, spousal and survivors' benefit regulations now clash with women's changed roles and options in our society.

Indeed, Social Security's outmoded benefit structure is increasingly a source of discrimination and unfairness, pitting women against women. Among those adversely affected are millions of married women who have joined the workforce and many divorced and single women who are providing for themselves and their dependents. Social Security's 1935-era benefit structure means that the benefits of wealthier single-earner couples are subsidized by everyone else, including dual-earning couples, who also often receive disproportionately lower benefits. Furthermore, many divorced women are left with no claim to spousal or survivors' benefits.

Originally published as Cato Institute Social Security Paper no. 33, February 24, 2004.

Moreover, the discrimination and unfairness in today's system are likely to increase as Social Security wrestles with impending insolvency. After all, Social Security will begin running deficits in just 15 years.

Both the system's financing problems and the inequities in its benefit structure can be resolved by allowing younger workers, including younger women, the choice of privately investing at least a portion of their Social Security taxes through personal retirement accounts. Not only would personal accounts help to solve Social Security's financial problems by taking advantage of the higher returns available to private capital investment, they would give women true ownership and control of their retirement income and create a benefit structure far more tailored to the needs of the modern family.

Ironically, however, some of the groups and individuals that have historically been outspoken in defense of women's rights have opposed voluntary personal retirement accounts and therefore find themselves in the unusual position of opposing increased choice and opportunity for women.

Social Security reform is inevitable. It is vital, therefore, that any reforms be consistent with the diversity of women's roles and opportunities in the 21st century. Those organizations and individuals who have identified themselves as advocates of women's rights should be questioned about their opposition to allowing women choices under Social Security.

Women's Roles Have Changed Since 1935; Social Security Has Not

Nothing endangers the future of retirement security for women more than continuing the current system's pay-as-you-go (PAYGO) financing structure into the next generation. Simply put, because PAYGO systems tax current workers to pay the benefits of current retirees, the program's ability to pay promised benefits is dependent on the ratio of workers to retirees, a ratio that has shrunk from 16.5 workers per retiree in 1950 to just 3.3 today. Soon almost 80 million baby boomers will start to retire and begin drawing benefits. By 2040 there will be 2.1 workers for every beneficiary.[1] As a result, Social Security's financial condition and ability to pay benefits are steadily declining.

In just 15 years Social Security will begin running deficits, spending more on benefits than it takes in through taxes. The Social Security Trust Fund is an accounting measure, not real assets, and will do nothing to stave off the program's rapidly approaching insolvency.[2]

Despite the rhetoric surrounding recent Social Security debates, PAYGO systems "guarantee" benefits only to the extent that lawmakers can afford to pay them. A series of Supreme Court decisions has made it clear that a worker has no right to *any* of his or her Social Security contributions.[3] As a result, today's workers face sharp benefit cuts or massive tax increases.[4] Since women tend to have lower wages than men and to be more dependent on Social Security in retirement, tax increases or benefit cuts, or both, will disproportionately hurt women.

Perhaps even more important than Social Security's financial problem is the clash between the current benefit structure and the socioeconomic changes that have occurred since 1935, such as the large number of women who have entered the workforce, women marrying later or not at all, and the doubling of the divorce rate. As a result, Social Security no longer meets the needs of millions of today's families and today's women.

When Social Security was created in 1935, its authors not surprisingly designed its structure to benefit the family structure that existed at the time: a husband who earns an income outside the home and a wife who works as a homemaker and caretaker for children. But women's roles and family structure have changed since then. Today, most women work outside the home for a substantial portion of their lives. Many women marry later in life or not at all, even if they have children for whom they care. Divorce is far more common. By failing to keep pace with the changing nature of American families, Social Security's outdated benefit structure results in single women and dual-earner couples subsidizing the benefits of wealthier single-earner couples, thus creating a sharply regressive element in the current benefit structure. For example:

- Under what is known as the "dual entitlement rule" for spousal benefits, the spouse with the lower lifetime earnings in a dual-earning couple (usually the wife) receives either a benefit based on her own earnings or an amount equal to half of her spouse's benefits, but not both.[5] This provides a generous benefit for

113

spouses who have not earned benefits in their own right, which may have made sense in an era when few women worked outside the home. But this subsidy for stay-at-home spouses comes at the price of penalizing women who work outside the home, since they often do not receive additional benefits despite paying Social Security taxes.

- A divorced woman must have been married for 10 years to receive benefits based on her husband's earnings. Again, this may have been reasonable in an era when divorce was relatively uncommon. But today it leaves millions of women without benefits they would otherwise receive.

- A widow is eligible to receive the greater of either her husband's benefit or her own, but not both. As a result, her household income may be cut by one-third or more when her husband dies, even though her cost of living will not be reduced nearly as much.

- A single working woman without dependents who dies before retirement age forfeits all of her contributions to Social Security.

In the past 50 years women have increasingly asserted themselves in the workplace and made life-changing strides in achieving economic independence. Increased education, longer commitments to the workforce, and reduced barriers to traditionally male-only jobs have significantly raised the earning power of women above historical levels. In 1950 just over 30 percent of women aged 20 and older worked either full time or part time, a figure that has nearly doubled to 60 percent today.[6]

Consistent with the doubling of the number of women in the workforce, 70 percent of all married couples are now dual-earner families.[7] Likewise, in 1998, 51 percent of dual-earning couples had children, up from just 33 percent in 1976.[8] Viewed from another perspective, 73 percent of women aged 15 to 44 in the labor force have children, an increase from 28 percent in 1960.[9]

In 2002, 55 percent of mothers, married and unmarried, with infants under one year old participated in the workforce, almost double the 31 percent rate of 1976.[10] According to the U.S. Census Bureau, "The cumulative effect is that women's work schedules are less likely to be interrupted by the birth of their first child, and women today are making longer-term commitments to the labor force than women in the 1960s."[11]

Women are also attaining higher levels of education than ever before, earning roughly 60 percent of associate's degrees, 56 percent of all bachelor's degrees, 57 percent of all master's degrees, and 42 percent of doctoral degrees.[12] In 1970 only 11 percent of women in the labor force had completed four or more years of college; by 1997 that figure had risen to 28 percent.[13]

As a result, women today have access to countless career paths and opportunities. The number of female lawyers, physicians, financial managers, and other managers has more than doubled since 1975.[14] Women and men participate equally in managerial and "professional specialty" occupations, such as engineering, computer programming, architecture, and scientific fields.[15] Furthermore, the U.S. Census Bureau's Survey of Women-Owned Business Enterprises reports that women-owned businesses made up 26 percent of the nation's 20.8 million nonfarm businesses, employed 7.1 million paid workers, and generated $818.7 billion in sales and receipts in 1997.[16]

In 2002 two-thirds of all women aged 16 or older worked 35 hours or more per week. (Another 22 percent of workingwomen are part-time workers.) Indeed, women now work nearly as long as men, an average of 41.0 hours per week, compared to 44.2 hours for men.[17]

In the future even more women are likely to work and to move into more and more previously male-dominated professions. As economist and former head of the Congressional Budget Office June O'Neill has noted, an examination of the labor force participation of female age groups born 10 years apart showed that each group attained a higher level of participation at every stage of life than the previous group.[18] Thus, we can expect women in the future to be even better educated, wealthier, and more self-sufficient than women today.

As women's financial independence has grown, so too has their social independence. The last 50 years have seen an astounding shift toward women providing for themselves and their dependents, rather than relying solely on men. Reduced marriage rates, rising divorce rates, later marriages, single parenthood, and alternative lifestyles have changed our social structure. For those reasons, married couples no longer constitute the vast majority of the population, and single people are no longer the minority.

The number of divorced people has more than quadrupled, from 4.3 million in 1970 to 20.9 million in 2002, and represents nearly 10 percent of adults, up from 3 percent in 1970.[19] The exploding rate of divorce has resulted in millions of women entering or reentering the workforce or committing more time to their existing jobs.

Currently, the divorced population is the fastest growing marital status category. One of three marriages ends prior to the 10 years required to qualify for Social Security spousal and survivors' benefits.[20] Further, the National Center for Health Statistics reports that marriages ending in divorce have a median length of just 7.7 years. Unfortunately, those who remarry do not experience a significantly improved chance for long-term marital success.[21] Fifteen percent of all remarriages end in divorce after three years, and, again, one-third of remarriages end before 10 years.

Millions of children in this country are raised in one-parent households, the great majority of which are led by women. The number of children living with a single parent rose from 8.5 million in 1970 to nearly 20 million in 2002; 83 percent of those children live with their mothers.[22] Some of that increase is due to rising divorce rates, but a significant portion is due to the increase in out-of-wedlock childbearing. Approximately 1.2 million women gave birth outside marriage in 2000; that was 31 percent of all births that year.[23]

Raising children while working full time is an extraordinarily difficult challenge, and many single mothers are struggling to keep ahead of the financial demands on them. The regressive payroll tax takes an enormous toll on those single parents, yet they do not benefit from the spousal or widow's survivor benefits received by married couples. Sheila Zedlewski of the Urban Institute notes, "Single mothers have been a growing segment of American families, and many of these women will have no claim to a Social Security spouse benefit."[24]

For many reasons, men and women are marrying much later in life, and many are choosing to stay single. In 2000 the median age for men and women at marriage was 27 years and 25 years, respectively, whereas in 1970 the median age was 23 for men and 21 for women.[25] Much of the delay can be attributed to an increase in the number of men and women obtaining higher levels of education. At the same time, the economic factors that historically pushed women into early marriage have become less important as women have become better able to support themselves. In 2000 nearly three million women aged 35 to 44 were never married, more than double the number in 1970.[26] It is for those reasons, and many others, that today only 52 percent of all households are married households, compared with 78 percent in 1950.[27]

In addition, the increased longevity enjoyed by women means that more women face their retirement years alone. Women's life expectancies significantly exceed those of men. For example, a woman who is 65 years old today can expect to live to 84, whereas a 65-year-old man can expect to live to only 81.[28] That means that women make up a majority of the elderly population; just over half of all Americans aged 65–74, 60 percent of those aged 75–84, and fully 71 percent of those over the age of 85 are women.[29] Making the problem worse, of women 65 years and older, 45 percent are widows, and, of those, 70 percent live alone.[30]

In spite of the dramatic changes in women's roles in society and the economy, Social Security's benefit structure has remained basically unchanged since the program was founded in 1935. As Rep. Charlie Stenholm (D-Tex.) has pointed out: "Social Security's benefit structure is based on a portrait from 1940 of a family with a husband as the sole wage earner and a dependent wife who remains at home. As two-earner households become the norm and the typical family becomes harder to define, the failure of Social Security to adapt results in glaring inequities."[31]

An Outdated Benefit Structure

The failure of Social Security's benefit structure to keep up with the progress of women and the changing nature of the American family creates serious inequities.

For instance, Social Security's current benefit structure still provides a substantial subsidy to single-earner marriages, couples in which one spouse is the sole income producer for the family. In most cases the husband is the sole earner, and the wife is dependent on her husband to provide all of the family income.[32] At retirement, the income producer receives 100 percent of his earned benefit, and his spouse receives a "spousal benefit" of an additional 50 percent of his benefit even though she did not contribute to the system. In fact, a wife receives the spousal benefit even if there are no children and regardless of financial need. The result is that single-earner families receive this subsidy even though such couples tend to be wealthier than couples in which both spouses work.

117

Moreover, this subsidy comes at the expense of dual-earner couples, both members of which earn income, contribute to Social Security, and have earned benefits at retirement. Unlike single-earner couples, dual-earner families are often penalized through the dual entitlement rule. The Social Security Administration explains this rule by stating that the lower-earning spouse receives her earned benefit, and if it is less than 50 percent of her husband's earned benefit, she also receives the difference between the two. However, the effect is that the spouse with the smaller earned benefit from Social Security, usually the working wife, is entitled to the higher of *her own earned benefit or a spousal benefit equal to one-half of the benefit received by the higher earning spouse, but not both.* As a result, if a woman has spent time in the workforce and paid Social Security taxes but has not earned enough to receive Social Security benefits equal to 50 percent of her husband's, she collects a benefit that is based solely on her husband's wage history (half of his benefit) and receives no benefit based on her own earnings or taxes paid. In this case, she would receive exactly the same benefit as a financially dependent spouse who never contributed a dime to the Social Security system.

The bias against two-earner couples has a regressive effect on Social Security benefits, taking retirement benefits from those families that depend on two incomes and subsidizing couples that can afford for only one of the spouses to work outside the home. Simply put, dual-earner couples often receive a smaller benefit than single-earner couples with exactly the same income and having paid exactly the same amount of Social Security taxes.

In a study published by the Urban Institute titled "Social Security: Out of Step with the Modern Family," the authors give the following example of two couples with the same earnings who receive different benefits at retirement.

> The Greens and the Whites each earn twice the average wage. But while Tom Green is the sole breadwinner, Ted and Becky White each earn the same amount. When Tom Green retires in 2032, the couple earns a Social Security benefit of $37,769, Tom's retired benefit of $25,179 plus Beth Green's spousal benefit of half that amount, $12,590. When Ted and Becky retire in 2032, each spouse gets a retired worker benefit of $17,358, a family total of only $34,716. That's $3,053 less than Tom and Beth's benefit.[33]

In addition to the dual entitlement rule that governs retirement income, the rules governing survivors' benefits can also lead to situations in which couples with identical household earnings and contributions receive very different monthly Social Security benefits. Social Security regulations state that a widow is eligible for the greater of her husband's benefit or her own, but not both. As a result, women from households with similar total incomes could find themselves with significantly different benefits once widowed, depending on whether the woman worked or not. Again, from the Urban Institute study:

> Tom Green dies. Beth Green moves up from spousal benefit to survivor benefit and receives $25,179. But, when Ted White dies, Becky White continues to get only her retired worker benefit of $17,358.[34]

Ekaterina Shirley and Peter Spiegler of Harvard's Kennedy School of Government point out, "Generally, the more of the couple's earnings the widow earned, the smaller the share of the couple's retirement benefits she receives after he dies."[35]

Another way to look at this problem is to determine by how much a widow's Social Security income will be reduced after her husband's death. A widow who receives a retirement benefit based on her own earned income will receive a benefit as little as one-half of the couple's combined retirement income. However, a widow who receives the 50 percent spousal retirement benefit, based solely on her husband's earned benefit, will still receive two-thirds of the couple's combined benefits after his death. According to the federal government, an adequate income for a surviving spouse is approximately 80 percent of a couple's income prior to the husband's death. The poverty line for a single individual aged 65 and older was $8,628 in 2002, only about 20 percent less than the $10,874 poverty line for couples as determined by the federal government.[36] It is clear that, as does the spousal benefit, the survivors' benefit formula favors single-earner households over dual-earner households.

As we have seen, both dual-income couples and widows from dual-earner couples suffer under Social Security's current benefit structure. Another group that is disadvantaged by the current benefit structure is divorced women. According to Social Security's benefit formula, a divorced woman must have been married for at least 10 years to be entitled to the 50 percent spousal benefit based on her former husband's earnings. A divorced woman with grown children is also entitled to the survivor's benefit after her ex-husband's death, but again only if the marriage lasted at least 10 years. For example:

> John and Judy Hall end their marriage after 9 years and 11 months. George and Rita Ball obtain a divorce after 10 years and 1 month of marriage. Despite a difference of only two months in the longevity of their marriages, Judy receives no spousal or survivors' benefits while Rita gets full spousal and survivor benefits.[37]

According to the U.S. Census Bureau, the average duration of the one million marriages that end in divorce each year is approximately 7.7 years. The result is that each year hundreds of thousands of dissolved marriages are unrecognized by the Social Security system. More than half of the women divorced each year are not eligible for spousal or survivors' benefits "earned" during their marriage. They will receive no share of their ex-husbands' benefits. The arbitrary 10-year requirement compounds the unfairness of the way spousal and survivors' benefits are calculated.

Finally, Social Security's benefit structure denies any benefit to the worker who dies before retirement age without a spouse or dependents. Thus, a single or divorced woman, without dependent children, who dies before age 62 receives not one dollar for the thousands of dollars she contributed to the system. And, as stated earlier, there are now millions of women in their 30s and 40s who have never married, and the percentage of married households has dropped by one-third since 1950.

As Eugene Steuerle and Melissa M. Favreault of the Urban Institute state: "Most of the inequities noted here are illegal under the private pension system. But that still has not prompted the Social Security Administration to take the first reform step: providing measures that assess the success of different reform options in reducing inequities as well as poverty among the elderly."[38]

Personal Accounts Provide Solutions

Given Social Security's financial crisis, it is not surprising that many proposals for Social Security reform are currently being debated in Washington. But the traditional ways of tinkering with Social Security's financing, raising taxes or cutting benefits, would do nothing to fix the inequities discussed above. However, one reform would both help to restore Social Security to solvency *and* make the program fairer for women and today's families: allowing workers to invest at least part of their Social Security taxes through individual accounts.[39]

Proposals for personal retirement accounts range from diverting just 2 percent of wages to the full 10 percent of wages currently paid to Old-Age and Survivors Insurance into an individually owned and controlled account. In addition, some proposals are progressive in nature, allowing low-wage workers to divert and invest a greater percentage of wages than high-wage workers. Because women are a large proportion of those in the lower-wage group, many women would have the choice of investing more of their income.

One, but by no means the only, approach to progressive personal retirement accounts was incorporated in the President's Commission to Strengthen Social Security's Model 2, the preferred plan of the majority of the commissioners. That plan recommended that all workers have the option of investing 4 percent of their payroll taxes up to $1,000 in a personal retirement account annually. The accounts would mirror the progressive benefit structure of Social Security by allowing lower-wage workers to invest a greater percentage of their payroll taxes than higher-wage workers.

Another study done by Marianne Baxter of Boston University suggests that, indeed, "women would have more to gain, compared with men, from a reformed Social Security system that would permit investment of retirement funds in other forms of financial assets."[40] Personal accounts would eliminate the distortions that exist under the current system that favors single-earner couples.

How Would Personal Accounts Help Two-Earner Couples?

Personal accounts would help a woman who is part of a two-earner couple because she would be proportionately rewarded for her time in the workplace. Whatever funds a woman contributed to her individual account would belong to her. In contrast, as stated earlier, with the current spousal benefit, many working wives receive no extra benefits at the margin. More work doesn't necessarily equal higher benefits. Personal accounts would increase the incentive to work by allowing a woman to own and control a portion of her Social Security contributions.

How Would Personal Accounts Help Young Widows?

Under the current system, a widow is not entitled to a Social Security survivor's benefit until she reaches age 60 unless she has dependent children. However, if her husband had had a personal retirement account, the funds in the account would be part of his estate and inheritable by his wife. She could use those funds to get additional training, start a small business, or in whatever way she chose to help her adjust to a different lifestyle.

How Would Personal Accounts Help Retirement-Age Widows?

Under a system of individual accounts, a couple could choose among different distribution methods. The couple could convert the personal account into an inflation-adjusted annuity for life or leave it in safe investments and take programmed withdrawals in retirement. In the latter case, a widow would be entitled to all the remaining funds that had accumulated in the account. If the couple chose, they could leave the funds in the account to their children, grandchildren, or others. As the President's Commission to Strengthen Social Security states: "Unlike Social Security, assets held in personal retirement accounts can be bequeathed to heirs if the account owner dies before retirement. In this way, wealth accumulation in the family need not be cut short with the death of the primary earner."[41]

How Would Personal Accounts Help a Single Woman Retiree?

Private investment through personal retirement accounts would bring a better rate of return than can be provided by the current Social Security system.[42] Higher rates of return translate directly to higher benefits. Moreover, single women without dependents—a growing demographic group in our society—who die before retirement forfeit all of the money they have paid in taxes to Social Security. However, if those women had had the option of a personal retirement account, they could pass the account on to a relative, partner, or other person of their choice.

How Would Personal Accounts Help Divorced Women?

Personal retirement accounts would provide a fair solution for all divorcees by establishing property rights in spousal benefits regardless of the duration of the marriage. At divorce, the accumulations in a couple's accounts during their marriage would be split and added to their individual accounts regardless of the length of the

Figure 1
LUMP SUMS AVAILABLE AT AGE 67 TO SPOUSE OF AVERAGE EARNER DIVORCED AT 10 YEARS

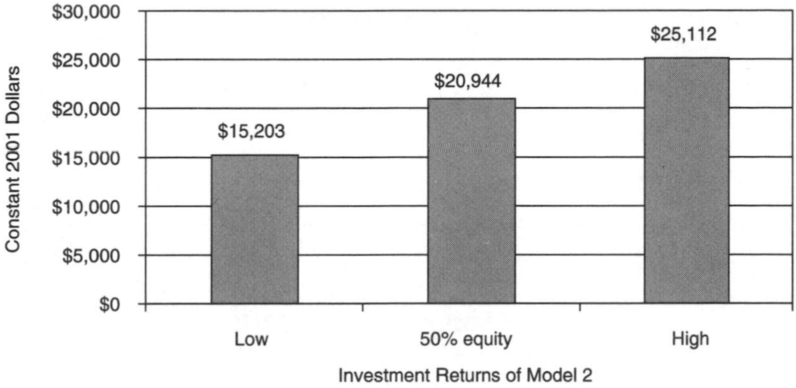

SOURCE: Andrew Biggs, "Perspectives of the President's Commission to Strengthen Social Security," Cato Institute Social Security Paper no. 27, August 22, 2002, p. 20.

marriage.[43] Thus, from "day one" of a marriage, a woman would own wealth.

Consider the following example: A woman marries at age 20. After 9 years, 11 months, and two young children, she divorces her husband. Thus, at age 30, she must enter the workforce without any experience or earnings history and support two children. Current Social Security rules leave this woman without entitlement to a spousal benefit from her past marriage. However, under proposed systems of personal retirement accounts, she would have accumulated the start of a nest egg upon which to build for her retirement. For example, under the commission's Model 2, the preferred approach, for a divorced spouse of an average earner, nearly 10 years of marriage would provide a lump sum upon retirement ranging from $15,000 to $25,000 (Figure 1). Annuitized distribution of those assets at retirement could increase her monthly income by nearly $200.

How Would Personal Retirement Accounts Help Low-Income Workers?

Low-income workers have the most to gain from a system of personal retirement accounts. Unlike wealthier workers, low-wage

123

Figure 2
Estimated Accumulation of Personal Account Assets at Retirement at Age 65 for Commission Model 2 for a Scaled Low-Income Worker

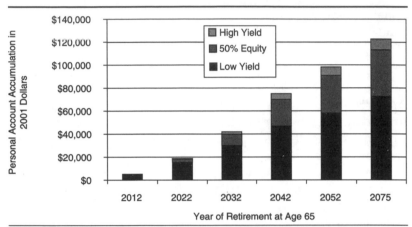

SOURCE: President's Commission to Strengthen Social Security, "Strengthening Social Security and Creating Personal Wealth for All Americans," p. 73.

earners lack the discretionary income necessary to take advantage of private investment opportunities. As a result, they are unable to accumulate real wealth. And, because Social Security benefits are not inheritable, they are unable to pass wealth on to their children. The result is a continuing cycle of poverty and growing inequality.[44]

Social Security reform would allow all workers to put part of their taxes in a personal retirement account. Low-income workers would have the opportunity, many for the first time in their lives, to save and own wealth. If the accounts were progressive, allowing an account of 4 percent up to $1,000, as under commission Model 2, low-income workers would have even more to gain. A worker who invested $1,000 annually, after 40 years would have $141,465. If she invested that money over 45 years, she would have $191,723.[45] Figure 2 illustrates the wealth that would be available to low-income workers under a system of individual accounts.

Rep. Charles Stenholm (D-Tex.) concludes: "Individual accounts address many of the inequities concerning divorce, dual-earner families, and widows' benefits. Individual accounts reward the two-earner household. Both spouses contribute to the accounts and assets accumulate in the name of the family. Individual accounts [remain] in the family. If there is a death, the property reverts to the surviving spouse. In a divorce, it is an asset that can be divided ... giving every woman who is facing a divorce a property stake in the personal account accumulations that the couple's racked up during a marriage."[46]

Women's Right to Choose Personal Accounts

Women—and to their credit, women's advocacy groups—have broken down many walls that for centuries kept women dependent and politically unrepresented. As a society, we have come to recognize that women are as capable as men of making decisions about their own lives.

There is no longer a legal barrier to women independently achieving positions of fame, power, or wealth. Women can expect to choose where to live, what work to do, what to study, where to travel, and with whom to partner. They can choose whether to marry, divorce, conceive children, travel the world, run for public office, and so on.

It is ironic, therefore, that the largest women's advocacy groups in the United States are flatly opposed to giving women the right to have a choice between the existing insolvent system and one that gives them more control and ownership of their retirement funds.[47] After all, this is, ultimately, a question of choice. Under all the major reform proposals, individual accounts would be *voluntary*. A woman could choose, if she wished, to continue to direct all of her Social Security contributions to the current government system. But she would also have the choice of directing part of her taxes to an individual account.

This position of women's rights organizations—opposing the expansion of women's rights and women's freedom to choose—is strangely inconsistent with the stated goals of those organizations.

The unwillingness of these women's organizations to support individual accounts becomes even more perplexing given the unsustainability of the current Social Security system. On several occasions at public forums, including hearings before the President's Commission to Strengthen Social Security, some of the groups critical of voluntary personal retirement accounts were asked if they would be willing to put forward their own plan for correcting the fiscal shortfalls in the system. In other words: "We know what you oppose.

What do you support? Further, would you be willing to have your plan modeled by the objective Social Security Administration actuaries so that each reform proposal would be compared with others using the same criteria?" Several witnesses stated that they would, but no plan has ever been offered.[48]

More recently, at an April 2002 Conference on Women and Social Security at the Cato Institute, I asked the same question of Heidi Hartmann of the Institute for Women's Policy Research and got the same response: they oppose voluntary personal retirement accounts and agreed to put forward their own plan. Those of us who have already put a great deal of work into detailed and fully evaluated proposals are still waiting.

The organizations that persist in seeing the ailing Social Security system as the Holy Grail of retirement security for women, without putting forward a plan for overhauling the system, are not acting responsibly and cannot be taken seriously in this debate. At a minimum, they should consider the advice of Rudy Penner, a senior fellow at the Urban Institute and former director of the Congressional Budget Office, who said: "Those looking out for older women need to steer clear of subtle traps as the debate over Social Security's future gathers force. One is turning a blind eye to the difficult problems facing the system. More grievous would be to overlook the benefits of individual accounts."[49] Indeed, the women's advocacy groups that are unwilling to move forward with a legitimate proposal are helping to put women's future at risk.

Conclusion

Social Security reform is inevitable. Given the program's huge unfunded liabilities, changes will have to be made. In making them, we should recognize that our society has dramatically changed since the 1930s and Social Security's original benefit structure has not. As a result, Social Security's benefit structure has become increasingly unfair to millions of workingwomen. The Social Security taxes of workingwomen who are married subsidize, in large measure, the free spousal benefits granted to wealthier married women who do not work outside the home. Likewise, divorced and single workingwomen, many of whom are raising children, are disadvantaged under traditional Social Security. As Rochelle Stanfield and Corrina Nicolaou of the Urban Institute write, "Unless the program is adjusted to reflect the reality of today's families, important segments of the aging population—particularly widows, divorcees, other unmarried women, and minorities—face an increasingly uncertain future."[50]

In addition to Social Security's unfair benefit structure, the program's future cash shortfall puts the expected benefits of *all* workers at risk. Indeed, the last 50 years have swelled Social Security to the point where it now consumes one of every eight dollars that average Americans earn. Projections show that, if payroll taxes were increased to cover the future cash shortfall, workers would be paying one of every *five* dollars to Social Security.[51]

Low-income workers—the majority of whom are women—would bear the biggest burden of such a tax hike. Worse, they are forced to participate in a system that takes their money but denies them a legal right to a benefit in retirement, denies them ownership, denies them the opportunity to see their savings grow, and denies them the right to pass along those savings to their families. Every generation of these families must start afresh, and the common American hope that children and grandchildren will have better lives because of their hard work is lost to the taxing system.

Allowing workers the *option of redirecting* at least a portion of their payroll taxes into personal retirement accounts would be a partial but meaningful solution to all those problems. First, a system of proportional contributions and real property rights to those contributions would reduce the subsidization inequities caused by the dual entitlement rule and could help low- and middle-income women accumulate real wealth. Furthermore, creating a larger, separate source of income for those without additional means to save would decrease dependence on a bankrupt system and alleviate some of Social Security's future benefit obligations.

Surprisingly, some traditional women's organizations advocate that we maintain the current outdated Social Security system, forcing workingwomen to pay into a system that is increasingly discriminatory and, in exchange, ask them to accept unfunded future promises and remain insecure. But, if we followed the advice of those organizations, we would be turning our backs on the progress that has been made by the courageous women who fought to allow each woman the right to make her own choices and shape her own life.

Women deserve a choice. Women deserve individual accounts.

Notes

1. *2003 Annual Report of the Board of Trustees of the Federal Old-Age and Survivors Insurance and Disability Insurance Trust Funds,* p. 51, ftp://ftp.ssa.gov/pub/OACT/TR/TR03/tr03.pdf.

2. According to the Clinton administration's fiscal year 2000 budget: "These [Trust Fund] balances are available to finance future benefit payments and other Trust Fund expenditures—but only in a bookkeeping sense. . . . They do not consist of real economic assets that can be drawn down in the future to fund benefits. Instead, they are claims on the Treasury that, when redeemed, will have to be financed by raising taxes, borrowing from the public, or reducing benefits or other expenditures. The existence of large Trust Fund balances, therefore, does not, by itself have any impact on the Government's ability to pay benefits." Executive Office of the President of the United States, *Budget of the United States Government, Fiscal Year 2000, Analytic Perspectives,* p. 337.

3. For example, the U.S. Supreme Court concluded in *Flemming v. Nestor,* 363 U.S. 603, 610–11 (1960), "To engraft upon the Social Security system a concept of 'accrued property rights' would deprive it of the flexibility and boldness in adjustment to ever-changing conditions which it demands."

4. A large and permanent tax increase would bring Social Security's finances into balance. Former Cato Institute Social Security analyst Andrew Biggs calculates the tax increases necessary to keep Social Security solvent: "To achieve permanent solvency under traditional Social Security financing would demand an immediate tax increase equal to 4.47 percent of payroll: 0.67 percent to redeem the trust fund's bonds from 2018 through 2042, 1.92 percent to maintain solvency from 2042 through 2075, and 1.88 percent to achieve permanent solvency thereafter." Andrew Biggs, "Failing by a Wide Margin: Methods and Findings in the 2003 Social Security Trustees Report," Cato Institute Briefing Paper no. 82, April 22, 2003, p. 2.

5. The Social Security Administration interprets this rule somewhat differently, stating that the lower-earning spouse receives her earned benefit, and if it is less than 50 percent of her husband's earned benefit, she also receives the difference between the two.

6. U.S. Department of Labor, Bureau of Labor Statistics, "Employment Status of the Civilian Population by Sex and Age, Historical Data," table A.1, "Women 20 Years and Over Participating in the Civilian Labor Force," http://data.bls.gov/servlet/SurveyOutputServlet.

7. U.S. Department of Labor, Bureau of Labor Statistics, "Employment Characteristics of Families in 2002," July 2003, http://www.bls.gov/news.release/pdf/famee.pdf. The 2001 and 2002 estimates are based on data from U.S. Bureau of the Census, Current Population Survey. The information relates to the labor force participation of persons 16 years and older in the civilian noninstitutional population.

8. U.S. Bureau of the Census, "Fertility of American Women," Current Population Survey, Series P20-526, June 1998, table G, http://www.census.gov/prod/2000pubs/p20-526.pdf. In the 1998 survey, there were 28,344 married couples, 14,316 of which had one or more children. In the 1976 survey, there were 25,420 married couples, 8,331 of which had one or more children.

9. U.S. Bureau of the Census, "Fertility of American Women," Current Population Survey, Series P20-526, June 1998, table F, http://www.census.gov/prod/2000pubs/p20-526.pdf.

10. U.S. Bureau of the Census, "Fertility of American Women," Current Population Survey, Historical Time Series, table H.5, "Women 15–44 Years Old Who Have Had a Child in the Last Year and Their Percentage in the Labor Force: Selected Years, 1976 to Present," October 2003, http://www.census.gov/population/socdemo/fertility/tabH5.pdf.

11. Kristin Smith, quoted in U.S. Bureau of the Census, "New Census Bureau Analysis Indicates Women Making Longer-Term Commitments to Workplace," news release, December 5, 2001, http://www.census.gov/Press-Release/www/2001/cb01-192.html.

12. U.S. Department of Education, National Center for Education Statistics, 1998 Integrated Postsecondary Education Data System, "Completions Survey" (IPEDS-C:97-98) and "Consolidated Survey" (IPEDS-CN:FY98).

13. U.S. Bureau of the Census, "Educational Attainment," Current Population Survey, Historical Time Series, table A-1, "Years of School Completed by People 25 Years Old and Over, by Age and Sex, 1940–2002," March 2003.

14. Barbara Wootton, "Gender Differences in Occupational Employment," *Monthly Labor Review*, April 1997, p. 16, http://www.epf.org/ff/ff4-6.pdf.

15. In 2002 men and women had roughly equal participation in managerial and professional specialty occupations: 20,901,000 men and 21,267,000 women. U.S. Bureau of Labor Statistics, "Annual Averages: Household Data," table 9, "Characteristics of the Employed," http://www.bls.gov/cps/cpsaat9.pdf (accessed December 2, 2003).

16. U.S. Department of Labor, Women's Bureau, "Facts on Working Women," Factsheet no. 2, November 2002, http://www.dol.gov/wb/factsheets/wbo02.htm.

17. U.S. Department of Labor, Bureau of Labor Statistics, Employment and Earning, "Annual Averages: Household Data," table 23, "Persons at Work in Nonfarm Occupations by Sex and Usual Full- or Part-Time Status," 2002, ftp://ftp.bls.gov/pub/special.requests/lf/aat23.txt.

18. June O'Neill, "The Causes and Significance of the Declining Gender Gap" (speech at Bard College, September 22, 1994), cited in "Where's My 26 Cents?" Employment Policy Foundation Newsletter, June 1998, www.epf.org/research/newsletters/1998/ff4-6.asp.

19. U.S. Bureau of the Census, "Families and Living Arrangements," Current Population Survey, Historical Time Series, table MS–1, "Marital Status of the Population 15 Years Old and Older, by Sex and Race, 1950–Present," June 2003, http://www.census.gov/population/socdemo/hh-fam/tabMS-1.pdf.

20. U.S. Department of Health and Human Services, Centers for Disease Control and Prevention, "Cohabitation, Marriage, Divorce, and Remarriage in the United States," *Vital and Health Statistics*, no. 22 (July 2002): table 21, http://www.cdc.gov/nchs/data/series/sr_23/sr23_022.pdf.

21. Although the probability of remarriage is higher for women who were under age 25 at divorce (81 percent), the probability of those women facing a second divorce before 10 years is also higher, 47 percent, compared to women over 25 at remarriage, who are significantly less likely to divorce a second time (34 percent). Ibid., table 41.

22. U.S. Bureau of the Census, "Families and Living Arrangements," Current Population Survey, Historical Time Series, table CH–1, "Living Arrangements of Children," June 12, 2003.

23. U.S. Bureau of the Census, "Fertility of American Women: June 2000," Current Population Reports, Series P20-543RV, October 2001.

24. Sheila Zedlewski, "Social Security and Single Mothers: Options for 'Making Work Pay' into Retirement," in *Social Security and the Family* (Washington: Urban Institute, 2000), http://www.urban.org/url.cfm?ID=900385.

25. U.S. Bureau of the Census, "America's Families and Living Arrangements: 2000," Current Population Reports, Series P20-537, June 2001, figure 3.

26. Ibid., table 5. In the survey, 2,951,000, or 13.0 percent of, women aged 35 to 44 had never married, up from 5.2 percent in 1970. Similarly, 1.6 million, or 8.6 percent of, women aged 45 to 54 had never married in 2000, up from 4.9 percent in 1970.

27. Of the nearly 110 million households in 2002, 56.7 million were married-couple households. In 1950, however, of 43.5 million households, 34 million were married-couple households. U.S. Bureau of the Census, "Families and Living Arrangements," Current Population Survey, Historical Time Series, table HH–1, "Households," March 2002, http://www.census.gov/population/socdemo/hh-fam/tabHH-1.pdf.

28. U.S. House of Representatives, Committee on Ways and Means, *2000 Green Book: Background Material and Data on Programs within the Jurisdiction of the Committee on Ways and Means* (Washington: Government Printing Office, 2000), p. 993, http://www.utdallas.edu/~jargo/green2000/contents.html.

29. U.S. Bureau of the Census, "The 65 Years and Over Population: 2000," Current Population Reports, Series C2KBR/01-10, October 2001, figure 2.

30. U.S. Bureau of the Census, "Marital Status and Living Arrangements: March 1998," Current Population Reports, Series P20-514, December 1998.

31. "Social Security and the Family," special event held at the Urban Institute, June 19, 2000.

32. In 2001 there were 2.6 million women and 26,000 men who were dual beneficiaries receiving spousal benefits. Similarly, 4.6 million women and 37,000 men received nondisabled widows' or widowers' benefits in 2001. *Social Security Bulletin, Annual Statistical Supplement*, 2002, tables 5.G2 and 5.F8.

33. Rochelle Stanfield and Corinna Nicolaou, "Social Security: Out of Step with the Modern Family," Urban Institute, April 1, 2000, p. 9, http://www.urban.org/UploadedPDF/out_of_step.pdf.

34. Ibid.

35. Ekaterina Shirley and Peter Spiegler, "The Benefits of Social Security Privatization for Women," Cato Institute Social Security Paper no. 12, July 20, 1998, p. 5.

36. U.S. Bureau of the Census, "Poverty 2002," http://www.census.gov/hhes/poverty/threshld/thresh02.html.

37. Stanfield and Nicolaou, p. 13.

38. Eugene Steuerle and Melissa M. Favreault, "Social Security for Yesterday's Family," *Straight Talk on Social Security and Retirement Policy*, no. 35 (November 2002), Urban Institute http://www.urban.org/UploadedPDF/310598_Straight35.pdf.

39. To the degree that some Social Security reform provides for a two-tiered structure, with some benefits continuing to be paid by the government, the author supports some additional reforms within the context of traditional Social Security. For example, the minimum benefit could be increased so that individuals who work 30 years or more would receive a benefit that equals 120 percent of the U.S. poverty line. The benefit enhancement could be phased in beginning with a 20-year worker. According to an internal agency memo at the Policy Office at SSA, if this provision were implemented immediately, it would raise significantly more than half a million of today's elderly out of poverty. Furthermore, as stated earlier, widows of beneficiaries are among the most vulnerable to poverty in our society. Currently, a widow's benefit

is at least one-third less than the total benefits she and her spouse received. The benefit structure should be changed to ensure that widows of below-average wage earners receive 75 percent of the total couple's benefit. If this were implemented today, several million widows would receive an increased monthly benefit check from Social Security.

It is appropriate that policymakers reconsider the eligibility requirements for receiving the 50 percent spousal benefit. For example, should non-income-producing spouses be eligible for the spousal benefit if there are not children in the family? Should the spousal benefit be means tested?

These and other suggestions should be thoughtfully analyzed and considered in the context of a system that cannot fulfill its promises. Indeed, it is essential to consider making these changes as part of a plan to make Social Security permanently solvent in the future.

40. Marianne Baxter, "Social Security as a Financial Asset: Gender-Specific Risks and Returns," National Bureau of Economic Research Working Paper 8329, June 2001, p. 3, http://papers.nber.org/tmp/63745-w8329.pdf.

41. President's Commission to Strengthen Social Security, "Strengthening Social Security and Creating Personal Wealth for All Americans," Report of the President's Commission, December 2001, p. 55, http://csss.gov/reports/Final_report.pdf. In addition to personal retirement accounts, the author supports an increased traditional benefit for widows as described in Model 2. Andrew Biggs notes that Model 2 "increases survivors benefits to 75 percent of the couple's prior benefit. . . . For a couple with equal incomes, this would mean a 50 percent increase in benefits to the widow. An estimated 2 to 3 million widows could receive increased benefits as a result of this new provision." Andrew Biggs, "Perspectives on the President's Commission to Strengthen Social Security," Cato Institute Social Security Paper no. 27, August 22, 2002, p. 20, http://www.cato.org/pubs/ssps/ssp-27es.html.

42. See Michael Tanner, "The Better Deal: Estimating Rates of Return under a System of Individual Accounts," Cato Institute Social Security Paper no. 31, October 28, 2003.

43. There are several ways in which this might be accomplished. One of the most commonly discussed is known as "earning sharing" under which half of a husband's or wife's individual account contributions are immediately deposited in the spouse's account. A second method would be to treat account accumulations as community property at the time of divorce. For further discussion, see Karl Borden and Charles Rounds, "A Proposed Legal, Regulatory, and Operational Structure for an Investment-Based Social Security System," Cato Institute Social Security Paper no. 25, February 19, 2002.

44. See, for example, Jagadeesh Gokhale, "The Impact of Social Security Reform on Low-Income Workers," Cato Institute Social Security Paper no. 23, December 6, 2001.

45. Author's calculations. Funds invested at 5.5 percent annually.

46. Charles Stenholm, Comments, in *Social Security and the Family*.

47. Those groups include the National Organization for Women, the Institute for Women's Policy Research, and the National Council of Women's Organizations Task Force on Women and Social Security. See, for example, Heidi Hartmann and Catherine Hill, "Why Privatizing Social Security Would Hurt Women: A Response to the Cato Institute's Proposal for Individual Accounts," Institute for Women's Policy Research

and National Council of Women's Organizations Task Force on Women and Social Security, February 25, 2002.

48. Indeed, the commission's final report points out the following: "The Commission also notes that several witnesses who were especially critical of personal retirement accounts were specifically asked to offer alternative plans. The Commission offered to have Social Security Actuaries score the plans so we could fairly compare them with other constructive suggestions received. The Commission regrets that it has not yet received plans from some witnesses who offered to provide them." President's Commission to Strengthen Social Security, p. 151.

49. Rudolph Penner, "How Women Fare in Social Security Reform," *Indianapolis Star*, August 5, 2001.

50. Stanfield and Nicolaou.

51. 2003 *Annual Report of the Board of Trustees of the Federal Old-Age and Survivors Insurance and Disability Insurance Trust Funds*, p. 60.

8. The Impact of Social Security Reform on Low-Income Workers

Jagadeesh Gokhale

It is now generally acknowledged that Social Security is facing a large financial shortfall. Under the Social Security Administration's intermediate economic and demographic assumptions, the system's annual outlays (benefits plus administrative costs) will begin exceeding tax revenues after 2018. Official projections indicate that meeting future Social Security funding shortfalls by issuing debt would require additional debt accumulation of $47 trillion by 2075.[1]

Such a large financial imbalance makes changes in Social Security inevitable. However, it is important to realize that any change will have a significant impact on the lives of millions of Americans. That is especially true for low-income Americans, who disproportionately depend on Social Security for their retirement income. The poorest 20 percent of the elderly, for example, depend on Social Security for 78 percent of their retirement income, while Social Security provides only 24 percent of retirement income for the wealthiest fifth of retirees.[2]

There are relatively few options for restoring Social Security to solvency: we can, of course, increase taxes or cut benefits, but these would have to be quite severe. In 2001, the President's Commission to Strengthen Social Security estimated that it would take benefit reductions of 26 percent or tax increases of 37 percent to keep the program in actuarial balance over the next 75 years.[3] Either of these alternatives would have a devastating effect on the economy. Even if we were able to impose such drastic policies, they would result in a considerable increase in tax distortions and economic inefficiency.

It would therefore be desirable to alter our system of retirement security by making benefits more attractive than they are at present

Originally published as Cato Institute Social Security Paper no. 23, December 6, 2001, and updated to reflect current information.

by investing in additional "benefit features." One such feature is wealth ownership and the ability to control rather than passively accept the full annuitization of "Social Security assets." One way to do so—introducing individual accounts—may provide an opportunity to address some of the other problems associated with the current Social Security system—in particular its impact on the intergenerational transfer of wealth and wealth inequality in America.

Many less-well-off households—particularly minority households and those with low education and earnings—currently save very little and therefore own almost no financial wealth at retirement. As a result, the distribution of bequeathable wealth among retirees in the United States is highly unequal. There is strong evidence that Social Security, which forces the poor to annuitize a large fraction of what would otherwise be their retirement savings, may be contributing to this inequality. In contrast, a system of individual accounts would allow workers to accumulate bequeathable wealth and could lead ultimately to greater wealth mobility.

Individual accounts therefore become the truly progressive option for Social Security reform—one that is most likely to benefit the poor.

Tax Hikes, Benefit Cuts, and the Poor

If we wanted to maintain the current financing structure of Social Security, achieving solvency would require tax increases or benefit cuts or some combination of the two policies. Given the vulnerability of low-income workers and their disproportionate reliance on Social Security for retirement income, it is important to look at how such policies would affect this group.

One simple way to measure the impact of any Social Security reform proposal is to examine how that proposal affects lifetime net tax rates (the excess of present value of Old-Age and Survivors Insurance payroll taxes over the present value of OASI benefits, measured as a percentage of the present value of lifetime earnings).[4]

Table 1 uses this method to show the impact of various Social Security reforms on the lowest, middle, and highest quintiles of income earners (average lifetime income) sorted by date of birth. The first four columns in Table 1 show section-specific lifetime net tax rates under "current rules" and alternative policy reforms that do not involve an option for private investment.[5] The last four columns show policy-specific increases in lifetime net tax rates relative to those under current rules.

Table 1

THE IMPACT OF POTENTIAL OASI REFORMS ON LIFETIME NET TAX RATES (DISCOUNT RATE = 5%)

Policy	Lifetime Net Tax Rate by Quintile of Lifetime Earnings				Increase from Current Rules by Quintile of Lifetime Earnings			
	Lowest	Middle	Highest	All	Lowest	Middle	Highest	All
	Birth Cohort 1945–49							
0 Current Rules	−4.2	6.1	5.0	5.3				
1 38% tax hike beginning in year 2000	−3.9	6.4	5.3	5.7	0.3	0.3	0.3	0.4
2 25% tax hike beginning in year 2000	−0.2	7.1	5.4	6.0	4.0	1.0	0.4	0.7
3 Accelerated increase in normal retirement age	−1.7	6.9	5.4	5.9	2.5	0.8	0.4	0.6
4 CPI indexing of covered earnings	−3.0	6.4	5.1	5.6	1.2	0.3	0.1	0.3
5 Indexing benefits by CPI minus 1%	−2.5	6.5	5.1	5.6	1.7	0.4	0.1	0.3
6 Stabilize real per capita benefits	−2.3	6.6	5.2	5.7	1.9	0.5	0.2	0.4
7 Freeze bend points in real ceiling	−3.8	6.3	5.0	5.4	0.4	0.2	0.0	0.1
8 Eliminate earnings ceiling	−4.4	6.1	5.3	5.5	−0.2	0.0	0.3	0.2
9 Eliminate earnings ceiling w/o benefit change	−4.2	6.1	5.4	5.6	0.0	0.0	0.4	0.3
10 Increase computation years from 35 to 40	−3.5	6.3	5.0	5.4	0.7	0.2	0.0	0.1

(continued next page)

135

Table 1
THE IMPACT OF POTENTIAL OASI REFORMS ON LIFETIME NET TAX RATES (DISCOUNT RATE = 5%) (continued)

Policy	Lifetime Net Tax Rate by Quintile of Lifetime Earnings				Increase from Current Rules by Quintile of Lifetime Earnings			
	Lowest	Middle	Highest	All	Lowest	Middle	Highest	All
	Birth Cohort 1970–74							
0 Current Rules	−3.4	5.7	5.3	5.4				
1 38% tax hike beginning in year 2000	−1.1	8.4	7.1	7.6	2.3	2.7	1.8	2.2
2 25% tax hike beginning in year 2000	0.0	6.9	5.7	6.1	3.4	1.2	0.4	0.7
3 Accelerated increase in normal retirement age	−1.6	6.5	5.6	5.9	1.8	0.8	0.3	0.5
4 CPI indexing of covered earnings	−2.2	6.1	5.4	5.6	1.2	0.4	0.1	0.2
5 Indexing benefits by CPI minus 1%	−1.9	6.2	5.4	5.7	1.5	0.5	0.1	0.3
6 Stabilize real per capita benefits	1.9	7.5	5.9	6.5	5.3	1.8	0.6	1.1
7 Freeze bend points in real ceiling	−2.2	6.3	5.5	5.8	1.2	0.6	0.2	0.4
8 Eliminate earnings ceiling	−4.1	5.7	7.7	6.9	−0.7	0.0	2.4	1.5
9 Eliminate earnings ceiling w/o benefit change	−3.4	5.7	8.2	7.3	0.0	0.0	2.9	1.9
10 Increase computation years from 35 to 40	−2.6	5.9	5.3	5.5	0.8	0.2	0.0	0.1

(continued)

Policy	Lifetime Net Tax Rate by Quintile of Lifetime Earnings				Increase from Current Rules by Quintile of Lifetime Earnings			
	Lowest	Middle	Highest	All	Lowest	Middle	Highest	All
Birth Cohort 1995–2000								
0 Current Rules	-2.9	5.5	5.4	5.4				
1 38% tax hike beginning in year 2000	0.9	9.3	8.0	8.4	3.8	3.8	2.6	3.0
2 25% tax hike beginning in year 2000	0.4	6.7	5.8	6.1	3.3	1.2	0.4	0.7
3 Accelerated increase in normal retirement age	-1.3	6.2	5.6	5.8	1.6	0.7	0.2	0.4
4 CPI indexing of covered earnings	-1.7	5.9	5.5	5.6	1.2	0.4	0.1	0.2
5 Indexing benefits by CPI minus 1%	-1.5	5.9	5.5	5.6	1.4	0.4	0.1	0.2
6 Stabilize real per capita benefits	6.8	9.0	6.6	7.5	9.7	3.5	1.2	2.1
7 Freeze bend points in real ceiling	-0.9	6.4	5.7	5.9	2.0	0.9	0.3	0.5
8 Eliminate earnings ceiling	-3.3	5.5	8.2	7.1	-0.4	0.0	2.8	1.7
9 Eliminate earnings ceiling w/o benefit change	-2.9	5.5	8.7	7.5	0.0	0.0	3.3	2.1
10 Increase computation years from 35 to 40	-2.2	5.5	5.4	5.5	0.7	0.2	0.0	0.1

It is evident that the poorest lifetime earners suffer disproportionately large increases in their lifetime net tax rates under the majority of proposed reforms. For example, a direct tax hike hits the poorest and middle lifetime earners the hardest. A direct cut in benefits increases the lifetime net tax rates of the poorest old and middle-aged portions of the population by more than does a direct tax hike. Increases in lifetime net tax rates as the result of a direct benefit cut are larger for the poorest than for middle- and upper-income households.

Policies 3 through 7 and policy 10 impose indirect benefit cuts by manipulating different aspects of Social Security's benefit formula.[6] In each case, the poorest lifetime earners suffer the largest increase in lifetime net tax rates. The poorest earners face the same or lower lifetime net tax rates only under policies 8 and 9, both of which are exclusively aimed at increasing the burden on high lifetime earners. Moreover, the conclusion that the poorest lifetime earners suffer the largest increases in lifetime net tax rates under most traditional Social Security reforms remains unchanged under alternative assumptions about the present value of future Social Security payments.

This study does not address the impact of individual accounts. But such accounts would benefit the poor in two ways. First, to the degree that individual accounts reduce Social Security's long-term deficit, they would reduce the need to cut benefits or increase tax rates. Second, the accumulation in individual accounts would offset any reduction in government-provided benefits that Congress deemed necessary to balance the system.[7]

Bequeathable Wealth

Social Security reform may also affect the poor in a less visible, but perhaps even more important, way. Many less-well-off households—particularly minority households and those with low education and earnings—save very little and own almost no financial wealth at retirement. Low saving by low lifetime earners renders the distribution of bequeathable wealth among retirees in the United States highly unequal. Calculations based on the Federal Reserve's "Survey of Consumer Finances" show that of all the wealth (net worth) owned by married households around the time of retirement (age 60–69), one-third is owned by the richest 1 percent of households. About one-half of wealth is owned by the top 5 percent of households, and nearly two-thirds is owned by the top 10 percent of households.[8] Contrary to conventional wisdom, Social Security may be contributing to this high level of inequality.

Wealth in the form of an entitlement to future Social Security and Medicare benefits—annuitized wealth—helps finance retirement consumption. However, it is widely appreciated that such annuity income alone is not enough. Access to wealth in assets that are freely transferable (stocks and bonds in an individual account) provides additional options for spending during retirement. For example, financing a child's college education, helping a child with a down payment on a house, entering a nursing home, and leaving a bequest are options that remain open with bequeathable wealth but are foreclosed when most of one's "wealth" is a monthly check received from the government. Hence, the fact that the United States exhibits a sizable degree of inequality in bequeathable wealth at retirement is a matter of some concern.

Another issue that is not as evident and is hardly ever discussed (probably because we lack appropriate data) is that, because of the disparity in bequeathable wealth among retirees, economic (and social) mobility among families across generations is not as great as we might desire. Again, the reason for this may be Social Security.

Social Security and Bequeathable Wealth

According to a recent simulation study, Social Security is an important contributor to inequality in bequeathable wealth in the United States.[9] Moreover, because Social Security contributes significantly to inequality in the size of inheritances, it induces greater persistence in inequality across household "dynasties."

The study assumes that households seek to maintain a "smooth" affordable consumption standard based on their expected lifetime earnings level. Thus, they save when income is high in order to maintain living standards when it is low—as in retirement. Because Social Security imposes a payroll tax when people are working and provides benefits during retirement, it reduces or eliminates low lifetime earners' incentives to arrive at retirement with significant personal savings. This effect is more pronounced for low earners because Social Security benefits finance a larger fraction of their target postretirement consumption. Low bequeathable wealth accumulation through retirement, of course, implies that low-wage workers pass on little to their offspring at death.

In contrast, high earners—who receive only a very small fraction of their retirement "wealth" from Social Security—accumulate considerable personal savings through retirement (again, to finance their higher target postretirement consumption). Therefore, they arrive at retirement with a stock of bequeathable wealth that is almost as great as it would be in the absence of Social Security. This implies that the children of the rich continue to receive large inheritances upon their parents' deaths.

Because it generates an asymmetric impact on retirement saving by low and high lifetime earners, Social Security may be reducing or eliminating the inheritances of children in poor households but not of those in rich households. In turn, this may reinforce the chance that the children of the poor, in contrast to those of the rich, themselves arrive at retirement with low levels of bequeathable wealth.

This suggests that by making the distribution of bequests more unequal, Social Security may increase the persistence of inequality in bequeathable wealth in poorer households. Showing that this is true for an economy is difficult, if not impossible, because the required data on bequests and inheritances are unavailable and, indeed, may be impossible to collect. However, the aforementioned dynamic simulation calibrated to the U.S. economy can help to provide ballpark estimates of Social Security's influence on inequality in bequeathable wealth at retirement and on the transmission of that inequality across generations.[10]

Results from a Simulation Study

Using this relatively simply stylized life-cycle simulation model, one can construct simple experiments to answer questions about wealth inequality.[11] Calibrating the simulation under current Social Security tax and benefit benchmarks yields a Gini coefficient of 0.674 for the distribution of bequeathable wealth at retirement.[12] This is quite close to the observed value of 0.73 (as calculated from the "Survey of Consumer Finances"). Moreover, the simulated distribution of bequeathable wealth at retirement closely approximates the concentration of wealth at the upper tail of the observed distribution. In the simulated distribution, of all bequeathable wealth held by households that are about to retire, 32.8 percent is held by the top 1 percent of households, 49.4 percent is held by the top 5 percent of households, and 58.5 percent is held by the top 10 percent of households.

An obvious question to pose is whether there would be less or greater inequality in bequeathable wealth among those at retirement age in the absence of Social Security.[13] Eliminating Social Security in the simulation model is equivalent to replacing it with individual accounts: Without Social Security, all households save in their own personal accounts for financing their target retirement consumption. When Social Security is eliminated from the simulation, the model's Gini value falls to 0.608. This suggests that Social Security causes greater inequality in bequeathable wealth among retirees.

The Transmission of Inequality across Generations

The simulation can be used to perform another interesting experiment—to address questions about the intergenerational transmission of wealth inequality via bequests. The question posed here is, Given that some households in a given generation have low bequeathable wealth at retirement, how likely are their children to retire with similarly low bequeathable wealth? This question about intergenerational wealth mobility is just as important as the previous one about wealth inequality. Low upward wealth mobility—which means that those who are poor today have little chance (or their children have little chance) of emerging wealthy tomorrow—is obviously undesirable. It detracts from the ideal of equality of opportunity and provokes calls for public intervention on behalf of those stuck in poverty.

The results on the influence of Social Security on intergenerational wealth mobility are striking. In Tables 2 and 3, rows show parental wealth positions at retirement and columns show children's wealth positions when they retire.[14]

They show the probability (as a percentage) that the child will appear in any particular wealth quintile given the parents' position in the bequeathable wealth distribution. Table 2 shows the probabilities under current Social Security's benchmarks. For example, 40 percent of the children of those who hold less than $99,000 in bequeathable wealth at retirement will also retire with $99,000 or less. On the other hand, those children have only a 5 percent chance of accumulating more than $455,000 by retirement. In contrast, children of parents retiring with more than $455,000 have an almost 50

141

Table 2

Intergenerational Mobility in Bequeathable Wealth under Current Social Security

Parent Wealth at Retirement ($ thousands)	Parent Wealth at Retirement ($ thousands)				
	0–99	99–159	159–245	245–455	455–117,576
0–99	40.0%	27.3%	17.8%	10.2%	4.7%
99–159	24.2%	24.4%	22.1%	18.1%	11.3%
159–245	15.4%	21.0%	22.8%	22.7%	18.1%
245–455	8.1%	15.2%	22.6%	27.8%	26.3%
455–117,576	3.5%	7.0%	14.4%	28.5%	46.6%

percent chance of themselves retiring with more than $455,000. The probability that the children of rich retirees will accumulate less than $99,000 by retirement is less than 4 percent. These results suggest that upward intergenerational wealth mobility is quite low under the current Social Security system and that lack of bequeathable wealth is likely to be persistent among some household dynasties.

Table 3 shows the same probabilities without Social Security. Table 3's wealth cutoffs are the same as those of Table 2. When there is no Social Security (or, alternatively, if Social Security were replaced with private accounts) children of parents in the poorest wealth category at retirement have only a 16 percent chance of retiring as members of the poorest group of their generation—much lower than the 40 percent chance in Table 2. As might be expected, the likelihood that those children will be in the richer categories at retirement increases significantly. For example, it more than doubles to 10.8 percent for the highest wealth category. The offspring of the rich, of course, have a much higher chance of themselves retiring rich and an even lower chance of retiring poor in the absence of Social Security.

One caveat is worth mentioning: reforming Social Security in the direction of setting up personal accounts may not improve intergenerational wealth mobility if households purchase annuities in the same amounts that Social Security provides today. However, given that owning bequeathable wealth enables households to improve the configuration of spending during retirement, and given that Social Security forcibly annuitizes a greater fraction of low earners' retirement resources, households with low earnings are likely to prefer a lower degree of annuitization under a reformed system. Hence, the simulation results should be taken as revealing the direction but not necessarily the magnitude of the potential improvement in wealth mobility across generations.

Conclusion

The results discussed above suggest that, in the absence of investment in private capital assets, we will have no choice but to pursue a Social Security reform that continues to disadvantage the poor and their offspring. Owning wealth in bequeathable form during retirement improves retirees' spending choices. However, by forcing

Table 3

Intergenerational Mobility in Bequeathable Wealth under Privatized Social Security

Parent Wealth at Retirement ($ thousands)	Parent Wealth at Retirement ($ thousands)				
	0–99	99–159	159–245	245–455	455–117,576
0–99	16.3%	20.3%	24.2%	28.4%	10.8%
99–159	9.1%	14.6%	22.3%	33.5%	20.5%
159–245	6.4%	11.3%	18.4%	33.0%	31.0%
245–455	3.8%	7.2%	13.4%	30.0%	45.6%
455–117,576	0.9%	2.1%	5.2%	18.3%	73.5%

the annuitization of a disproportionate fraction of low earners' retirement resources, Social Security increases inequality of bequeathable wealth within each generation. This occurs because Social Security reduces the ability and the incentive of low earners to accumulate personal savings for retirement. In addition, greater inequality of retiree wealth due to meager wealth accumulation by low earners prevents their children from receiving sizable inheritances. This means that such children have a greater likelihood of themselves retiring with low bequeathable wealth. This process implies a persistent social and economic schism between household dynasties that are trapped in poverty and other dynasties that continue to enjoy wealthy lifestyles.

In contrast, an individual account Social Security system would repair the current high degree of wealth inequality and low wealth mobility across households, moving America closer to the ideal of equality of opportunity—at least from an intergenerational perspective. Private accounts, therefore, becomes the truly progressive option for Social Security reform. Lawmakers who are concerned about the interest of the poor should be among the first to embrace individual accounts.

Note

1. See *2003 Annual Report of the Board of Trustees of the Federal Old-Age and Survivors Insurance and Disability Insurance Trust Funds* (Washington: Government Printing Office, March 17, 2003); and *Interim Report of the President's Commission to Strengthen Social Security* (Washington: Government Printing Office, July 2001).

2. See "Income of the Population 55 or Older, 2000," Social Security Administration Office of Policy, February 2002, p. 107, Table 6.A2.

3. *Interim Report of the President's Commission*, p. 18.

4. Jagadeesh Gokhale and Laurence J. Kotlikoff, "Social Security's Treatment of Postwar Americans: How Bad Can It Get?" in *The Distributional Aspects of Social Security and Social Security Reform*, ed. Martin Feldstein and Jeffrey Liebman (Chicago: University of Chicago Press, 2002).

5. The alternatives considered are based on popularly suggested reform proposals, and all improve Social Security's financial position. However, none except the first two restores the system to full, long-term solvency.

6. Policy 3 accelerates the scheduled increases in Social Security's normal retirement age; policy 4 uses the consumer price index (CPI) rather than the average annual wage series to index covered earnings when calculating the primary insurance amount (PIA); policy 5 increases retiree benefits by CPI minus 1 percent; policy 6 reduces future PIA amounts by productivity growth, preventing benefits from rising in real terms in the future; policy 7 grows future bend points in the PIA calculation according to the CPI rather than the nominal wage index; policy 8 eliminates current and future

ceilings on taxable income without altering the method of calculating benefits; policy 9 is the same as policy 8 except that it eliminates the resulting addition to future benefits; and policy 10 increases the number of computation years from 35 to 40.

7. David Koitz, Geoffrey Kollmann, and Dawn Nuschler, "Social Security: What Happens to Future Benefit Levels under Various Reform Options," Congressional Research Service, August 20, 2001.

8. These calculations are reported in Jagadeesh Gokhale et al., "Simulating the Transmission of Inequality via Bequests," *Journal of Public Economics* 79 (2001): 93–128.

9. Other contributing factors are skill (earning) differences and assortative marriage by skills. Ibid.

10. The model simulates an 88-period, overlapping-generations economy, with each generation consisting of 2,000 married households with demographic and economic characteristics calibrated to the U.S. population of married households. The factors studied in this model are the process of involuntary bequests and inheritance, fertility differences, skill (earnings) differences, partial marital sorting by skill levels, partial inheritance of skills, rate of return heterogeniety, progressive income taxation, and Social Security.

11. The estimates reported here should be viewed with caution as they are based on a stylized life-cycle simulation model. First, life-cycle behavior may not be an accurate representation of individual behavior, and, second, for tractability, the model abstracts from a number of features of the real-world U.S. economy—for example, all households are assumed to be married, fertility among all households is always positive, and the observed negative correlation of mortality with skills and wealth is ignored.

12. A Gini coefficient is a measure of dispersion within a group of values, calculated as the average difference between every pair of values divided by two times the average of the sample. The larger the coefficient, the higher the degree of dispersion.

13. Focus is maintained on the just-retired population for two reasons. First, all potential inheritances have generally been received by the time one retires and uncertainty about future receipts is negligibly small. Hence, measuring bequeathable wealth inequality among the just-retired fully takes into account the influence of past inheritances. Second, it is the bequeathable wealth of the just-retired that determines the future inheritances of their offspring. As suggested later in the text, greater inequality in this wealth implies greater persistence of inequality across generations.

14. In the simulated economy, all uncertainty about potential inheritances is fully resolved by the age of retirement—66. The wealth ranges specified in Tables 2 and 3 are the result of benchmarking the simulation's aggregate wage flow to that of the U.S. economy in 1995.

9. Disparate Impact: Social Security and African Americans

Michael Tanner

The debate over Social Security reform is vital to all Americans, but no group has as much at stake as do African Americans. To start with, African-American seniors are disproportionately dependent on Social Security for their retirement income. Three of four older African-American households rely on Social Security for half or more of their retirement income. Over a third of older African Americans rely on Social Security for *all* of their income.[1] As a result, they would be among the people most affected by Social Security's looming financial crisis and the potential reduction in benefits that could result.

In addition to the Social Security system's coming problems, African Americans face distinct problems and disadvantages under the current system. Because lifetime Social Security benefits are so closely related to the length of life, African Americans, who have shorter life expectancies, are left at a disadvantage, receiving a far poorer rate of return on their taxes than do comparable whites.

Social Security also contributes to the growing wealth gap between blacks and whites. Because Social Security taxes squeeze out other forms of saving and investment, especially for low-income workers, many African Americans are unable to accumulate real wealth. And, since Social Security benefits are not inheritable, that wealth inequity is compounded from generation to generation.

Any Social Security reform should take into account the needs and circumstances of African Americans. Such frequently discussed reforms as raising the retirement age, reducing benefits, or increasing

Originally published as Cato Institute Briefing Paper no. 61, February 5, 2001, and updated to reflect current information.

Table 1
BLACK AND WHITE LIFE EXPECTANCY, 2000

Age	White Male	Black Male	White Female	Black Female
0	74.8	68.2	80.0	74.9
5	70.3	64.4	75.5	71.0
10	65.4	59.5	70.5	66.1
15	60.5	54.6	65.6	61.2
20	55.7	49.9	60.7	56.3
25	51.1	45.5	55.8	51.5
30	46.4	41.1	50.9	46.8
35	41.7	36.6	46.1	42.1
40	37.1	32.3	41.3	37.5
45	32.6	28.1	36.6	33.1
50	28.2	24.2	32.0	28.9
55	24.0	20.7	27.5	24.9
60	20.0	17.5	23.2	21.0
65	16.3	14.5	19.2	17.4
70	13.0	11.7	15.5	14.1
75	10.1	9.4	12.1	11.2
80	7.6	7.3	9.1	8.6

SOURCE: Centers for Disease Control, National Center for Health Statistics, "United States Life Tables, 2000," *National Vital Statistics Reports* 51 (December 19, 2002): Tables 5-6, 8-9.

taxes would only make things worse. On the other hand, transforming the system into one based on individually owned, privately invested accounts would treat African Americans far more fairly.

The Current System: Unequal Benefits

Lifetime Social Security benefits depend, in large part, on longevity. As a result, people with identical earnings histories receive different total benefits depending on how long they live. Individuals who live to be 100 receive far more in benefits than do individuals who die at 66. Therefore, those groups in our society with shorter life expectancies, such as the poor and African Americans, are put at a severe disadvantage.

As Table 1 shows, at every age African American men and women both have shorter life expectancies than do their white counterparts.

148

Although some observers have suggested that this lower life expectancy is income related (lower-income individuals have shorter life expectancies than do wealthy individuals, and African Americans, on average, have lower incomes than whites), the shorter life expectancy of African Americans appears to hold across all income levels.

As a result, a black man or woman earning exactly the same lifetime wages, and paying exactly the same lifetime Social Security taxes, as his or her white counterpart will likely receive a far lower rate of return. Because African Americans have lower average incomes than do whites, they do benefit from Social Security's progressive benefit formula, which generates a higher rate of return for low-wage workers. However, that progressivity is not enough to offset the lower return due to life expectancy.[2] Sylvester Schieber, vice president for research at Watson Wyatt Worldwide and a member of the 1984–86 Advisory Council on Social Security, and John Shoven, professor of economics at Stanford University, examined the effect of race and life expectancy on rates of return for individuals born between 1917 and 1921 and concluded that not only did African Americans have lower rates of return than did whites at every income level but that an African-American worker earning $10,000 per year received the same rate of return as a white earning $22,000 per year.[3]

A 1996 study by Constantijn Panis and Lee Lillard for the RAND Corporation found that the redistributional effects of Social Security were significantly affected by life expectancy, resulting in a substantial loss to African Americans.[4] African Americans' rates of return were approximately 1 percent lower than those earned by whites. Even adjusting for marital status and income (African Americans' excess mortality is due in part to their lower incomes and lower marriage rates), African Americans earned rates of return half a percent lower than whites. The result was a net lifetime transfer of wealth from blacks to whites averaging nearly $10,000 per person.

A 1998 study by the Heritage Foundation found that African Americans in general, and African-American men in particular, had the lowest rates of return of any group in society. In fact, the study found that an average single black man will pay $13,377 more in payroll taxes over his lifetime than he will receive in benefits, a return of just 88 cents on every dollar paid in taxes.[5]

Life expectancy is not the only factor reducing the rate of return that African Americans receive on Social Security taxes. Social Security benefits are calculated on the basis of the highest 35 years of earnings over a worker's lifetime. Workers must still pay Social Security taxes during years outside those 35, but those taxes do not count toward or earn additional benefits.[6] Generally, those low-earning years occur early in an individual's life. That is particularly important to African Americans because they are likely to enter the workforce at an earlier age than whites.

Only 17.9 percent of African Americans graduate from college compared to 33 percent of whites.[7] Indeed, more than 25 percent of African Americans do not complete high school.[8] As a result, more African Americans enter the workforce early, paying additional Social Security taxes but failing to receive additional benefits.

Some observers suggest that this is offset by gaps in employment later on. African Americans are far more likely than are whites to experience periods of unemployment. However, although African-American men do have more periods of zero earnings during their careers, it does not appear to be enough of a difference to significantly change the disparities in the rate of return. Moreover, there is almost no difference in the number of zero-earnings years for black and white women.[9]

The lower rate of return is not just an abstract number; it translates directly into lower benefits. For example, assume that a 30-year-old black man and a 30-year-old white man both earn an equivalent of $30,000 per year over their working lifetimes. By the time they retire, they will each have paid $136,740 in Social Security taxes over their lifetimes[10] and will be entitled to monthly Social Security benefits of $1,162. However, the white man can expect to live until age 81. If he does, he will receive $199,400 in total Social Security benefits. The black man, in contrast, can expect to live only to age 79.[11] He can expect to receive only $174,300, almost $25,000 less than his white counterpart. This may actually understate the unfairness of the current sysem, since it is based on life expectancies at age 65. However, if both men are age 30 today, the life expectancy for the white man is 76; for the black man it is only 71.[12] If those projections are accurate, the black man can expect to receive nearly $70,000 less in lifetime Social Security benefits than his white counterpart.

It is this perverse redistribution that has led Ron Walters, professor of political science at the University of Maryland and a leading black activist, to brand Social Security a form of "reverse reparations."[13] It is amazing that this disparate impact, which would not be tolerated in any other government program, is so easily accepted within the current Social Security system.

The Wealth Gap

On average, African Americans' incomes continue to trail those of whites. African-American men, as a group, earn only 71 percent of what white men earn, while African-American women earn 97 percent of what white women earn.[14] However, progress is being made, and most of the current inequality can be explained by education and family structure. For example, whereas in 1949 a nonelderly two-parent black family earned only 44 percent of what a white family earned, today they earn more than 84 percent of what their white counterparts do.[15]

Unfortunately, this progress disguises a much more significant problem: Even as the "income gap" shrinks, the "wealth gap" is growing larger. The typical black household has a net worth of only $7,500. That's less than one-tenth of the figure for whites.[16] More than half of black families have no significant financial assets at all.[17]

These figures are distorted slightly because a large portion of white net worth comes from home equity, and whites are more likely than blacks to own their own homes (although home equity makes up a larger percentage of net worth for blacks than for whites). However, even subtracting the value of homeownership, blacks dramatically trail whites in terms of household wealth.[18]

In addition, African Americans are far less likely than whites to have private pension coverage. Moreover, participation rates may overstate African-American pension coverage because African Americans are somewhat less likely to vest in their plans' benefits. Only 36.8 percent of African Americans are fully vested in their company's pension plan, compared to 41 percent of whites.[19]

When African Americans do have pension coverage, it is usually a defined-benefit program, not the type of defined-contribution plan that allows for the accumulation of wealth. Roughly 41 percent of white workers are eligible to participate in defined-contribution plans, but only 32 percent of African Americans are offered such programs.[20] Even when their employers do offer such plans, African Americans are less likely to participate. For instance, only 53 percent

Table 2
PERCENTAGE OF HOUSEHOLDS OWNING FINANCIAL ASSETS, 2001

Type of Assets	White Non-Hispanic	African American
Transaction accounts	94.9	78.2
CDs	18.5	6.7
Savings bonds	19.4	7.8
Bonds	3.8	0.4
Stocks	24.5	11
Mutual funds	20.9	7.2
Retirement accounts	56.9	37.3
Life insurance	29.8	22.3
Any financial asset	96.5	82.4

SOURCE: "Recent Changes in U.S. Family Finances: Evidence from the 1998 and 2001 Survey of Consumer Finances," *Federal Reserve Bulletin*, January 2003.

of eligible African Americans participate in their employers' 401(k) plans, while 68 percent of eligible white workers do.[21]

Most African Americans do not own stock outside of retirement plans. Overall, only about 11 percent of black families own stock, compared to 24.5 percent of white families. Approximately 7.2 percent of African Americans own mutual funds; 20.9 percent of whites do (Table 2).[22] As a result, white families are growing wealthier, and black families are not.

There is no single reason why African Americans invest at lower rates than whites, but Social Security is a contributing factor. Participation in voluntary savings and investment arrangements is highly dependent on income.[23] For low-income workers, the primary reason for lack of savings is not a lack of incentives but a lack of disposable income. After paying daily living expenses, they simply have no funds left over to invest. Given that African Americans, on average, have lower incomes than whites and are disproportionately represented among low-wage workers, it is not surprising that they have lower rates of saving and investment.

They are, however, required to pay 12.4 percent of their income into Social Security. This extracts a terrible opportunity cost, because the money they are forced to pay into Social Security, with its poor rate of return and lack of personal ownership, is money that they could otherwise invest in real assets—assets that they would own and that would earn far higher returns.

This last point is especially important. African Americans are, in essence, being forced to substitute Social Security "wealth" for other types of wealth. But Social Security is not wealth in any traditional sense. A person does not own it. There is no legal property or contractual right to that wealth. It is merely a political promise that may or may not be kept.

Moreover, Social Security is not inheritable. Unlike other forms of wealth, it cannot be passed on to future generations. Numerous scholars have stressed inheritance as a means of increasing wealth in the African-American community and the role that the lack of such inherited wealth plays in widening the black-white wealth gap. Darrell Williams, professor of economics at the University of California at Los Angeles, calls inheritance "the single biggest factor that explains the wealth gap."[24] But, as Jagadeesh Gokhale, an economist at the Federal Reserve Bank of Cleveland, and others have noted, Social Security essentially forces low-income workers to annuitize their wealth, preventing them from making a bequest of that wealth to their heirs.[25]

Moreover, because this forced annuitization applies to a larger portion of the wealth of low-income workers than of high-income workers (in this case a larger proportion of black income than white), it turns inheritance into a "disequalizing force," leading to greater inequality of wealth in America. The wealthy are able to bequeath their wealth to their heirs, while the poor cannot.[26] The wealth gap has an impact beyond individual families; it helps to impoverish entire communities.

Most economists recognize that when investment capital grows scarce the areas that are the first to feel the lack of capital are areas where investments are most risky—inner-city neighborhoods with high crime rates, a poorly educated workforce, and high business bankruptcy rates.[27] As economist Jude Wanniski explains, "The people who lose the most . . . are the poorest, the youngest, those at the beginning of their careers, those who are furthest from the sources of capital."[28]

Social Security has the perverse result of transferring capital out of areas where it is needed most, such as the inner city, to comfortable retirement communities. The South Bronx loses; the Florida coast gains.

The Current System: Inadequate Benefits

Without other assets to rely on in retirement, African-American seniors are disproportionately forced to rely on Social Security for their retirement income. Unfortunately, Social Security benefits are quite low, leaving one of four African-American seniors in poverty.

Perhaps the easiest way to look at this is to examine Social Security's "replacement rate," or the proportion of a person's preretirement income that Social Security benefits equal or "replace." Because of Social Security's progressive benefit formula, the program's benefits replace a higher proportion of income for low-wage earners than for high-wage earners. The actual replacement rate fluctuates slightly from year to year on the basis of a variety of factors. For an average-wage earner who retires this year, Social Security can be expected to replace approximately 41.6 percent of preretirement income. A low-wage worker will receive benefits equal to 56.1 percent of preretirement income, and the replacement rate for a maximum-wage worker will be 29.8 percent.[29]

For people who are 25 years old today and will retire in 2045, projected replacement rates are 55.2 percent for low-wage workers, 40.9 percent for average-wage earners, and 27.3 percent for maximum-wage earners.[30] However, the relatively higher replacement rate for low-wage workers should be considered in light of their greater dependence on Social Security. The poorest 20 percent of the elderly depend on Social Security for 78 percent of their retirement income. Thus, total annual retirement income for the 25-year-old low-wage worker (from Social Security and other sources) will equal only 71 percent of preretirement income. In comparison, Social Security accounts for only 24 percent of postretirement income for the wealthiest fifth of retirees.[31] Therefore, when a high-wage worker retires, his income will actually equal 114 percent of his income before retirement despite the lower replacement rate.

Most financial planners suggest that if one's preretirement standard of living is to be maintained, retirement benefits of between 60 and 85 percent of preretirement income are probably necessary.[32] Clearly, then, Social Security fails to provide sufficient income to afford poor workers a dignified and secure retirement.

A Bad Situation Will Get Worse

As unfair as Social Security currently is to African Americans, the situation will soon get worse. Social Security faces an unfunded liability of more than $25 trillion. By 2018 the program will begin to run a deficit. At that point, Social Security will be forced to either reduce benefits or increase taxes. Either of those choices will severely impact African Americans.[33]

The payroll tax is an extremely regressive tax. First, it is a tax only on wages, leaving other income sources, such as capital gains, interest, profits, gifts, inheritances, and other types of investment income untaxed. Since wages represent a higher proportion of African Americans' income, a payroll tax will take a higher percentage of total income from blacks than from whites. This effect is compounded because the amount of income subject to the payroll tax is capped. Therefore, wealthy individuals actually pay a smaller percentage of their total income in payroll taxes than do poor workers.

Under the SSA's intermediate projections, in order to continue paying all promised benefits, the combined employer-employee OASDI portion of the payroll tax would have to be increased from the current 12.4 percent to more than 18 percent. That would push more working blacks into poverty. Likewise, as we have seen, a reduction in benefits will also disproportionately hurt African Americans since elderly blacks are more likely than elderly whites to be poor and, therefore, dependent on Social Security benefits. Those poor elderly who receive most or all of their retirement income from Social Security can ill afford any reduction in benefits. Yet benefit cuts of as much as one-third may be required to keep the system solvent. A one-third reduction in Social Security benefits would leave the elderly poor with a postretirement income equal to only 50 percent of their preretirement wages. Such a benefit cut would plunge millions of elderly African Americans into poverty.

Reducing benefits indirectly by, for instance, raising the retirement age would also work to the severe disadvantage of African Americans because of their shorter life expectancies. Few would live long enough to see even a single Social Security benefit check.

The Solution: Individual Accounts

Although African Americans are disadvantaged under both the current Social Security system and many of the most commonly discussed solutions to the program's future financial crisis, they

155

would be among those who would benefit most from individual accounts.

First, by transforming Social Security from a defined-benefit to a defined-contribution plan, individual accounts would disconnect total benefits from life expectancy. The benefits an individual received would depend on what was paid into the system plus the investment return on those payments, not on how many years the person received benefits.

In addition, individuals who begin work earlier, and therefore contribute for additional years, would earn additional benefits as a result of their contributions.

Moreover, under an account system, individuals would have a property right to their Social Security benefits. If a person were to die with money still in his or her retirement account, that money would become part of the estate to be inherited by that person's heirs.

The importance for African Americans of this inheritance right cannot be overstated. The ability to accumulate wealth and pass that wealth on to one's heirs is critical to the future of black-white equality. If African Americans are going to be full partners in the American economy, the "wealth gap" must be closed. African Americans must become investors. After all, as both Jesse Jacksons say, "Capitalism without capital is just an 'ism.'"[34] Individual accounts would give low-income workers in general, and African Americans in particular, a chance to accumulate that capital.

There are more immediate advantages to individual accounts as well. Not only would a privately invested Social Security system provide a fairer rate of return to African Americans, but that rate of return would be far higher, lifting many more African-American seniors out of poverty. Figure 1 shows the difference in the rate of return that African Americans receive under Social Security and what they could expect to receive from private capital investment.[35]

The increased rate of return translates into higher lifetime benefits. However, if you ignore the impact of life expectancy and look only at monthly retirement benefits, private capital investment still leaves African-American seniors far better off. As Figure 2 shows, even low-income African Americans would receive significantly higher benefits under private accounts.

The higher retirement benefits provided by individual accounts would lift many African-American seniors out of poverty. A new

Figure 1
COMPARATIVE RATES OF RETURN ON SOCIAL SECURITY
AND PRIVATE INVESTMENT FOR SELECTED CATEGORIES
FOR AFRICAN AMERICANS

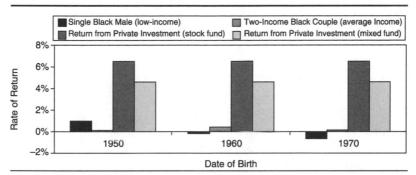

SOURCE: Derived from William Beach and Gareth Davis, "Social Security's Rate-of-Return," Heritage Center for Data Analysis, January 15, 1998; Michael Tanner, "A Better Deal: Estimating Rates of Return under a System of Individual Accounts," Cato Institute Social Security Paper no. 31, October 28, 2003.

Figure 2
MONTHLY BENEFIT FOR AN AFRICAN-AMERICAN WORKER BORN IN
1970 WHO EARNS $15,000 A YEAR

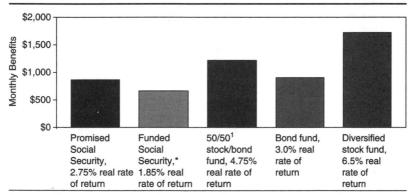

SOURCE: Cato Institute Social Security calculator at www.socialsecurity.org.

*When this worker retires, the Social Security Administration projects that it will be able to pay only 73 percent of legislated benefits.

study by Harvard professors Martin Feldstein and Jeffrey Liebman (a former Clinton administration official) concludes that allowing individuals to invest a portion of their Social Security would reduce poverty among elderly married African-American couples by 23.4 percent and among widowed, divorced, and never-married African-American seniors by 61.5 percent.[36]

Conclusion

Our current Social Security system contains a great many inequities. Minority groups, such as African Americans, are among those who are most disadvantaged by Social Security. Elderly African Americans are much more likely than their white counterparts to be dependent on Social Security benefits for most or all of their retirement income. But despite a progressive benefit structure, Social Security benefits are inadequate to provide for the retirement needs of the elderly poor. As a result, one of four elderly African Americans lives in poverty.

In addition, the nominal progressivity of Social Security is undermined by differences in life expectancy. Because African Americans generally have shorter life expectancies, they receive less total Social Security payments over the course of their lifetimes than do whites. In effect, Social Security transfers wealth from poorer blacks to wealthier whites. It seems unlikely that this inequity would be permitted to continue in any other government program.

Finally, because Social Security taxes squeeze out private savings and investment, they make it more difficult for African Americans to accumulate wealth. The result is a growing wealth gap, with African Americans falling further and further behind.

Therefore, African Americans are among those with the most to gain from transforming the program into a system of individually owned, privately invested accounts, similar to individual retirement accounts or 401(k) plans. A Social Security program that allowed for private investment would provide poor African-American retirees with higher benefits, would not be dependent on life expectancy, and would increase the pool of capital available for investment in poor inner-city neighborhoods.

African Americans understand this and are increasingly coming to embrace individual accounts for Social Security. According to a Zogby International poll conducted for the Cato Institute, African

Americans support individual accounts by a margin of 58 to 39 percent.[37] Other polls show similar results.[38]

Everyone interested in racial equality in America should recognize that Social Security reform is rapidly becoming a civil rights issue. In their own way, individual accounts will do as much for future generations of African Americans as ending Jim Crow did for past generations.

Notes

1. Social Security Administration, "Social Security Is Important to African Americans," October 2003.

2. Because there are so many variables to be considered, including earnings patterns, income, marital status, family status, and employment and unemployment, studies of rates of return for African Americans have not been as consistent in their results as have those looking at other factors such as income or gender. A small number, including those by Dean Leimer of the Social Security Administration, "Lifetime Redistribution under the Social Security Program," *Social Security Bulletin* 2 (1999): 43–51, and Treasury Department Researchers James Duggan, Robert Gillingham, and John Greenlees, "Progressive Returns to Social Security? An Answer from Official Records," Department of the Treasury Research Paper no. 9501, November 1995, have found that the system's progressivity offsets the longevity problem. Charles Meyer and Nancy Wolf, "Intercohort and Intracohort Redistribution under Old-Age Insurance: The 1962–1972 Retirement Cohorts," *Public Finance Quarterly* (July 1987): 259–81, found mixed results. Married African Americans were at an advantage under Social Security, but single African Americans were disadvantaged. However, the weight of evidence increasingly supports the idea that returns for African Americans are lower than those for whites. See, for example, Alan Frieden et al., "Internal Rates of Return to Retired Worker-Only Beneficiaries under Social Security," *Studies in Income Distribution* 5 (October 1976): 490–94; Michael Hurd and John Shoven, "The Distributional Impact of Social Security," in *Pensions, Labor, and Individual Choice*, ed. David Wise (Chicago: University of Chicago Press, 1985), pp. 193–215; and Ronald Lee, "Race—Ethnicity and Social Security Transfers: Who Gains and Who Loses?" Paper presented at the 1994 Annual Meeting of the Population Association of America, Miami, Florida, May 1994.

3. Sylvester Schieber and John Shoven, *The Real Deal: The History and Future of Social Security* (New Haven, Conn.: Yale University Press, 1999), pp. 225–26.

4. Constantijn W. A. Panis and Lee Lillard, "Socioeconomic Differentials in the Return to Social Security," RAND Corporation Working Paper no. 96-05, 1996, p. 14.

5. William Beach and Gareth Davis, "Social Security's Rate of Return," Heritage Center for Data Analysis, Report no. 01-98, January 1998.

6. One of the earliest works to address this problem was Milton Friedman and Wilbur Cohen, *Social Security: Universal or Selective?* (Washington: American Enterprise Institute, 1972).

7. U.S. Department of Education, National Center for Education Statistics, "The Condition of Education: 2002," Educational Attainment, Table 25-3.

8. U.S. Department of Education, National Center for Education Statistics, "Drop Out Rates in the United States: 2000," High School Completion Rates, Table B7.

9. Alexa Hendley and Natasha Bilimoria, "Minorities and Social Security: An Analysis of Racial and Ethnic Differences in the Current Program," *Social Security Bulletin* 62 (1999): 59–64.

10. Counting only the OASI portion of the payroll tax. This figure does not include the disability portion.

11. Projected life expectancy at age 65. Centers for Disease Control, "United States Abridged Life Tables, 2000," *National Vital Statistics Report* 51, no. 3 (December 19, 2002): Table 5, 8. At 65, a white male can expect to live an additional 16.3 years, whereas a black male can expect to live for an additional 14.5 years.

12. Projected life expectancy at age 30. Ibid. At 30, a white male can expect to live an additional 46.4 years whereas a black male can expect to live an additional 41.1 years.

13. Quoted in Jodi Kantor, "Race Bait and Switch," *Slate.com*, April 21, 1999.

14. U.S. Bureau of the Census, "Money Income in the United States: 2001," September 24, 2002, Table 7.

15. Ibid.

16. U.S. Bureau of the Census, "Net Worth and Asset Ownership of Households: 1998 and 2000," *Current Population Reports*, May 2003, Figure 6.

17. Ibid., Table H.

18. Ibid.

19. Elayne Robertson Demby, "Unequal Opportunity," January 1997, p. 17, www.assetpub.com.

20. "Examining the Minority Gap in Social Security and Pensions," *Aging Today*, March–April 1998, p. 3.

21. Glenn Springstead and Theresa Wilson, "Participation in Voluntary Individual Savings Accounts: An Analysis of IRAs, 401(k)s, and the TSP," *Social Security Bulletin*, no. 1 (2000): 34–39.

22. Ana M. Aizcorbe, Arthur B. Kennickell, and Kevin B. Moore, "Family Finances in the U.S.: Recent Evidence from the Survey of Consumer Finances," *Federal Reserve Bulletin*, January 2003, p. 13.

23. Springstead and Wilson.

24. Quoted in Eric Smith, "Prescription for Wealth," *Black Enterprise*, January 2000, p. 87.

25. Jagadeesh Gokhale et al., "Simulating the Transmission of Wealth Inequality via Bequests," *Journal of Public Economics* 79, no. 1 (2001): 93–128.

26. Jagadeesh Gokhale and Laurence Kotlikoff, "The Impact of Social Security and Other Factors on the Distribution of Wealth," National Bureau of Economic Research, October 1999.

27. Stephen Moore and John Silvia, "The ABCs of the Capital Gains Tax," Cato Institute Policy Analysis no. 242, October 4, 1995, p. 34.

28. Jude Wanniski, Testimony before the Senate Finance Committee, 104th Cong., 1st sess., committee transcript, February 15, 1995.

29. Board of Trustees, Federal Old-Age and Survivors Insurance and Disability Insurance Trust Funds, *2003 Annual Report of the Board of Trustees of the Federal Old-Age and Survivors Insurance and Disability Insurance Trust Funds* (Washington: Government Printing Office, March 17, 2003), Table VI.F11.

30. Ibid.

31. See Social Security Administration Office of Policy, "Income of the Population 55 or Older, 2000," February 2002, p. 107, Table 6.A2.

32. A. Haeworth Robertson, *Social Security: What Every Taxpayer Should Know* (Washington: Retirement Policy Institute, 1992), p. 218.

33. Board of Trustees, Federal Old-Age and Survivors Insurance and Disability Insurance Trust Funds, *2000 Annual Report of the Board of Trustees of the Federal Old-Age and Survivors Insurance and Disability Insurance Trust Funds* (Washington: Government Printing Office, March 30, 2000), p. 25.

34. Jesse L. Jackson Sr. and Jesse L. Jackson Jr., *It's about the Money!* (New York: Random House, 1999), p. 33.

35. Some opponents of Social Security privatization have argued that such rate-of-return comparisons are misleading because they fail to account for transition costs. See, for example, John Geanakopolis, "Generation X: Does Bush Understand His Social Security Plan?" *New Republic*, October 23, 2000, pp. 18–20. They point out that the rate of return is the ratio of how much a person pays in to how much he actually gets out. Therefore, any measure of the return must take into account not just the amount paid into private investment but also anything paid to continue providing benefits to current beneficiaries. Consider a simple overlapping-generations model describing Social Security: Generation A's benefits are paid by Generation B, B's by C, and so forth. Imagine that generation C wishes to privatize. To be able to invest its own payroll taxes in the market, generation C must also cover B's benefits. Imagine that generation C does so at a 5 percent rate, while investing its own money at a 7 percent rate of return. The net gain is only 2 percent—the 7 percent gain from investment minus the 5 percent interest to service the money borrowed. And, in a properly functioning market, the 2 percent differential will be purely a function of risk. Therefore, there is no real gain to generation C. Moreover, the debt would never end. The 5 percent interest rate cited is purely for servicing the debt, not for repaying it. Thus, it is arguable that no one ever receives a higher rate of return under privatization.

This argument is correct as far as it goes. Privatization is not simple arbitrage, and all costs must be taken into account. However, the critics are mistaken in assuming that all methods of paying those costs are the same. If, for example, the costs were paid purely through an increased payroll tax, the critics would be correct. Workers would see no increase in their rate of return. But if the transition is financed by cutting government spending, that is a different story. Most economists would agree that government makes far less productive use of capital than does the private sector. In many cases, government spending is actually harmful to the economy, producing, in a sense, a negative rate of return. Therefore, cutting government spending to fund the transition would not entail a loss in current welfare equivalent in present value to future gains in welfare.

In short, the critics are correct to note that the transition to a privatized system ultimately requires an increase in national savings. If we wish to support a larger retiree population in the future, the only choices are to redistribute wealth to the old at the expense of the young or to increase economic output so that both groups can be made better off. Increasing savings is the most straightforward way to increase future economic output. All things being equal, therefore, the cost of the transition is simply the cost of increased savings. In order to increase savings, someone must forgo consumption today. The critics imply that that someone must be the individual worker. However, under a properly structured privatization scenario, it would be the government that forwent consumption. Hence, workers would be better off because they would receive a higher rate of return.

Two other points should be made. First, if the transition were paid for by taxes rather than reductions in government spending, it would far more likely be paid for out of income taxes than out of payroll taxes. Because the income tax system is highly progressive, low-wage workers would see the full rate of return from their individual accounts, there being little or no offsetting increase in their income taxes, while high-income workers would bear most of the cost and see reduced rates of return. An income tax–funded transition would be a large transfer from today's wealthy to both today's poor and workers of the future. Thus African Americans would clearly benefit.

36. Martin Feldstein and Jeffrey Liebman, "The Distributional Effects of an Investment-Based Social Security System," National Bureau of Economic Research Working Paper no. 7492, September 2000. Feldstein and Liebman assume that 9 percentage points of a worker's payroll taxes are invested in individual accounts. Their model takes into account all transition costs and was based on actual work histories.

37. The poll of 1,109 likely voters nationwide conducted July 7, 2002, posed the following question: "There are some in government who advocate changing the Social Security system to give younger workers the choice to invest a portion of their Social Security taxes through individual accounts similar to IRAs or 401(k) plans. Do you strongly agree, agree, disagree, or strongly disagree?" The margin of error is + / − 3.1 percent.

38. See Michael Tanner, "Public Opinion and Social Security Privatization," Cato Institute Social Security Paper no. 5, August 6, 1996, citing polls by Public Opinion Strategies and others.

PART III

SOLVING THE PROBLEM

10. No Second Best: The Unappetizing Alternatives to Individual Accounts

Michael Tanner

While proposals for Social Security choice have been much debated, there has been far less discussion of the alternatives. Indeed, opponents of individual accounts often critique these proposals as if those reforms existed in a vacuum. They compare individual account proposals with "current law" and suggest that those proposals will provide lower benefits, or at least lower government-provided benefits. Or they suggest that the costs of transition to a private investment-based system will require tax increases.

But as Charles Blahous, executive director of the President's Commission to Strengthen Social Security, has pointed out, "The essential problem with comparing reform plans with 'current law' is that 'current law' allows the system to go bankrupt."[1]

Impending bankruptcy is not the only problem facing Social Security. Payroll taxes are already so high that younger workers will receive an extraordinarily poor rate of return. In addition, Social Security contains a host of inequities that penalize working women, minorities, and low-income workers.

Most critics of Social Security choice focus only on insolvency. They implicitly assume that the structure of the current program is fine and changes are needed only in the program's financing. Therefore, the solutions they offer generally do not deal with establishing property rights, making benefits fairer to women or minorities, allowing low-wage workers to accumulate wealth, or even increasing rates of return.

Yet, even judging by their own limited standards, opponents of Social Security choice offer few concrete proposals.

Originally published as Cato Institute Social Security Paper no. 24, January 29, 2002, and updated to reflect current information.

President Clinton identified the limited range of options available to restore Social Security to solvency: raise taxes, cut benefits, or get a higher rate of return through investment in real capital assets.[2] Henry Aaron, a noted opponent of individual accounts at the Brookings Institution, agrees. "Increased funding to raise pension reserves is possible only with some combination of additional tax revenues, reduced benefits, or increased investment returns from investing in higher yielding assets," he told Congress in 1999.[3]

The question, then, is since opponents of Social Security choice have rejected individual investment to earn a higher rate of return, which of the other alternatives do they support—raising taxes? cutting benefits? or some nonindividual form of investment?

As Reps. Jim Kolbe (R-Ariz.) and Charles Stenholm (D-Tex.) have pointed out in a recent letter to the bipartisan congressional leadership, "All participants in the debate over the future of Social Security must be held to the same standard so that the different approaches to strengthening Social Security can be compared on a level playing field."[4]

Unfortunately, few if any opponents of individual accounts have put an actual scoreable proposal on the table. Indeed, the President's Commission to Strengthen Social Security specifically invited opponents of Social Security choice to submit detailed proposals for reforming the system, offering to have those proposals scored by the Social Security Administration on the same basis as the commission's own proposals. However, no opposition group chose to take advantage of the offer.[5]

Still, from their writing, testimony, and speeches, it is possible to piece together what opponents of individual accounts offer as an alternative. Generally, those proposals boil down to some pretty unpopular alternatives—tax increases, benefit cuts, or government investing.

All of those proposals contain significant costs and risks for both individuals and the American economy.

Tax Increases, Explicit and Otherwise

Not surprisingly, since their primary goal is to preserve the structure and benefits of the current system, the solution most commonly offered by opponents of individual accounts is some form of tax increase. The National Academy on an Aging Society suggests that there is no limit to the amount of taxes American society can bear if they are used for a good cause such as preserving Social Security. The academy specifically rejects the notion, widely accepted by economists, that total taxes should not exceed 20 percent of national income. "Perhaps the question for the public has more to do with what government is doing with taxes, than the relative size of government."[6]

Joseph White, a fellow with the Century Foundation and professor of public policy at Case Western University, takes a similar approach. In his book *False Alarm: Why the Greatest Threat to Social Security and Medicare Is the Campaign to "Save" Them,* White argues:

> We have a responsibility to maintain a decent society. Social Security and Medicare are part of that. We have a responsibility not to confuse solving the government's problems (by cutting its expenditures) with solving society's. No matter where we started, cutting Social Security and Medicare would be good for the budget. Eliminating them would be better. But the government does not exist just for its budget. The government exists to make the country a better place to live. Social Security and Medicare do make this a better country, and they can and should be preserved from the attack on entitlements.[7]

Ken Apfel, social security commissioner under President Clinton, says that successful Social Security reform will require us to abandon the notion that "future tax revenues should not be increased—even modestly." Apfel warns that "over the next several decades Social Security taxes are projected to decline by more than 10 percent as a percentage of GDP. With a doubling of the senior population, more revenue will be needed, not less."[8]

Lisa Maatz, formerly of the Older Women's League, argues that, "while not a favorite of most taxpayers, [tax increases have] a place in the solvency discussion. If it helps preserve the universal nature of Social Security, where no individual is left to sink or swim on their own, it may be worth the cost."[9]

This is ultimately the point, an admittedly philosophical one, of those who would raise taxes to preserve Social Security. They see Social Security as a good thing; therefore, in their view, we should be willing to pay whatever it takes to preserve the program in its current form. The first place to look for tax increases is the payroll

Table 1
TAX INCREASES REQUIRED TO PRESERVE
SOCIAL SECURITY'S SOLVENCY

Year	Covered Workers (in thousands)	Deficit Balance ($ in billions)	Taxes per Worker ($)
2020	175,428	94	535.83
2025	178,369	312	1,778.51
2030	181,372	568	3,237.80
2035	184,433	823	4,691.38
2040	187,554	1069	6,093.67

SOURCE: Author's calculations derived from data in Board of Trustees, Federal Old-Age and Survivors Insurance and Disability Insurance Trust Funds, *2003 Annual Report* (Washington: Government Printing Office, 2003), Tables VI.F10, IV.B2.

tax itself. For example, Vincent Sombrotto, president of the National Association of Letter Carriers, has urged the President's Commission to "reject the notion that taxes can never be raised to overcome the projected shortfalls in the Social Security Trust Fund. If Americans are living longer, why shouldn't we pay higher payroll taxes to handle it?"[10] Likewise, former Social Security commissioner Robert M. Ball, writing for the Century Foundation, proposes "moderately" increasing future payroll taxes.[11] Jeff Faux of the Economic Policy Institute would not only raise payroll taxes but would index them to future increases in longevity.[12] Various levels of payroll tax increases are also supported by Notre Dame economist Teresa Ghilarducci;[13] Mark Weisbrot of the Center on Economic and Policy Research;[14] and Robert Myers, former chief actuary at the Social Security Administration, who suggests that they would not be "too terribly painful."[15]

As Table 1 illustrates, the tax increase needed to restore Social Security to solvency is extremely large. The government must acquire new funds to maintain benefits after the system begins running a deficit in 2018. In 2020 an additional $536 per worker will be necessary to maintain solvency. By 2030 the tax burden increases to $3,238 per worker, and it continues to rise thereafter.

Tax increases of this magnitude would have a serious impact on the U.S. economy. A look at the impact of the last rounds of payroll tax hikes shows how increasing payroll taxes can destroy jobs and reduce economic growth. For example, according to the Congressional Budget Office, payroll tax hikes between 1979 and 1982 resulted in the permanent loss of 500,000 jobs.[16] A study of the 1988 and 1990 payroll tax hikes, by economists Gary and Aldona Robbins, estimated 510,000 jobs lost permanently and a reduction of the U.S gross domestic product of $30 billion per year.[17] The reason for this is that workers view payroll taxes as a "pure tax," not as an investment. Higher payroll taxes create a "wedge" between what employers are able to pay and what employees are willing to accept, thereby lowering take-home wages and making employment less attractive.

Projecting the potential impact of future tax increases is more difficult, but the CBO estimates that a 5 percent increase in payroll taxes would reduce marginal after-tax compensation by 10 percent. The CBO further concludes that every 10 percent drop in after-tax wages will lead to as much as a 3 percent contraction in the labor supply. This would, in turn, likely lead to an unspecified, but significant, decline in U.S. GDP.[18]

Moreover, a payroll tax hike would fall heaviest on low-income workers, who are least able to afford it. According to Jagadeesh Gokhale, a senior economic adviser with the Federal Reserve Bank of Cleveland, increasing the payroll tax would result in a 3.8 percent increase in Social Security's lifetime net tax rate for workers in the lowest quintile of income.[19]

As an alternative to across-the-board payroll tax hikes, some people have suggested targeting the tax increase to upper-income workers by removing the current cap on income subject to the tax. In 2003, workers pay Social Security taxes on the first $87,000 of wage income. Income above that level is exempt from Social Security taxes (though not Medicare payroll taxes). Approximately 84 percent of all wage income earned in the United States falls under that cap and is subject to the tax.

It is unclear whether advocates of this approach would remove the cap altogether or simply raise it. The National Committee to Preserve Social Security and Medicare, for example, suggests that the cap be raised so that 90 percent of covered earnings are subject to the tax,[20] as does the AFL-CIO.[21] Hans Reimer of the 2030 Center appears to advocate total repeal of the cap,[22] as do the National Council of Women's Organizations[23] and the Older Women's

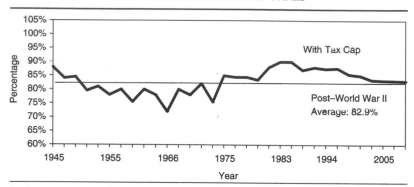

Figure 1
PERCENTAGE OF WAGES SUBJECT TO OLD-AGE
AND SURVIVORS PAYROLL TAXES

SOURCE: D. Mark Wilson, "Removing Social Security's Tax Cap on Wages Would Do More Harm Than Good," Heritage Foundation Center for Data Analysis Report no. 01-07, October 17, 2001.

League.[24] Dean Baker of the Center for Economic and Policy Research would remove the cap as well, but only on the employer's portion of the payroll tax.[25] Ball would raise the cap, but only to 87.5 percent of covered earnings.[26]

Advocates of raising or eliminating the cap on payroll taxes often suggest that the current level of covered wages is significantly below the roughly 90 percent of earnings subject to the tax in 1983, at the time of the Greenspan Commission's reform. What they fail to note, however, is that the 1983 rate was unnaturally high. In fact, as Figure 1 shows, from 1945 to 1965, the proportion of wages covered by the payroll tax declined steadily from 88 percent to roughly 71 percent. However, beginning in 1965, in order to pay for increased benefits, the cap was gradually increased, reaching a high of 90 percent in 1983. Since that time, it has again begun to decline, but it remains above the post–World War II average of 82.9 percent.[27]

The multiplicity of proposals and their vagueness make it difficult to analyze their impact. However, there is no doubt that any change in the payroll tax cap would be a significant tax increase. In fact, total elimination of the cap would amount to the largest tax increase in U.S. history, $461 billion over the first five years.[28] For workers with wages over the cap, it would amount to an immediate 12.4

percent increase in their marginal tax rates, such that many workers would be paying more than half their income in federal taxes alone.

While the economic consequences of raising or eliminating the payroll tax cap would be less than those of an across-the-board tax hike, they would still be considerable. The Heritage Foundation estimates that removing the cap would reduce the rate of U.S. economic growth by 2–3 percent. Over the next 10 years it would cost the U.S. economy nearly $136 billion in lost growth. In addition, roughly 1.1 million jobs would be lost over the next 10 years.[29]

However, in exchange for this massive tax increase and its attendant costs, Social Security would gain very little. Even total repeal of the cap would extend the payroll tax solvency of Social Security by only an estimated seven years.[30]

Less direct tax increases are also contained in proposals to redirect general tax revenue to Social Security. The result would be to rely, not on payroll tax hikes, but on increases in income or other taxes to make up for any gap in Social Security's financing.[31]

Of course, tax increases are not necessary to support general revenue financing of Social Security. The federal government could always reduce other spending and devote the savings to Social Security. Indeed, advocates of Social Security choice have suggested that as a way to help finance the transition to a system of individual accounts.[32] However, such spending reductions would be considerable, and most opponents of Social Security choice are not advocates of cutting government spending. In fact, their statements and publications show that they are talking about an increase in income tax revenue.

Instead of advocating new taxes, one common approach calls for repeal of the tax reductions that passed Congress in 2001 but have not yet taken effect. However, one suspects that this position stems more from opposition to the tax cut than from concern about Social Security. The tax cuts, after all, expire by 2009, meaning that Social Security will be running a surplus throughout the period during which the tax cuts are in effect. Social Security's deficit doesn't start until approximately 2018. Presumably, then, when advocates of repealing the tax cut speak of applying the funds to Social Security, they mean somehow crediting the money to the Social Security Trust Fund.

All of those proposals reflect a fundamental misunderstanding of the nature of the trust fund. Social Security payroll taxes are currently bringing in more revenue than the program pays out in benefits, a surplus that is projected to continue until approximately 2018. Thereafter, the situation will reverse, with Social Security paying out more in benefits than it brings in through taxes. The surplus is used to purchase special issue Treasury bonds. The Social Security surplus used to purchase the bonds becomes general revenue and is spent on the government's annual general operating expenses. What remains behind in the trust fund is the bonds, plus an interest payment attributed to the bonds (also paid in bonds, rather than cash). Government bonds are, in essence, a form of IOU. They are a promise against future tax revenue. When the bonds become due, the government will have to repay them out of general revenue.[33]

Adding more money to the trust fund now would simply increase the number of bonds. The money from purchase of those bonds would revert to general revenue and be spent. It is an endless cycle that does nothing to change Social Security's actual solvency.

That is why the more sophisticated proponents of tax increases would not actually apply the increased revenue to Social Security but to paying down the national debt. As Robert Shapiro, former under secretary of commerce in the Clinton administration explains, "Getting rid of the debt will save hundreds of billions of dollars a year in interest payments, significantly pushing back the day of reckoning on redeeming those trust fund assets. . . . If the next generation decides to borrow to redeem those assets, becoming debt-free first will make it a lot cheaper to do so."[34]

In short, paying down the debt will save money currently spent on interest payments. Presumably, this will provide extra revenue to pay benefits after 2018. Moreover, if it becomes necessary to borrow in order to cover Social Security's post-2018 shortfall, it will be easier to do so if the current national debt has been paid off. There is a kernel of truth to both these points. But eventually both fall short.

Despite budget shortfalls caused by the slowing economy after the terrorist attacks of September 11 and increased government spending, the Bush administration still projects future non–Social Security surpluses, much of which would be dedicated to paying down the national debt. It is true, of course, that repaying government debt reduces the interest payments the government must pay each year. These savings in debt service costs could, in theory, assist in maintaining the solvency of the Social Security system. But the extent of the help should not be overestimated. In 2000 the government paid approximately $225 billion to service the publicly held debt. If that debt were repaid (or had never been run up in the first place), the government would have, in theory, an extra $225 billion annually with which it could increase spending or reduce taxes.

But how far would those interest savings take Social Security? Assume that the publicly held debt is retired by 2018, the year in which Social Security begins to run payroll tax deficits, thereby adding an extra $225 billion annually to Social Security's balance sheets. While this would help, it would take only until 2021 for Social Security to run payroll tax deficits exceeding $225 billion. In other words, those debt service savings would buy Social Security another five years of payroll tax solvency.

The larger case for debt repayment, however, isn't based on reducing debt service costs or increasing the government's capacity to borrow. It is that repaying debt frees investment dollars that were previously used to finance government operations so those dollars can be dedicated to more productive, private investment. Retiring government debt injects capital into the economy; more capital means better tools and technology for each worker, which raises worker wages and increases the nation's productivity. A more productive economy is better able to support larger populations of retirees with a relatively smaller supply of workers. The economics of debt repayment are relatively simple; the politics, which determines whether debt is retired, how much is retired, and how the benefits of a reduced debt burden are allotted, is substantially more complicated.[35]

Roger Hickey, director of the Campaign for America's Future, while strongly advocating repeal of the Bush tax cut, seems to acknowledge that repeal will have little direct impact on Social Security, since he does not even pretend to advocate applying the new revenue to the Social Security system. Nor would he use the new revenue to pay down the debt. Rather, he would increase government spending generally in the belief that increased government spending would lead to increased economic growth, making additional revenues available in the future.[36] Hickey's Social Security plan, therefore, amounts simply to a dose of old-fashioned "tax and spend" economics.

These tax increases would not be without consequences. Interestingly, many of the people advocating repeal of the Bush tax cuts also favor removing the cap on payroll taxes. The combined result of the two actions would be an astounding increase of more than 15 percent in top marginal tax rates (Table 2). But most economists would agree that high marginal tax rates are very likely to restrict economic output and, potentially, economic growth.[37]

Some opponents of individual accounts go beyond repealing the Bush tax cut and advocate other forms of general tax increases. For example, several opponents of individual accounts have suggested increasing the tax on Social Security benefits. Communitarian author and commentator Amitai Etzioni, for example, would extend income taxes to all Social Security benefits, ignoring the fact that the employee's portion of the payroll tax has already been taxed.[38] (Social Security taxes are not deducted from gross income for income tax purposes.) Less drastically, the AFL-CIO[39] and Aaron[40] would tax Social Security in the same way as other pension income.

Going still further on the tax front, Baker calls for a tax on all stock transactions. Both the buyer and the seller of stocks would be taxed at 0.25 percent of the transaction price.[41] Baker would also increase the capital gains tax from its current 18 percent to 28 percent, the rate prior to 1997.[42]

To the degree that these tax increases bring in revenue before 2018, they suffer from the same problems as does repealing the Bush tax cut. However, presumably they would also increase revenues after 2018, which would allow revenues to be used to pay Social Security benefits.

There is one final revenue-raising proposal that appears to be gaining support among some opponents of individual accounts. Currently, some 5 million state, county, and municipal workers do not participate in the Social Security system. Instead, they participate in their own retirement programs, which provide far better benefits than does Social Security.[43] However, the National Committee to Preserve Social Security and Medicare would require all newly hired public employees to be brought into the Social Security system,[44] as would Aaron.[45] This would be a 12.4 percent tax hike for those workers and could potentially force them to curtail contributions to their far more lucrative private pension plans.

Table 2
RESULTS OF REPEALING TAX CUT AND REMOVING CAP
ON PAYROLL TAXES

Income ($)	Tax Rate after Bush Cuts (%)	Payroll Tax (%)	Total Tax (%)	Tax Rate if Tax Cuts Repealed (%)	Payroll Tax if Cap Removed (%)	Total Tax with Increases (%)
0–27,050	10.0	15.3	25.3	15.0	15.3	30.3
27,050–65,550	15.0	15.3	30.3	28.0	15.3	43.3
65,550–84,900	25.0	15.3	40.3	31.0	15.3	46.3
84,900–136,750	25.0	2.9	27.9	31.0	15.3	46.3
136,750–297,350	33.0	2.9	35.9	36.0	15.3	51.3
Over 297,350	39.6	2.9	42.5	39.6	15.3	54.9

Benefit Cuts

The flip side of tax hikes is benefit cuts. Most opponents of individual accounts have been reluctant to propose any reduction in currently promised Social Security benefits. After all, their goal is to preserve the current benefit structure. Still, a few have put benefit cuts on the table.

In fact, Baker suggests that benefit cuts might not be such a bad thing. He points out that, because of scheduled increases in the benefits baseline, even after required cuts, retirees would receive checks for higher dollar amounts than they do today.[46] Baker is not necessarily incorrect in this. Indeed, the President's Social Security Commission makes a similar argument.[47] However, it does render rather hypocritical the argument of opponents of Social Security choice that reductions in government-provided benefits included in some individual-account plans are automatically bad.

Indeed, many of the cuts proposed by opponents of individual accounts sound very much like the cuts they warn would result from such individual accounts. For example, one of the most widely criticized proposals by the president's commission was a plan to change the indexing formula used to determine benefits. The formula is now adjusted for wage productivity; the change would be to adjust it for prices. Benefits would remain constant on an inflation-adjusted basis but would no longer increase at a rate greater than that of inflation. Opponents of individual accounts, including Aaron and colleagues, called this a deep cut in benefits.[48] But in 1976 Aaron supported a very similar proposal by a congressional commission, which included such anti-choice stalwarts as MIT professor Peter Diamond, who said that it "would leave more options open for spending the productivity dividend of economic growth. Congress could still raise pensions in the future, but it could also decide that other programs such as housing, health insurance, or defense have greater claims on available funds."[49] The same holds true for other proposed cuts. Shapiro, while joining the chorus calling for repeal of the Bush tax cuts, also suggests increasing the retirement age and reducing cost-of-living adjustments.[50] Apfel, while not providing any specific proposals for cuts, suggests that "modest measures should be taken to keep Social Security benefit levels from growing as fast as the economy."[51]

Ball suggests that the increase in benefits for future retirees, scheduled under current law, should be slowed by about 3 percent. He would accomplish that primarily through increasing the benefit computation period from the present law's 35 highest years' wages to 38 years.[52] Alicia Munnell of Boston University would also increase the benefit computation period,[53] as would Aaron. Lengthening the computation period means that more years of low or no wages would be included when determining the average wage on which to base benefits.[54]

In fact, Aaron probably supports the most extensive cuts in benefits of any foe of Social Security choice. For example, while opponents of individual accounts often accuse supporters of favoring increases in the retirement age, Aaron would raise not only the normal retirement age but also the early retirement age.[55] He is supported in this approach by fellow Brookings scholar Gary Burtless.[56] Myers would speed up already scheduled increases in the normal retirement age but would leave early retirement untouched. Ghilarducci would also agree to speed the increase in the normal retirement age to 67, but only if disability criteria are loosened to include sector unemployment.[57]

Aaron would consider still further benefit cuts, including reducing or even eliminating spousal benefits.

> The simplest and least costly way to end the lesser earner problem would be to eliminate the spouse's benefit altogether. However, this step would significantly reduce benefits for many older couples in which one spouse worked outside the home little or not at all. It would also make it far more costly for one parent to stay home to care for children. But a large majority of mothers, even those with preschool age children, now work, and that proportion has been rising. To aid parents who stay at home to care for children, Vice President Al Gore proposed, as part of his 2000 campaign for president, to give earnings credits of one half the average wage for up to five years spent caring for young children. Such a provision would further reduce the need for the spouse's benefit. A gradual reduction in the spouse's benefit over a decade or so from one-half of the principal earner's benefit to one-third or even one-quarter would free-up funds that could be used to lower the projected long-term deficit or applied to improving benefits in other ways.[58]

However, with the exception of his coauthor Robert Reischauer, few opponents of Social Security choice are willing to embrace such significant benefit cuts.

Government Investing

The third alternative identified by President Clinton is to find a way to achieve a higher rate of return on monies paid into the Social Security system. In practice, this means investing Social Security funds in private capital assets. That is precisely the point made by many advocates of Social Security choice. However, because opponents of individual accounts reject the idea of allowing workers to invest their Social Security taxes through individual accounts, they are forced to turn to a different entity for investing, namely, the government itself.

Supporters of this approach seldom refer to it as government investing; instead, they've devised an impressive collection of euphemisms for the concept. For example, Munnell calls it "broadening the portfolio" of the Social Security Trust Fund.[59] Reimer refers to it as "diversifying the Social Security Trust Fund's investment strategy."[60] To Aaron, it is "improving the management of Social Security's reserves."[61]

Whatever it is called, the concept of government investing is a central part of many reform plans supported by opponents of individual accounts. Ball proposed such an approach to the Social Security Advisory Council as long ago as 1996. Former president Clinton included it in his proposal for Social Security reform. It is at the heart of the proposal advanced by Aaron and is also supported by the National Committee to Preserve Social Security and Medicare,[62] *New York Times* columnist Paul Krugman, and the Older Women's League,[63] as well as Munnell, Reimer, and others.

Allowing the federal government to purchase stocks would give it the ability to obtain a significant, if not a controlling, interest in virtually every major company in America. Experience has shown that even a 2 or 3 percent block of shares can give an activist shareholder substantial influence over the policies of publicly traded companies.[64] The result could be a government bureaucrat sitting on every corporate board, a prospect that has divided advocates of government investing.

Even if the government avoids directly using its equity ownership to influence corporate governance, there is likely to be an enormous temptation to allow political considerations to influence the types of investments that the government makes. Approximately 42 percent of state, county, and municipal pension systems require that some portion of investment be targeted to projects designed to stimulate the local economy or create jobs. This includes investment in local infrastructure and public works projects as well as investment in in-state businesses and local real estate development.[65] In addition, 23 percent of the pension systems have prohibitions against investment in specific types of companies, including companies that fail to meet the "MacBride Principles" for doing business in Northern Ireland; companies doing business in Libya and other Arab countries; companies that are accused of pollution, unfair labor practices, or failing to meet equal opportunity guidelines; the alcohol, tobacco, and defense industries; and even companies that market infant formula to Third World countries.[66]

In fairness, most advocates of government investing believe that sufficient "firewalls" can be built-in to prevent government from politicizing its investment decisions. However, given the dismal history of government investment policies, that seems to be based far more on hope than on experience. As Federal Reserve chairman Alan Greenspan observed: "I don't know of any way that you can essentially insulate government decisionmakers from having access to what will amount to very large investments in American private industry. . . . I have been around long enough to realize that that is just not credible and not possible. Somewhere along the line, that breach will be broken."[67]

Some proponents of government investment don't even pretend to insulate the investment process from politics. For example, Gerald Shea of the AFL-CIO has suggested that it would be a good thing if the government exercised its new influence over the American economy, claiming that government involvement would "have a good effect on how corporate America operates."[68]

This danger led Greenspan to warn that proposals for government investing "have very far reaching potential dangers for a free American economy and a free American society."[69]

International experience also provides ample warning against allowing the government to direct investment in private capital markets. A recent study by the World Bank found nearly universal politicization of government investment policy, resulting in rates of return well below those earned by private-sector investments. Indeed, in many countries returns on government investment were below what could be earned on ordinary bank deposits.[70]

The Ostrich Approach

Some opponents of Social Security choice would prefer to offer no alternative at all. They simply deny that Social Security is in need of reform. For example, Rep. Jerrold Nadler (D-N.Y.) has called Social Security "a crisis that doesn't exist."[71] Baker and Weisbrot wrote an entire book devoted to the idea that Social Security was "a phony crisis."

Their argument is, essentially, that current projections of Social Security's insolvency are too pessimistic. They contend that, if the economy grows faster than projected, then wages and payroll tax revenue will rise, providing more than enough revenue to keep the program going, without any need to make significant changes.

However, as Cato analyst Andrew Biggs has shown, keeping Social Security solvent would require levels of economic growth unprecedented in American history. Moreover, even if the economy does grow more quickly than projected, Social Security's benefit liabilities and funding shortfalls will rise along with it. In short, even under assumptions vastly more optimistic than can be expected, Social Security remains insolvent.[72]

In fact, a new study by a pair of demographers and economists at the University of California–Berkeley suggests that projections about Social Security's future might not be pessimistic enough! Ronald Lee and Ryan Edwards report that "the chance for a really bad outcome is far higher than commonly expected."[73]

As a result, even most opponents of Social Security choice admit that something must be done to reform Social Security, but they won't tell us what.

Beyond Solvency

While most opponents of individual accounts offer no proposal to fix Social Security's problems beyond solvency, it is worth noting that at least some of their plans would make those problems worse.

Rate of Return

Payroll taxes are already so high relative to benefits that most young workers will receive an extremely poor rate of return, a return far below that provided by private capital markets. The Social Security Administration estimates that 30-year-old medium-wage workers will receive rates of return ranging from a high of 3.42 percent (for a single-earner couple) to just 1.13 percent (for a single male). Those returns will decline even further in the future.[74]

Raising taxes or reducing benefits, as many opponents of individual accounts advocate, will simply make the rate of return even worse (at least compared with promised benefits). This is particularly true of proposals to increase the payroll tax. The impact on rates of return of other proposals for tax hikes is less easily measured and falls more unevenly. However, any increase in the revenue going into the system without a corresponding increase in benefits will mean lower returns.

Minorities and Women

The current Social Security system contains a host of inequities, many of which disadvantage minorities and women. For example, because lifetime Social Security benefits are closely linked to longevity, people with shorter life expectancies can expect to receive less in retirement benefits. At every age and every income level, African Americans have shorter life expectancies than do whites. As a result, an African American who has the same lifetime earnings and pays the same payroll taxes as a white person can expect to receive a lower rate of return. This problem is exacerbated by the facts that African Americans are more likely to begin working earlier than whites and that African-American marriages are more likely to end in divorce in less than 10 years. Indeed, no group may be as poorly treated by Social Security as African Americans.[75]

None of the proposals advanced by opponents of individual accounts would change this unfair situation—and many would make it worse. For example, African Americans, who on average earn lower wages, would be disproportionately affected by proposed increases in the payroll tax. Even worse would be increases in the retirement age supported by Aaron and other foes of individual accounts.

The current system also penalizes many women, especially women who work outside the home. For instance, under Social Security's "dual entitlement rule" for spousal benefits, the spouse with lower lifetime earnings, nearly always the wife, is eligible to receive either a benefit based on her own earnings or one-half of her spouse's benefits, but not both. Effectively, this means that many women pay Social Security taxes but receive no additional benefits

181

for those taxes. Moreover, the current spousal system may set up situations in which a two-earner couple may actually receive less in benefits than a single-earner couple with the same lifetime earnings.[76]

In addition, the loss of up to 50 percent of a couple's benefits at the husband's death throws every fifth widow into poverty.[77] And current rules for spousal benefits deny benefits to women who were married less than 10 years. Since the average marriage lasts only 7 years, millions of women lose benefits under the current system.[78]

Some women's organizations have proposed changes in the current system to address some of those inequities. For example, they would increase benefits for widows and decrease the number of years of marriage required to qualify for spousal benefits from 10 to 7. They would also give women a $5,000 per year credit for years spent raising children outside the workforce.[79] These proposals would make the current system fairer, but they would also be costly, requiring additional revenue equal to more than 1 percent of payroll.[80]

Aside from women's groups, few opponents of Social Security choice have proposed reforms to eliminate the current system's inequities for women. And, once again, many of their proposals would make the problems worse. Proposals to lengthen the period used to compute Social Security benefits would particularly disadvantage women, since women are far more likely than men to have years with zero or low earnings.

And, of course, Aaron's proposal to drastically reduce spousal benefits would directly affect women.[81]

Wealth Creation

One of the strongest arguments for Social Security choice is that a system of individual accounts would give low-income Americans an opportunity to accumulate wealth. In contrast, the current Social Security system contributes to the growing "wealth gap" in the United States. Because it forces the poor to annuitize their savings, it prevents them from accumulating real wealth and passing that wealth on to future generations.[82]

None of the anti-choice proposals would directly deal with the wealth creation issue. However, some opponents of individual accounts have proposed creating personal accounts to supplement the current Social Security system as a way to help the poor accumulate wealth. These would be funded, depending on the proposal, through voluntary individual contributions, general tax revenues, or mandatory payroll tax increases.[83] However, studies show that voluntary "add-on" accounts are unlikely to benefit low-income workers. Low-wage workers simply don't have enough discretionary income to be able to contribute more to their retirement savings, even if the government provides generous matching funds.[84] On the other hand, if the add-on accounts are funded by mandatory contributions, they become simply another tax increase. If that increase is combined with the tax increases needed to keep the current system solvent, the burden on low-income workers could become intolerable.

A Right to Benefits

Under the current Social Security system, workers have no legal right to their retirement benefits.[85] In two important cases, *Helvering v. Davis* and *Flemming v. Nestor,* the U.S. Supreme Court has ruled that Social Security taxes are simply taxes and convey no property or contractual rights to Social Security benefits. As a result, a worker's retirement security is entirely dependent on political decisions made by the president and Congress. Benefits may be reduced or even eliminated at any time and are not directly related to Social Security taxes paid into the system. Therefore, retirees are left totally dependent on the whims of politicians for their retirement income.

None of the proposals advanced by opponents of individual accounts would change this situation in any way.

Conclusion

Opponents of Social Security choice have generally preferred to attack proposals for individual accounts without discussing their own alternatives for reforming Social Security. That is most probably because their alternatives boil down to some very unpopular options—raising taxes, cutting benefits, or government investment in private financial assets.

The debate over Social Security choice is not over a choice between individual accounts and a mythological Social Security system that can pay all promised future benefits without any increase in taxes. Individual accounts would win even that debate, since they give workers ownership of and control over their money, increase rates of return and therefore benefit levels, and allow low-income workers to accumulate wealth. The real debate, given the financial unsustainability of the current system, is over alternative proposals for reforming the system.

On one side of the debate are proposals to allow workers to privately invest some or all of their payroll taxes through individual accounts. These proposals may, or may not, include changes in the current system, such as reductions in government-provided benefits. Some may include using additional revenues, particularly general revenue, as a method of financing the transition. On the other side are proposals to prop up the current system by raising taxes, slashing benefits, or allowing the government to invest in private capital markets. These proposals contain significant costs and risks for both individuals and the American economy. And they offer none of the benefits of individual accounts.

The American people deserve a fair and honest debate about Social Security reform. They deserve to see the various proposals side by side so that they can compare the alternatives. Given the choice, we can be confident that Americans will choose to take control over their retirement funds through individual accounts.

Perhaps that's why opponents of Social Security choice prefer not to talk about their alternatives.

Notes

1. Charles Blahous, *Reforming Social Security for Ourselves and Our Posterity* (Westport, Conn.: Praeger, 2000), p. 140.

2. William Jefferson Clinton, Speech at the Great Social Security Debate, Albuquerque, N.M., July 27, 1998.

3. Henry Aaron, Testimony before the Senate Committee on Finance, 106th Cong., 1st sess., January 19, 1999.

4. Jim Kolbe and Charles Stenholm, Letter to House Speaker Dennis Hastert and Minority Leader Richard Gephardt, November 21, 2001.

5. President's Commission to Strengthen Social Security, *Strengthening Social Security and Creating Personal Wealth for All Americans: Report of the President's Commission*, December 21, 2001, p. 151.

6. Robert Friedland and Laura Summer, "Demography Is Not Destiny," National Academy on an Aging Society, Washington, 2001, p. 61.

7. Joseph White, *False Alarm: Why the Greatest Threat to Social Security and Medicare Is the Campaign to "Save" Them* (Baltimore: Johns Hopkins University Press, 2001), pp. 12–13.

8. Kenneth Apfel, "Social Security Standoff," *Washington Post*, April 11, 2001.

9. Lisa Maatz, Testimony submitted to the President's Commission to Strengthen Social Security, August 2001.

10. Vincent R. Sombrotto, Testimony before the President's Commission to Strengthen Social Security, October 18, 2001.

11. Robert M. Ball (with Thomas N. Bethell), *Straight Talk about Social Security: An Analysis of the Issues in the Current Debate* (New York: Century Foundation Press, 1998).

12. Jeff Faux, Statement submitted to the White House Conference on Social Security, December 8, 1998.

13. Teresa Ghilarducci, Statement submitted to the White House Conference on Social Security, December 8, 1998.

14. Dean Baker and Mark Weisbrot, *Social Security: The Phony Crisis* (Chicago: University of Chicago Press, 1999), p. 117.

15. Robert Myers, Statement submitted to the White House Conference on Social Security, December 8, 1998.

16. Congressional Budget Office, "Aggregate Income Effects of Changes in Social Security Taxes," August 1982, p. 30.

17. Aldona Robbins and Gary Robbins, "Effects of the 1988 and 1990 Social Security Tax Increases," Institute for Research on the Economics of Taxation, Washington, 1991, pp. 14–15.

18. Ralph Smith et al., *Social Security: A Primer* (Washington: Congressional Budget Office, 2001), pp. 76–79.

19. The lifetime net tax rate can be defined as the excess of the present value of lifetime Old Age and Survivors Insurance taxes over the present value of lifetime Social Security benefits. Jagadeesh Gokhale, "The Impact of Social Security Reform on Low-Income Workers," Cato Institute Social Security Paper no. 23, December 6, 2001, pp. 2–3.

20. National Committee to Preserve Social Security and Medicare, Statement to the President's Commission to Strengthen Social Security, September 6, 2001.

21. AFL-CIO, "Social Security: Options to Strengthen Social Security for Working Families," www.aflcio.org/socialsecurity/strength/htm.

22. Hans Reimer, Testimony before the President's Commission to Strengthen Social Security, October 5, 2001.

23. Heidi Hartmann, Catherine Hill, and Lisa Witter, "Strengthening Social Security for Women," National Council of Women's Organizations, Task Force on Women and Social Security, July 1999, p. 11.

24. Maatz.

25. Baker and Weisbrot, p. 117.

26. Ball (with Bethell), pp. 10–11.

27. D. Mark Wilson, "Removing Social Security's Tax Cap on Wages Would Do More Harm Than Good," Heritage Foundation Center for Data Analysis Report no. 01-07, October 17, 2001, p. 5.

28. Ibid., p. 6.

29. Ibid., pp. 9–10.

30. Ibid., p. 3. Total repeal of the cap would do considerably more for trust fund solvency, but that would be the result of running fat surpluses today, which would be spent, then "redeeming" the bonds in the trust fund in the future. Unless today's surpluses were actually saved, a very problematic scenario, we would actually be worse off, because benefit obligations would rise.

31. In addition to the economic consequences of using general tax revenues to finance the current system, it is also worth noting that general revenue financing would represent a significant departure from Social Security's traditional structure as

a payroll-tax-financed contributory social insurance program. That would transform Social Security into something much more closely resembling traditional welfare programs, something the designers sought to avoid.

32. See, for example, Peter Ferrara and Michael Tanner, *A New Deal for Social Security* (Washington: Cato Institute, 1998), pp. 187–94.

33. As President Clinton's fiscal year 2000 budget explained: "[Trust fund] balances are available to finance future benefit payments . . . but only in a bookkeeping sense. . . . They do not consist of real economic assets that can be drawn down in the future to fund benefits. Instead, they are claims on the Treasury that . . . will have to be financed by raising taxes, borrowing from the public, or reducing benefits or other expenditures. The existence of large Trust Fund balances, therefore, does not, by itself, have any impact on the Government's ability to pay benefits." Office of Management and Budget, *Budget of the United States Government, Fiscal Year 2000* (Washington: Government Printing Office, 2000), p. 337.

34. Robert Shapiro, "Nest Eggs, Over Easy," *Washington Monthly*, November 2001.

35. There is also the question of whether cutting taxes may do more to stimulate the economy than repaying debt. For example, $1 in tax cuts may save people and the economy more than just a dollar. In fact, because tax cuts reduce economic distortions (such as reducing savings and investment), a $1 tax cut saves the economy at least $1.25. Moreover, $1 in tax cuts doesn't actually cost the government $1 in lost revenue. Because taxpayers will save and invest more, work more, start more businesses, and evade taxes less, the government will lose only about 75 percent of the officially scored tax cut. So the $1.35 trillion tax cut will cost the government only about $1 trillion over 10 years. U.S. Congress, Joint Economic Committee, "Economic Benefits of Personal Income Tax Reductions," April 2001.

36. Roger Hickey, Testimony before the President's Commission to Strengthen Social Security, October 5, 2001.

37. U.S. Congress. A number of empirical studies have examined the responsiveness of taxable income to changes in marginal tax rates. In a 1987 paper, Lawrence Lindsey found an elasticity ranging from 1.05 to 2.75 with a midpoint estimate of 1.6 to 1.8. Lawrence Lindsey, "Individual Taxpayer Response to Tax Cuts, 1982–84, with Implications for the Revenue Maximizing Tax Rate," *Journal of Political Economy* 33 (1987). Other studies report similar levels of responsiveness. Martin Feldstein, "The Effect of Marginal Tax Rates on Taxable Income: A Panel Study of the 1986 Tax Act," *Journal of Political Economy* 103, no. 3 (1995); and Gerald Auten and Robert Carroll, "Taxpayer Behavior and the 1986 Tax Reform Act," U.S. Treasury, Office of Tax Analysis, July 1994. Recent studies suggest a somewhat lower, but still substantial, response. See, for example, Jonathan Gruber and Emmanuel Saez, "The Elasticity of Taxable Income: Evidence and Implications," National Bureau of Economic Research Working Paper no. 7512, January 2000; and Gerald Auten and Robert Carroll, "The Effect of Income Taxes on Household Income," *Review of Economics and Statistics* 81 (1999).

38. Amitai Etzioni, "Should We End Social Security? A Community Approach," *Dow Jones News Service*, September 1, 1998.

39. AFL-CIO.

40. Henry Aaron and Robert Reischauer, *Countdown to Reform: The Great Social Security Debate* (New York: Century Foundation, 2001), pp. 113–14.

41. Dean Baker, "False Poverty: The Nation Can Afford to Pay for Its Elderly," *Aging Today*, March–April 2000.

42. Baker and Weisbrot, p. 118.

43. Carrie Lips, "State and Local Government Retirement Programs: Lessons in Alternatives to Social Security," Cato Institute Social Security Paper no. 16, March 17, 1999.

44. National Committee to Preserve Social Security and Medicare.

45. Aaron and Reischauer, pp. 112–13.

46. Dean Baker, "Social Security Myth #2184—There Won't Be Anything for Me," Center for Economic and Policy Research Issue Brief, February 20, 2001.

47. President's Commission to Strengthen Social Security, *Strengthening Social Security and Creating Personal Wealth for All Americans.*

48. Henry Aaron, Alicia Munnell, and Peter Orszag, "Social Security Reform: The Questions Raised by the Plans Endorsed by President Bush's Social Security Commission," Washington, Century Foundation and Center on Budget and Policy Priorities, November 30, 2001.

49. Quoted in "Propping Up Social Security," *Business Week*, July 19, 1976.

50. Shapiro.

51. Apfel.

52. Robert Ball, Testimony before the House Ways and Means Committee, Subcommittee on Social Security, 105th Cong., 2d sess., June 3, 1998.

53. Alicia Munnell, Testimony before the House Ways and Means Committee, Subcommittee on Social Security, 105th Cong., 2d sess., June 3, 1998.

54. Current benefits are determined on the basis of wages during the highest-earning 35 years, with all years before the worker reaches age 65 indexed to reflect real wage growth and inflation. These earnings are then divided by 420 months to yield Average Indexed Monthly Earnings. Social Security benefits are then calculated by a progressive formula: 90 percent of the first $606 of the AIME, 32 percent of the next $3,653, and 15 percent of the remaining AIME. Obviously, including additional low-income years or years with zero earnings in the AIME calculation would lower that amount and therefore benefits.

55. Aaron and Reischauer, pp. 106–10.

56. Gary Burtless, Testimony before the Senate Budget Committee, 106th Cong., 1st sess., January 19, 1999.

57. Ghilarducci.

58. Aaron and Reischauer, p. 104.

59. Munnell.

60. Reimer.

61. Aaron, Testimony.

62. National Committee to Preserve Social Security and Medicare.

63. Maatz.

64. Theodore Angelis, "Investing Public Money in Private Markets: What Are the Right Questions?" Presentation to a conference on "Framing the Social Security Debate: Values, Politics, and Economics," National Academy of Social Insurance, Washington, January 29, 1998.

65. James Packard Love, *Economically Targeted Investing: A Reference for Public Pension Funds* (Sacramento: Institute for Fiduciary Education, 1989).

66. Ibid.; and Carolyn Peterson, *State Employee Retirement Systems: A Decade of Change* (Washington: American Legislative Exchange Council, 1987).

67. Alan Greenspan, Testimony before the Senate Committee on Banking, 105th Cong., 2d sess., July 21, 1998.

68. Quoted in Michael Eisenscher and Peter Donohue, "The Fate of Social Security," *Z Magazine*, March 1997.

69. Greenspan.

70. World Bank, "Public Management: How Well Do Governments Invest Pension Fund Reserves?" World Bank, Washington, 2001.

71. Jerrold Nadler, Constituent Newsletter, 1997, Issue 2, p. 1.

72. Andrew Biggs, "Social Security: Is It 'A Crisis That Doesn't Exist'?" Cato Institute Social Security Paper no. 21, October 5, 2001.

73. Ronald Lee and Ryan Edwards, "The Fiscal Impact of Population Aging in the U.S.: Assessing the Uncertainties," National Bureau of Economic Research Working Paper, October 2, 2001, p. 8.

74. President's Commission to Strengthen Social Security, *Interim Report*, August 2001, p. 7.

75. For a fuller discussion, see Michael Tanner, "Disparate Impact: Social Security and African Americans," Cato Institute Briefing Paper no. 61, February 5, 2001. See also Jeffrey Lieberman, "Redistribution in the Current U.S. Social Security System," Harvard University, July 2001; and Constanjin Panis and Lee Lillard, "Socioeconomic Differentials in the Return to Social Security," RAND Corporation Working Paper no. 96-05, 1996.

76. For further discussion, see Leanne Abdnor, "Social Security Choices for 21st-Century Women," Cato Institute Social Security Paper no. 33, February 24, 2004. See also Darcy Ann Olsen, "Greater Financial Security for Women with Personal Retirement Accounts," Cato Institute Briefing Paper no. 38, July 20, 1998.

77. Ibid., pp. 4–5.

78. President's Commission to Strengthen Social Security, *Interim Report*, p. 25.

79. Hartmann, Hill, and Witter, pp. 6–11.

80. Ibid., Table 1, p. 11.

81. Aaron would partially offset the impact for low-income women by increasing survivors' benefits and establishing "earnings sharing" between spouses.

82. Gokhale, pp. 4–7.

83. For a discussion of these proposals, see Darcy Ann Olsen, "Social Security Reform Proposals: USAs, Clawbacks, and Other Add-Ons," Cato Institute Briefing Paper no. 47, June 11, 1999.

84. For evidence from participation in 401(k) programs, see William Bassett, Michael Flemming, and Anthony Rodriguez, "How Workers Use 401(k) Plans: The Participation, Contribution, and Withdrawal Decisions," *National Tax Journal* 11, no. 2 (June 1998).

85. For a thorough discussion of this issue, see Charles Rounds, "Property Rights: The Hidden Issue of Social Security Reform," Cato Institute Social Security Paper no. 19, April 19, 2000.

11. Empowering Workers: The Privatization of Social Security in Chile

José Piñera

A specter is haunting the world. It is the specter of bankrupt government-run Social Security systems. The pay-as-you-go system that reigned supreme through most of the 20th century has a fundamental flaw, one rooted in a false conception of how human beings behave: it destroys, at the individual level, the link between contributions and benefits—in other words, between effort and reward. Whenever that happens on a massive scale and for a long period of time, the final result is disaster.

Two exogenous factors aggravate the consequences of that flaw: the global demographic trend toward decreasing fertility rates and medical advances that are lengthening life. As a result, fewer workers have to support more and more retirees. Since increasing payroll taxes generates unemployment, sooner or later promised benefits have to be reduced, a telltale sign of a bankrupt system. Whether benefits are reduced through inflation, as in most developing countries, or through legislation, the result is the same: anguish about old age is created, paradoxically, by the inherent insecurity of an unfunded "Social Security" system.

In Chile, the Pension Reform law of 1980 introduced a revolutionary innovation. The law gave every worker the choice of opting out fully from the government-run pension system and instead putting the former payroll tax in a privately managed personal retirement account (PRA). Since 95 percent of the workers chose the PRA system, the end result was a "privatization from below" of Chile's Social Security system.

Originally published as Cato's Letters no. 10, 1996.

When we celebrated the first 21 years of this reform, the results spoke for themselves. Retirement benefits in the PRA system already are 50 to 100 percent higher—depending on whether they are old-age, disability, or survivors' retirement benefits—than they were in the pay-as-you-go system. The resources administered by the pension funds amount to $40 billion, or around 55 percent of GNP. By improving the functioning of both the capital and the labor markets, the pension reform has been one of the key changes that have substantially increased savings and doubled the growth rate of the economy.[1]

The success of the Chilean pension reform has led another 15 countries in Latin America and Europe to follow suit.[2] In January 2001, even Sweden, once an emblematic welfare state, allowed its workers to put 2.5 percentage points of their 18.5 percent payroll tax contribution into individual retirement accounts. Those developments led *The Economist* to state: "Radical reform of Social Security is the next great liberal reform, easily as significant a change as privatization of state owned enterprises—also dismissed in its time as Utopian. On retirement benefits Latin America has led the way. Let the world follow."[3]

How It Works

Under Chile's new Social Security system, what determines a worker's retirement benefit is the amount of money he accumulates in his PRA during his working years. Neither the worker nor the employer pays a payroll tax. Nor does the worker collect a government-funded benefit. Instead, 10 percent of his wage is deposited, tax-free, by his employer each month in his own PRA.[4] The 10 percent rate was calculated on the assumption of a 4 percent average real return on a PRA during a whole working life, so that the typical worker would have sufficient money in his account to fund a retirement benefit equal to approximately 70 percent of his final salary. A worker may contribute up to an additional 10 percent, also deductible from taxable income, of his wage each month as a form of voluntary savings. The return on the PRA is tax-free. Upon retirement, when funds are withdrawn, taxes are paid according to the income tax bracket at that moment.

A worker may choose any one of the private pension fund companies (called Administradoras de Fondos de Pensiones, or AFPs) to manage his PRA. A key provision is totally free entry to the AFP industry, for both domestic and foreign companies (foreign companies can own up to 100 percent of an AFP) in order to provide competition and thus benefit workers. Those companies can engage in no other activities and are subject to strict supervision by a government entity, the Superintendency of AFP, that was created to provide highly technical oversight to prevent theft or fraud.[5]

Each AFP operates five mutual funds, with different bond/share proportions. (The original scheme allowed only one fund for each AFP.) Older workers have to own mutual funds highly invested in fixed income securities, while young workers can have up to 80 percent of their funds in shares. Investment decisions are made by the AFP, but the worker can choose both the AFP and, within limits, the preferred fund. The law sets only maximum percentage limits both for specific types of instruments and for the overall mix of the portfolio; and the spirit of the reform is that those regulations should be reduced progressively as the AFP companies gain experience and capital markets work better. There is no obligation whatsoever to invest in government bonds or any other security. Legally, the AFP companies and the mutual funds are separate entities. Thus, should an AFP go under, the assets of the mutual funds—that is, the workers' investments—are not affected at all and only the AFP's shareholders lose their capital.

Workers are free to change from one AFP company to another, and from one fund to another. There is then competition among the companies to provide a higher return on investment, better customer service, or a lower commission. Each worker is given a PRA passbook (to use if he wants to update his balance by visiting his AFP) and receives a statement by mail every three months informing him of how much money has been accumulated in his retirement account and how well his investment fund has performed. The account bears the worker's name, is his property, and will be used to pay his old-age retirement benefit (with a provision for survivors' benefits).

As should be expected, individual preferences about old age differ as much as any other preferences. Some people want to work forever; others cannot wait to cease working and indulge in their true vocations or hobbies. The pay-as-you-go system does not permit the satisfaction of such preferences, except through collective pressure to have, for example, an early retirement age for powerful political constituencies. It is a one-size-fits-all scheme that may exact a high price in human happiness.

The PRA system, on the other hand, allows individual preferences to be translated into individual decisions that will produce the desired outcome. In the branch offices of many AFPs, there are user-friendly computer terminals on which a worker can calculate the expected value of his future retirement benefit, based on the money in his account, the life expectancy of his age group, and the year in which he wishes to retire. Alternatively, the worker can specify the retirement benefit he wishes to receive and determine how much extra money he must deposit each month if he wants to retire at a given age. Once he gets the answer, he simply asks his employer to withdraw that new percentage from his salary. Of course, he can adjust that figure as time goes on, depending on the actual yield of his pension fund or other relevant variables (for example, longer life expectancies).

All workers, whether employed by private companies or by the government, were given the opportunity to opt out of the pay-as-you-go system.[6] Self-employed workers are not compelled to participate in the PRA system, as they were not in the government pay-as-you-go system, because of the practical difficulties in a country like Chile of enforcing any mandatory system for self-employed people. But the pension reform allows them to enter the PRA system if they wish, thus creating an incentive for informal workers to join the formal economy.

The Social Security reform system maintained a "safety net." A worker who has contributed for at least 20 years but whose benefit, upon reaching retirement age, is below what the law defines as a "minimum pension" is entitled to receive that benefit level from general government revenue sources once his PRA has been depleted. (Those without 20 years of contributions can apply for a welfare-type retirement benefit at a lower level.)

The government-run disability and survivors' program, a source of systematic abuse, given the nonexistence of incentives to control its fair use, was also fully privatized. Each AFP has to provide this service to its affiliated workers by taking out, through open and transparent bidding, group life and disability coverage from private life insurance companies. This coverage is paid for by an additional worker contribution of around 2 percent of salary, which includes the commission to the AFP for administrative and investing expenses.

192

A key feature of the reform was the change in the meaning of "retirement." The legal retirement age is 65 for men and 60 for women. (Those were the ages in the former pay-as-you-go system and were not discussed or changed during the reform process because they are not a structural characteristic of the PRA system.) But in the PRA system, workers with sufficient savings in their accounts to buy a "reasonable annuity" (defined as 50 percent of the average salary of the previous 10 years, as long as it is higher than the "minimum pension") can cease working, begin withdrawing their money, and stop contributing to their accounts. Of course, workers can continue working after beginning to retire their money. A worker must reach the legal retirement age to be eligible for the government subsidy that guarantees the minimum pension. But in no way is there an obligation to cease working, at any age, nor is there an obligation to continue working or saving for retirement benefit purposes once you have assured yourself a "reasonable" benefit as described above.

Upon retiring, a worker may choose from three general payout options. In the first case, a retiree may use the capital in his PRA to purchase an annuity from any private life insurance company. The annuity must guarantee a constant monthly income for life, indexed to inflation (there are indexed bonds available in the Chilean capital market so that companies can invest accordingly), plus survivors' benefits for the worker's dependents (wife and orphans under the age of 21). Second, a retiree may leave his funds in the PRA and make programmed withdrawals, subject to limits based on the life expectancy of the retiree and his dependents; with this option, if he dies, the remaining funds in his account form a part of his estate and can be given to his heirs basically tax-free. In both cases, he can withdraw as a lump sum the capital in excess of that needed to obtain an annuity or programmed withdrawal equal to 70 percent of his last wages. And third, he can choose any mix he wishes of the previous two.

The PRA system solves the typical problem of pay-as-you-go systems with respect to labor demographics: in an aging population the number of workers per retiree decreases. Under the PRA system, the working population does not pay taxes to finance the retired population. Thus, in contrast with the pay-as-you-go system, the potential for intergenerational conflict and eventual bankruptcy is avoided. The problem that many countries face—huge unfunded government social security liabilities—does not exist under the PRA system.

In contrast to company-based pension systems that generally impose costs on workers who leave the company before a given number of years and that sometimes result in the loss of the workers' retirement funds—thus depriving workers of both their jobs and their pension rights (as did the infamous Enron case in the United States)—the PRA system is completely independent of the company employing the worker. Since the PRA is tied to the worker, not the company, the account is fully portable. Given that the pension funds must be invested in tradable securities, the PRA has a daily value and therefore is easy to transfer from one AFP to another. The problem of "job lock" is entirely avoided. By not impinging on labor mobility, the PRA system helps create labor market flexibility and neither subsidizes nor penalizes immigrants. As PRA systems spread around the world, I envision portability between countries as well, which will help people who are more internationally mobile, such as professionals or unassimilated immigrants.

A PRA system also can accommodate flexible labor styles. In fact, some people are deciding to work only a few hours a day or to interrupt their working lives—especially women and youngsters. In pay-as-you-go systems, those decisions create the problem of filling the gaps in contributions and, in some cases, may entail no right at all to a retirement benefit, despite years of contributing to the system. Not so in a PRA scheme where stop-and-go contributions do not impinge on the right to get back the totality of (plus the return on) one's contribution.

The Transition

In countries that already have a pay-as-you-go system, one crucial challenge is to design and implement the transition to a PRA system. In Chile we set three basic policy rules:

1. The government guaranteed those already receiving a Social Security check that their benefits would not be touched by the reform. It would be unfair to the elderly to break the promises made. I stated this basic rule in this way: "Nobody will take away your grandmother's check."

2. Every worker was given the choice of staying in the pay-as-you-go system or moving to the new PRA system. Those who opted out of the former system were given a "recognition bond" that was deposited in their new PRAs. That bond was indexed to inflation and carried a 4 percent real interest rate. It was basically a zero-coupon treasury bond maturing when the worker reaches the legal retirement age. The bonds can be traded in secondary markets, so as to allow the worker to use them to build the capital necessary for early retirement. The bond was calculated to reflect the rights the worker had already acquired in the pay-as-you-go system. The exact formula was in the law and was widely and simply explained to the people. Thus, a worker who had paid Social Security contributions for years did not have to start at zero when he entered the PRA system.
3. All new entrants to the labor force were required to enter the PRA system. This requirement ensured the complete end of the pay-as-you-go system once the last worker who remained in it reaches retirement age. From then on, and for a limited period of time, the government has only to pay benefits to retirees of the old system.

To give all those who might be interested in doing so an equal opportunity to create AFPs, the law established a six-month period during which no AFP could begin operations (not even advertising). Thus, the AFP industry is unique in that it had a clear day of conception (November 4, 1980) and a clear date of birth (May 1, 1981). Note that in this way we transformed May Day into a day celebrating the empowerment of workers through Social Security choice.

We also ended the illusion—artificially maintained by lawmakers around the world—that both the employer and the worker contribute to Social Security. As economists know well, all the contributions are ultimately paid from the worker's marginal productivity, and employers take into account all labor costs—whether termed salary or Social Security contributions—in making their hiring and pay decisions. So, by renaming the employer's contribution an additional gross wage, our reform made it clear, without reducing workers' take-home pay, that all contributions are paid ultimately by the worker and that he can control his own money. Of course, at the end of the day, wage levels will be determined by the interplay of market forces.

The financing of the transition is a complex technical issue that we addressed successfully without raising taxes and that each country must resolve according to its own circumstances. The key insight in this regard is that, contrary to the widely held belief, there is no "economic" transition cost, because there is no cost to GNP due to this reform (on the contrary). A completely different, and relevant, issue is how to confront the "cash-flow" transition cost to the government of recognizing, and ultimately eliminating, the unfunded liability created by the pay-as-you-go-system.

The implicit pay-as-you-go debt of the Chilean system in 1980 has been estimated by a World Bank study at around 80 percent of GDP. As that study states, "Chile shows that a country with a reasonably competitive banking system, a well-functioning debt market, and a fair degree of macroeconomic stability can finance large transition deficits without large interest rate repercussions."[7]

We used five "sources" to finance the fiscal costs of changing to a PRA system:

1. Using debt, the transition cost was shared by future generations. In Chile, roughly 40 percent of the cost has been financed by issuing government bonds at market rates of interest. These bonds have been bought mainly by the AFPs as part of their investment portfolios, and that "bridge debt" should be completely redeemed when the beneficiaries of the old system are no longer with us (a source of sadness for their families and friends but, undoubtedly, a source of relief for future treasury ministers).

2. Since the savings rate needed in a defined-contribution system, like the PRA, to finance adequate retirement benefit levels was lower than the existing payroll taxes, a fraction of the difference between them was used as a temporary "transition tax" (which was gradually reduced to zero, lowering the cost of hiring labor and leading to more employment).

3. In a government's balance sheet there are liabilities—such as Social Security and health obligations—but also government-owned enterprises, land, and other types of assets. Since we were also at that time privatizing government-owned assets,

especially companies, that was one way to finance the transition that had several additional benefits, such as increasing efficiency, spreading ownership, and depoliticizing the economy.

4. The need to finance the transition was a powerful incentive to reduce wasteful government spending. Prior to the reform, the government deliberately created a budget surplus, and for many years afterwards the treasury minister was able to use the need to "finance the transition" as a powerful argument to contain the permanent pressure from all sources to increase government expenditures.

5. The increased economic growth fueled by the PRA system substantially increased tax revenues, especially those from the value-added tax.

The Results

Since the system began to operate on May 1, 1981, the average real return on investment has been 10.7 percent per year (during 21 years). Of course, the annual yield has shown the oscillations that are intrinsic to the free market—ranging from minus 3 percent to plus 30 percent in real terms—but the important yield is the average one over the working life of a person (say 40–45 years) or the full working plus retired life (say 55–60 years) if a person chooses the programmed withdrawal option.

Retirement benefits under the PRA system (with a mandatory savings rate of only 10 percent) have been significantly higher than under the old, state-administered system, which required a much higher payroll tax. According to one study, the average AFP retiree was receiving, after 15 years of operation of the system, a retirement benefit equal to 78 percent of his mean annual income over the previous 10 years of his working life. Upon retirement, workers may withdraw in a lump sum their "excess savings" (above the 70 percent of salary threshold). If that money were included in calculating the value of the retirement benefit, the total value would come close to 84 percent of working income. Recipients of disability retirement benefits also receive, on average, 70 percent of their working income.[8]

The pension funds have already accumulated an investment fund equivalent to 55 percent of GNP, and some experts forecast that that percentage will rise to 100 percent of GNP when the system reaches full maturity. This long-term investment capital not only has helped fund economic growth but has spurred the development of efficient financial markets and institutions. The decision to create the PRA system first, and then privatize the large state-owned companies second, resulted in a "virtuous sequence." It gave workers the possibility of benefiting handsomely from the enormous increase in productivity of the privatized companies by allowing workers, through higher stock prices that increased the yield of their PRAs, to capture a large share of the wealth created by the privatization process.

One of the key results of the new system has been, then, to increase the productivity of capital and thus the rate of economic growth in the Chilean economy. The vast resources administered by the AFPs have encouraged the creation of new kinds of financial instruments while enhancing others already in existence but not fully developed. Another of Chile's pension reform contributions to the sound operation and transparency of the capital market has been the creation of a domestic risk-rating industry and the improvement of corporate governance. (The AFPs appoint independent directors of the companies in which they own shares, thus shattering complacency at board meetings.)

The new Social Security system has made a significant contribution to the reduction of poverty by increasing the size and certainty of old-age, survivors', and disability benefits; by the indirect but very powerful effect of promoting economic growth and employment; and by eliminating the unfairness of the old system. According to conventional wisdom, pay-as-you-go schemes redistribute income from the rich to the poor. However, when certain income-specific characteristics of workers and the modus operandi of the political system are taken into account, those systems generally redistribute income to the most powerful groups of workers, who are obviously not the most vulnerable or poor.

Social Security issues in Chile have ceased to concentrate the energy and focus of the government, thus depoliticizing a huge sector of the economy and giving individuals more control over their own lives.[9]

It is not surprising that the PRA system has survived intact three center-left governments in the last 12 years, since it really has become the "third rail" of Chilean politics. Not only has it been untouched in its structural design, but technical adjustments have improved it, for example, by allowing more competition in the management of voluntary retirement savings and enlarging the choices of funds from one to five.

When the PRA system was inaugurated in May 1981, one-fourth of the eligible work force signed up in the first month of operation alone, and today 95 percent of covered Chilean workers are in the PRA system. When given a choice, Chilean workers have voted with their money overwhelmingly for a free-market-based retirement system.

For Chileans, their PRAs now represent real and visible property rights—indeed they are the primary sources of security for retirement, and the typical Chilean worker's main asset is not his used car or even his small house (probably still mortgaged) but the capital in his PRA. The new Social Security system has given Chileans a personal stake in the economy. A typical Chilean worker is not indifferent to the behavior of the stock market or interest rates. He knows that a bad economic policy can harm his retirement benefits. When workers feel that they themselves own a part of their country's assets, not through party bosses or a Politburo, they are much more attached to the free market and a free society.

The overwhelming majority of Chilean workers who chose to move into the new system freely decided to abandon the government system even though some of the national trade union leaders and most of the political class advised against it. I have always believed that common workers care deeply about and pay a lot of attention to matters close to their lives, such as Social Security, education, and health, and make their decisions for the well-being of their families, not according to political allegiances or collectivist ideologies.

The ultimate lesson of the Chilean experience is that the only revolutions that are successful are those that trust the individual and the wonders that individuals can do when they are free.[10]

Notes

1. According to economist Klaus Schmidt-Hebbel, the rate of growth of the Chilean economy went from an average of 3.7 percent per year, in the period from 1961 through 1974, to 7.1 percent per year in the period from 1990 through 1997. To that extra growth of 3.4 percentage points per year, the pension reform would have contributed .9 percentage points per year, that is, more than a quarter of the total. Of the total increase of 12.2 percentage points in the rate of savings during those two periods, this reform contributed 3.8 percentage points, that is, 31 percent of the total increase. See Klaus Schmidt-Hebbel, "Does Pension Reform Really Spur

Productivity, Saving, and Growth?" *Documentos de Trabajo del Banco Central*, no. 33 (April 1998): 25, 29.

2. See my companion essay, "The Global Pension Revolution," Cato's Letters no. 15, Cato Institute, 2001.

3. *The Economist*, June 12, 1999.

4. This mandatory percentage applies only to the first $15,000 of annual income. Therefore, as wages go up with economic growth, the "mandatory savings" content of the system decreases as a percentage of the worker's total wage. It should be noted that this cap, which is expressed in the law in indexed pesos, has not been touched in 21 years by four different governments.

5. For complete statistical information on the 21 years of the system, visit the Web site of the Superintendency of AFP, www.safp.cl.

6. Members of the armed forces and the national police were not given the choice to opt out. Since then, the deficit of their pay-as-you-go system has increased to unsustainable levels. The original pension reform project included them, but that provision was vetoed by the Defense Ministry on the grounds that it was its legal prerogative to introduce such changes.

7. World Bank, *Averting the Old Age Crisis* (New York: Oxford University Press, 1994), p. 268.

8. Sergio Baeza, *Quince Años Después: Una Mirada al Sistema Privado de Pensiones* (Santiago: Centro de Estudios Públicos, 1995).

9. For more information, see L. Jacobo Rodríguez, "Chile's Private Pension System at 18: Its Current State and Future Challenges," Cato Institute Social Security Paper no. 17, July 30, 1999.

10. The labor reform was approved in 1979, and the full story is in my book, *La Revolución Laboral en Chile* (Santiago: Zig Zag, 1990). I told the story about the Social Security reform in a companion book, *El Cascabel al Gato* (Santiago: Zig Zag, 1991).

12. Perspectives on the President's Commission to Strengthen Social Security

Andrew G. Biggs

In May 2001 President Bush appointed the President's Commission to Strengthen Social Security to formulate proposals that would maintain Social Security's promise for today's retirees while improving that promise for younger workers through personal accounts. That was their task, and in the end they accomplished it well.

The commission began its work with an interim report, issued in August 2001, outlining the state of the current program. The interim report generated significant controversy—particularly its criticism of the Social Security trust fund and the overall progressivity of the program.

The commission's final report and recommendations, delivered to the president in December 2001, contains three separate reform proposals based on personal retirement accounts. Although the plans encompass a broad range of ideas on how to maintain Social Security, each would pay benefits at least as high as the current program at a lower long-term cost, while giving workers the opportunity to build assets and wealth in personal accounts that they would own and control.

The commission's Plan 1 would do nothing more than give workers the option to voluntarily invest a portion of their Social Security payroll taxes in a personal retirement account. Because it makes no other changes to the system, it is politically attractive in the short term, but it does not address long-term concerns. Nevertheless, even this "accounts only" approach would pay higher benefits to all retirees while reducing long-term general revenue costs by 8 percent compared with the current program.

Originally published as Cato Institute Social Security Paper no. 27, August 22, 2002, and updated to reflect current information.

Plan 2 would go further by allowing workers to voluntarily invest 4 percent of their wages up to $1,000 while indexing traditional benefits for new retirees to increases in prices rather than wages. This step would make Social Security sustainable indefinitely, reducing the long-term general revenue costs of supporting the program by 68 percent while paying retirees higher benefits than under current law.

Plan 3 incorporates a combination add-on and carve-out account, wherein a worker who voluntarily invests an additional 1 percent of his wages may redirect 2.5 percentage points of his payroll taxes, up to $1,000 annually. Plan 3 would pay benefits higher even than those promised by Social Security while putting 52 percent less pressure on general revenues than the current program. More problematic is the fact that Plan 3 incorporates new, ongoing general revenue transfers to the traditional pay-as-you-go program. Although these funding increases are consistent with the desire of the plan's sponsors for workers to continue to receive a combination of defined benefit and defined contribution benefits that exceeds levels promised by the current program, it is believed that revenues are better applied to establishing the funded portion of Social Security reform rather than to bolstering the existing pay-as-you-go element.

The latter two plans incorporated significant new protections for the most vulnerable Americans. Both plans would guarantee 30-year minimum-wage workers a retirement above the poverty line, a promise the current program cannot make. This guarantee would lift up to one million retirees out of poverty by 2018. Survivors' benefits for lower-wage individuals would be increased to 75 percent of the couple's prior benefit, increasing benefits for two to three million retired women.

The commission's plans would also assist divorced persons, who for the first time would gain a right to benefits on the basis of their spouses' earnings even if they divorced before 10 years of marriage. Coupled with the progressive funding of the personal accounts in Plans 2 and 3, these steps make reform based on personal accounts unequivocally beneficial to lower-income Americans.

The commission attracted considerable criticism from opponents of personal accounts. What the commission's work did not attract was substantive counterproposals on how to keep Social Security solvent and sustainable over the long term in the absence of personal accounts. The next stage of the Social Security debate is for account opponents to make their case and for the public and policymakers to decide what they want. Inaction, the "policy" most often put forward by account opponents, is not a viable option.

Background

The President's Commission to Strengthen Social Security was appointed with a mandate to "provide bipartisan recommendations to the President for modernizing and restoring fiscal soundness to the Social Security System."[1]

The 16-member commission, split evenly between Democrats and Republicans, was co-chaired by former senator Daniel Patrick Moynihan (D-N.Y.) and Richard Parsons, soon to be chief executive officer of AOL Time Warner. The other members of the commission included

- Leanne Abdnor (R), former vice president of the Cato Institute and executive director of the Alliance for Worker Retirement Security;
- Sam Beard (D), founder and president of Economic Security (2000);
- John Cogan (R), former deputy director of the Office of Management and Budget, now a resident scholar at the Hoover Institution at Stanford University;
- Bill Frenzel (R), former U.S. representative from Minnesota, now a resident scholar at the Brookings Institution;
- Estelle James (D), consultant with the World Bank and lead author of the bank's influential 1994 book, *Averting the Old Age Crisis;*[2]
- Robert Johnson (D), chief executive officer of Black Entertainment Television;
- Gwendolyn King (R), former commissioner of Social Security (1989–92);
- Olivia Mitchell (D), professor of insurance and risk management at the University of Pennsylvania's Wharton School and executive director of the Pension Research Council;
- Gerry Parsky (R), former assistant secretary of the Treasury (1974–77), now chairman of Aurora Capital Partners;

- Tim Penny (D), former U.S. representative from Minnesota, now senior fellow at the University of Minnesota's Hubert H. Humphrey Institute of Public Affairs;
- Robert Pozen (D), former vice chairman of Fidelity Investments, now lecturer in public policy at Harvard University;
- Mario Rodriguez (R), president of Hispanic Business Roundtable;
- Thomas Saving (R), professor of economics at Texas A&M University and public trustee of the Social Security program; and
- Fidel Vargas (D), vice president of Reliant Equity Investors and member of the 1994–96 Advisory Council on Social Security.

The commission, which was instructed to submit its recommendations to President Bush by December 21, 2001, worked according to the following principles outlined by the president.

1. Modernization must not change Social Security benefits for retirees or near-retirees.
2. The entire Social Security surplus must be dedicated to Social Security only.
3. Social Security payroll taxes must not be increased.
4. Government must not invest Social Security funds in the stock market.
5. Modernization must preserve Social Security's disability and survivors' components.
6. Modernization must include individually controlled, voluntary personal retirement accounts, which will augment the Social Security safety net.

These principles were the starting point for the commission's deliberations. However, they did not dictate the commission's conclusions. The president's principles are flexible enough, in fact, not to rule out the approach advocated by former vice president Gore—retention of the traditional Social Security defined benefit, augmented by supplementary personal accounts. Nor do they dictate that accounts must be financed by redirecting existing payroll taxes. Indeed one of the commission's plans includes new contributions by workers. In short, although critics claimed that the commission was "stacked" in a certain direction, the principles it worked under—not to mention the proposals it arrived at—were anything but preordained.

Interim Report

The commission's first task was to complete an interim report[3] outlining the challenges facing the current Social Security system— that is, to define the problem the commission and the country have to address. Given the intense reaction to the report from reform opponents, it seemed at times that the commission, rather than the program, was viewed as the problem. Nevertheless, despite allegations that the report contained numerous factual errors,[4] it in fact holds up quite well under scrutiny.

In many ways, the commission's interim report simply echoed the annual reports of Social Security's trustees, who noted that the program faces substantial and ongoing deficits over the long term. Much like the trustees, the commission urged that reform be undertaken sooner rather than later.

In its interim report, the commission reached the following conclusions regarding the current Social Security program, which complement the principles for reform outlined by the president.

- If we are to support tomorrow's retirees without overburdening tomorrow's workers, this generation of Americans must save and invest more.
- The existing Social Security program does not save or invest for the future. It was not designed to facilitate saving, and the political process cannot be relied upon to save on behalf of American families.
- Under the existing system, Americans will soon face inescapable choices: cut Social Security benefits, raise taxes, cut other government spending, or borrow on an unprecedented scale.
- Arguments for doing nothing amount to direct advocacy of one or more of these options.[5]

In addition, the commission established eight criteria by which to evaluate proposals to strengthen the Social Security system:

1. Encouragement of workers' and families' efforts to build personal retirement wealth by giving citizens a legal right to a portion of their benefits.
2. Equity of lifetime Social Security taxes and benefits, both between and within generations.
3. Adequacy of protection against income loss due to retirement, disability, death of an earner, or unexpected longevity.

4. Encouragement of increased personal and national saving.
5. Rewarding individuals for actively participating in the workforce.
6. Movement of the Social Security system toward a fiscally sustainable course that reduces pressure on the remainder of the federal budget and can withstand economic and demographic changes.
7. Practicality and suitability to successful implementation at reasonable cost.
8. Transparency: Analysis of reform plans should measure all necessary sources of tax revenue, and all benefits provided, including those from the traditional system as well as from personal accounts.[6]

Taken together, these criteria provide a basis for formulating and assessing proposals to reform Social Security.

The policy reasons for reform are fundamentally demographic. Because Social Security is a pay-as-you-go system in which taxes paid by today's workers are used to pay benefits for today's beneficiaries, the relative sizes of the working and retired populations are crucial to determining the tax rates or benefit levels the system must apply.

To illustrate these basic but important relationships, the commission's interim report contained a one-page section titled "Basic Social Security Math." Although the trustees' long-term projections encompass myriad economic factors such as wage growth, interest rates, and changes in hours of work and general workforce participation, the basic math of pay-as-you-go Social Security financing is driven almost entirely by demographics.

Consider the equation presented by the commissioners:

$$\frac{Average\ benefits\ as\ percentage\ of\ average\ taxable\ wage}{Worker\text{-}to\text{-}beneficiary\ ratio}$$

$$= Program\ cost\ as\ percentage\ of\ average\ wage$$

Because today's Social Security benefit averages 36 percent of the average worker's wage, and because there are currently 3.4 workers per beneficiary, the payroll tax required to support today's beneficiary is around 10.5 percent of a worker's earnings ($36/3.4 = 10.5$).

Figure 1
SOCIAL SECURITY'S COST RISES AS POPULATION AGES

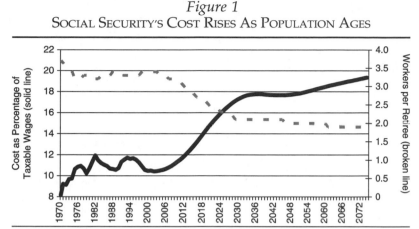

SOURCE: The 2001 Annual Report of the Board of Trustees of the Federal Old-Age and Survivors Insurance and Disability Insurance Trust Fund.

Because today's payroll tax rate is set by law at 12.4 percent of wages, Social Security currently runs a surplus.

Notice how the equation is structured, with one variable that we assume to be exogenous (i.e., whose value is not determined by the other variables): the worker-beneficiary ratio.[7] If the number of workers per retiree falls, then either the average benefit must fall (to maintain a constant tax rate) or the tax rate must increase (to maintain constant benefit levels). Under the current pay-as-you-go financing, these are the constraints policymakers and the public face (see Figure 1).

For instance, if the worker-beneficiary ratio falls from 3.4 to 2, one of two things must happen: The average benefits must fall from 36 percent of the average worker's wage to just 25 percent, or the payroll tax rate must rise to around 18 percent of wages to maintain the 36 percent benefit rate. No amount of kind words about "sacred trusts" can change that unfortunate fact. It is not a matter of political commitment or concern for the elderly, as reform opponents charge. It is a matter of simple mathematics: Under the current system we can pay promised benefits or we can maintain current tax rates, but we cannot do both. No amount of kind words justifies promising benefits without specifying how those benefits are to be paid.

Table 1
TAX AND BENEFIT BASELINES MUST MATCH

Benefits			Taxes	
Promised	100 percent of currently scheduled benefits	⟷	Pay-as-you-go[a]	18.3 percent
Payable	72 percent of currently scheduled benefits[b]	⟷	Current law	12.4 percent

SOURCE: 2001 Trustees Report, "Estimated Income Rates and Cost Rates, Calendar Years 2001–2075," Table IV.B1.

[a] Average of years 2038–2075, ranging from 17.8 to 19.4 percent of taxable payroll.
[b] Average of years 2038–2075, ranging from 74 to 69 percent of scheduled benefits.

Tax and Benefit Baselines: Not Mix and Match

The above discussion shows that the current 12.4 percent payroll tax rate is mathematically incompatible with currently legislated benefit levels under today's pay-as-you-go financing. One or the other—or both—must change.

In comparing benefits paid under the commission's (or any other) reform plans with the current program's, it is very important to recognize the distinction between "promised" and "payable" benefits. Promised benefits are exactly that: what Social Security's benefit formula *promises* a worker with a given wage history. Social Security's payable benefit, by contrast, is what the underfunded system will in fact pay under current law. As Table 1 shows, the promised and payable benefit baselines must be matched with the appropriate tax baselines, which have been termed pay-as-you-go and current law. Pay-as-you-go is the rate required to pay promised benefits, while current law is the 12.4 percent rate currently in effect.

These tax and benefit baselines are not like a menu from which you may choose one baseline from the tax column and another from the benefit column. Each benefit baseline has only one appropriate tax baseline.

Opponents of personal accounts often violate this rule. Critics cite Social Security's promised benefits when making comparisons with reform proposals, which is perfectly acceptable as long as they produce a plan that can actually pay that promised level of benefits. Unfortunately, most reform opponents don't have such a plan and, when challenged by the President's Commission to produce one, failed. Again, account opponents are not required to have a reform plan as long as they're satisfied to cite only Social Security's payable level of benefits.

If the reform debate is simply going to be an exercise in promising benefits without paying for them, why not promise everyone 10 times the benefits without any question of where the money will come from? Consistency of baselines is probably the single most important thing to remember to avoid being deceived in the Social Security debate. Without a reform plan, promised benefits are just a pipe dream.

A related issue involves clarifying what "current law" benefit levels truly are. Many commentators use the phrase current law to denote promised benefits. Under the Social Security Act, taxes trump benefits. As the Concord Coalition puts it:

> All of the long-term spending projections for Social Security—by the Congressional Budget Office, the GAO, and the Social Security Administration itself—assume that current-law benefits will be paid in full, even after the trust funds are empty. This cannot happen. If Social Security is simply left on autopilot, the law leaves no doubt that the contradiction will be resolved the other way around—with massive benefit cuts. Making this fact more widely known would have two salutary consequences. In general, it would cause the public to take a more active interest in reform. And in particular, it would allow a fairer comparison of reform proposals with current law. As things stand, reformers face the hopeless task of trying to out-promise a system that is unsustainable.[8]

The Social Security Administration is authorized to issue benefit checks only when sufficient funds exist in the trust fund. Because these funds are ultimately derived from legislated payroll tax rates, under current law, when the fund becomes insolvent in 2042, taxes will remain constant while benefits for all Social Security beneficiaries (not simply new retirees) will be reduced to the level payable by payroll tax receipts.[9]

The current Social Security system's finances are driven almost entirely by tax rates, benefit levels, and the ratio of workers to retirees. Other factors, including economic growth and interest rates, play relatively minor roles. The problem is that currently legislated tax rates, when combined with the projected worker-retiree ratios, simply cannot equal the benefit levels promised under current law.

The Interim Report and the Trust Fund

Although much of the interim report's discussion was unremarkable, two issues in particular attracted attention—most of it unfavorable. The first was the commissioners' claim that the Social Security trust fund has not been effective in prefunding the program for the future. The fund, the commission argued, is an asset to Social Security but an equal and opposite liability to the rest of the federal government. From the point of view of the taxpayer, it changes very little.

Commissioners and staff knew that the interim report would ruffle a few feathers. Nevertheless, there was genuine surprise at the reaction to the report's argument that the Social Security trust fund has not effectively prefunded the system for the future.

Upon release of the report, the commission's view of the trust fund came under immediate attack in a paper written by Henry Aaron, Alan Blinder, Alicia Munnell, and Peter Orszag and issued by the Century Foundation and the Center on Budget and Policy Priorities:

> The commission asserts that the Social Security Trust Fund does not hold real assets. The Social Security Trust Fund, however, currently holds more than $1 trillion in Treasury securities. These assets are backed by the full faith and credit of the U.S. Government, the benchmark of security in global financial markets.[10]

Similar statements came from Rep. Bob Matsui (D-Calif.), who said, "This report falsely asserts that the Social Security system will be unable to meet its obligations because the assets held by the Trust Fund are 'not real.' To the contrary . . . because U.S. Treasury Bonds are the benchmark for security in global financial markets and to

210

assert otherwise is to suggest that the U.S. Government will no longer honor its debt obligations."[11] For these and other assertions, Matsui said, the commission should have been disbanded.

Congressional Democrats such as House Minority Leader Richard Gephardt (D-Mo.) echoed these remarks. Gephardt claimed:

> The president's commission has published a misleading, mis-guided report that is one of the most skewed documents that I have seen in many, many years. . . . The assertion that Social Security is going bust in [2018] flies in the face of all reality. The facts are Social Security has enough reserves in the trust fund to last until at least [2042].[12]

As discussed below, the foregoing statements do not accurately reflect the arguments made by the commission. Moreover, the commission's arguments were in the past supported by the very critics who attacked them.

Given this controversy, it is worth outlining what the commission's interim report did and did *not* say about the trust fund.

- The commission did *not* say the trust fund's trillion dollars in government bonds are not "real," nor that they are not assets of the Social Security system.
- Moreover, the commission did not say that the government would default on the trust fund's bonds, despite what some commentators have repeatedly charged.[13] On the contrary, on p. 18 of the interim report the commissioners specifically declared that "the bonds in the Social Security Trust Fund will be honored." Nothing could be clearer than that, and the commission's own reform proposals bore out that pledge.

What the commission said about the trust fund is subtler than the caricature presented by reform opponents, and in retrospect the interim report could have been clearer and more comprehensive in its presentation. Whether this would have quieted the opposition is debatable, but it would at least have reduced misunderstandings among the public.

First, the commission pointed out that although the trust fund's bonds are an asset to Social Security, they are an equal and opposite debt to the rest of the government. This is not a matter of economics, but merely of accounting: an asset to Social Security must be a debt to someone, and that someone is the federal Treasury and, by extension, the taxpayer. The interim report illustrated this point with a number of quotations from the Clinton administration and such nonpartisan sources as the Congressional Budget Office, the Congressional Research Service, and, here, the General Accounting Office:

> [Social Security] Trust Funds are not like private Trust Funds. They are simply budget accounts used to record receipts and expenditures earmarked for specific purposes. A private Trust Fund can set aside money for the future by increasing its assets. However, under current law, when the Trust Funds' receipts exceed costs, they are invested in Treasury securities and used to meet current cash needs of the government. These securities are an asset to the Trust Fund, but they are a claim on the Treasury. Any increase in assets to the Trust Funds is an equal increase in claims on the Treasury.[14]

Hence, the trust fund is indisputably not a *net* financial asset with which the government can pay Social Security benefits. That is, the fund's bonds do not put off the need for tax increases or spending cuts by a day or a dollar, because precisely the same steps must be taken to repay trust fund bonds as would be needed to pay full benefits directly via tax increases or spending cuts. After all, without a trust fund, beginning in 2018 we would have to raise taxes, borrow, or cut other spending to pay full Social Security benefits. With a trust fund, beginning in 2018 we must raise taxes, borrow, or cut other spending to repay the trust fund bonds that will pay full Social Security benefits. In terms of timing and cost, from the perspective of the overall budget—and the taxpayer—there is no substantive difference between having a trust fund and not having a trust fund.

A second point, however, is more important. The accounting identity pointed out by the commission—assets to Social Security equal debts to the government—does not mean that the trust fund did not or could not effectively prefund future benefits at the economic level. There was an economic argument in the interim report that is more important than the accounting point of view, and it addresses not what happens when trust fund bonds are redeemed in 2018 but what actually happened in the period from 1985 to today when those bonds were amassed.

In essence, the commission argued that the Social Security payroll tax surpluses seen since the mid-1980s were never "saved" in a

212

true economic sense. Although the trust fund was "credited" with government bonds equal in size to these cash surpluses, thereby saving them in a financial or accounting sense, the cash itself was not used to reduce government borrowing or repay existing government debt. Rather than increase government saving, these payroll tax surpluses tempted Congress to either spend more or tax less than it otherwise would have. In this case, though the trust fund was still credited with bonds, paying future Social Security benefits would still require raising future taxes. Future workers would suffer a net loss as taxes rose to repay the trust fund's bonds.

The commission's critics rejected this view as well. The authors of the Century Foundation paper, for instance, stated:

> The commission asserts that in the future, "the nation will face the same difficult choices as if there had been no Trust Fund at all." This assertion ignores the real economic contribution of the Trust Fund. The accumulation of Trust Fund reserves raises national saving, reduces the public debt and thereby reduces the annual cost of paying interest on that debt, and promotes economic growth.[15]

Along the same lines, Munnell and Weaver argue that trust fund surpluses have made unequivocal additions to national saving: "The excess payroll taxes that have been used to build up reserves in the Trust Funds have increased national saving and in recent years have helped pay down the debt. In this way, the very real sacrifice of today's workers has boosted investment and enhanced our capacity to pay future benefits."[16] How this process is thought to have worked merits some explanation.

According to this view, past payroll tax surpluses reduced government borrowing and, in several years, allowed existing government debt to be repaid. In doing so, they increased national saving, which in turn increased the amount of capital per worker, thereby increasing productivity. Because productivity lies at the root of wages, these too would increase. By the time Social Security needed to tap the trust fund, wages and national income in general would have risen by an amount greater than the tax increases needed to repay the trust fund's bonds. Hence, the trust fund could be repaid without making future workers worse off than they would have been had the entire enterprise never taken place.

In a 1989 study, Aaron, Bosworth, and Burtless conclude that trust fund financing could, in theory, succeed through precisely this mechanism:

> If national saving and domestic investment are increased by the additions to Social Security reserves, wages will rise about 7 percent more than trend growth. That increase would pay for the added pension costs generated by the rising propor- tion of beneficiaries in the total population. Workers active during the twenty-first century would actually enjoy a higher standard of living than in a world where the proportion of pensioners did not increase. *The central question is whether Social Security surpluses will be used to add to national saving or to finance current consumption.*[17]

Indeed that is the central question, as the commission stated directly in its interim report.

In the Century Foundation paper, however, the authors—Aaron included—overlook this central question and treat Social Security's impact on national saving as a fairly cut-and-dried affair in which, as a matter of accounting, Social Security surpluses raise saving on a dollar-for-dollar basis:

> If the non–Social Security portion of the budget had a deficit of $300 billion in a given year, and Social Security ran a $100 billion surplus, the net deficit would be $100 billion smaller— and national saving $100 billion higher—than otherwise. The only way in which Social Security surpluses would fail to increase government saving is if Congress decided to increase spending or reduce taxes in the non–Social Security part of the budget because of the surplus in Social Security.[18]

Of course, it is this last option that the commission considered to be most consistent with the historical evidence.[19] As shown below, in their more academic work the commission's critics acknowledge the very same issues the commission noted. And, by and large, these critics' own work lends support to the commission's position.

The Century Foundation authors are, of course, correct that, all other things being equal, a dollar of Social Security surpluses equals a dollar of extra saving. But, as many argued from early in the post-1983 period, all things aren't equal: rather than save surplus Social Security funds, the government could use them to hide the size of the deficit in non–Social Security federal spending. For instance, in 1995 President Clinton acknowledged,

> We clearly have been using payroll taxes for 12 years now, long before I ever came here, to minimize the size of the deficit exclusive of the payroll tax, so that from 1983 forward, previous Democratic congresses and Republican presidents made judgments that it was better and politically more palatable to tax payroll than income, even though it's a burden on working people and small businesses.[20]

Similarly, North Dakota senators Kent Conrad and Byron Dorgan wrote in 1995 that the payroll tax "is dedicated solely for working Americans' future retirement, it shouldn't be used either for balancing the operating budget or masking the size of the budget deficit." If it is used for those purposes, they warned, when needed "the retirement fund would have nothing but IOUs in it."[21] That is to say, if payroll tax surpluses are devoted to consumption rather than saving, then the overall burden on future workers is not reduced and the overall capacity of the economy to support Social Security payments is not enhanced.

Unfortunately, that is exactly what took place. In a 1989 report to Congress, the General Accounting Office stated:

> The changes to Social Security enacted in 1983 are not producing the result of lessening the burden of paying for the retirement benefits of the baby boom generation. The budgetary reality is that the payroll taxes are being used to finance the current operations of government and are masking the size of the on-budget deficit. *The economic reality is that the Trust Fund reserves consisting of Treasury securities that are financing current consumption rather than productive investment are illusory.* They will remain so until the rest of the government achieves approximate balance between revenues and outlays.[22]

For the record, it was only in 1999–2000 that on-budget government finances reached surplus. In 1990 testimony to Congress, the GAO's head, Comptroller General Charles A. Bowsher, said, "The luxury of these reserves has provided a convenient excuse for avoiding the tough choices needed to cut the general fund deficit."[23]

In other words, the GAO found that the on-budget balance was not independent of the Social Security balance; larger surpluses in Social Security facilitated larger deficits elsewhere. In that case, Bowsher said, "The growing Social Security surpluses are serving more as a substitute for other deficit reduction action than as a net addition to national savings. . . . If we do not use the accumulating Social Security reserves to increase our national savings rate, we will be in no better position to meet our obligations to future retirees than we would be if we had remained under pay-as-you-go financing."[24]

Lawrence H. Thompson, the GAO's assistant comptroller general, put it most plainly: "We shouldn't kid the American people into thinking extra savings is going on."[25]

The Commission's Opponents Share Its View of the Trust Fund

Although the commission's view of the trust fund clearly has support among politicians of both parties and from the nonpartisan General Accounting Office, it is ironic that perhaps the strongest support for its view comes from the very analysts who so severely criticized the commission's interim report.

As pointed out above, it is possible—indeed plausible—that payroll tax surpluses would tempt Congress to spend more or tax less than it otherwise would. Doing so would not change Social Security's finances on paper, but would greatly alter the economic realities of paying future benefits. In the early 1980s, soon after the decision to "prefund" Social Security via trust fund surpluses was made, Munnell feared this could be the outcome:

> If the payroll taxes earmarked to pay future retirement and disability benefits are used to cover current outlays from the general fund, then the government debt held by the Trust Funds will be no more than paper claims. When the baby boom generation retires after the turn of the century, the Trust Funds will redeem their claims on the Treasury in order to pay promised benefits. The Treasury, however, will not have accumulated resources to meet its obligations but rather will be forced to raise taxes at that time to pay off its debts. Thus, the full burden of supporting the beneficiaries will come from the future taxpayers—just as if the system had been financed on a pay-as-you-go basis all along.[26]

This is precisely the fear expressed by the commission.

216

It is, of course, difficult to know what the level of non–Social Security federal spending and taxation would have been had there been no payroll tax surpluses.[27] Nevertheless, the surprising fact was that most of those arguing against the commission's portrayal of the trust fund had in the past actually agreed with it—at least until the commission's argument was used to buttress the case for personal accounts.

For instance, while Congressman Matsui attacked the commission's depiction of the trust fund, in the past he had clearly embraced both the commission's reasoning and its conclusions. In a 1990 op-ed co-authored with Sen. Bob Graham (D-Fla.), Matsui's rhetorical attack against the fund went beyond anything stated in the interim report:

> Trust Fund reserves are growing at the pace of a billion dollars a week. But these billions won't be available to the next generations of America's retirees. As quickly as the surpluses amass, they are being siphoned off to help finance the deficit. Bluntly put, the federal government is spending more than $1 billion a week of the Social Security surplus as though it were general revenues. All that the Trust Fund gets for these expenditures are chits from the U.S. Treasury.... If those monies are really to be there, if when we retire we are going to be left with anything more than a vault full of Treasury Department IOUs, integrity must be restored to the use of the Trust Fund surpluses.[28]

To prevent further government spending of Social Security surpluses, Matsui and Graham proposed investing those funds in nonfederal municipal bonds, though the lower rates of return on those bonds relative to the fund's current holdings would require ongoing general revenue subsidies to make up the losses. In other words, Matsui and Graham apparently believed so strongly that Social Security surpluses were being spent rather than saved that they proposed a plan that was, in financial terms, a money-loser simply to get those surpluses out of the hands of the federal government.

This aspect of Matsui's proposal is particularly interesting given Matsui's charge that a fault of reform is "plans to allow people to direct part of their payroll taxes into individual accounts make Social Security's financing problem worse, not better"[29] and "privatization proposals would only make Social Security's challenges harder to solve."[30] Of course, Social Security's actuaries state, "If the personal accounts are considered as part of 'Social Security,' it is reasonable to combine the amounts of Trust Fund assets and personal accounts for a representation of total system assets."[31] By this standard, as detailed below, the commission's three reform proposals make an immeasurable improvement over current law.

Moreover, as recently as the summer of 2000, Matsui warned his constituents, "When the Baby Boomers begin to retire in the next 10 years, Social Security will begin to pay out more in benefits than it receives in revenue,"[32] apparently giving credence to the deficit date stressed in the interim report.

A similar warning was sounded by the co-authors of the Century Foundation paper. In 1988, for instance, Henry Aaron took a very skeptical view of the trust fund:

> The economic justification for additions to Social Security reserves is that such surpluses increase national saving, add to the U.S. capital stock, and boost productive capacity in anticipation of the extra costs a growing population of retirees will generate. *Current budget policy overwhelms this sound policy. Instead of adding to U.S. national saving, current fiscal policy simply diverts a part of payroll taxes to pay for ordinary operations of government.*[33]

It's worth pointing out that the budget policy Aaron was decrying in 1988 is the same budget policy that, with brief exceptions, has held every year since 1985.

Moreover, in 1988, Aaron, Bosworth, and Burtless clearly rejected the idea that it was being effectively carried out:

> If OASDHI [Old Age, Survivors, Disability and Hospital Insurance] revenues exceed annual expenditures, the resulting surpluses may be used to pay for current public or private consumption (either through increases in non-OASDHI government expenditures or through reductions in non-OASDHI taxes). As the OASDHI surpluses increase, so would deficits elsewhere in the federal budget. *Although this policy may seem peculiar, it closely resembles the course on which the United States is embarked today. Under this policy, the reserve does not add to national saving (because it does not reduce the overall government budget deficit) and, hence, it does not add to future productive capacity.* In effect, the OASDHI surpluses are borrowed to pay for current government services, replacing

income tax revenues or cuts in other government programs sufficient to balance the non-OASDHI budget.

Although such a policy might hold down future payroll tax rates, it cannot protect future taxpayers from shouldering the expense of rising benefit costs. When and if the Trust Funds are drawn down to pay for future benefits, other federal taxes will have to be increased to finance the repurchase of government debt previously bought by the OASDHI Trust Funds. In addition, the incomes against which those taxes are imposed will be no larger than if the reserves never existed. Since future benefits must be paid out of future production, the burden on future taxpayers would not be reduced.

The authors concluded:

> The growing surpluses in the Social Security system camouflage a major deterioration in the budget balance for non-OASDHI operations ... In effect, the current policy is to borrow the OASDHI surplus to finance a deficit in the rest of the budget. As a result the payroll tax, ostensibly earmarked for retirement, survivors, disability, and hospital insurance, is being used increasingly to pay for other government expenditures, such as defense and interest on the public debt.[34]

Aaron has not, to the author's knowledge, explained whether or why he changed his view. It is arguable that trust fund surpluses were at least partially saved during the years of on-budget surpluses in 1999–2000, yet Aaron appears to have changed his mind about what took place *before* those years as well, without providing evidence as to why.

Alicia Munnell expressed similar skepticism toward trust fund financing in the 1980s on the basis of evidence from other countries that attempted trust fund financing and the factors that influenced their success or failure. Three factors that reduce the prospects for successful trust fund financing:

- Whether the pension fund's surpluses are considered part of a unified budget.
- Whether the fund can invest in private securities or is a "captive market" of the Treasury.
- Whether the government fluctuated political control from party to party.

As Munnell noted, all of these criteria apply to the United States:

> One factor in this regard is probably whether the Social Security programs are included in some type of unified budget or are accounted for separately. If Trust Fund activity is integrated with other federal functions and the total reported as a single figure, as has been true in the United States since 1969, Congress and the public would be encouraged to think that the Trust Fund reserves are available to cover general government outlays.
>
> Another closely related factor is the ease with which the Treasury can borrow from the Trust Funds. This depends on the extent to which the administration and the finances of the Social Security Trust Funds and the rest of the government are intertwined.

In addition, Munnell argued, the use of a "unified budget" concept in the United States tends to blend Social Security and non–Social Security funds in the eyes of lawmakers:

> In the United States the finances of the Social Security Trust Funds and the rest of the budget are closely intermingled. The Treasury Department, rather than the Social Security Administration, collects the earmarked payroll taxes and deposits them in a general account with other revenues it receives. The Trust Funds are then issued with special federal securities in a compensating amount. While the balances of the securities reflect the resources available to the Social Security programs, they more closely resemble spending limitations than control over resources. One would expect less use of Trust Fund revenues for general government expenditures in situations where the Trust Funds are more than a bookkeeping activity on the part of the Treasury Department.

Munnell goes on to point out:

> The likelihood of the members of Congress responding to the Social Security surpluses in this manner probably depends largely on their ability to count the surpluses toward overall budget deficit reduction. All three countries studied keep their Social Security accounts very separate from the rest of the budget, and this appears to have discouraged the legislatures from incorporating Social Security surpluses in their general budget decisions or their deficit reduction efforts. As long as the United States retains a unified budget

and frames its deficit targets in these terms, Congress will be tempted to keep one eye on the surpluses when voting on tax and expenditure proposals.

A somewhat discouraging result, for those committed to increasing national saving through accumulating reserves in the Social Security Trust Funds, is that the greatest success has occurred in countries with stable and disciplined political environments, where one party has been in power almost continuously since the experiment began.[35]

For these reasons, soon after the 1983 reforms Munnell argued against running Social Security surpluses at all.

With her co-author Lynn Blais, now of the University of Texas School of Law, Munnell elaborated:

> The assumption that an increase in Trust Fund reserves will represent a net increment to national saving may not be valid. Instead, surpluses in the Social Security Trust Funds may very likely be offset by deficits in the rest of the budget, so that they are, in effect, used to finance general government expenditures. Indeed, the pattern shown in Table 2 [showing Social Security and general budget balance from 1946 to 1983] indicates that this may have been the case in the past. Of course, these figures are far from conclusive because it is difficult to determine what the balance would have been in the federal budget without the surpluses in the Social Security Trust Funds. *Nevertheless, our best guess is that the scheduled buildup of assets in the Social Security Trust Funds over the next 35 years would be used to offset deficits elsewhere in the federal budget and thus would contribute little to overall saving and capital accumulation.*
>
> In this country it appears it would be difficult as a practical matter to stockpile real resources in anticipation of future benefit payments. It is more likely that Congress would divert surpluses in the Trust Fund to offset deficits in other parts of the federal budget.

Munnell and Blais concluded at the time that it would be preferable to abandon efforts to prefund Social Security through the trust fund financing mechanism:

> In view of the improbability that Social Security surpluses will increase national saving and the possibility that, if increased saving did materialize, it would have adverse fiscal

> implications or disrupt financial markets, the authors con-
> clude that it would be preferable to return the Social Security
> system to pay-as-you-go financing with a substantial contin-
> gency reserve.[36]

Incidentally, Senator Moynihan took the same view when, in 1989–90, he argued that if Social Security surpluses were not truly being saved, the system's finances should return to a pay-as-you-go basis. "We cannot continue to use regressive payroll taxes to finance general government expenses. This is not acceptable," he said.[37]

Alan Blinder of Princeton University has written less on Social Security trust fund surpluses and national saving than Aaron or Munnell. Nevertheless, in a 1990 commentary on a paper by Nobel laureate James Buchanan in which Buchanan argues that "a small dose of public choice theory might have dampened the enthusiasm of those who sought to ensure the integrity of the system" by running Social Security surpluses within the context of the overall budget,[38] Blinder stated his agreement with Buchanan on this point: "Buchanan asserts that the Social Security surpluses of the next thirty years or so will make the government prone to do more non–Social Security spending than it otherwise would have done. As I have already made clear, I suspect he is right."[39]

Peter Orszag of the Brookings Institution, another author of the Century Foundation paper, has also written less in the past on the impact of trust fund accumulations on national saving. Nevertheless, in recent congressional testimony Orszag implicitly acknowledges that past surpluses may not have contributed to national saving in the dollar-for-dollar manner outlined in the Center on Budget and Policy Priorities paper. Orszag argues, in much the same way as the commission, that it is important to

> distinguish between "narrow" and "broad" prefunding. In
> its narrow sense, prefunding means that the pension system
> is accumulating assets against future projected payments.
> In a broader sense, however, prefunding means increasing
> national saving. The broader definition of prefunding—
> higher national saving—should be our ultimate objective.
> But we can sometimes be led astray, because prefunding in
> the narrow sense need not imply prefunding in the broader
> sense (i.e., higher national saving).[40]

Orszag points out, correctly, that both trust fund and personal account financing could create narrow, but not broad, prefunding if extra saving through the pension system were offset by lack of saving elsewhere. Individuals could reduce contributions to non–Social Security investment accounts or the government could increase spending or lower taxes elsewhere in the budget. This is precisely the distinction made in the commission's interim report: although Social Security surpluses have clearly funded the system in a narrow sense, in the broader sense of raising national saving, they have fallen short.

Orszag follows the above passage with the statement that "the emerging political consensus not to spend the Social Security and Medicare surpluses is *precisely what ensures that the narrow prefunding in the Trust Funds also corresponds to higher national saving* (i.e., broad prefunding)."[41]

But if a lock box is needed to ensure that Social Security surpluses translate into increased national saving, then we can assume that when the lock box budget mechanism was absent—from 1983 through 1999—increased saving is less likely to have occurred. Viewed another way, if Social Security surpluses were saved as a matter of course, as Orszag and the other authors of the CBPP paper maintain, any lock box would be redundant. Orszag's comments appear to acknowledge this. Moreover, although lock-boxing future Social Security surpluses may raise national saving, it cannot change the fact that past surpluses were not treated in this way.

Other congressional leaders held similar views of the efficacy of the trust fund. In 1989 Rep. Richard Gephardt (D-Mo.) argued that the government "should stop borrowing on workers' retirement benefits. People should be secure in the knowledge that the system will be able to send out their monthly Social Security checks. If the practice of borrowing against Social Security monies continues, that security is threatened."[42] In 1990, Gephardt said, "What Democrats want to do is we want to stop the stealing of [trust] funds to mask the deficit." According to the article, Gephardt said, "The government would have to pay interest on the borrowed money. To pay back Social Security by 2015 or 2018, taxes would have to increase."[43] That is precisely the point the commission's interim report made. It should now be clear that most of the commission's most prominent critics agreed with it.

As an aside, many commentators who have criticized the tax cuts passed by Congress in 2001 as weakening Social Security simultaneously take the view that Social Security's trust fund is "real" regardless of whether accompanying payroll tax surpluses are spent or saved. But the bookkeeping balance of Social Security's trust fund is unaffected by the balance of the non–Social Security budget; whether the tax cut was passed or not, Social Security would be credited with the same amount of bonds. Critics are free to argue that funds sent back to the public in last year's tax cut could have been better used by saving them for Social Security.[44] If that is the case, though, those critics must also accept the commission's logic that the "raids" on the trust fund that took place practically every year from 1985 to the present must have weakened Social Security far more because these prior "raids" were used to finance additional government spending. There is at least a theoretical argument that the recent tax cuts will stimulate long-term economic growth. In their responses to the commission's interim report, account opponents failed to reconcile their short-term arguments against tax cuts with their longer-term defense of the current trust fund financing structure.

Now, one might ask, "Why do these arguments about the trust fund even matter?" In one sense, they don't: the assets we have are the assets we have, and nothing we do today can change the past. This was the point of the commission's accounting argument: as benefit costs begin to rise, there is no separate store of wealth with which to pay them. Looking forward, though, the trust fund issue is extremely important. If we conclude that trust fund financing doesn't truly reduce burdens on future taxpayers, we have only three other options:

- Return to pay-as-you-go financing.
- Have the government invest the trust fund in private assets.
- Invest individually through personal accounts.

Few wish to return to pay-as-you-go financing, which entails a 50 percent increase in payroll tax rates to meet current benefit promises. And, politically speaking, a battle between government investment and personal accounts would be a rout. The economics may be the same, but the politics are worlds apart: the public simply doesn't trust the government to invest in private corporations, and even after two years of weak market performances public support for personal accounts remains strong.[45]

What made the trust fund controversy surprising was that the very people who most prominently disagreed with the commission's view last summer had prominently agreed with it before—before, that is, it was used to support the case for personal accounts.

Progressivity

The second point of controversy in the interim report was the commission's contention that the current Social Security system isn't nearly as progressive as many of its proponents claim. If Social Security's progressivity is called into doubt, the transition to personal accounts—which are often designed with less explicit regard to progressivity—would not significantly alter the distribution of costs and benefits to the system as a whole.

This idea, like the commission's views on the trust fund, came under attack. For instance, Peter Coy of *Business Week* wrote:

> Today's Social Security is progressive—that is, it transfers money from rich to poor in large part because of the benefits formula. The higher your average lifetime income, the less of it is replaced by your benefit check in retirement. That Robin Hood formula largely offsets the fact that low-income people tend to collect fewer checks because they die younger.

"Privatizing Social Security may have some merits," Coy said, "but the argument that it would benefit the poor is deeply flawed."[46]

In fact, the academic research that Coy relied on in his critique of private accounts shows clearly how little Social Security's so-called Robin Hood benefit formula actually takes from the rich and gives to the poor. Social Security's complex benefit formula does a great deal of redistribution on the basis of longevity, marital status, and the relative wages of spouses, but very little on the basis of income. Personal account reform proposals—even proposals with no redistributive intent—would leave system progressivity largely unchanged. In fact, the commission's personal account plans are consciously progressive, and enhance benefits for low-wage workers, as discussed later.

Research on redistribution in Social Security is complex and ongoing, and ranges from the construction of models of representative workers to the statistical analysis of large numbers of actual earnings

Figure 2
SOCIAL SECURITY REDISTRIBUTION IS ONE-FIFTH OF WHAT BASIC
BENEFIT FORMULA IMPLIES

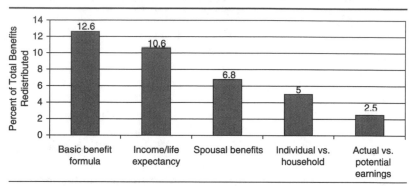

SOURCE: Alan Gustman and Thomas Steinmeier, "How Effective Is Redistribution under the Social Security Benefit Formula?" *Journal of Public Economics* 82, no. 1 (October 2001): 1–28.

records. The following summary relies on a recent study by Alan Gustman of Dartmouth College and Thomas Steinmeier of Texas Tech, who used Social Security earnings records contained in the National Institute on Aging's Health and Retirement Study to disaggregate the various factors influencing Social Security's overall progressivity.[47] Although details differ among researchers, the Gustman and Steinmeier article is representative of the general direction in which academic research on Social Security's progressivity is flowing. Some other research finds even less progressivity in the current program.[48] Nevertheless, the Gustman and Steinmeier article is reasonably representative of current research.

On its face, Social Security is highly redistributive because its progressive benefit formula replaces a substantially higher portion of a low-income worker's preretirement earnings than of that a high-income worker. On the basis of the benefit formula alone, Gustman and Steinmeier find that Social Security should redistribute 12.6 percent of total benefits from higher- to lower-income workers (see Figure 2). This would be sufficient to substantially increase the benefits for low-wage retirees.

But Gustman and Steinmeier find four major factors that substantially reduce Social Security's true progressivity. First, the correlation between income and life expectancy means that, while low-income retirees may receive relatively higher monthly benefits, total lifetime benefits are not nearly so progressive. Once differential mortality is factored into the equation, net progressivity is reduced by 16 percent, leaving 10.6 percent of total benefits redistributed.

The influence of differential mortality on Social Security's progressivity could increase in the future. Although life expectancies for all Americans are increasing, there is evidence that they are increasing more slowly for individuals with lower wages and educations. If that is the case, Social Security could become even less progressive in this regard.[49]

A second factor is that Social Security pays spousal benefits. The spouses of high earners on average live longer and receive higher benefits than the spouses of lower-wage earners, which reduces progressivity by another 30 percent. This leaves 6.8 percent of total benefits redistributed.

Although Gustman and Steinmeier make no projections regarding the future, this issue could be complicated in coming years. On the one hand, as more women have entered the workforce and gained benefit eligibility on the basis of their own earnings, the spousal benefit may play a smaller role in the future than it does today. On the other hand, the spousal benefit could increase disparities in benefits between individuals of different races, as the "marriage gap" between blacks and whites has widened in recent decades. In 1960, some 67 percent of white females aged 15 and over were married, versus 57 percent of black females. In 1998, however, although the percentage of white married females had dropped to 58 percent, for black females it had fallen to 36 percent, making most black females ineligible for spousal benefits at retirement.[50]

A third factor that reduces Social Security's progressivity is that much of the program's apparent redistribution is from the richer to the poorer spouse *living in the same household,* rather than from an upper-income household to a lower-income household. In other words, when benefits are redistributed from husband to wife, there is no effect on household progressivity. Because spouses share income and expenses, the household is the more relevant standard for public policy purposes. From that perspective, Social Security's progressivity is reduced another 14 percent, leaving 5 percent of total benefits redistributed.

Finally, although many individuals with low lifetime incomes have worked full careers at low wages, many others are *high*-income workers who took time out of the workforce.[51] In fact, Gustman and Steinmeier found that most of the individuals with the lowest lifetime earnings were women with total household incomes far above what could be expected on the basis of their own earnings. That is to say, having a high-income spouse enabled some of these women to have lower incomes themselves. Adjusted for potential lifetime earnings—earnings if individuals worked a full career— Social Security's total progressivity is reduced by another 20 percent, so that just 2.5 percent of total benefits are redistributed.

To sum up, Social Security's true progressivity is just one-fifth of what it seems to be on the surface. For that reason, Gustman and Steinmeier state:

> It is clear from these results that the general perception that a great deal of redistribution from the rich to the poor is accomplished by the progressive Social Security benefit formula is greatly exaggerated. As a result, adoption of a Social Security scheme with individual accounts designed to be neutral with regard to redistribution would make much less difference to the distribution of Social Security benefits and taxes among families with different earnings capacities than is commonly believed.[52]

In fact, the plans adopted by the commission included personal accounts, but these accounts were not neutral with regard to progressivity and made Social Security a better deal for the poor and for other vulnerable members of society. Although Peter Coy argued that "attempts to insulate the poor from the regressive features of a privatized Social Security system would require so many awkward compromises that it might leave no one happy," the commission's plans enhanced progressivity in ways that would be seamless from the point of view of the individual and the administrators of the program.

Moreover, though Coy acknowledged that aspects of the commission's proposals would at the least maintain system progressivity— such as the progressive funding of the accounts themselves, in Plans 2 and 3—he argued that such provisions might not "survive the budgeters' axe" to be enacted.[53] But this objection can be applied to any reform proposal, as well as to current law, because Congress

Table 2
PERSONAL ACCOUNT PLANS WOULD MAINTAIN OR ENHANCE SYSTEM PROGRESSIVITY

	Current Law	Plan 1	Plan 2	Plan 3
Benefit to low-wage retiree	$767	$770	$868	$823
Benefit to high-wage retiree	$1,673	$1,684	$1,556	$1,646
Low as a percentage of high	46%	46%	56%	50%

SOURCE: Derived from Stephen C. Goss and Alice H. Wade, "Estimates of Financial Effects for Three Models Developed by the President's Commission to Strengthen Social Security," Memorandum dated January 31, 2002, pp. 74–76. Based on workers retiring in 2022 and holding the default investment portfolio.

changes laws as it wills. Coy's is simply not an intellectually respectable objection to the commission's progressive reform plans, which were designed from the bottom up with progressivity in mind. The commission's plans without their provisions to enhance retirement security and wealth building for the least advantaged Americans are simply not the commission's plans; to pretend otherwise is to caricature the commission's proposals.

In addition, Coy argued, "It's not clear, however, that those offsets alone, even if they survived the budgeters' axe, would leave Social Security as progressive as it is today." Although comprehensive measures of progressivity are complex, an easy shorthand measure is simply to compare benefits received by low-wage retirees with those received by high-wage retirees.

As Table 2 shows, under current law, a low-wage retiree in 2022 would receive benefits equal to 46 percent of those received by a high-wage retiree.[54] Under Plan 1, the current 46 percent progressivity ratio would be maintained, while under Plan 2 it would increase substantially to 56 percent, and under Plan 3 to 50 percent. It is worth noting that although Plan 1 would not enhance progressivity per se, benefits would be higher for all recipients.

Some critics argue, of course, that although Social Security's retirement and survivors' programs may not be progressive, its disability program disproportionately benefits the poor, thereby making up the difference. The commission noted in its interim report that the poor and minorities are more likely to receive Social Security's disability payments.[55] But even when disability benefits are counted, a low-income single male still receives a lower return from Social Security than does a high-income, single-earner couple, according to Social Security's actuaries.[56] Moreover, changes to Social Security's retirement program, such as personal accounts, need not reduce the progressivity of the disability program. Although the commission's treatment of disability provisions is discussed at greater length later, under the commission's plans the special provisions for low-wage workers apply to their disability as well as their retirement benefits, so disabled workers would not be disadvantaged relative to higher-wage earners.

The Commission's Reform Plans—Common Characteristics

In its report to the president in December, the commission outlined three reform proposals. Although they all contain personal accounts, beyond that they cover a spectrum of reform options. Nonetheless, the plans have a number of features in common.

Optional Personal Accounts

Under all three models, workers would have the option to invest part of their payroll taxes in a personal retirement account. Note that these personal accounts would be voluntary. No worker would be forced to take an account, and no worker with an account would be forced to invest in the stock market. Workers seeking extra security could invest solely in government or corporate bonds.

For simplicity's sake, Social Security's actuaries estimate personal account benefits under three stylized portfolios:

1. The standard portfolio is assumed to consist of 50 percent stocks (with an annual rate of return of 6.5 percent after inflation); 30 percent corporate bonds (3.5 percent annual return); and 20 percent government bonds (3 percent annual return). Assuming administrative costs of 0.3 percent of assets managed, the net annual return is assumed to be 4.6 percent after inflation.
2. The low-yield portfolio is assumed to hold only government bonds, with a yield, net of administrative costs, of 2.7 percent annually.
3. The high-yield portfolio assumes that 60 percent of the portfolio is invested in equities or, alternately, that the equities held in the default portfolio return the historical average of 7.1 percent after inflation rather than the assumed return of 6.5 percent.

Analysis of the three reform plans produced by Social Security's actuaries assumes that a worker holds a particular portfolio throughout his working lifetime. More realistically, workers would likely adjust their portfolios as they age, beginning with greater stock allocations and moving toward fixed income investments as they near retirement. Most workers aged 60 to 65 hold approximately 40 percent of their 401(k) account portfolios in equities.[57] Asset allocations could be expected to differ somewhat with personal accounts for Social Security, but the trend from equities to fixed income investments over the course of the life cycle should be expected to continue.

Under all three commission plans the personal account would be the property of the worker: The government could not "raid" it to pay for other programs, and it could be passed on to the worker's heirs in case of premature death. The ownership aspect of personal accounts is of particular benefit to African-American males, one-third of whom do not survive to age 65.

Common Administrative Structure

All three plans would use a centralized and simplified administrative structure similar to that of the federal Thrift Savings Plan, which would keep administrative costs to just 0.3 percent of assets managed while simplifying account management for first-time investors. Account holders would choose from a range of simplified index funds; no individual stocks or sector funds (such as the NASDAQ) could be chosen, which would ensure adequate diversification for long-term investment purposes.

Cost-of-Living Adjustments Maintained

All three proposals would maintain annual adjustments to traditional benefits to maintain purchasing power in the face of inflation. In addition, the actuaries' analysis assumes that, at retirement, workers would convert their entire accounts into fixed or variable annuities, though the commission made no formal recommendation that workers be required to do so.[58] Benefit numbers cited herein assume conversion to a fixed annuity that pays constant benefits for life, adjusted annually for inflation. Workers who chose variable annuities would receive benefits 4 to 9 percent higher than those with fixed annuities, assuming that the annuities are invested in the default portfolio of 50 percent stocks, 50 percent bonds.[59]

Offset Interest Rate

A worker choosing to invest part of his payroll taxes in a personal account accepts an offset to his traditional Social Security benefits equal to the amount of his account contributions compounded at the designated offset interest rate (3.5 percent, 2 percent, and 2.5 percent for Plans 1, 2, and 3, respectively). As long as a worker's account interest rate exceeds the offset interest rate, the worker will be assured of receiving higher total benefits by taking the account. In two of the three plans, a worker would receive higher total benefits simply by investing in government bonds, which are assumed to return 3 percent after inflation. This offset is applied up-front, at the time contributions are made to the account, and simply represents the decision to invest those contributions in the account (instead of investing them in the traditional system and earning an assumed interest rate of 3.5, 2, or 2.5 percent). There is no diminution of personal account balances at the point of retirement as a consequence of the offset.[60]

Minimum Benefit

Plans 2 and 3 incorporate new minimum benefit guarantees, such that by 2018 a minimum wage worker would be assured of a benefit equal to 120 percent of the poverty line in Plan 2, or 100 percent of the poverty line in Plan 3. Under Plan 2, the minimum benefit would rise annually with inflation. Under Plan 3, the minimum benefit, while initially lower than under Plan 2, would rise at the faster rate of wage growth. One-half million to one million seniors could be lifted out of poverty by virtue of these new protections, according to Social Security's actuaries.

Increased Survivors' Benefit

Plans 2 and 3 also increase survivors' benefits to 75 percent of the couple's prior benefit, for below-average-income widow(er)s (see Figure 3). For a couple with equal incomes, this would mean a 50 percent increase in benefits to the widow. An estimated 2 to 3 million widows would receive increased benefits as a result of this new provision.

Assets Split in Divorce

All three plans dictate that account assets be split in the event of divorce (see Figure 4). Under current law, before 10 years of marriage

Figure 3
LOWER-INCOME SURVIVOR'S BENEFIT INCREASED FROM 32 TO 50 PERCENT COMPARED WITH CURRENT LAW

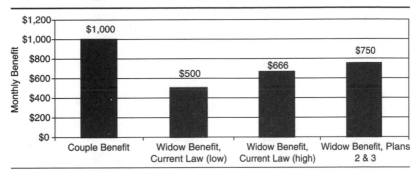

SOURCE: President's Commission to Strengthen Social Security, final report, p. 107.

Figure 4
LUMP SUMS AVAILABLE AT AGE 67 TO SPOUSE OF AVERAGE EARNER DIVORCED BEFORE 10 YEARS OF MARRIAGE

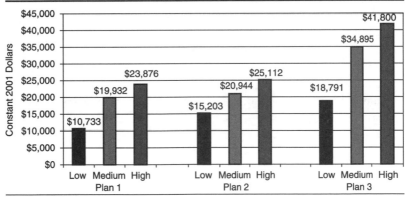

SOURCE: Author's calculations. Assumes marriage at age 25 to average earner, no account contributions during marriage, and divorce just before 10 years of marriage. Account assets split at divorce and compounded until age 67.

a spouse is not eligible to receive any benefits on the basis of the husband's or wife's earnings. Under the reform plans, that spouse would receive half the husband's or wife's account assets. These assets, if simply left to accumulate until retirement, could result in

233

lump sums ranging from $10,000 to $40,000 for the spouse of an average-wage worker. At retirement, the account could increase the spouse's monthly income by $55 to $215. Given that women divorced at an early age are among those most vulnerable to poverty in retirement, this provision could assist a particularly vulnerable group.

Commission Plan 1

Plan 1 was designed as a flexible framework to demonstrate the power of personal accounts, absent any other considerations. In other words, it is an "accounts only" plan that does nothing to the current Social Security program other than to give workers the opportunity to invest through personal retirement accounts. This is both its strength and its weakness. On the one hand, Plan 1 shows the power of personal retirement accounts to increase Social Security's financial rate of return and to give workers the rewards of personal asset accumulation. Moreover, a number of different account options could be integrated into Plan 1's basic framework.

On the other hand, Plan 1 makes no attempt to address larger system-solvency issues. And although solvency is by no means the only criterion of a successful reform proposal, it is a very important one. Plan 1, while bringing Social Security marginally closer to solvency and long-term sustainability, does not go nearly far enough to satisfy that important criterion.

Plan 1 includes an optional account into which workers could invest 2 percentage points of their taxable wages. As the commissioners noted, Plan 1 presents a flexible framework:

> The accounts could be made larger, or smaller. They could be funded in a progressive fashion (with a higher contribution rate based on the first dollars of earnings than on higher earnings amounts). Some have proposed that such accounts be supplemented with extra contributions for younger workers or that such accounts be funded from general revenues. . . . Others have suggested that the accounts be made larger, with the requirement that a certain amount be invested in federal securities as a means of limiting the total size of the transition investment. Though the plan scored here envisions a 2 percent account for all wage earners, any of the above variations could be fit within this framework.[61]

Figure 5
MONTHLY BENEFITS FOR LOW-WAGE RETIREE UNDER PLAN 1

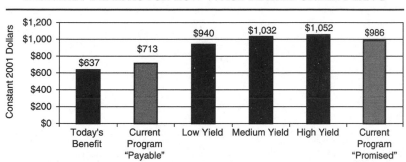

SOURCE: Stephen C. Goss and Alice H. Wade, "Estimates of Financial Effects for Three Models Developed by the President's Commission to Strengthen Social Security," Memorandum dated January 31, 2002, p. 74.

As a flexible structure, Plan 1 leaves open the possibility of the account being funded as an "add-on" with general revenues rather than a "carve-out" with payroll taxes.

In exchange for the personal account, individuals would accept an offset to their traditional benefits at an interest rate of 3.5 percent. This offset rate, being higher than the bond rate, means that account holders must accept some minimal risk to receive higher expected benefits than under the traditional system.

Under Plan 1, a low-wage married worker retiring in 2052 could expect total benefits some 5 percent higher than the current system promises (see Figure 5). I use such a worker to illustrate benefit levels under all three commission reform models because low-wage workers illustrate the special protections built into Plans 2 and 3. Because opponents of personal accounts claim that the poorest would be left behind, it is useful to show that this is not necessarily so. Note that single workers would receive benefits approximately 10 percent higher from their accounts, as they would not be required to purchase joint-and-survivors annuities providing spousal coverage.

In financing terms, Plan 1 is clearly a mixed bag. If funded as a "carve-out," Plan 1 increases Social Security's 75-year actuarial deficit by 0.32 percent of payroll, so in theory it makes the system "worse off" over the measurement period. However, this actuarial decline

Figure 6
COST OF PLAN 1 COMPARED WITH COST OF CURRENT SYSTEM

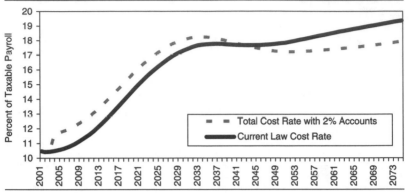

SOURCE: President's Commission to Strengthen Social Security, final report, p. 115.

is purely a function of timing. In the early years, account contributions are counted as lost income and it is only when workers with accounts actually retire that the account offset reduces liabilities to the traditional system and thereby results in cost savings. If funded as an "add-on," the general revenue requirements would be identical.

Moreover, by the year 2042, Plan 1 would be cheaper than the current system and would remain cheaper thereafter, while paying higher expected benefits to all retirees (see Figure 6). Social Security would still be running annual payroll tax deficits as of 2075, which merely shows that a 2 percent account is not enough to fix the current program, but these deficits would be 24 percent smaller than under the current system.[62] More comprehensive measures of the three plans' financing are available in the appendices.

For those who argued that personal accounts by themselves hurt Social Security rather than help it, Plan 1 comes as a surprise.[63] It reduces the size of general revenue infusions needed to pay full benefits by 8 percent, versus the current program, while paying higher benefits to all retirees, and by 2042 its costs are permanently lower than those of the current system.

Since Plan 1 is by design a flexible framework, Figure 7 shows the impact of a larger account funded with 6 percent of payroll,

Figure 7
PLAN 1 USING 6 PERCENT ACCOUNTS VERSUS 2 PERCENT ACCOUNTS COMPARED WITH CURRENT PROGRAM

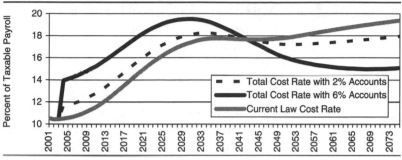

SOURCE. Author's calculations.

compared with the 2 percent account of Plan 2 and the current law. The results are exactly as would be expected: the up-front costs are larger, as the government must fund the larger personal accounts while simultaneously maintaining benefits to current retirees, but once the program "turns the corner" the savings are greater as well. Moreover, total expected benefits for workers would also be proportionately higher.

In short, Plan 1 has the following characteristics:

- Workers may voluntarily invest 2 percent of their taxable wages in personal accounts.
- Traditional Social Security benefits are offset by the worker's personal account contributions compounded at an interest rate of 3.5 percent above inflation.
- No other changes are made to traditional Social Security.
- All retirees could expect higher benefits than under the current program.
- Beginning in 2042, Plan 1 would cost less than the current program.
- Additional revenues would be needed to keep the trust fund solvent beginning in the 2030s.
- Although Social Security's finances would be improved, the program would still not be sustainable over the long term.

237

Commission Plan 2

Broadly speaking, the commission's Plan 2 reflects the outlook that Social Security should maintain a real inflation-adjusted foundation on which other retirement savings could build but that this foundation should not grow at a rate unsustainable under current payroll tax rates. In other words, it considers the adequacy of the real, inflation-adjusted resources provided to retirees more important than other considerations, particularly income replacement rates. This point of view generated controversy, but it has attracted much support in the past, even from account opponents. Plan 2 was preferred by most of the commissioners and would be, from my point of view, the preferred direction for Social Security reform.

In Plan 2 the commission analyzed the rate of benefit growth the current program can sustain without raising taxes, regardless of whether personal accounts are introduced. This affordable rate of benefit growth is slightly faster than the rate of inflation. Plan 2, then, ensures that benefits for all workers at least keep pace with inflation and, for lower-wage workers, rise at a faster rate. It is important to understand that Plan 2 incorporates Social Security's affordable rate of benefit growth, whether or not personal accounts are integrated into the program. Hence, steps taken in Plan 2 to restrain benefit growth to affordable levels are not due to the introduction of personal accounts but to the inherent fiscal constraints faced by the current program. Personal accounts in Plan 2 are not a source of the program's fiscal limitations but are introduced to overcome the current program's inherent fiscal limitations and allow the payment of total retirement benefits substantially higher than the current pay-as-you-go system is capable of paying.

The commission's Plan 2 allows each worker to invest 4 percentage points of his payroll taxes in a personal account, up to an annual maximum of $1,000. Plan 2 therefore creates a progressive personal account, with relatively larger contributions for lower-income workers.

In exchange, the worker would forgo traditional benefits at an offset interest rate of 2 percent. Because the offset rate is below the government bond rate of 3 percent, workers can increase their total retirement benefits merely by investing in risk-free government bonds, which are fully backed by the government and are the legal property of the holder. Since Plan 2's low offset rate means that

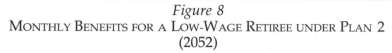

Figure 8
MONTHLY BENEFITS FOR A LOW-WAGE RETIREE UNDER PLAN 2
(2052)

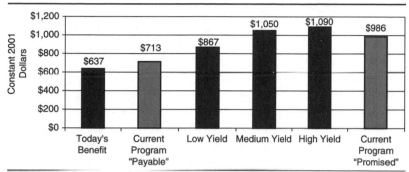

SOURCE: Stephen C. Goss and Alice H. Wade, "Estimates of Financial Effects for Three Models Developed by the President's Commission to Strengthen Social Security," Memorandum dated January 31, 2002, p. 75.

workers can increase their benefits without risk, its progressive account structure particularly benefits low-wage workers.

Under Plan 2, a low-wage worker retiring in 2052 and holding the standard investment portfolio would receive $1,050 per month versus the $986 per month promised by the current system and the $713 that could actually be paid (see Figure 8). Even if that worker held only government bonds in his account, he would receive a total monthly benefit of $867 (in 2001 dollars), 22 percent higher than would be paid under current law.[64]

This point is relevant to the charge that the commission reform plans would "cut guaranteed benefits." What critics reference as Social Security's "guaranteed benefit" is not guaranteed in law, as the Supreme Court has ruled.[65] Nor is it guaranteed in an economic or financial sense because the resources will not be available to provide promised benefits. Quite the contrary: We can be reasonably sure legislated resources—current payroll tax rates—won't provide nearly what has been promised. Hence, the proper baseline for "guarantees" is what the law provides and what payroll taxes can afford to pay: that is, the so-called payable benefit. On this basis, there is simply no truth to claims that Plan 2 would "cut guaranteed benefits."

239

Moreover, a worker who opted for a personal account would have a stronger "guarantee" to his benefits in that, unlike the current program's benefits, the account assets are his legal property and, in the case of government bonds, are backed by the full faith and credit of the government. Plan 2's benefit increase for low-wage workers is not simply a function of throwing money at the problem. Although Plan 2 pays low-wage workers higher retirement benefits than those promised by the current program, it does so at a cost 68 percent lower than that needed to maintain the current system.

One reason for this is that under Plan 2, higher-wage earners do not do quite as well as low-wage earners. A high-wage worker with the default portfolio, for instance, would receive just 88 percent of his full promised benefit, and an average-wage worker 94 percent. Nevertheless, even high-wage earners receive 25 percent more than the current system can afford to pay while avoiding the massive income tax increases many account opponents favor to keep the current program solvent.[66]

Some may charge that the general revenue infusions required to finance the transition to personal accounts are unaffordable. However, concern over fiscal pressures should be a reason to favor the commission's plans, not reject them. Account opponents who decry the revenue transfers under the commission's plans should detail how they would afford the much larger general revenue transfers necessary to maintain the current program. It is only if account opponents choose the true "do nothing" option, in which Social Security becomes insolvent and large benefit cuts are enacted, that pressures on general revenue will be less than under the commission's proposals.

To balance the current program, beginning in 2009 Plan 2 indexes the initial wages each cohort receives to the growth of prices, instead of the generally higher rate of wages indexed under current law (see Figure 9). Price indexing brings Social Security back to solvency and makes it sustainable over the long term.

This shift from wage to price indexing of initial benefits has generated controversy and merits a close look. Social Security's current benefit formula replaces a higher percentage of low-wage workers' pre-retirement earnings than that of higher earners. For workers retiring in 2003, Social Security replaces 90 percent of the first $606 in average monthly pre-retirement earnings, 32 percent of monthly

Figure 9
Cost of Plan 2 Compared with Cost of Current System

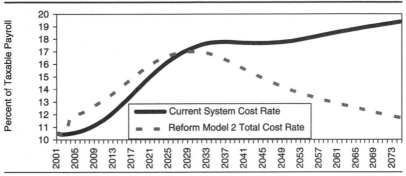

Source: President's Commission to Strengthen Social Security, final report, p. 126.

Figure 10
Social Security's "Bend Point" Formula Provides Higher Monthly Benefits to Those with Lower Average Wages

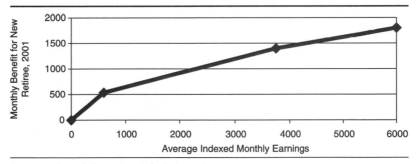

Source: Social Security Administration.

earnings between $606 and $3,653, and 15 percent of any amount between $3,653 and the taxable maximum. The benefit formula's pairings of monthly income levels and income replacement rates are known as "bend points" (see Figure 10).

For instance, a new retiree with $20,000 average indexed earnings would receive $877 per month, or 53 percent of his pre-retirement monthly earnings. A $50,000 worker, by contrast, would receive $1,567 per month. Although this is almost twice what the $20,000

241

Figure 11
WAGE INDEXING GIVES HIGH-WAGE WORKERS LARGEST INCREASE

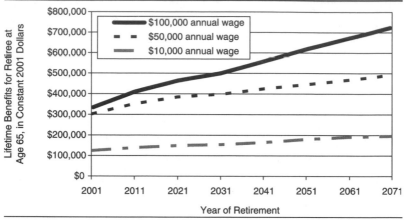

SOURCE: Author's calculations.

worker receives, it is only 38 percent of the $50,000 worker's pre-retirement earnings. This progressivity is intentional: higher-wage workers can save more outside of Social Security, and those outside assets can provide income during retirement.

To maintain progressivity, Social Security's bend points are increased annually according to the growth of wages. In 2001, for instance, Social Security's 90 percent bend point was placed at the first $561 of a new retiree's average indexed monthly pre-retirement earnings, while in 2003 the 90 percent bend point rose to $606. By 2015 the 90 percent replacement level will rise to the first $661 in earnings (in today's dollars), and so forth ($767 by 2030 and $991 by 2050). The upper bend points, marking replacement rates of 32 and 15 percent, are similarly indexed to wage growth and increase each year.

Put another way, a $20,000 worker would retire today with monthly benefits of about $877, equal to 53 percent of his pre-retirement earnings. By 2050, the same worker earning the same $20,000 (in today's dollars) would receive $1,091 monthly, or 64 percent of his pre-retirement earnings. In other words, the 2050 retiree would receive 25 percent higher benefits simply because of the passage of time, even if he paid precisely the same taxes.

Moreover, under the current benefit formula, future increases in benefits will be greatest for the highest earners (see Figure 11).

For instance, a worker earning $10,000 today already receives the maximum 90 percent replacement rate on much of his wages. A similar worker making $10,000 (in 2002 dollars) in 2031 will receive a 25 percent real benefit increase, and in 2071 a 58 percent increase. By contrast, higher-income workers today have much of their wages covered under the upper bend points offering lower replacement rates. Over time, wage indexing pushes more of those wages into the bend points offering higher replacement rates. For instance, a $100,000 worker retiring at 65 in 2001 can expect to receive about $330,000 in lifetime retirement benefits. By 2031, lifetime benefits increase by 51 percent to $499,000, and by 2071 by 120 percent to $725,000, under today's (unsustainable) benefit formula.[67]

It should be stressed that these are workers earning the same annual wages in real, inflation-adjusted dollars. Clearly, the current wage-indexed benefit formula provides vastly unequal benefits to otherwise identical workers retiring at different points in time. Wage indexing increases benefits over time, and the largest increases go to the highest earners. In fact, these figures underestimate differences in lifetime benefits, as they assume identical life expectancies for upper- and lower-wage workers. Because life expectancies are correlated to income, the true results are likely to be even more extreme.[68]

Moreover, as the commission noted in its interim report, wage indexing of initial benefits prevents the system from gaining much from increases in long-term economic growth.

> Initial Social Security benefit levels are currently indexed to the growth in national wage levels. Consequently, even if there were no demographic problem, Social Security costs would grow almost as fast as the economy as a whole. Faster economic growth means more tax contributions in the short term, and higher benefit obligations in the long term. Though this faster growth helps, it does far less than many people believe. Mostly it creates the illusion of improvement because short-term revenue gains postpone the projected date of Trust Fund depletion, whereas increased costs would occur mostly after the projected depletion date.[69]

Even if the economy grew twice as fast as the trustees project, Social Security would still become insolvent within the 75-year scoring period.[70] Social Security's wage indexing formula is in large part responsible for that.

A solution to the problems of financing and equity is to switch from wage to price indexing of Social Security's benefit bend points. In doing so, the bend points would increase annually along with increases in the Consumer Price Index.[71] Under Plan 2, price indexing is instituted beginning in 2009, so current retirees and those over age 55 are entirely unaffected, and those under age 55 are affected only to the degree that their working careers extend past 2009.[72] In addition, Plan 2 is not a "pure" price indexing approach, as it contains special provisions targeted toward the most vulnerable Americans—low-wage workers and widows—so that they receive higher benefits than the current benefit formula promises, much less can actually afford to pay. Whatever the large-scale financing impact of the switch to price indexing, it is difficult to portray this principle as unfair; it simply treats relevantly similar individuals in a similar way.

These facts blunt criticisms, such as those made by Kilolo Kijakazi and Robert Greenstein of the CBPP, that "replacing 'wage indexing' with 'price indexing' would result in deep reductions over time in Social Security benefits."[73] As we have seen, under a pure price indexing approach, workers with similar wages would receive similar benefits, at whatever point in time they retired.

Greenstein and Kijakazi are correct that price indexing reduces the replacement rate for an average-wage worker in any given year,[74] which they illustrate with an average-wage worker retiring in 2040: Under the current wage indexing approach, that worker would be promised a benefit equal to 37 percent of his pre-retirement earnings. Under pure price indexing, they say, his benefit would equal only 28 percent of his pre-retirement earnings. Greenstein and Kijakazi extend their example to a worker retiring in 2070, making the notional "cuts" even larger.

Several points are worth making. First, under current law, after trust fund depletion in 2042 benefits would equal whatever level payroll tax receipts are capable of paying, regardless of the wage-indexed benefit formula. Thus, under current law that 2040 retiree will actually receive a 27.4 percent replacement rate even if price indexing weren't introduced. Moreover, under Plan 2 the personal account provides retirees with benefits higher than those that a pure price indexing approach implies. The 2040 retiree could expect total retirement benefits equal to about 34.8 percent of pre-retirement earnings, assuming investment in the default 50 percent stock, 50 percent bond portfolio.[75]

Beyond this point, there is a more important difference between average-wage workers in the future and average-wage workers today: average workers in the future will earn substantially more money. The average-wage worker in 2040 will earn some 48 percent more than that of today; in 2070, almost double today's average (and more than 20 percent greater than the SSA's hypothetical "high earner" in 2001). Compared with today's workers, these future Americans will have substantially higher standards of living while working and several years greater life expectancy in retirement.

Now, workers retiring today with earnings 50 to 100 percent higher than the average would of course receive a lower income replacement rate than would an average-wage worker, and Greenstein and Kijakazi would surely be the first to defend that practice. Yet they argue that treating a similar worker in the future in a similar way is a "deep reduction."

To be fair, Greenstein and Kijakazi acknowledge that the "benefit cuts" inherent in price indexing would not, in fact, actually cut benefits: "To be sure," they say, "benefit levels would keep pace with changes in prices.'"[76] In other words, benefits would not be cut. But, they say, "Beneficiaries would be precluded from partaking in the general increase in the standard of living from one generation to the next. Upon retiring, workers would essentially drop back to a standard of living prevalent in an earlier generation.'"[77]

Of course, price indexing also precludes workers from "partaking" in the 50 percent increase in payroll tax rates necessary to maintain the current wage-indexed benefit formula. The question, which Greenstein and Kijakazi don't address, is whether workers should be forced to pay those extra taxes to achieve promised replacement rates, particularly when individuals desiring a higher retirement income could invest their tax savings privately at rates of return two to three times higher than under Social Security. Why must the government force people to do something they could easily do voluntarily if they so wished?

In effect, Greenstein and Kijakazi argue that a $100,000 annual wage worker retiring in 2070 should receive some $725,000 in lifetime retirement benefits, even if payroll taxes must top 19 percent, despite the fact that a similar worker retiring today can expect just $330,000 in lifetime benefits. But why? If it is so important to give a $100,000 worker $725,000 in lifetime retirement benefits, why not raise taxes today? Greenstein and Kijakazi argue that tomorrow's taxpayers should shoulder a tax burden that they are unwilling to ask today's taxpayers to bear, but provide neither the economic nor philosophical rationale for doing so.[78]

The question remains: if higher earners today receive lower replacement rates because they are able to save more outside of Social Security, shouldn't the same reasoning apply to identical earners in the future? Isn't this particularly true given the financing burden the wage-indexed benefit formula places on the system and on the taxpayer?

In testimony before the president's commission, Hans Riemer of the Campaign for America's Future and the 2030 Center declared that "the level of guaranteed protection that Social Security provides today is about right."[79] Plan 2, and all of the other plans put forward by the commission, would maintain the level of benefits provided today and enhance benefits substantially for those in greatest need.

Despite charges made by reform opponents against price indexing today, in the past it has received support even among those who oppose personal accounts. Peter Diamond of MIT, one of the most prominent academic critics of personal accounts, was a member of a government panel in the 1970s that recommended price indexing, calling it "fair and necessary."[80] As the panel's report pointed out:

> The wage-indexing method provides a sharp tilt in favor of workers retiring in the future. The increases in benefits for workers already retired are limited to increases in the rise in the Consumer Price Index. Yet workers who retire five years later will receive increments due to both price changes and increases in real wages. This difference in retirement benefits can be substantial.[81]

When President Carter appeared to be favoring wage indexing over a price-indexed approach, Diamond and the other panel members chided him for fiscal and generational irresponsibility:

> President Carter would be displeased with his predecessors if he were currently faced with the choice of cutting Social Security benefits for present recipients or raising the same amount of revenue as would be raised by an increase in the payroll tax rate of five percentage points. Yet that is precisely what the best current estimates say he is proposing to do to some future President. . . . It appears to us that correction of

> overindexing by choice of a price indexing method would
> be greatly superior [to wage indexing]. . . . Use of the price
> indexing method would eliminate the need for a tax rise
> when the percentage of retirees increases sharply early next
> century. . . . While the price indexing method implies protec-
> tion from inflation and a growth in benefits with the real
> growth of the economy, the wage indexing method calls for
> a much larger growth in benefits for future retirees at a time
> when the country may not be able to afford it. Use of the price
> indexing method would permit moderate tax and benefit
> increases to aid those recipients with greatest need as percep-
> tions of those needs arise.[82]

The same charges could be made today against those who wish to
saddle future taxpayers with economic burdens they themselves are
unwilling to bear today.

Henry Aaron of the Brookings Institution concurred with Diamond, arguing that price indexing "would leave more options open
for spending the productivity dividend of economic growth. Congress could still raise pensions in the future, but it could also decide
that other programs such as housing, health insurance, or defense
have greater claims on available funds."[83] As chairman of the
1978–79 Advisory Council on Social Security, Aaron again argued
for price indexing, but the change was not adopted.

> As per capita income rises, the case for increasing the amount
> of mandatory "saving" for retirement and disability through
> Social Security is far weaker than was the rationale for estab-
> lishing a basic floor of retirement and disability protection
> at about the levels that exist today.
>
> At the levels of real income prevailing in the 1930s (or
> perhaps even in the 1950s), it can well be argued that it
> was appropriate, indeed, highly desirable—perhaps even
> necessary for the preservation of our society—that govern-
> ment should, by law, have guaranteed to the aged and disa-
> bled and their dependents replacement incomes sufficient to
> avoid severe hardship, and to have required workers (and
> their employers) to finance this system with a kind of "forced
> saving" through payroll tax contributions. But as real
> incomes continue to rise, it is not easy to justify the require-
> ment that workers and their employers "save" through pay-
> roll tax contributions to finance ever higher replacement
> incomes, far above those needed to avoid hardship. Perhaps
> not all workers will want to save that much, or to save in
> the particular time pattern and form detailed by present law.

Aaron and his co-authors go on to say:

> Future Congresses will be better equipped than today's Congress to determine the appropriate level of and composition of benefits for future generations. . . . Congress might elect to give more to certain groups of beneficiaries than to others, or to provide protection against new risks that now are uncovered. But precisely because we cannot now forecast what form those desirable adjustments might take, we feel the commitment to large increase in benefits and taxes implied under current law will deprive subsequent Congresses, who will be better informed about future needs and preferences, of needed flexibility to tailor Social Security to the needs and tastes of the generations to come.[84]

The primary difference between the price indexing advocated by Diamond and Aaron and that applied in Plan 2, besides certain technical factors of implementation, is that Plan 2 provides a personal account to make up for the reduction in the growth of traditional benefits.

Subsequent to the release of the commission's recommendations, Diamond disowned his prior support for price indexing and strongly criticized the commission for having advocated it.[85] Diamond argued that he had favored price indexing in the 1970s because the financing problems facing Social Security at the time were much greater than those at present. It is true that Social Security faced a short-term financing crisis in the late 1970s due to an error in the benefit formula introduced in the 1972 amendments that implied a quantum leap in future benefit levels. But price indexing, which is extremely slow to take effect, would have done nothing to avert insolvency in the short term. Moreover, the wage-indexing alternative that Diamond and the rest of the panel argued so strongly against entailed long-term system costs barely higher than those projected by Social Security's actuaries today.[86] In addition, the Hsiao panel rejected the view that income replacement rates should be the basis of Social Security's benefit formula, as is the case under wage indexing.

To summarize Plan 2:

- Workers can voluntarily redirect 4 percent of their payroll taxes up to $1,000 annually to a personal account (the maximum contribution is indexed annually to wage growth). Traditional Social Security benefits are offset by the worker's personal account contributions compounded at an interest rate of 2 percent above inflation.

- Workers opting for personal accounts can reasonably expect total benefits greater than those paid to current retirees, to workers without accounts, and than future benefits payable under current law.
- Plan 2 establishes a minimum benefit payable to 30-year minimum-wage workers of 120 percent of the poverty line. Survivors' benefits for below-average-wage workers would be increased by 33 to 50 percent.
- Beginning in 2009, calculation of traditional benefits would switch from wage indexing to price indexing. Current retirees and workers aged 55 and over would be entirely unaffected.

Commission Plan 3

Plan 3 aimed to match or exceed benefits currently promised by Social Security for all workers, but to do so at lower cost than the current program. In this, it succeeds.

Plan 3's accounts are designed as a combination add-on and carve-out. That is to say, if a worker agrees to contribute an additional 1 percent of his earnings to the account, he may "carve out" 2.5 percentage points of his payroll taxes up to an annual maximum of $1,000.

Workers opting for personal accounts would accept an offset at a 2.5 percent interest rate. Again, for a low-wage worker investing in government bonds, the guaranteed benefit is both higher and more "guaranteed" than under the current system.

Under Plan 3, a low-wage worker with the default investment portfolio would receive $1,103 per month in total expected retirement benefits, as opposed to the $986 promised by the current program and the $713 actually payable (see Figure 12). All other workers, at all other times, could expect benefits at least as high as those promised by the current program.

To bring the traditional program back to balance, Plan 3 requires new ongoing sources of general revenue, equivalent in size to increasing the payroll tax cap to 90 percent of taxable payroll and redirecting to Social Security the portion of benefits taxation that currently flows to Medicare.

Figure 12
MONTHLY BENEFITS FOR LOW-WAGE RETIREES UNDER PLAN 3
(2052)

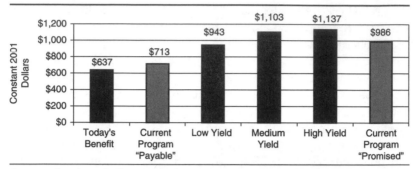

SOURCE: Stephen C. Goss and Alice H. Wade, "Estimates of Financial Effects for Three Models Developed by the President's Commission to Strengthen Social Security," Memorandum dated January 31, 2002, p. 76.

Two points are worth making in this regard. First, it should be emphasized that Plan 3 describes only the size of the general revenue transfers and not the means. The commission worked under the president's principle that payroll taxes would not be raised, and this was taken to encompass increases in the taxable wage base as well as the payroll tax rate. Second, increased revenue commitments were included for ensuring that benefits for all retirees exceeded the replacement rates promised in the current benefit schedule. However, it is not clear why current replacement rates should be the standard many decades in the future, as the prior section on price indexing points out. Third, even if meeting promised replacement rates were the goal, given the relative efficiencies of pay-as-you-go and funded systems it would make sense to meet this goal with a larger personal account rather than increased taxation. Doing so would entail greater prefunding, but on the whole that is a desirable thing.

One problem with Plan 3 is that mandating additional worker contributions to take advantage of the personal account might discourage lower-wage workers from taking part, even if the additional contributions are partially subsidized by the government. Indeed, experimental individual development account trials aimed at lower-income workers often have far from universal participation, even with substantially more generous matches than included in Plan 3.[87] And according to the 1998 Retirement Confidence Survey conducted by the Employee Benefit Research Institute, some 40 percent of workers said they could not save even an extra $20 per week for retirement.[88] Among low-wage workers, this percentage would likely be even higher. Adverse selection in terms of account participation could complicate overall system financing, and would also prevent lower-wage workers from reaping the benefits of asset ownership under Plan 3. In terms of both participation rates and administrative simplicity, the poor might do better if the progressive carve-out approach used in both Plans 2 and 3 were simply expanded. This would make achieving actuarial balance within the 75-year window more challenging, but from a public policy perspective it would do more to enhance retirement income and asset accumulation among the poor.

To balance system finances, Plan 3 makes several changes to Social Security's benefit structure. First, it would adjust benefits for future retirees to account for increases in longevity. In addition, the benefit penalties for retiring early—and the rewards for working later— are increased to encourage people to stay in the work force longer. Some would argue that these changes constitute an increase in the retirement age.[89] This is incorrect: under Plan 3, the normal retirement age would remain the same as under current law. Thus, workers could still retire at any age past 62 and still receive more than current law would pay them. It is ironic that the Campaign for America's Future has issued press releases attacking Plan 3's purported increase in the retirement age, while in testimony before the commission Roger Hickey of the CAF praised a reform proposal by Henry Aaron and Robert Reischauer that explicitly raises both the normal and the early retirement ages.[90]

Moreover, Plan 3's changes to benefits would not even begin until 2009, so current retirees and those over age 55 are not subject to any changes. For individuals retiring soon after 2009, the changes would be tiny—just a penny on the dollar—and that offset would be more than made up by gains from the personal account.

Over the long term, Plan 3's changes would pay higher benefits for a lower cost than under the current program (see Figure 13). If the new general revenue transfers were included, it would bring Social Security back to cash surpluses and long-term sustainability for half the cost of maintaining the current program.

Figure 13

COST OF PLAN 3 COMPARED WITH COST OF CURRENT SYSTEM

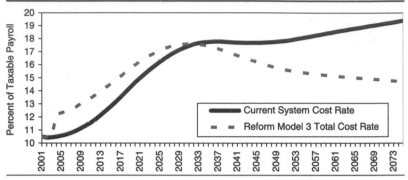

SOURCE: President's Commission to Strengthen Social Security, final report, p. 13.

The commission's treatment of disability benefits has been received with some level of confusion. For instance, a memo prepared by the staff of Rep. Robert Matsui (D-Calif.) alleged, "The President's Social Security commission recommended cutting disability benefits to help pay for the cost of private accounts."[91] In fact, the commission made no specific recommendations regarding the long-term financing of Social Security's Disability Insurance program, which provides benefits to workers who through illness or injury are unable to continue to work.

Under the commission's proposals, a worker with a personal account who became disabled would receive the traditional Social Security benefit without any offset for holding the account. Only at retirement would he access his account balance, and only at retirement would his traditional benefit be offset on the basis of his account contributions. A worker who became disabled early in life would have made few contributions, and thus would have a very small offset to his traditional benefits. But as long as his account earned more than the offset interest rate, he could still anticipate higher total benefits than if he had remained in the current program.

For instance, low-wage disabled workers scheduled to retire in 2055 would receive under Plan 1 disability benefits before retirement equal to those promised by the current system and 30 percent higher than current law; Plan 2 would pay benefits 13 percent higher than

Table 3
MONTHLY BENEFIT PAYABLE TO LOW-WAGE DISABLED WORKER SCHEDULED TO RETIRE IN 2055 (IN 2001 DOLLARS)

Promised	$986
Plan 1	$986
Plan 2	$807
Plan 3	$857
Payable	$713
Benefit payable to low-wage worker in 2001	$637

SOURCE: Derived from data presented in Stephen C. Goss and Alice H. Wade, "Estimates of Financial Effects for Three Models Developed by President's Commission to Strengthen Social Security," Memorandum dated January 31, 2002.

current law; and Plan 3, 20 percent higher than current law. As these disabled workers would receive more than current law could pay them, it is clear that disability benefits have not been cut to fund personal accounts.

Charges of "cuts" come about because disabled workers under the three commission proposals would receive the benefits dictated under those proposals, which under Plans 2 and 3 are somewhere between those promised and those actually payable under current law (see Table 3). But, as noted, the "promised" benefit is not a valid benchmark of comparison because no means of funding that promise is available at present. The current program cannot keep its promises past the year 2042 without increasing the payroll tax by 50 percent. Moreover, any reductions in promised benefits are due to the system's insolvency, not to the introduction of personal accounts. Accounts are designed to make up for Social Security's inability to pay promised benefits.

It is worth noting the complications facing any reform's treatment of disability insurance. On one hand, the Disability Insurance program is distinct from the Old-Age and Survivors Disability Insurance program, having its own dedicated tax and its own trust fund. At the same time, the two sides of Social Security share a common formula for calculating benefits, and changes to the calculation of retirement benefits can also affect the DI program. Moreover, the DI program faces financing challenges even steeper than those of

OASDI—without change, the DI program will run payroll tax deficits by 2009 and its trust fund will be exhausted by 2028.

Lacking comprehensive disability reform, several options are open to reformers of the retirement program, none of them ideal:

- Separate the OASI and DI programs so they run independently. At present, although the programs have separate taxes and trust funds, they share a common benefit formula. Although this would isolate DI from any changes to OASI, DI is even more severely underfunded and would therefore become insolvent sooner.
- Retain the integration of OASI and DI but allow DI to continue under pre-reform criteria. While this would protect DI recipients from any changes, it would also create an incentive for workers nearing retirement to seek to qualify for disability benefits. An increase in DI applications could speed the program's insolvency.
- Apply changes to OASI and DI universally, acknowledging that further steps must be taken to protect disabled workers as well as to reform the DI program in general.

It was the third option that the commissioners took.

In doing so, the commission emphasized that "in the absence of fully developed proposals, the calculations carried out for the commission and included in this report assume that defined benefits will be changed in similar ways for the two programs." However, *"this should not be taken as a commission recommendation for policy implementation. . . .* The commission recognizes that changes in Social Security's defined benefit structure and the role of personal accounts may have different implications for DI and OASI beneficiaries. The commission urges the Congress to consider the full range of options available for addressing these implications."[92] In other words, the commissioners anticipated that additional steps would be taken to address the DI program, and that these steps could require additional funding as well as broader structural reform.

The commissioners agreed with the Social Security Advisory Board, which declared, "After two additional years of study of the disability programs . . . we are convinced that the issues facing the disability programs cannot be resolved without making fundamental changes."[93] Unfortunately, the deliberate focus of the president's commission on the financing problems of the retirement portion of Social Security and the short period available for the commission's work made the development of comprehensive disability reform proposals impossible. The commission did recommend, however, "that the President address the DI program through a separate policy development process."

As the independent Social Security Advisory Board has argued, the disability program requires reforms extending beyond mere financing changes.[94] Decisions on disability eligibility vary greatly between states, with some states approving DI claims at over twice the rate of others, and are many times resolved only through adjudication. Moreover, awards based on mental conditions have more than doubled as a percentage of total DI claims between 1980 and 1990, and now make up the largest single reason for DI claims. State agency administrators and examiners report that at least half of the claims processed now involve issues relating to mental impairment.[95] Clearly, the nature of disability claims is changing quickly and radically, and the program requires a comprehensive assessment of how it is to function and what claims should be met. The complexity of DI's structure and function causes its administrative costs to be five times higher than those of OASDI relative to its income.[96] Without a doubt, more changes will be needed to bring DI back to long-term health.

To summarize Plan 3:

- Workers who invest an additional 1 percent of wages in a personal account may also invest 2.5 percentage points of payroll taxes, up to $1,000 annually. The add-on contribution is progressively subsidized by a refundable tax credit, enhancing the progressivity of the account.
- Account holders accept an offset to their traditional Social Security benefits at a real annual interest rate of 2.5 percent. Hence, under Plans 2 and 3, workers could increase their total retirement benefits by simply investing in government bonds.
- Plan 3 increases system progressivity by establishing a minimum benefit payable to 30-year minimum-wage workers of 100 percent of the poverty line (111 percent for a 40-year worker). This minimum benefit would be indexed to wage growth. Benefits for below-average-wage earners would be increased as well.

- The growth rate of traditional benefits would be adjusted to reflect increases in life expectancy; the offset for early retirement and bonus for later retirement would be increased; and the third bend point factor affecting higher-wage retirees would be reduced from 15 to 10 percent.
- Benefits payable to workers who do not opt for personal accounts would be more than 50 percent higher than those paid to today's retirees.
- New sources of dedicated revenue would be added in the equivalent amount of 0.6 percent of payroll over the 75-year period, and continuing thereafter.
- Additional temporary transfers from general revenues would be needed to keep the trust fund solvent between 2034 and 2063. Total cash requirements would be 52 percent of those needed to maintain the current program.

Summary of the Three Plans

Taken together, the commission's three reform plans show the power of personal accounts to address the problems associated with Social Security.

- Each of the three commission proposals would pay future beneficiaries higher expected benefits than those received by today's retirees.
- Each of the three proposals would increase expected benefits relative to what the current system can pay.
- Each of the three proposals would increase expected benefits for those who opt for personal accounts relative to those who stay in the traditional system.
- Each of the comprehensive reform proposals (Plans 2 and 3) would increase expected benefits for those who opt for personal accounts, even if participants invested in the most conservative portfolio available (government bonds).
- Each of the three proposals would increase expected benefits for low-income participants even relative to currently promised benefits (which cannot be paid without significant tax increases). These low-wage participants would receive higher benefits than if Social Security were fully funded and faced no financial crisis whatsoever. Two of the proposals institute, for

Figure 14
ALL THREE PLANS WOULD PAY HIGHER BENEFITS THAN UNDER CURRENT LAW

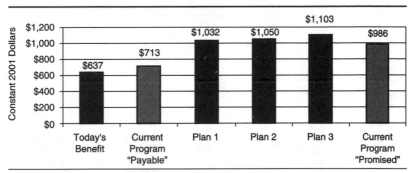

SOURCE: President's Commission to Strengthen Social Security, final report. Low-wage worker retiring in 2052; assumes investment in 50-50 stock-bond portfolio.

the first time, a guarantee that minimum-wage workers not retire in poverty.

- Two of the three proposals would institute special benefit increases for widows of low-income participants, raising incomes for millions of Americans most vulnerable to poverty in retirement.
- Two of the three proposals would increase expected benefits for all of the participants in personal accounts even relative to the benefits the current system promises, much less can afford to pay.
- One proposal makes no changes whatsoever to Social Security's benefit structure other than to offer workers the opportunity to increase their total benefits by owning a personal retirement account.
- Under all of the proposals, participants receive more benefits for less money relative to the current system.

All three plans would pay higher benefits than are paid under the current system (see Figure 14), and lower-income workers—those whom account opponents claim to be most concerned about—receive benefits higher than those the current program even promises.

Figure 15
ALL THREE PLANS WOULD REQUIRE LESS GENERAL REVENUE THAN THE CURRENT PROGRAM

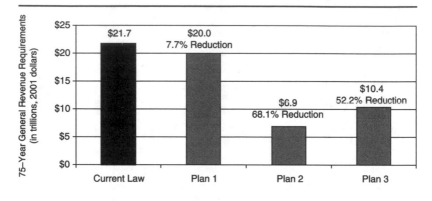

SOURCE: President's Commission to Strengthen Social Security, final report, p. 22. Based on current program finances as projected in 2001 Social Security Trustees Report.

Moreover, all three plans would produce those benefits at lower general revenue costs than the current program (see Figure 15). Assuming future payroll tax surpluses are unavailable for transition financing, the transition cost of Plan 1 is $1.1 trillion; Plan 2, $0.9 trillion; and Plan 3, $0.4 trillion. If future payroll tax surpluses were made available to fund reform, as they should be, costs would decline to $0.7 trillion for Plan 1, $0.4 trillion for Plan 2, and $0.1 trillion for Plan 3. These latter values equal 0.29 percent, 0.33 percent, and 0.10 percent of GDP during the scoring period, substantially less than the cost of maintaining the current program.

Even Plan 1, the "accounts only" approach, cuts 75-year general revenue costs by 8 percent, while Plan 2 reduces costs by 68 percent and Plan 3 by 52 percent. In other words, the government could devote twice as much extra money to the traditional system and low-wage workers would still receive lower benefits than they would under Plans 2 and 3. The commission's success was that it showed how to deliver higher long-term benefits at lower long-term costs.

Finally, all three plans would leave Social Security with substantially greater assets over the long term. As noted previously, Social Security's actuaries opine that although personal accounts are the property of individuals, for accounting purposes their assets should be treated as part of total system assets. A comprehensive view of Social Security's asset position combines account balances with the balance of the traditional trust.

Table 4 details the increases in total system assets as of 2076, the end of the traditional 75-year actuarial scoring period. Clearly, any arguments that the commission's personal account plans "defund" Social Security are rebutted by these figures. By 2076 the current Social Security program would be underfunded by $3.23 trillion, in present value terms. By contrast, even under Plan 1, which makes no structural changes to Social Security's revenue or benefit formulas other than to incorporate optional personal retirement accounts, Social Security's deficit is reduced to $2.75 trillion, assuming that two-thirds of eligible workers choose to participate in personal accounts. Under Plan 2, Social Security would have net assets worth $1.67 trillion, and under Plan 3, $1.79 trillion. All of these figures are present values, that is, the amount those future lump sum assets—or debts—would be worth to individuals today.

Where from Here?

With the commission's work done, where does the Social Security debate go from here? The events of September 11, 2001, clearly reshaped many of the government's priorities, pushing national security concerns to the front burner, and rightly so.

That said, baby boomers will still begin to retire in 2008, the American population will still continue to age, and low birth rates will still reduce the ratio of workers to retirees. Like it or not, Social Security's problems remain as real and as pressing since September 11 as they were before that date. In fact, the latest report from Social Security's trustees, released in March 2003, shows the program's long-term cash deficits increasing, from $23.9 trillion in the 2002 report to $25.3 trillion in the latest edition.

259

Table 4
TOTAL SYSTEM ASSETS AS OF 2076 UNDER CURRENT LAW AND
COMMISSION REFORM PLANS (PRESENT VALUE IN BILLIONS OF
DOLLARS, DISCOUNTED TO JANUARY 1, 2001)

	Likely Participation Rate	OASDI Trust Fund Assets[a]	Current Personal Account and Annuity Assets	Total
	Present law	−3,230	N/A	−3,230
Plan 1	67% account participation	−3,826	1,080	−2,746
	100% account participation[b]	−4,124	1,619	−2,505
Plan 2	67% account participation	380	1,290	1,670
	100% account participation	423	1,935	2,358
Plan 3	67% account participation	185	1,602	1,620
	100% account participation	270	2,401	2,671

SOURCE: Based on table from Stephen C. Goss and Alice H. Wade, "Estimates of Financial Effects for Three Models Developed by the President's Commission to Strengthen Social Security," Memorandum dated January 31, 2002, p. 24. The net current accrual for future benefit offset equals the net future savings to the traditional system as the result of benefits offset before the end of the scoring period.

[a]Negative values are the OASDI unfunded obligation for the period 2001 through 2075.

[b]For Model 2, 67 percent participation is considered more likely if the benefit offset yield rate is computed as 2 percent above the realized or expected inflation rate, but 100 percent participation is considered more likely if the offset yield rate is computed as 1 percent below the market yield on Treasury bonds. Based on the intermediate assumptions of the 2001 trustees report and other assumptions described in the text.

If anything, the war on terrorism reminds us that the federal government has other important functions to accomplish, and allowing Social Security and other entitlement programs to grow out of control clearly threatens the government's ability to conduct those duties.

Some have treated Social Security reform as a luxury to be undertaken when the government happens to be flush with cash. In fact, it is a necessity that becomes even more important when the government finds itself squeezed between its various duties. Those who introduced Social Security reform plans before the era of budget surpluses understood this, and the rest of the reform community should as well. The correct question isn't whether we can afford to reform Social Security, but whether we can afford not to.

Nevertheless, all of the commission's proposals demand an upfront investment. That's what pre-funding is: putting aside extra money now to save money later. When surpluses have disappeared and their reappearance is questionable, how can we muster the courage—not to mention the cash—to move reform forward?

The common objection to the commission's plans is that they don't say where they'll get the money to fund the transition. The quick answer to that is that reformers will get it from the same place reform opponents will get the money to keep the current system afloat, except they'll need a lot less of it—up to 68 percent less, to be precise.

The more thoughtful answer is that tough decisions indeed need to be made, but if we make them now in the context of reforms using personal accounts they'll be a lot less tough and be accomplished a lot sooner than if we don't. Yes, there will be a transition period of moving to personal accounts, but after that we're off the hook. If we don't move to personal accounts and simply let the program stagnate, we're on the hook forever. It is reform opponents who need to come up with the most cash, and most of them refuse to put forward any proposals for doing so.

At this point, the Social Security debate is like a sporting event at which only one team has shown up. The president has confronted one of the most contentious issues in politics and taken the heat for doing so. Congressional reformers such as Reps. Jim Kolbe (R-Ariz.) and Charlie Stenholm (D-Tex.); Sens. Judd Gregg (R-N.H.) and John Breaux (D-La.); and Reps. Richard Armey (R-Tex.), Jim DeMint (R-S.C.), and Clay Shaw (R-Fla.) have introduced their own reform plans and continue to fight for change. Each proposal has its pros and cons, but at least these reform plans are in the public arena where the costs and benefits can be discussed and assessed.

But where is Senator Daschle's reform plan? What does Dick Gephardt think we should do? Rep. Robert Matsui in press releases denounces the commission's proposals, "I could have done this by myself in two hours,"[97] yet he apparently hasn't found any spare time in a 24-year congressional career to actually sponsor a legislative proposal other than one that would have the trust fund invest in municipal bonds that pay a lower return than the fund's current bonds.

Account opponents sometimes refer to the reformers' "secret plan," but the biggest secret is what they would do to address the solvency and sustainability of a program that constitutes the biggest tax most workers pay as well as the biggest source of income to most retirees.

This fact was made embarrassingly clear in testimony before the commission by representatives of the Campaign for America's Future, a coalition of personal account opponents who were active in opposing the commission. While calling for "bipartisan dialogue," the CAF took every opportunity to poison the well of public debate. Before the commission even met, the CAF issued "biographies" of the commissioners that, for instance, described commission cochairman Richard Parsons as having a "proven track record as a corporate executive willing to undermine the retirement security of his employees," Robert Johnson of Black Entertainment Television as "refusing to pay fair wages" to entertainers, and highlighted any and all links commission members may have to the investment sector. Throughout the process, the CAF issued press releases and published op-eds charging the commission with "ignoring key critics of President Bush's privatization proposal." (As it happens, key critics of personal accounts such as Rep. Robert Matsui were invited to meet with the commission, in public or private, but declined to do so.)

Given these charges, one would assume that when two leading members of the Campaign for America's Future were invited to testify before the commission, they would have come prepared with constructive alternatives to personal accounts. Indeed, at the commission's public hearing in San Diego it at first seemed that specific options would be debated, when CAF founder Roger Hickey stated:

> It is well known that there are proposals to strengthen Social Security without privatizing and without across-the-board benefit cuts or tax hikes. They have been put forward by many experts: Henry Aaron, former commissioner Robert

Ball, economist Peter Diamond at MIT, Dean Baker and others. We should be debating the details of these pragmatic plans, we believe.[98]

What appeared less well known to Hickey was that the plans he cited are far from lacking "across-the-board benefit cuts or tax hikes":

- Henry Aaron's proposal with Robert Reischauer increases both the early and the normal retirement ages as well as increasing the benefit computation period, both of which constitute across-the-board cuts in promised benefits (and are termed as such by Aaron and Reischauer); the Aaron-Reischauer plan also includes increases in the maximum taxable wage, government investment in the stock market, and other changes.
- Robert Ball's proposal with the 1994–96 Advisory Council on Social Security would increase payroll tax rates in the future, reduce annual cost-of-living adjustments, and increase the benefit computation period, along with other changes such as government investment in the stock market.
- Dean Baker of the Center for Economic and Policy Research would increase payroll tax rates on all workers as well as the base wage on which taxes are levied.
- Peter Diamond of MIT would force state and local workers to enter the system; raise the maximum wage subject to payroll taxes; increase taxes on benefits and eliminate the current tax exemption for low-income retirees; index benefits for life expectancy to about half the degree done in Plan 3; and phase in payroll tax increases.[99] This proposal, however, has never been fully analyzed for solvency.

Hickey eventually acknowledged to Commissioner Fidel Vargas that his preferred course of action was to repeal the recent tax cuts passed by Congress and spend the proceeds on non–Social Security programs, in hopes that this would spur economic growth and benefit Social Security. The probability that additional federal spending will spur economic growth is for individuals to judge, but it is worth pointing out that economic growth would need to double for Social Security to remain technically solvent throughout the 75-year actuarial scoring period.[100]

Hans Riemer, Roger Hickey's colleague at the Campaign for America's Future, exhibited better knowledge of existing reform proposals when he testified before the commission in Washington, D.C., but he demonstrated the same lack of seriousness when it came to discussing the alternatives to personal accounts. Riemer offered general prescriptions, such as repealing the recent tax cuts, increasing or removing the "cap" on income to which the payroll tax applies, and investing the trust fund in the stock market (this last option is particularly puzzling given that Riemer simultaneously endorses the view that future stock returns cannot exceed 3.5 percent annually, which would make trust fund investment practically worthless in terms of achieving solvency).[101] When pressed for a more specific, comprehensive plan that could be scored by Social Security's actuaries and compared with the plans put forward by the commission, Riemer agreed to do so, and reiterated this agreement at later dates.[102] In the end, though, Riemer never delivered the promised proposal.

The commissioners did not claim that their plans constitute a free lunch. Rather, they merely maintained that their proposals met the president's principles for reform and are superior to the alternatives. Account opponents' determination to keep those alternatives a secret implicitly acknowledges that the commissioners are right. The sad state of the political discussion over Social Security is revealed, not in reformers' disagreement with their opponents' policy proposals, but in the difficulty of discerning precisely what policy proposals reform opponents actually favor. Realistically, however, an unwillingness to embrace any reform plan is an acceptance of the status quo. This is fine, as long as everyone recognizes that the status quo allows Social Security to go broke. Until both sides lay their cards on the table and declare specifically what they wish to do, there is little taking place in the way of debate.

Conclusion

The President's Commission to Strengthen Social Security took seriously its task to formulate proposals incorporating voluntary personal accounts that would not merely ensure the solvency of Social Security but contribute to its long-term sustainability as well. Sustainability means more than making Social Security's assets equal its liabilities in a bookkeeping sense over a 75-year period. Reform must ensure that, in an overall economic and budgetary sense, Social

Security truly saves for the future, preparing the program and the country to support a growing population of retirees through 2075 and beyond.

The commission's three reform proposals represent a range of ways to use private, individually controlled investment to strengthen Social Security and to build assets and wealth for Americans who need them most. None of the plans is perfect, and each constitutes a compromise between commission members. The Appendix includes the author's own criteria for reform, against which the commission proposals can be assessed.

Nevertheless, all three commission plans move Social Security toward a sustainable future and contribute to the overall reform effort. The commission's Plan 2, in particular, would allow workers to regain control over their retirement savings while giving the federal government the budgetary flexibility that comes from a pension program that can live within its means.

In his 2002 State of the Union address, President Bush said that the fight against terrorism wasn't just our responsibility, but our privilege. That sentiment applies just as well to Social Security reform. It would be very easy to sit back and do nothing—to keep spending the program's surpluses and pretending the problem will fix itself, then feigning surprise when it doesn't. But to do so would sell us all short. Addressing Social Security's problems today, making the tough choices now instead of passing them off to others, is not just this generation's obligation, it is its privilege.

Appendix: Analytical Framework

What follows is a basic analytical framework of the primary policy issues that must be addressed regarding Social Security reform. Answers to these four questions—whether to fund, where to fund from, how much to fund, and what to fund—do not depend on any particular philosophical or ideological beliefs.

Whether to Fund

The first question, whether to fund, asks whether it is desirable to move away from Social Security's current pay-as-you-go financing, in which each working generation pays the benefits of the current retired generation, to a funded status, in which each working generation accumulates and holds assets to provide income in its own retirement. Note that, at this stage, no distinction need be made between funding through a central investment strategy or through personal accounts.

The advantage of pay-as-you-go funding is that it can begin paying benefits quickly: the Social Security Act was passed in 1935 and the program began paying out retirement benefits just five years later. By contrast, a funded system demands a full working lifetime before it can begin paying full retirement benefits.[103]

The advantage of a funded system is that at any given time it pays a substantially higher rate of return than does a pay-as-you-go program. This rate-of-return difference is not simply the opinion of right wing economists; liberal economists Paul Samuelson of MIT and Henry Aaron of the Brookings Institution established during the 1950s and 1960s that a pay-as-you-go system like Social Security will pay a rate of return roughly equal to the growth rate of the taxable wage base—that is, labor force growth plus wage growth.[104] From 1960 to 2000, this pay-as-you-go rate of return equaled 2.9 percent after inflation.

By contrast, the return to capital during that same period was 8.5 percent after inflation.[105] The difference was based not on risk—both "returns" fluctuated over time—but on the economic fundamentals involved.[106] Peter Diamond of MIT, a prominent opponent of personal accounts, found that under typical circumstances the return from a funded system should exceed that of a pay-as-you-go system, and historically this difference has been wide.[107]

The upshot is that a funded system, however structured, can pay the same benefits at substantially lower cost than a pay-as-you-go system. This advantage goes for a funded defined-benefit government-run system just as much as for a decentralized personal account program. Over a 45-year working lifetime, a funded system at the historical return to capital pays benefits at one-sixth the cost of a pay-as-you-go plan. Even at a more modest return of 5 percent, which is closer to what could be expected from an actual investment portfolio, the long-term cost is just half that of a pay-as-you-go system.[108]

The conclusion then, based on the work of economists opposed to personal accounts, is that over the long term a pay-as-you-go system is simply less efficient than a funded program.

Yet, while vastly inefficient over the long term, pay-as-you-go programs like Social Security are highly efficient in the short term:

266

not in the sense that the program's administrative costs are low—though for the retirement and survivors' programs, they are—but in that under a pure pay-as-you-go system all of the money paid in today is used today to pay benefits.[109] There is no "waste, fraud, and abuse" to cut, no way to use the money actually paid to retirees more efficiently. In short, to move from an unfunded system to a funded system you have to come up with additional funds. This raises the obvious question, "From where?"

Where to Fund From

To move from an unfunded pension system to a funded system, several sources of funding are available. The first source, and the least likely on a large scale, is current retirees. If we were to reduce benefits to today's retirees, workers could simply shift their payroll taxes from supporting today's generation to saving for their own. But this would constitute a changing of the rules after the game has been played, which most people would consider unethical.[110] The fact that the current system does not and cannot guarantee benefits does not mean that policymakers should fund reforms at retirees' expense. Moreover, many retirees have few resources other than Social Security, so large-scale reductions in payments to current retirees would throw many into poverty. This is hardly the goal of reform.

Some reform plans have adopted tax increases as a funding source. In one sense, it seems like an obvious solution: why not simply obtain the money from the same place government gets all its other money? Although revenue increases are feasible on a small scale, if not desirable from a philosophical viewpoint, any tax increase is likely to fall on higher-wage workers who already save large portions of their incomes. Because these workers may reduce personal saving in response to such a tax increase, this route could give the appearance of increasing saving without actually accomplishing it.

Similar objections apply to debt financing the transition to reform. It is common sense that you can't increase saving through borrowing. The economic benefits of a funded system flow from increases in saving, and increased saving means reduced consumption, at least in the short term.[111] Under a debt-financed transition to "funding," based on either personal accounts or centralized government investment, the increased benefits from the funded system would be offset by higher debt service costs, and the higher return from the funded system would be offset by the rate of return on the outstanding debt. Debt financing, again, gives the appearance of economic pre-funding without the substance.[112]

The fourth possible source of funding is reductions in other government spending. It is said that a government program is the closest thing to immortality on this earth. Programs can continue year after year because they benefit the interests of those who sponsor them, even if their net benefit to society and the economy is small or even negative.

Recalling the real return to capital cited before—8.5 percent after inflation—it is difficult to imagine many government programs yielding this return at the margin, or even well in from the margin. There are exceptions, of course; as certain government functions such as national defense or police forces are prerequisites to most nongovernment economic activities, basic government services presumably produce average returns above those available in the market.

In general, however, existing estimates suggest below-market returns from most public investment. Paul Evans and Gregorios Karras examined state government spending on education, highways, health and hospitals, police and fire protection, and sewers and sanitation, measuring whether increased government investment in those functions raised state economic output. In general, they found the opposite: "We find fairly strong evidence that current government educational services are productive but no evidence that the other government activities considered are productive. Indeed, we typically find statistically negative productivity for government capital."[113] Because the federal government spends relatively little on education, we may infer that the losses from reductions in federal investment spending would be outweighed by gains to Social Security were those funds invested on its behalf.

From this perspective, the preferred route to a funded pension system is through reductions in existing or projected federal government spending rather than through increased taxation or public debt. That said, though, how much funding is desirable? And thus, how big should those reductions in spending be?

How Much to Fund

How much funding to seek is as much a value judgment as an economic question. From an efficiency standpoint, it stands to reason that over the long term a public pension program should be fully converted from an unfunded to a funded status. Although some argue that a mix of pay-as-you-go and funded financing diversifies risks, it is my view that—all other things being equal—the greater efficiency of funded pensions outweighs the benefits of diversification with pay-as-you-go financing.

That said, however, preferring funding over pay-as-you-go is only half the question. The other half is, even in the absence of pay-as-you-go financing, how much funding do we wish to do? Do we wish to devote the entire 12.4 percent current payroll tax rate to a future funded program, or should we settle for a smaller amount? At the rate of return to capital, a funded program can produce the same benefits as the current system at a payroll tax rate of less than 3 percent. Assuming a 5 percent return, the required payroll tax rate would be approximately 6 percent, though a cushion would obviously be necessary to account for fluctuations in the market. If we were to devote the entire 12.4 percent payroll tax to a funded system, the levels of retirement, survivors', and disability benefits would be substantially higher than those produced by the current program. Many workers, particularly those with shorter life expectancies, would prefer greater consumption opportunities during their working lifetimes to the higher level of retirement income such a program would provide.

At the same time, more funding—that is, more saving today— requires more forgone consumption today. Even assuming the transition is financed from current government expenditures, the public has substantial sentimental and personal interest attachments to many of these programs. Moreover, the further one moves from government expenditures at the margin toward the core functions of government, the higher the presumed return on those programs and the greater the cost to present generations of giving them up.

If the goal of a personal account is merely to fill the gap between Social Security's promised and payable benefits, then an account can be smaller still. However, while a relatively small account may fill this gap, its long-term benefits are also proportionately smaller.

What to Fund

It is possible to go almost all the way through the analytical framework with no significant mention of personal retirement

269

accounts. The reason is that the economic case for a funded Social Security system has little to do with accounts per se, and the public debate over the costs and benefits of funding can take place outside of the personal account context. Even among account opponents there is a clear preference for funding over pay-as-you-go financing. For instance, the Clinton administration's Social Security proposals, first to invest the trust fund in the stock market and later to prefund through debt reduction, both acknowledge the case for a funded pension system.

On a permanent basis, however, there are only two viable ways to fund Social Security. Debt reduction is not one of them. Although it has the same economic effects as other means of funding, there is only a limited amount of publicly held debt to reduce. Any large-scale movement toward funding would soon exhaust current supplies of debt to retire.[114] (No, it is not permissible to run up new debt for the purpose of repaying it later.)

Hence, the realistic choices for a funded system are between centralized investment of the trust fund and decentralized investment through personal accounts. The advantages of centralized investing are reduced administrative costs and the spreading of investment risks away from retirees and onto taxpayers. That may be of value, since even under current demographic trends, the working population will always be larger than the retired population. Shifting investment risk onto the working public may encourage the retired or near-retired population to lobby for more aggressive investment policies than taxpayers would be wise to bear.[115]

The main disadvantage of centralized investing is that it risks political influence over capital markets. Commentators ranging from Al Gore to Alan Greenspan have argued that the dangers of political investing are simply too great to be risked. Gore, a former supporter of government investment, said, "The magnitude of the government's stock ownership would be such that it would at least raise the question of whether or not we had begun to change the fundamental nature of our economy. Upon reflection, it seemed to me that those problems were quite serious."[116]

Defenders of centralized trust fund investing insist that no firewall will be left unconstructed to safeguard the nation's stock and bond markets from politically influenced investing of trust fund reserves. That may be so at the beginning, but others may soon find it in their interests to leverage the equity power of trust fund investing to accomplish goals they see as worthwhile. Few firewalls cannot be breached if those assigned to preserve them are uncommitted to the task.

Indeed, overseas experience confirms these risks. A World Bank study of centralized investment of government pension reserves found that in most cases investment returns did not exceed those available from an ordinary bank savings account. The principal reason, the bank found, is that investment decisions "are largely determined by the mandates and restrictions imposed on public pension fund managers. Asset allocation decisions are largely political and have little to do with any application of portfolio theory. In short, the problem is that investment policy is driven by political motives." Both Ireland and Canada began investing their Social Security funds passively but will soon begin active targeted investments in infrastructure and domestic industries, raising concerns that political concerns will trump the financial needs of pensioners.[117]

Personal accounts would largely bypass the risks of political influence, as workers would have the incentive to monitor the investment choices available to them and protest any manipulation of investment choices toward nonfinancial goals. Moreover, personal accounts, unlike central investing, give workers a true property right to their retirement savings. Individuals desiring low-risk investment choices could opt for government bonds, making their benefits truly backed by the full faith and credit of the United States. Younger workers could invest in equities or corporate bonds, according to their needs and their willingness to live with risk. Personal accounts could also benefit those who, having shorter life expectancies, do not fare as well in the current system in which benefits are effectively annuitized. Finally, as the commission pointed out, personal accounts carry significant nonfinancial benefits, entirely separate from the benefits they deliver. In testimony before the commission, Washington University professor Michael Sherraden summarized research on asset holding that has been conducted using experimental Individual Development Accounts. Among the findings—

- Asset holding has substantial positive effects on long-term health and marital stability, even when studies control for income, race, and education.[118]

271

- Among participants in trial programs of Individual Develop-ment Accounts, 84 percent feel more economically secure, 59 percent report being more likely to make educational plans, and 57 percent report being more likely to plan for retirement because they are involved in an asset-building program.[119]
- Individuals with investment assets, as well as their children, perform better on educational tests and reach higher educa-tional attainment, even after accounting for income.[120]
- Single mothers and their children are less likely to live in pov-erty if the mother came from a family with asset holdings, even after controlling for education and socioeconomic status.[121]
- Saving patterns are passed on from parents to children; parents who save are more likely to have children who save, even after other factors are counted. Hence, asset holding could be a means to establish long-term patterns of greater saving.[122]
- Ninety-three percent of individuals with Individual Develop-ment Accounts say they feel more confident about the future and 85 percent more in control of their lives because they are saving. Approximately half of account holders report that hav-ing accounts makes them more likely to have good relationships with family members, and 60 percent say that they are more likely to make educational plans for their children because they are saving.[123]

In this context, it is worth noting that the commission's Plans 2 and 3 deliberately established progressive personal accounts mostly to build savings and wealth most among those who currently have the least.

Opinions may differ, and policymakers and the public must make up their own minds in the course of the political debate, but the criteria outlined above establish a strong prima facie case for funded personal accounts as part of a larger Social Security reform package.

Notes

1. Executive Order 13210, President's Commission to Strengthen Social Security, May 2, 2001.

2. Estelle James, *Averting the Old Age Crisis* (Oxford: Oxford University Press, 1994).

3. President's Commission to Strengthen Social Security, interim report, August 2001. Hereinafter cited as interim report.

4. Henry J. Aaron, Alan S. Blinder, Alicia H. Munnell, and Peter R. Orszag, "Per-spectives on the Draft Interim Report of the President's Commission to Strengthen

Social Security," The Century Foundation Center on Budget and Policy Priorities, July 23, 2001, p. 3.

5. Interim report, p. 9.

6. Ibid., p. 32.

7. It is not wholly true to say that the worker-retiree ratio is fixed. Steps such as the scheduled increase in the normal retirement age should alter the ratio slightly in the program's favor, though such steps are also comparable to reductions in benefit payments at any given age.

8. Neil Howe and Richard Jackson, "What Happens to Benefits When Social Security Goes Bankrupt?" The Concord Coalition, April 19, 2000.

9. In practice, rather than reduce each check sent to beneficiaries, checks would be withheld until sufficient funds existed to pay "full" benefits; over the course of a year, however, total benefits received would be the same as if each monthly benefit had been reduced.

10. Henry Aaron, Alan Blinder, Alicia Munnell, and Peter Orszag, "Perspectives on the Draft Interim Report of the President's Commission to Strengthen Social Security," Century Foundation and the Center on Budget and Policy Priorities, July 23, 2001, p. 3.

11. Robert T. Matsui, U.S. House of Representatives, Remarks from the Capital Hilton Hotel, Washington, July 24, 2001.

12. Quoted in P. Mitchell Prothero, "Social Security Panel Draws Fire," United Press International, July 24, 2001.

13. See Dean Baker, "Defaulting on the Social Security Trust Fund Bonds: Winners and Losers," Center for Economic and Policy Research, July 23, 2001.

14. David M. Walker, Comptroller General of the United States, "Social Security and Surpluses: GAO's Perspective on the President's Proposals," February 23, 1999.

15. Aaron, Blinder, Munnell, and Orszag, "Perspectives on the Draft Interim Report of the President's Commission to Strengthen Social Security," p. 3.

16. Alicia H. Munnell and R. Kent Weaver, "Social Security's False Alarm," *Christian Science Monitor*, July 19, 2001.

17. Henry Aaron, Barry Bosworth, and Gary Burtless, *Can America Afford to Grow Old?* (Washington: Brookings Institution, 1988), p. 14. Emphasis added.

18. Aaron, Blinder, Munnell, and Orszag, p. 14.

19. Interim report, p. 17.

20. Quoted in Eric Black, "Memo to My Editor; Re: Social Security, Politics and the Balanced Budget Amendment," *Minneapolis Star Tribune*, March 10, 1995, p. 14A.

21. Byron Dorgan and Kent Conrad, "Unfair Looting," *Washington Post*, March 16, 1995, p. A21.

22. General Accounting Office, *Social Security: The Trust Fund Reserve Accumulation, the Economy, and the Federal Budget*, Washington, January 1989, p. 6. Emphasis added.

23. Statement of Charles A. Bowsher, Comptroller General of the United States, before the Senate Committee on Finance, "The Question of Rolling Back the Payroll Tax: Unmasking the Deficit Illusion," February 5, 1990.

24. Ibid., pp. 6, 8.

25. Quoted in "Warning Issued by GAO about Social Security," *St. Louis Post-Dispatch*, January 29, 1989, p. 1A.

26. Alicia Munnell, "At Issue: Social Security and the Budget," *Fiscal Policy Forum* 4, no. 1 (Winter 1986). Emphasis added.

27. However, regression analysis of Social Security surpluses and on-budget expenditures from 1979 to 2001 indicates that improvements in Social Security cash balances are more than offset by reductions in non–Social Security surpluses. See Kent Smetters, "Has Mental Accounting Been Effective in 'Lock-Boxing' Social Security's Assets? Theory and Evidence," University of Pennsylvania and National Bureau of Economic Research, August 2001.

28. Bob Graham and Robert Matsui, "Social Security Safeguard," *Washington Times,* September 12, 1990, p. G3.

29. Robert Matsui, Testimony submitted to the President's Commission to Strengthen Social Security, August 15, 2001.

30. Robert Matsui, "Trustees' Report Shows Social Security Health Improving," press release, March 26, 2002.

31. Stephen C. Goss, chief actuary, and Alice H. Wade, deputy chief actuary, "Estimates of Financial Effects for Three Models Developed by the President's Commission to Strengthen Social Security," Memorandum dated January 31, 2002, pp. 23–24.

32. Office of Rep. Robert Matsui, constituent newsletter, Summer 2000.

33. Henry Aaron, "Costs of an Aging Population: Real and Imagined Burdens of an Aging America," in *Social Security and the Budget,* ed. Henry Aaron (Lanham, Md.: University Press of America, 1988), p. 57. Emphasis added.

34. Aaron, Bosworth, and Burtless, *Can America Afford to Grow Old?* pp. 7, 11. Emphasis added.

35. Alicia Munnell and C. Nicole Ernsberger, "Public Pension Surpluses and National Saving: Foreign Experience," *New England Economic Review,* March/April 1989.

36. Alicia Munnell and Lynn Blais, "Do We Want Large Social Security Surpluses?" *New England Economic Review,* September/October 1984. Emphasis added.

37. Quoted in Pat Wechsler, "Will Social Security Be There for You?" *Newsday,* January 14, 1990, p. 79.

38. James Buchanan, "The Budgetary Politics of Social Security," in *Social Security's Looming Surpluses: Prospects and Implications,* ed. Carolyn L. Weaver (Lanham, Md: University Press of America, 1990).

39. Alan Blinder, "The Budgetary Politics of Social Security," in ibid. Disagreeing with Buchanan, Blinder argued that trust fund decumulations post-2018 would have an equal and opposite effect on government spending, reducing it to less than it would otherwise be. The commission's interim report notes this possibility and outlines the degree of spending restraint that would be required under such a scenario.

40. Peter Orszag, Testimony to the Social Security Subcommittee of the House Ways and Means Committee, "Global Aging and Social Security Crises Abroad," September 21, 2000. See also Peter R. Orszag and Joseph E. Stiglitz, "Rethinking Pension Reform: Ten Myths about Social Security Systems," presented at the World Bank Conference, New Ideas about Old Age Security, September 14–15, 1999.

41. Ibid. Emphasis added.

42. Quoted in Steve Gerstel, "Senate Begins Debating $1.1 Trillion Fiscal 1990 Budget," United Press International, May 2, 1989.

43. Quoted in Leo Fitzmaurice, "Republicans Masking Deficit, Gephardt Says," *St. Louis Post-Dispatch,* February 13, 1990, p. 10A.

44. But they must first devise a way for Social Security to truly save these funds rather than merely crediting them to the trust fund and transferring them to general revenue to be spent.

274

45. For instance, an August 2, 1999, Zogby International poll asked, "If Social Security funds are invested in stocks and bonds, who should do the investing—the government through a central fund, or individual workers through private accounts like an IRA or 401(k)?" Respondents favored private accounts by a more than four-to-one margin. A January 25–27, 2002, CNN/USA/ Gallup Today poll showed that, by a margin of 63 to 33 percent, respondents favor the option to invest part of their payroll taxes in a personal retirement account, despite a lengthy period of low market returns.

46. Peter Coy, "Who Loses under Social Security Reform?" *Business Week Online*, December 19, 2001.

47. Alan L. Gustman and Thomas L. Steinmeier, "How Effective Is Redistribution under the Social Security Benefit Formula?" *Journal of Public Economics* 82, no. 1 (October 2001): 1–28.

48. See Julia Lynn Coronado, Don Fullerton, and Thomas Glass, "The Progressivity of Social Security," National Bureau of Economic Research, March 2000.

49. See Gregory Pappas, Susan Queen, Wilbur Hadden, and Gail Fisher, "The Increasing Disparity in Mortality between Socioeconomic Groups in the United States, 1960 and 1986," *New England Journal of Medicine* 329 (July 8, 1993): 103–109.

50. U.S. Bureau of the Census, *Current Population Reports*, Series P20-514; *Marital Status and Living Arrangements: March 1998 (Update)*; and earlier reports.

51. This could happen in two ways: by working part-time or by withdrawing entirely from the workforce for a time. In either case, Social Security's benefit formula has difficulty distinguishing between those who worked full-time at low wages and those who worked part-time at high wages. For instance, Ms. Smith is a single mother who works full-time at half the average wage ($15,000) while simultaneously raising her children. Ms. Jones is married and worked for nine years at twice the average wage ($60,000) before leaving work to raise her children. At retirement, these two very different women would receive similar benefits—about $620 per month. Even though Ms. Smith worked full-time at low wages and Ms. Jones part-time at high wages, their average wage—upon which their benefits are based—is the same. And because that average is low, both benefit from Social Security's "progressivity" even if only one actually needs it.

52. Alan L. Gustman and Thomas L. Steinmeier, "How Effective Is Redistribution under the Social Security Benefit Formula?" National Bureau of Economic Research Working Paper no. 7597, March 2000, p. 33.

53. Coy.

54. As defined by the Social Security Administration, a low-wage worker receives 45 percent of the average wage, while a high-wage worker receives 160 percent of the average wage.

55. Interim report, p. 26.

56. Orlo R. Nichols, Michael D. Clingman, and Milton P. Glanz, "Internal Real Rates of Return under the OASDI Program for Hypothetical Workers," Social Security Administration, Office of the Chief Actuary, Actuarial Note no. 144, June 2001.

57. Robert L. Clark, Gordon P. Goodfellow, Sylvester J. Schieber, and Drew A. Warwick, "Making the Most of 401(k) Plans: Who's Choosing What and Why," in *Forecasting Retirement Needs and Retirement Wealth*, ed. Olivia S. Mitchell, P. Brett Hammond, and Anna M. Rappaport (Philadelphia: University of Pennsylvania Press, 2000), pp. 95–138.

58. The commission recommended, "personal account distributions should be permitted to be taken as an annuity or as gradual withdrawals, and balances above a threshold can also be taken as a lump-sum distribution. The threshold amount should be chosen so that the yearly income received from an individual's defined benefit plus the joint (if married) annuity keeps both spouses safely above the poverty line during retirement, taking into account expected lifetimes and inflation." Final report, pp. 41–42. Some account critics charge that requirements to annuitize eliminate the possibility of wealth building and bequests, popular features of personal accounts. (See, for example, Bernard Wasow, "Setting the Record Straight: Two False Claims about African Americans and Social Security," Century Foundation, March 2002, p. 2.) The increased poverty protections incorporated into the traditional program as part of Plans 2 and 3, however, mean that relatively small fractions of the account balance would be required to be annuitized to maintain an income above the poverty line, thus enabling retirees to leave lump sums to their heirs. Moreover, account balances of workers who die before retirement could also be passed on, which is of considerable value to groups with shorter life expectancies.

59. Whereas the current Social Security program offers a de facto inflation-adjusted annuity, which is often touted as superior to anything the market could provide, private inflation indexed annuities are now on the market. Moreover, there is evidence that individuals would prefer variable annuities that invest in equities to real, inflation-indexed annuities. See Jeffrey R. Brown, Olivia S. Mitchell, and James M. Poterba, "The Role of Real Annuities and Indexed Bonds in an Individual Accounts Retirement Program," in *Innovations in Financing Retirement*, ed. Zvi Bodie, P. Brett Hammond, and Olivia S. Mitchell (Philadelphia: University of Pennsylvania Press, 2002), pp. 175–97.

60. For instance, assume that a worker invested the maximum of $1,000 annually into his or her personal account. Compounding these contributions at 2 percent would total $60,644 after 40 years, and computing this notional lump sum through an annuity formula would reduce traditional benefits by approximately $360 per month. However, the true account balance, growing at an assumed interest rate of 4.6 percent, would equal $112,265—an amount sufficient to increase monthly benefits by $672. Again, as long as the account's interest rate exceeds the offset interest rate, total retirement benefits will increase.

61. Final report, p. 98.

62. Ibid., p. 113.

63. See Henry J. Aaron, Alan S. Blinder, Alicia H. Munnell, and Peter R. Orszag, "Governor Bush's Individual Account Proposal: Implications for Retirement Benefits," Century Foundation Issue Brief no. 11, June 2000.

64. This amount would be 88 percent of what Social Security promises but cannot pay. With a net return of around 4.2 percent, the 2052 retiree could receive more than his promised benefit.

65. *Flemming v. Nestor*, 363 U.S. 603 (1960).

66. If payroll tax shortfalls were financed through income tax revenues, rates would have to rise by approximately 17 percent across the board by 2052. If income tax increases were restricted to upper rates, the increases would be even larger. See Andrew G. Biggs, "The Cost of Not Reforming Social Security," *The Dismal Scientist*, April 17, 2001, www.economy.com.

67. Author's calculations.

68. For discussion of differential mortality according to income, see Eugene Steuerle and Jon M. Bakija, *Retooling Social Security for the 21st Century: Right and Wrong Approaches to Reform* (Washington: Urban Institute Press, 1994), pp. 115–119.

69. Interim report, p. 13.

70. The latest report from Social Security's trustees illustrates this point, albeit on a smaller scale. The trustees increased their projections for future productivity growth, but this had little effect on system solvency, and, overall, the program's actuarial balance declined and its long-term deficits increased.

71. In practice, there are several means to accomplish price indexing. Under the commission's Plan 2, price indexing would actually be implemented by multiplying the PIA bend point factors (i.e., 90, 32, and 15 percent replacements) by the ratio of the Consumer Price Index to the Average Wage Index in successive years. The bend point dollar amounts would remain indexed to wages. By indexing the factors rather than the dollar amount, the progressivity of the benefit formula is retained. If the bend point dollar amount were indexed to prices, over time retirees would see practically all of their pre-retirement wages covered under the 15 percent bend point, creating a de facto flat replacement rate throughout the income distribution.

72. In other words, a worker retiring just after 2009 would have his working years before 2009 calculated under the old system, with only years past 2009 calculated under the new formula.

73. Kilolo Kijakazi and Robert Greenstein, "Replacing 'Wage Indexing' with 'Price Indexing' Would Result in Deep Reductions over Time in Social Security Benefits," Center on Budget and Policy Priorities, December 14, 2001.

74. Replacement rates would also fall for workers with wage levels derived from the average in any given year. The Social Security Administration's "low-wage" earner, for instance, is defined as earning 45 percent of the average wage, whatever that average wage may be.

75. Assuming an all-bond portfolio, the replacement rate would be approximately 29.4 percent, while with a 60-40 stock bond portfolio it would be approximately 36 percent.

76. Greenstein and Kijazaki, p. 6.

77. This, of course, is untrue when benefits from the personal accounts are counted in. All workers would receive more than the current system can pay, and many low-wage workers would receive more than is even promised.

78. Their position is valid only when workers' economic well-being is judged not by their absolute incomes but by their incomes relative to others. In this sense, the low-wage worker in 2070 will be disadvantaged in a way that an average-wage worker today is not, despite their having virtually identical incomes.

79. Hans Riemer, Testimony before the President's Commission to Strengthen Social Security, August 22, 2001, p. 27, www.csss.gov.

80. Peter Diamond, James Hickman, William Hsiao, and Ernest Moorhead, "Report of the Consultant Panel on Social Security to the Congressional Research Service," August 1976, p. 23.

81. Ibid., p. 9.

82. Peter Diamond, James Hickman, William Hsiao, and Ernest Moorhead, letter to the *New York Times*, May 29, 1977, sec. 4, p. 14.

83. "Propping up Social Security," *Business Week*, July 19, 1976, p. 34.

84. Statement of Henry Aaron, Gardner Ackely, Mary Falvey, John Porter, and J. W. Van Gorkom, *Social Security Financing and Benefits, Report of the 1979 Advisory Council* (Washington: Government Printing Office, 1979), pp. 212–15.

85. "Will Voluntary Personal Accounts Save Social Security?" American Enterprise Institute Seminar Series in Tax Policy, April 5, 2002.

86. For instance, the wage indexing plan advocated by the Ford administration implied system costs in 2030 of 18.9 percent of payroll, contrasted with 17.24 percent projected in the 2002 Social Security trustees report. The Hsaio panel faulted the Ford administration's plan for leaving "a significant actuarial deficit in the financing of the OASDI system" and highlighted "the stability of the tax rates needed to finance promised benefits under this Panel's recommendation—a stability not enjoyed by other major recommendations that Congress is considering." *Report of the Consultant Panel on Social Security to the Congressional Research Service*, p. 6.

87. See Michael Sherraden, "Saving in IDA Programs: Supplement to Invited Testimony to the President's Commission on Social Security," October 28, 2001, p. 1, which noted that even with a 2-to-1 match, participants contributed to their accounts an average of only 7 out of 12 months of the year and saved only 67 percent of the maximum eligible for the match.

88. Paul Yakoboski, Pamela Ostuw, and Jennifer Hicks, "What Is Your Savings Personality? The 1998 Retirement Confidence Survey," Employee Benefits Research Institute Issue Brief no. 200, August 1998, p. 11, www.ebri.org/rcs/T114.pdf.

89. Hans Riemer, "Bush Social Security Commission Proposes Benefit Cuts to Pay for Privatization," Institute for America's Future, December 6, 2001.

90. Roger Hickey, Testimony before the President's Commission to Strengthen Social Security, September 6, 2001, p. 226, www.csss.gov. Hickey cited the Aaron-Reischauer proposal as one of several plans he approved of that reached actuarial balance "without privatizing and without across-the-board benefit cuts or tax hikes" (p. 204). On being reminded that the Aaron-Reischauer plan increased the retirement age Hickey declared his opposition to that provision, but fully 38 percent of the plan's progress toward solvency is achieved through changes in the retirement age. Aaron-Reischauer also contains another across-the-board benefit cut in the form of an increase in the benefit computation period from 35 to 38 years, which constitutes another 13 percent of the plan's progress toward solvency. See Henry J. Aaron and Robert D. Reischauer, *Countdown to Reform: The Great Social Security Debate* (New York: Century Foundation Press, 2001).

91. Staff of Robert Matsui, U.S. House of Representatives, "Six Problems with Privatizing Social Security," March 6, 2002.

92. Interim report, p. 138; emphasis in original.

93. Social Security Advisory Board, "Charting the Future of Social Security's Disability Programs: The Need for Fundamental Change," January 2001, p. 11.

94. Ibid., p. 11.

95. Ibid., p. 5.

96. "Administrative Expenses as a Percentage of Contribution Income and of Total Expenditures, Fiscal Years 1996–2000," Table III.A8 of the *2001 OASDI Trustees Report*.

97. Quoted in Robert A. Rosenblatt, "Options Given to Save Social Security; Privatization: Panel Will Let President Bush Choose among Varied Plans to Restore Retirement Program to Solvency," *Los Angeles Times*, November 30, 2001.

98. Roger Hickey, Testimony before the President's Commission to Strengthen Social Security, p. 204.

99. Peter Diamond, Remarks at "Will Voluntary Personal Accounts Save Social Security?" American Enterprise Institute Seminar Series in Tax Policy, Friday, April 5, 2002.

100. On the effect of economic growth on system solvency, see Andrew G. Biggs, "Social Security: Is It 'A Crisis That Doesn't Exist'?" Cato Institute Social Security Paper no. 21, October 5, 2000.

101. Hans Riemer, "Young Social Security Beneficiaries in the 50 States," 2030 Center, October 2, 2000, p. 5.

102. Hans Riemer, Testimony before the President's Commission to Strengthen Social Security, October 18, 2001, p. 44ff.

103. Individuals who pay into a funded system for only part of their working lifetimes would, of course, still receive proportionate benefits at retirement.

104. See Paul A. Samuelson, "An Exact Consumption-Loan Model of Interest with or without the Contrivance of Money," *Journal of Political Economy*, December 1958, pp. 467–482; Henry J. Aaron, "The Social Insurance Paradox," *Canadian Journal of Economics and Political Science* 32, no. 3 (1966). In practice, Social Security's pay-as-you-go return is slightly lower than the sum of its two components because the number of hours worked generally declines over time.

105. James Poterba, "The Rate of Return to Corporate Capital and Factor Shares: New Estimates Using Revised National Income Accounts and Capital Stock Data," National Bureau of Economic Research, April 1999, pp. 9–10. The standard deviation of returns on capital was 1.0 percent.

106. If the return to capital were lower than the pay-as-you-go return (a so-called dynamically inefficient economy), all generations would benefit by funding present consumption on a pay-as-you-go basis until such time as the capital stock was depleted sufficiently to raise the return from capital above the pay-as-you-go rate. This was the case in Canada during the 1960s when it established its pay-as-you-go pension program, though even then such a circumstance could not be expected to long continue. For the United States to reach dynamic inefficiency would require a national saving rate of approximately 30 percent, significantly above the present level. Countries with extremely high saving rates could theoretically benefit from pay-as-you-go financing, though only the highest saving countries such as Singapore could possibly qualify and globalized capital markets make such benefits even less likely. See, for example, Kenneth Kassa, "Does Singapore Invest Too Much?" *Economic Letter*, Federal Reserve Bank of San Francisco, May 15, 1997. Of course, this analysis leaves aside other aspects of reform, such as risk and ownership, which would also play into any decision.

107. See Peter A. Diamond, "National Debt in a Neoclassical Growth Model," *American Economic Review* no. 55 (1965): 1126–50.

108. The distinction between the real, pre-tax return to capital and the returns to investment accounts is most commonly made by Martin Feldstein; see "The Missing Piece in Policy Analysis: Social Security Reform," The Richard T. Ely Lecture, *American Economic Review* 86, no. 2 (May 1996): 1–14. Feldstein points out that while the individual receives the return to his investment only after state, local, and federal corporate taxes have been paid, the real return to new capital investment is in fact the pre-tax return to capital. Some Social Security reform plans attempt to "capture" that full return by estimating the amount of new saving the plan would create, deriving the increased federal corporate tax revenues based on that new saving, and crediting those new revenues to Social Security.

109. This is complicated somewhat in that Social Security currently runs payroll tax surpluses. Although these surpluses are credited to the trust fund, many analysts (as detailed above) believe they are not contributing to national saving.

110. However, if post-1983 payroll tax surpluses were consumed, then taxpayers during that period enjoyed more government services or lower taxes than they would have had those surpluses been saved. Moreover, future workers will earn lower

wages than if the surpluses had been saved. In this case, future workers could argue with past workers that they were not provided with the economic means to finance full promised benefits.

111. Over the long term, however, an economy with a higher rate of saving will in general also have a higher rate of consumption, up to the so-called golden rule level of saving.

112. There are, of course, other reasons for moving to a personal account–based pension system, such as personal ownership, control over investments, and the ability to pass investments on to an heir. These reasons could make the transition worthwhile even if debt financing were involved.

113. Paul Evans and Gregorios Karras, "Are Government Activities Productive? Evidence from a Panel of U.S. States," *Review of Economics and Statistics* 76, no. 1 (February 1994): 1–11. See also Douglas Holtz-Eakin, "Public Sector Capital and the Productivity Puzzle," *Review of Economics and Statistics* 76, no. 1 (February 1994): 12–21.

114. See General Accounting Office, *Federal Debt: Debt Management Actions and Future Challenges*, GAO-01-317 (Washington: Government Printing Office, February 28, 2001).

115. On the risk-related costs of centralized investment, see George M. Constantinides, John B. Donaldson, and Rajnish Mehra, "Junior Must Pay: Pricing the Implicit Put in Privatizing Social Security," National Bureau of Economic Research Working Paper no. 8906, April 2002.

116. Quoted in Richard W. Stevenson and James Dao, "Gore Defends Stock Investment Switch," *New York Times*, May 25, 2000, p. 27.

117. Canadian Chamber of Commerce, "Canada's Retirement Income System: Still in Need of Reform," February 2002; and Philip Lane, "Gambling with the Future of Our Pensioners," *Irish Times*, February 12, 2002.

118. R. J. Galligan and S. J. Bahr, "Economic Well-Being and Marital Stability: Implications for Income Maintenance Programs," *Journal of Marriage and the Family* (1978): 283–90; R. L. Hampton, "Family Life Cycle, Economic Well-Being and Marital Disruption in Black Families," *California Sociologist* 5 (1982): 16–32; and S. J. South and G. Spitze, "Determinants of Divorce over the Marital Life Course," *American Sociological Review* 51, no. 4 (1986): 583–90.

119. A. Moore, S. Beverly, M. Schreiner, M. Sherraden, M. Lombe, E. Cho, L. Johnson, and R. Vonderlack, *Saving, IDA Programs, and Effects of IDAs: A Survey of Participants. Downpayments on the American Dream Policy Demonstration: A National Demonstration of Individual Development Accounts* (Washington University in St. Louis, George Warren Brown School of Social Work, Center for Social Development, 2001).

120. S. Mayer, *What Money Can't Buy: Family Income and Children's Life Chances* (Cambridge, Mass.: Harvard University Press, 1997); M. S. Hill and G. J. Duncan, "Parental Family Income and the Socioeconomic Attainment of Children," *Social Science Research* 6 (1987): 39–73.

121. L. Cheng, "Asset Holding and Intergenerational Poverty Vulnerability in Female-Headed Families," Paper presented at the Seventh International Conference of the Society for the Advancement of Socio-Economics, Washington, April 7–9, 1995.

122. M. E. Pritchard, B. K. Meyers, and D. Cassidy, "Factors Associated with Adolescent Saving and Spending Patterns," *Adolescence* 24, no. 95 (1989): 711–23.

123. Moore et al., *Saving, IDA Programs, and Effects of IDAs.*

13. The 6.2 Percent Solution: A Plan for Reforming Social Security

Michael Tanner

For the past several years there has been a growing consensus about the need to reform Social Security. As the debate has developed, the Cato Institute has provided studies and other information on the problems facing Social Security and the advantages of individual accounts as a way to reform the system. But until now we have not suggested a specific plan for reform.

Now, however, the debate has advanced to the point where it becomes important to move beyond generalities and provide specific proposals for transforming Social Security to a system of individual accounts. The Cato Project on Social Security Choice, therefore, has developed a proposal to give workers ownership of and control over their retirement funds.

This plan would establish voluntary personal accounts for workers born on or after January 1, 1950. Workers would have the option of (1) depositing their half of the current payroll tax (6.2 percentage points) in an individual account and forgoing future accrual of Social Security retirement benefits or (2) remaining in the traditional Social Security system and receiving the level of retirement benefits payable on a sustainable basis given current revenue and expenditure projections.

Workers choosing the individual account option would have a variety of investment options, with the number of options increasing as the size of their accounts increased. The initial default option would be a balanced fund, weighted 60 percent stocks and 40 percent bonds. Workers choosing the individual account option would also receive bonds recognizing their past contributions to Social Security.

At retirement, workers would be able to choose an annuity, a programmed withdrawal option, or the combination of an annuity

Originally published as Cato Institute Social Security Paper no. 32, February 17, 2004.

and a lump-sum payment. The government would maintain a safety net to ensure that no senior would retire with income less than 120 percent of the poverty level.

We expect this proposal to restore Social Security to long-term and sustainable solvency and to do so at a cost less than the cost of simply continuing the existing program. And it would do far more than that.

Workers who chose the individual account option could accumulate retirement resources substantially greater than those that are currently payable under traditional Social Security. They would own and control those assets. At the same time, women and minorities would be treated fairly, and low-income workers could accumulate real wealth.

Most important, this proposal would reduce Americans' reliance on government and give individuals greater responsibility for and control over their own lives. It would provide a profound and significant increase in individual liberty.

The Social Security Crisis

Social Security as we know it is facing irresistible demographic and fiscal pressures that threaten the future retirement benefits of today's young workers. Although Social Security is currently running a surplus, according to the system's own trustees, that surplus will turn into a deficit within the next 15 years.[1] That is, by 2018 Social Security will be paying out more in benefits than it takes in through taxes (Figure 1).

In theory, Social Security is supposed to continue paying benefits after 2018 by drawing on the Social Security Trust Fund. The trust fund is supposed to provide sufficient funds to continue paying full benefits until 2042, after which it will be exhausted. At that point, by law, Social Security benefits will have to be cut by approximately 27 percent.[2]

However, in reality, the Social Security Trust Fund is not an asset that can be used to pay benefits. Any Social Security surpluses accumulated to date have been spent, leaving a trust fund that consists only of government bonds (IOUs) that will eventually have to be repaid by taxpayers. As the Clinton administration's fiscal year 2000 budget explained it:

282

Figure 1
SOCIAL SECURITY'S PAYROLL TAX SURPLUS OR DEFICIT

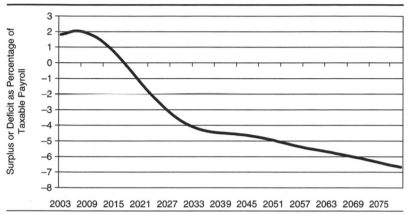

SOURCE: *2003 Annual Report of the Board of Trustees of the Federal Old-Age and Survivors Insurance and Disability Insurance Trust Funds*, table IV.B1.

> These [Trust Fund] balances are available to finance future benefit payments and other Trust Fund expenditures—but only in a bookkeeping sense. . . . *They do not consist of real economic assets that can be drawn down in the future to fund benefits*. Instead, they are claims on the Treasury that, when redeemed, will have to be financed by raising taxes, borrowing from the public, or reducing benefits or other expenditures. The existence of large Trust Fund balances, therefore, does not by itself have any impact on the Government's ability to pay benefits.[3]

Even if Congress can find a way to redeem the bonds, the trust fund surplus will be completely exhausted by 2042. At that point, Social Security will have to rely solely on revenue from the payroll tax—but that revenue will not be sufficient to pay all promised benefits. Overall, Social Security faces unfunded liabilities of nearly $26 trillion.[4] Clearly, Social Security is not sustainable in its current form.

There are few options for dealing with the problem. That opinion is held by people who are not supporters of individual accounts as well as by those who are. As former president Bill Clinton pointed out, the only way to keep Social Security solvent is to (1) raise taxes, (2) cut benefits, or (3) get a higher rate of return through private

283

Figure 2
INFLATION-ADJUSTED INTERNAL REAL RATE OF RETURN
FROM OASI

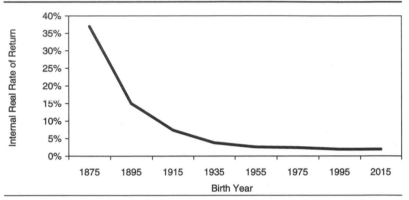

SOURCE: Dean R. Leimer, "Cohort-Specific Measures of Lifetime Net Social Security Transfers," Social Security Administration, Office of Research and Statistics, Working Paper no. 59, February 1994.

capital investment.[5] Henry Aaron of the Brookings Institution, a leading opponent of individual accounts, agrees. "Increased funding to raise pension reserves is possible only with some combination of additional tax revenues, reduced benefits, or increased investment returns from investing in higher yield assets," he told Congress in 1999.[6]

The tax increases or benefit cuts would have to be quite large. To maintain benefits in the first year after Social Security starts running a deficit, the government must acquire revenues equivalent to $197 per worker. By 2042 the additional tax burden increases to $1,976 per worker, and by 2078 it reaches an astounding $4,193 per worker (in constant 2003 dollars).[7] And it continues to rise thereafter. Functionally, that would translate into either a huge increase in the payroll tax, from the current 12.4 percent to as much as 18.9 percent by 2077, or an equivalent increase in income or other taxes.[8]

A Declining Rate of Return

Social Security taxes are already so high, relative to benefits, that Social Security has quite simply become a bad deal for younger workers, providing a low, below-market rate of return. As Figure 2 shows, that return has been steadily declining and is expected to be less than 2 percent for most of today's workers.

The poor rate of return means that many young workers' retirement benefits will be far lower than if they were able to invest their payroll taxes privately.[9] On the other hand, a system of individual accounts, based on private capital investment, would provide most workers with significantly higher returns. Those higher returns would translate into higher retirement benefits, leading to a more secure retirement for millions of seniors.

Savings and Economic Growth

Social Security operates on a pay-as-you-go (PAYGO) basis; almost all of the funds coming in are immediately paid out to current beneficiaries. This system displaces private, fully funded alternatives under which the funds coming in would be saved and invested for the future benefits of today's workers. The result is a large net loss of national savings, which reduces capital investment, wages, national income, and economic growth. Moreover, by increasing the cost of hiring workers, the payroll tax substantially reduces wages, employment, and economic growth.

Shifting to a private system, with hundreds of billions of dollars invested in individual accounts each year, would likely produce a large net increase in national savings, depending on how the government financed the transition. That would increase national investment, productivity, wages, jobs, and economic growth. Replacing the payroll tax with private retirement contributions would also improve economic growth because the required contributions would be lower and would be seen as part of a worker's direct compensation, stimulating more employment and output.

In 1997 Harvard economist Martin Feldstein estimated that, if all Social Security payroll taxes were privately invested, that investment would produce a net benefit of $10–$20 trillion in present value.[10] That is his estimate of the present value of the improved economic performance that would result from the reform. Most of that net benefit would probably come in the form of higher returns and benefits earned for retirees through the private investment accounts. But some would also come in the form of higher wages and employment for working people.

Helping the Poor and Minorities

Low-income workers would be among the biggest winners under a system of privately invested individual accounts. Private investment would pay low-income workers significantly higher benefits than can be paid by Social Security. And that does not take into account the fact that blacks, other minorities, and the poor have below-average life expectancies. As a result, they tend to live fewer years in retirement and collect less in Social Security benefits than do whites. Under a system of individual accounts, by contrast, they would retain control over the funds paid in and could pay themselves higher benefits over their fewer retirement years, or leave more to their children or other heirs.[11]

The higher returns and benefits of a private investment system would be most important to low-income families, as they most need the extra funds. The funds saved in individual retirement accounts, which could be left to the children of the poor, would also greatly help families break out of the cycle of poverty. Similarly, the improved economic growth, higher wages, and increased jobs that would result from an investment-based Social Security system would be most important to the poor. Moreover, without reform, low-income workers will be hurt the most by the higher taxes or reduced benefits that will be necessary if we continue on our current course. Averting a financial crisis and its inevitable results would consequently be most important to low-income workers.

In addition, with average- and low-wage workers accumulating huge sums in their own investment accounts, the distribution of wealth throughout society would become far broader than it is today. That would occur not through the redistribution of existing wealth but through the creation of new wealth, far more equally held. Because a system of individual accounts would turn every worker into a stockowner, the old division between labor and capital would be eroded. Every laborer would become a capitalist.

Ownership and Control

After all the economic analysis, however, perhaps the single most important reason for transforming Social Security into a system of individual accounts is that it would give American workers true ownership of and control over their retirement benefits.

Many Americans believe that Social Security is an "earned right." That is, they think that, because they have paid Social Security taxes, they are entitled to receive Social Security benefits. The government encourages this belief by referring to Social Security taxes as "contributions," as in the Federal Insurance Contributions Act (FICA). However, the U.S. Supreme Court has ruled, in the case of *Flemming v. Nestor*, that workers have no legally binding contractual or property right to their Social Security benefits, and those benefits can be changed, cut, or even taken away at any time.[12]

As the Court stated, "To engraft upon Social Security a concept of 'accrued property rights' would deprive it of the flexibility and boldness in adjustment to ever changing conditions which it demands."[13] That decision built on a previous case, *Helvering v. Davis*, in which the Court had ruled that Social Security is not a contributory insurance program, stating that "the proceeds of both the employer and employee taxes are to be paid into the Treasury like any other internal revenue generally, and are not earmarked in any way."[14]

In effect, Social Security turns older Americans into supplicants, dependent on the political process for their retirement benefits. If they work hard, play by the rules, and pay Social Security taxes their entire working lives, they earn the privilege of going hat in hand to the government and hoping that politicians decide to give them some money for retirement.

In contrast, under a system of individual accounts, workers would have full property rights in their private accounts. They would own their accounts and the money in them the same way they own their individual retirement accounts (IRAs) or 401(k) plans. Their retirement benefits would not depend on the whims of politicians.

Principles for Reform

In developing a proposal for Social Security reform, we relied on five basic principles:

1. *Solvency is not enough.* The goal of Social Security reform should be to provide workers with the best possible retirement option, not simply to find ways to preserve the current Social Security system. After all, if solvency were the only goal, that could be accomplished with tax increases or benefit cuts, no matter how bad a deal that provided younger workers. A successful Social Security reform will of course result in a solvent system, not just in the short run, but sustainable over time as well. And it

287

will also improve Social Security's rate of return; provide better retirement benefits; treat women, minorities, and low-income workers more fairly; and give workers real ownership of and control over their retirement funds.

2. *Don't touch grandma's check.* Although there is no legal right to Social Security benefits, workers who have relied on the program in good faith should not become scapegoats for the government's failures. Workers who are retired today or who are nearing retirement should not have their benefits reduced or threatened in any way.

3. *More investment is better than less.* You don't cut out half a cancer. Many proposals for Social Security reform would allow workers to privately invest only a small portion of their payroll taxes; they would continue to rely on the existing PAYGO Social Security system for the majority of Social Security benefits. But small account proposals will not allow low- and middle-income workers to accumulate real wealth or achieve other objectives of reform. Individual accounts should be as large as feasible.

4. *Individuals, not government, should invest.* The only way to increase Social Security's rate of return is to invest in private capital assets. This should be done through the creation of individually owned accounts, not by allowing the government to directly invest Social Security surpluses. Individual accounts would give workers ownership of and control over their retirement funds, allowing them to accumulate wealth and pass that wealth on to their heirs; it would also give them a stake in the American economic system. Government investment would allow the federal government to become the largest shareholder in every American company, posing a potential threat to corporate governance and raising the possibility of social investing. And government, not workers, would still own and control retirement benefits.

5. *Be Honest.* The American people can handle an open and honest debate about Social Security reform. Individual accounts will create a better, fairer, and more secure retirement system. But they cannot create miracles. They will provide higher retirement benefits than Social Security can pay. But they will not make everyone a millionaire. They will help solve Social Security's financial crisis and save taxpayers trillions of dollars over

the long run. But there is no free lunch. There are short-term costs that will require the president and Congress to make tough choices.

Promised vs. Payable Benefits

Opponents of individual accounts frequently suggest that the creation of such accounts would result in cuts in the promised level of Social Security benefits. Those critics are confusing changes necessary to restore the system to balance with changes resulting from individual accounts. As noted above, Social Security faces unfunded liabilities of nearly $26 trillion. Quite simply, unless there is a substantial increase in taxes, the program cannot pay the promised level of benefits.

That is not merely a matter of conjecture; it is a matter of law. The Social Security Administration is legally authorized to issue benefit checks only as long as there are sufficient funds available in the Social Security Trust Fund to pay those benefits. Once those funds are exhausted, in 2042 by current estimates, Social Security benefits will automatically be reduced to a level payable with existing tax revenues, approximately 73 percent of the current benefit levels.[15]

This, then, is the proper baseline to use when discussing Social Security reform. Social Security must be restored to a sustainable level regardless of whether individual accounts are created.

As the Congressional Budget Office puts it:

> A number of recent proposals to reform Social Security call for changes in the program's benefits. The effects of those proposals are frequently illustrated by comparing the new benefits to those expected to arise under the policies put in place by current law—showing whether they would be higher or lower and by how much. However, because of scheduled changes in benefit rules, a growing economy, and improvements in life expectancy, the benefits prescribed under current law do not represent a stable baseline. Their value will vary significantly across future age cohorts. Thus, focusing on differences from current law will not fully portray the effects of proposed benefit changes.[16]

It is wrong, therefore, to attribute to individual accounts benefit cuts that would be needed to bring the system into balance irrespective of whether individual accounts are created.

It is clear, in fact, that individual accounts by themselves do not cause any reduction in total retirement benefits (defined as the combination of account accumulations and traditional Social Security benefits). The best illustration of this concept is the first of three plans proposed by the President's Commission to Strengthen Social Security. That plan would create individual accounts (2 percent of payroll is used for illustrative purposes) but make no other changes to bring Social Security into solvency. The result is that Social Security remains insolvent (although the plan does improve financing by 8 percent), but the combined benefit received by workers is higher than benefits currently promised by Social Security.[17]

Because one goal of this reform plan is to bring the Social Security system into balance and eliminate the system's unfunded liabilities, changes are made to bring the system's finances into balance in a sustainable PAYGO system. Those changes are separate from the creation of individual accounts.

Therefore, in comparing benefit levels, payable benefits is the appropriate baseline.

A Proposal for Individual Accounts

Current workers should be given a choice. Beginning January 1, 2005, workers born on or after January 1, 1950, would have two options: Those who wish to remain in the traditional Social Security system would be free to do so, accepting a level of benefits payable with existing levels of revenue. Those workers would continue to pay the full 12.4 percent payroll tax and would continue to receive Social Security benefits as under current law. However, beginning in 2012, the formula used to calculate the accrual of benefits would be adjusted to index them to price inflation rather than national wage growth.[18]

That change would have no impact on people who are already retired, since benefits after retirement are already adjusted according to inflation (that's what cost-of-living adjustments, or COLAs, are). Nor would it reduce benefits for those nearing retirement. However, for younger workers, benefits would gradually be adjusted to a level sustainable under the current level of payroll taxation.

At the same time, those workers who wished to enter the new market-based system would be allowed to divert their half of the payroll tax (6.2 percentage points) to individually owned, privately invested accounts.[19] Those choosing to do so would agree to forgo all future accrual of retirement benefits under traditional Social Security. The remaining 6.2 percentage points of payroll taxes would be used to pay transition costs and to fund disability and survivors' benefits. Once transition costs were fully paid, this portion of the payroll tax would be reduced to the level necessary to pay survivors' and disability benefits.

Although they would forgo future benefits under traditional Social Security, workers who chose the individual account option would receive a bond in recognition of their past contributions to Social Security. That bond would be a zero-coupon bond calculated to provide a benefit based on accrued benefits under the current Social Security system as of the date that the individual chose an individual account.[20] The bonds would be fully tradable on secondary markets, but all proceeds would have to be fully redeposited in the worker's individual account until the worker became eligible to make withdrawals.

The recognition bonds may be valued at something less than the full present value of accrued benefits because we believe that workers will attach a value to receiving a tangible asset, making them willing to accept a discount in the face value of the bond. Indeed, polls show that a third of younger workers would opt out of Social Security even if they didn't get back a cent of the payroll taxes they've put in.[21] In addition, because the recognition bonds would be tradable, workers who wished to do so could sell them and allocate the sale price among higher-earning assets in the same way they do other contributions (see below). Finally, because the accrued benefits are calculated against current law, for some younger workers the level of those benefits would be higher than the level of benefits that would be payable under a sustainable PAYGO system. Those workers, therefore, receive something of a windfall through recognition bonds.

Workers would also have the option of depositing up to an additional 10 percent of their earnings in their accounts on a voluntary basis (that is, over and above the 6.2 percent payroll tax or contribution). Voluntary additional contributions would be made on an after-tax basis, and their investment, buildup, and distribution would be treated identically to the 6.2 percent account contribution discussed earlier.

Funds deposited in individual accounts would be invested in real capital assets under a three-tiered system.

> *Tier I.* Collection of payroll taxes, including individual account contributions, continues to be handled by the employer in much the same way as today. A worker's employer sends payroll taxes to the U.S. Treasury. The employer tells Treasury how much of the total payment is from employees who have chosen the personal retirement account option. Treasury then transfers that portion to a private-sector custodian bank, which invests the total amount in a money market fund that is always priced at one dollar, a standard industry convention. The following year, when the contribution is reconciled to the individual's name using the W-2 form, the fund's shares representing his contributions and interest credit are distributed to each worker and electronically transferred to the default account as specified under Tier II.
>
> *Tier II.* Workers initially have a choice of three investment options. As soon as a worker's contributions are reconciled, they are electronically deposited in one of three balanced funds, each highly diversified and invested in thousands of securities. The default portfolio, where one's money is invested if no choice is made, has 60 percent stocks and 40 percent bonds. The two other funds have the same asset classes but with different weights. For younger workers one fund with a higher concentration of stocks is created, and another, more geared toward less-volatile bonds, is created for those near retirement. Workers can move their funds from the default portfolio to either of the other two options.
>
> *Tier III.* Once a worker has accumulated some "trigger" level of funds, the worker is free to participate in a much larger range of investment options, closely approximating the options currently available under traditional 401(k) plans.[22]
>
> The institutions and providers managing funds under Tier III may choose to offer additional goods and services, such as retirement planning software, to attract assets from Tier II. Each worker can allocate his assets at will among Tier III providers. This ensures stiff competition as each provider strives to meet investors' needs. Costs would most likely be greater than in Tier II, but they would be incurred only if an individual chose to shift to Tier III.[23]

At retirement workers are able to choose an annuity, a programmed withdrawal option, or the combination of an annuity and a lump-sum payment. They can choose to annuitize their entire account holdings, or they can choose programmed withdrawals from the principal of their account, based on twice their life expectancy. If they choose the latter option, funds in their accounts will remain invested under the same provisions as before retirement. If a worker choosing the programmed withdrawal option dies before his assets are exhausted, those assets become part of his estate and are fully inheritable in the same way as any other asset. Finally, workers can choose to purchase an annuity providing annual income equal to 120 percent of the poverty level and take any funds available above this level as a lump sum.

Further, we believe that the system should adopt a "hold harmless point," such that once an individual can purchase an annuity equal to 120 percent of the poverty level, he or she can opt out of the system altogether and stop paying the 6.2 percent individual account contribution. For married couples, the hold harmless point would occur when the couple had accumulated sufficient combined funds to purchase a family annuity equal to 240 percent of the single-adult poverty threshold.

Contributions to individual accounts are on a posttax basis. Interest, dividends, and capital gains accruals on investments within individual accounts, plus all eligible withdrawals from the accounts, are exempt from income taxes. In most ways, individual Social Security accounts resemble Roth IRAs.[24]

Finally, the federal government provides a safety net ensuring that no worker's retirement income falls below 120 percent of the poverty level. Workers whose accumulations under the private investment option fall below the amount required to purchase an annuity at that level receive a supplement sufficient to enable them to purchase such an annuity.[25] This safety net is funded from general revenues rather than from the Social Security payroll tax.

Some proposals for Social Security reform provide much higher benefit guarantees; some guarantee that no one will ever receive less than payable or even promised Social Security benefits. Aside from the obvious expense of such guarantees, this approach is flawed in two respects. First, it seems wrong to make taxpayers responsible for guaranteeing investments by high-income workers who do not depend on Social Security for their retirement income. Should a factory worker really be on the hook to guarantee Bill Gates's investment choices? Second, guarantees inevitably create a "moral hazard" issue. Workers would be encouraged to speculate and make risky investment choices, knowing that they would reap the potentially higher gains from such investments and be protected from any possible losses. This is very similar to the type of moral hazard that led to the savings-and-loan crisis of the 1980s.[26]

Finally, although the individual account option is completely voluntary for current workers, it will eventually become mandatory for those workers who have not yet entered the labor force. As a result, the PAYGO Social Security system will eventually be replaced entirely by a market-based one.

Paying for the Transition

Although moving to a system of individual accounts will save money in the long run, there will almost certainly be a short-term requirement for additional revenues.[27] That is because, to the degree that workers choose the individual account option, payroll tax revenues are redirected from the payment of current benefits to personal accounts. But because most of the workers who choose accounts are likely to be young, it will be many years before the accounts result in significant savings to the traditional system.

Where, then, will the transitional financing come from? Ultimately, this is a decision for Congress, which will have to weigh the utility of various financing mechanisms, including debt, taxes, and reductions in current government spending.

However, three sources are worth special note. First, the portion of taxes on Social Security benefits currently used to fund Medicare should be redirected back to Social Security. That would provide an estimated $8.3 billion annually in additional revenue.[28]

Second, the Cato Institute has identified more than $87 billion annually in corporate welfare, roughly defined as "any government spending program that provides payments or unique benefits and advantages for specific companies or industries."[29]

Sen. John McCain (R-Ariz.) and Rep. Richard Gephardt (D-Mo.) have called for a commission to pinpoint and eliminate corporate subsidies. Congress should take this idea a step further and earmark the savings for individual accounts. Senator Graham has proposed such a commission as part of Social Security reform legislation that he has introduced.[30]

Third, to the degree that they actually represent an increase in national savings, contributions to individual accounts may, in themselves, prove to be a source of additional revenue for the federal government, revenue that could be used to help finance the transition.

It works in this way: The return on investment received by individuals is not the actual return earned by a given investment. A portion of the returns is actually taxed away through corporate taxes before returns are realized at the level of the individual investor. Therefore, a portion of the funds diverted to individual accounts is actually "recaptured" and available to help fund the transition.[31] The Social Security Administration estimates that this revenue recapture would provide "a substantial and growing source of income to the OASDI program."[32]

In a 1999 memo to Sen. Phil Gramm, the Social Security Administration estimated that, to the degree that contributions to individual accounts represent a net increase in savings, the recapture would be equal to 31.4 percent of the real, before-tax return on investments. This is based on an assumed average corporate tax rate of 35 percent applied against an assumed net new savings of 68.4 percent of assets invested through individual accounts.[33]

After using the three financing sources discussed above, we believe that any remaining transition costs could be financed through reductions in other wasteful government spending.[34] Simply restraining the projected growth in nondefense discretionary spending by 1 percent would generate more than $20 billion per year.[35]

We recognize that it may be necessary to issue some new debt to cover short-term year-to-year cash shortfalls. If that should become necessary, we believe that the issuance of such debt should be honest, explicit, and on budget. At the same time, we should understand that this would not really be new debt; it would simply be making explicit an already existing implicit debt.

It is also important to remember that the financing of the transition is a one-time event that actually serves to reduce the government's future liabilities. The transition moves the government's need for additional revenue forward in time, but—depending on the transition's ultimate design—it does not necessarily increase the amount of spending necessary. In fact, it will likely reduce the total cost of Social Security. In effect, it is a case of pay a little now or pay a lot later.

Why 6.2 Percent Accounts?

Some proposals for creating individual accounts as part of Social Security reform keep most of the traditional PAYGO Social Security structure in place and offer only very small accounts, allowing workers to privately invest just 2–3 percentage points of payroll taxes.

People who support plans with small individual accounts generally do so for one of three reasons:

- A political calculation that small accounts will avoid charges of "privatizing" Social Security;
- A desire to diversify risk by splitting responsibility for retirement income between markets and government, combining defined-contribution and defined-benefit programs; or
- Concern over short-term annual cash deficits.

However, given the clear advantages of larger accounts, none of those reasons holds up.

First, small account size seems unlikely to protect supporters from political attack. The recent Medicare reform debate provides a useful example. Despite rollbacks of attempts to introduce market competition to Medicare (the final bill contained only a handful of "demonstration projects" that don't begin until 2010), the bill was still attacked as an attempt to "privatize" Medicare. Opponents of individual ownership can be expected to be just as vociferous in their denunciations of 2 percent accounts as they would be in attacking 6.2 percent accounts.

At the same time, small account proposals may prove politically counterproductive by dissipating the enthusiasm of grassroots activists and others who support reform and failing to engage the attention of young workers. Opponents of individual accounts are entrenched and well organized. Washington politicians are fearful and reluctant to take on an issue of this magnitude. It will take strong public support to make reform happen.

Generating a sufficient level of support, particularly among generally apathetic younger voters, will require a reform proposal that makes clear how much those voters have to gain from reform. Bold colors, not pale pastels, will be needed to generate that kind of support.

The advantages of larger individual accounts are not lost on voters. A poll conducted by Zogby International for the Cato Institute asked voters how much of their Social Security taxes they wished to invest. A plurality of voters (27.9 percent) chose the full 12.4 percent. Only a slightly smaller group (26.5 percent) chose 6.2 percentage points, as provided for in this proposal. Only 11 percent of voters preferred 2–3 percent accounts. Support for large accounts was consistent across all political, ideological, and demographic groups, with younger voters showing particular support for bigger accounts (Table 1).[36]

Second, although risk diversification is generally a good thing, continued reliance on a government-provided benefit may actually increase the overall risk to workers. Those making this argument generally attach the most risk to the market-based component of a reformed Social Security system (individual accounts) and less or even no risk to the portion provided by government. In reality, however, this misreads both market and political risks.

Given the long-term investment horizon envisioned for workers choosing individual accounts under this proposal, market investment is remarkably safe. In fact, over the worst 20-year period of market performance in U.S. history, which included the Great Depression, the stock market produced a positive real return of more than 3 percent. At the same time, we know that, even under the best of conditions, Social Security will provide below-market returns. As Figure 3 shows, even with recent stock market declines, a worker investing all of his payroll taxes in stocks would receive benefits 2.8 times greater than he would receive had he "invested" the same amount of money in Social Security.[37]

Mixing private investments with traditional Social Security is therefore mixing a good investment (private accounts) with a bad investment (Social Security). That's not diversification, it's just bad investment policy.

Moreover, given the lack of property or other legal rights to Social Security benefits, and the program's enormous unfunded liabilities, traditional Social Security has political risks over and above its poor rate of return.

Besides, the proposed individual account plan provides an opportunity to diversify risk. The proposed default portfolio consists of

297

Table 1
PORTION OF TAXES TO BE INVESTED

	Overall	Political Preference			Age			
		Democrat	Republican	Independent	18–29	30–49	50–64	65 +
6.2%	26.5	26.7	21.7	32.5	41.3	29.9	29.2	11.5
2% or 3%	11.0	13.6	9.0	9.6	11.9	12.9	8.8	10.3
12.4%	27.9	22.0	36.2	25.9	32.6	40.2	27.5	11.8
None	20.4	23.2	17.4	20.4	8.4	11.2	22.3	35.4
Not sure	14.2	14.6	15.7	11.6	5.8	5.7	12.1	31.0

Figure 3
EVEN AFTER MARKET DROPS, PERSONAL ACCOUNTS WOULD PAY HIGHER RETURN THAN TRADITIONAL SYSTEM

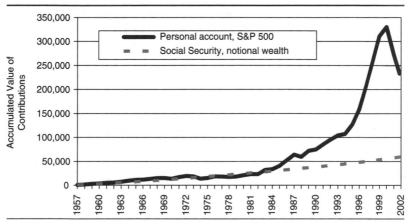

SOURCE: Andrew G. Biggs, "Personal Accounts in a Down Market: How Recent Stock Market Declines Affect the Social Security Debate," Cato Institute Briefing Paper no. 74, September 10, 2002.

both stocks and bonds. Risk-averse investors can opt for a portfolio even more heavily weighted toward bonds.

Finally, the truly risk averse can avoid private investment altogether. They can choose to remain entirely within the current Social Security system.

People concerned with short-term annual cash flows acknowledge that large accounts would save money in the long run, but they are equally concerned with maintaining the program's financial balance on an annual basis. This concern is due in part to the size of projected annual budget deficits and in part to skepticism about the ability of the federal government to use money saved in the future to repay debt incurred during the transition, rather than for tax cuts or new spending programs. In all honesty, Congress's recent spending habits give some cause for concern.

However, focusing only on short-term cash flows may be penny-wise and pound-foolish. It is much like paying only the minimum payment on a credit card, neglecting the opportunity to pay off the long-term debt altogether. Large account plans do incur greater short-term costs, but they also result in greater long-term savings.

299

More important, Social Security reform is about more than finances. Indeed, if system finances were the only issue, we could simply raise taxes or cut benefits. True Social Security reform must also provide increased rates of return and higher benefits; correct the inequities of the current system so as to treat workingwomen, African Americans, and others more fairly; and give low-income workers a greater opportunity to own and accumulate real wealth. By those measures, large accounts do a far better job of achieving true reform.

For example, increasing attention is being paid to the benefits of individual accounts as a way to give low-income workers an opportunity to build wealth. Although any increase in wealth should be encouraged, we should also be honest enough to admit that for low-wage workers 2 percent of their wages is not enough to allow for the accumulation of a real nest egg. Given that their Social Security accounts may often be the only form of savings that low-income workers have, the more we enable them to save, the better.

Finally, small accounts do little to advance the fundamental goals of reducing reliance on government and giving individuals greater responsibility for and control over their lives.

Of course, one might ask, if big accounts are better than small, then why not allow workers to privately invest the full 12.4 percent payroll tax, or at least the roughly 10 percentage points used for OASI benefits?

Although there is no doubt that even bigger accounts would provide higher benefits than those envisioned under our plan, accounts of 10 percent or more may actually result in too much forced savings for many workers.

Most high- and middle-income individuals do not rely solely on Social Security for their retirement income. In fact, the wealthiest fifth of retirees receives only 20 percent of its income from Social Security.[38] Those workers have other (non–Social Security) forms of saving and investment, including IRAs, 401(k) plans, and even individual equity ownership and other investments. Indeed, we can assume that many of those workers have already achieved the level of retirement savings that they desire. Forcing them to save more through Social Security accounts may simply result in their saving less through their other investments. Moreover, in most cases, the non–Social Security investments take place in a less regulated and less constrained environment than that envisioned for individual accounts under Social Security. The end result of excessively large accounts, therefore, might actually be a perverse decrease in the freedom to invest.

Finally, some people have suggested progressive accounts, with low-income workers able to invest a higher proportion of their payroll taxes than those with higher incomes.[39] Such an approach has a great deal of appeal. It would maximize the benefits of individual accounts to low-income workers while holding down overall transition costs and avoiding the problems of oversaving by higher-income workers.

However, there are serious practical and implementation problems with such an approach. In particular, proposals for progressive accounts would appear to shift compliance and administrative costs to employers. The additional record keeping could become a significant burden, particularly for small businesses.

Consider, for example, a worker who holds two jobs. During the day, he works at a well-paid manufacturing job. At night, he supplements his income as a minimum wage bartender. How would his two employers reconcile his total income to determine the amount that he is able to contribute to his individual account?

One last point: we believe that 6.2 percent accounts are a very easy concept to explain to the average worker. The worker can privately invest his half of the 12.4 percent payroll tax, while the employer's half is used to finance the transition (and fund survivors' and disability benefits). Of course we recognize that, from an economic point of view, there is no difference between the employer and the employee share of the tax. The employee ultimately bears the full cost, but most workers make the distinction in their own minds. A 6.2 percent account proposal, then, becomes clear, concise, and easy to understand in an age of eight-second sound bites.

Conclusion

More and more Americans agree on the importance of allowing younger workers an opportunity to privately invest their Social Security taxes, but advocates of individual accounts are divided over how large those accounts should be. Some proposals that call for large accounts have very large transition costs, which makes their political viability suspect. Other proposals are relatively less expensive but give workers control over and ownership of only a small portion of their retirement funds. We believe that it is possible both to have large accounts and to be fiscally responsible. This proposal is designed to meet that goal.

The proposed Social Security reform would restore Social Security to long-term and sustainable solvency and would do so at a cost less than that of simply propping up the existing program. It would also do far more than that.

Younger workers who chose the individual account option could receive retirement resources substantially higher than under traditional Social Security. At the same time, women and minorities would be treated more fairly, and low-income workers would be able to accumulate real wealth.

Most important of all, this is a proposal that would give workers ownership of and control over their retirement income. It is a plan that puts people, not government, first. It is a plan that is fiscally responsible and protects future generations of workers and taxpayers.

Notes

1. *2003 Annual Report of the Board of Trustees of the Federal Old-Age and Survivors Insurance and Disability Insurance Trust Funds*, ftp://ftp.ssa.gov/pub/OACT/TR/TR03/tr03.pdf. Cited hereafter as *2003 Trustees' Report*.

2. Ibid.

3. Executive Office of the President of the United States, *Budget of the United States Government, Fiscal Year 2000, Analytic Perspectives*, p. 337. Emphasis added.

4. *2003 Trustees' Report*.

5. William Jefferson Clinton, Speech to the Great Social Security Debate, Albuquerque, N.M., July 27, 1998.

6. Henry Aaron, Testimony before the Senate Committee on Finance, 106th Cong., 1st sess., January 19, 1999.

7. Author's calculations, derived from *2003 Trustees' Report*.

8. Ibid., p. 16.

9. See Michael Tanner, "The Better Deal: Estimating Rates of Return under a System of Individual Accounts," Cato Institute Social Security Paper no. 31, October 28, 2003.

10. Martin Feldstein, "Privatizing Social Security: The $10 Trillion Opportunity," Cato Institute Social Security Paper no. 7, January 31, 1997.

11. See Michael Tanner, "Disparate Impact: Social Security and African Americans," Cato Institute Briefing Paper no. 61, February 5, 2001.

12. *Flemming v. Nestor*, 363 U.S. 603 (1960). For a fuller discussion of this issue, see Charles Rounds, "Property Rights: The Hidden Issue of Social Security Reform," Cato Institute Social Security Paper no. 19, April 19, 2003.

13. *Flemming v. Nestor* at 616.

14. *Helvering v. Davis*, 301 U.S. 619 (1937), quoted in *Flemming v. Nestor* at 616.

15. In practice, rather than reduce each check sent to beneficiaries, the Social Security Administration would stop sending out checks altogether until it accumulated sufficient funds to pay "full" benefits. When those funds were exhausted, checks would again be withheld until sufficient funds accumulated, leading to checks starting and stopping several times over the course of a year. The net effect would be that total annual benefits would be reduced by the same amount as if each month's benefits had been proportionally reduced.

16. David Koitz, "Measuring Changes to Social Security Benefits," CBO Long-Range Fiscal Policy Brief no. 11, December 1, 2003.

17. The President's Commission to Strengthen Social Security, *Strengthening Social Security and Creating Personal Wealth for All Americans* (Washington: Government Printing Office, December 2001). For an analysis, see Andrew Biggs, "Perspectives on the President's Commission to Strengthen Social Security," Cato Institute Social Security Paper no. 27, August 22, 2002.

18. This is by no means the only method of reducing promised Social Security benefits to a level actually payable under a sustainable PAYGO system. There is a fairly lengthy menu of such proposals, including means testing, adjusting the retirement age, adding an additional bend point to the formula for determining benefits, and changing spousal benefits. See Michael Tanner, "No Second Best: The Unappetizing Alternatives to Individual Accounts," Cato Institute Social Security Paper no. 24, January 29, 2002. However, we believe that changing from wage to price indexing is one of the fairest ways to restore Social Security to PAYGO solvency. For a more in-depth discussion of the benefits of price indexing, see Matthew Miller, *The 2% Solution: Fixing America's Problems in Ways Liberals and Conservatives Can Love* (New York: Public Affairs, 2003), pp. 198–207. In addition, it would be possible to offer workers the choice of receiving the full level of *promised* benefits but requiring them to pay the level of payroll taxes necessary to support those benefits. Such a mechanism has been included in legislation proposed by Sen. Lindsey Graham (R-S.C.). See the Social Security Solvency and Modernization Act of 2003.

19. Technically workers currently contribute 5.3 percent toward Old-Age and Survivors Insurance (OASI) and 0.9 percent to Disability Insurance (DI). Under our proposal, the employer would assume responsibility for the entire DI contribution (1.8 percent) and would continue to pay 4.4 percent of capped payroll toward the OASI portion of Social Security.

20. The face value of recognition bonds would be calculated by applying the existing Social Security benefit formula (AIME/PIA) to the worker's past covered earnings. The actuarial present value of this accrued-to-date benefit would then be calculated using a discount rate equal to the long-term opportunity cost to government of capital (essentially the 30-year bond rate), or roughly 3.5 percent, and current age- and gender-specific expected mortality rates.

21. Polling conducted by Rasmussen Research Corporation, July 1999.

22. The advisory committee was not able to reach a consensus on what level should constitute the trigger for permitting movement from Tier-II investments to Tier-III. Several members favored a dollar amount, such as accumulations of at least $5,000. Others preferred a time-based trigger, for example 3 years. Still others suggested an accumulation equal to 120 percent of the poverty level. Any of these options would ultimately be acceptable.

23. Workers could also move some or all of their Tier III assets back to Tier II, a platform with fewer features but lower costs. The competition among Tier III providers, and between Tiers II and III, would ensure that workers received the greatest amount of goods and services at the lowest possible cost. For more information on how this three-tiered structure of investments would work, see William Shipman, "How Individual Social Security Accounts Would Work," *Investor's Business Daily*, December 1, 2003.

24. Counterintuitively, saving on a posttax basis, with accumulation and payout tax-free, benefits middle- and low-income individuals more than proposals that would make contributions tax-free but payouts taxable. For further discussion, see Jagadeesh Gokhale and Laurence Kotlikoff, "Who Gets Paid to Save?" *Tax Policy and the Economy* 17 (2003): 112–39.

25. The determination of eligibility for this safety net will take place at the normal retirement age, 67 for most workers covered under our plan, with workers at that age receiving the full subsidy, although payment would not take place until the worker annuitized his account. Workers choosing early retirement would have the amount of their subsidy reduced in much the same way as workers choosing early retirement have their current Social Security benefits reduced.

For married couples, the determination of the federal guarantee would take place at the time that the older spouse reached retirement age. The government would take into consideration the combined accrued assets in both accounts and provide sufficient additional funds to purchase both spouses an individual annuity equal to 120 percent of the poverty level for a single adult.

26. See Andrew Biggs, "The Archer-Shaw Social Security Plan: Laying the Groundwork for Another S&L Crisis," Cato Institute Briefing Paper no. 55, February 16, 2000.

27. The Cato Institute is currently preparing detailed cost projections for this proposal. Those results will be presented in a forthcoming paper.

28. *2003 Annual Report of the Board of Trustees of the Federal Hospital Insurance and Federal Supplementary Medical Insurance Trust Funds* (Washington: Government Printing Office, 2003), p. 3, table 1.C.1. In overall budgetary terms, of course, this does not produce a net gain, since it would ultimately increase Medicare shortfalls. But it seems fair to use Social Security funds for Social Security. Medicare will ultimately require its own reform to remain solvent, but that is an issue for another day.

29. Stephen Slivinski, "The Corporate Welfare Budget: Bigger Than Ever," Cato Institute Policy Analysis no. 415, October 10, 2001, p. 6.

30. The Social Security Solvency and Modernization Act of 2003.

31. For a full discussion of "revenue recapture," see Peter Ferrara and Michael Tanner, *A New Deal for Social Security* (Washington: Cato Institute, 1998), pp. 62–64, 180–81.

32. Stephen C. Goss, chief actuary, Social Security Administration, Memorandum to Sen. Phil Gramm, April 16, 1999.

33. Ibid. SSA also uses this method in calculating revenue feedback under a Social Security reform proposal offered by Peter Ferrara. Stephen C. Goss, Memorandum to Peter Ferrara, December 1, 2003.

34. See, for example, Andrew Taylor, "House Panels Identify 'Waste, Fraud and Abuse,' But Are Unlikely to End Them," *CQ-Today*, October 2, 2003.

35. See Peter Ferrara, "To Get Spending under Control," *Washington Times*, January 6, 2004. Ferrara notes that such spending restraint would still result in a government 59 percent larger than it is today.

36. The survey of 1,204 likely voters was conducted in July 1999 and has a margin of error of + / − 3.0 percent. http://www.socialsecurity.org/zogby/full report.pdf.

37. Andrew Biggs, "Personal Accounts in a Down Market: How Recent Stock Market Declines Affect the Social Security Debate," Cato Institute Briefing Paper no. 74, September 10, 2002.

38. Neil Gilbert and Neung-Hoo Park, "Privatization, Provision, and Targeting: Trends and Policy Implications for Social Security in the United States," *International Social Security Review* 49 (January 1996): 22.

39. See, for example, Peter Ferrara, "A Progressive Proposal for Social Security Accounts," Institute for Policy Innovation Policy Report no. 176, June 2003. Progressive accounts are also a feature of the Social Security Solvency and Modernization Act, sponsored by Sen. Lindsey Graham, and of the President's Commission to Strengthen Social Security's Model 2.

PART IV

THE TOUGH QUESTIONS

14. Speaking the Truth about Social Security Reform

Milton Friedman

The journalist Michael Barone recently summed up the conventional wisdom about reforming Social Security. "The content of the reform is fairly clear—individual investment accounts to replace *part* of the government benefits financed by the payroll tax, later retirement ages, adjusted cost of living increases," he wrote in the *American Enterprise*. And, he added, "suddenly the money to pay for the *costs of transition* is at hand, in the form of a budget surplus."

I have italicized "part" and "costs of transition" because they epitomize key defects in conventional wisdom.

Social Security has become less and less attractive as the number of current recipients has grown relative to the number of workers paying taxes, an imbalance that will only get bigger. That explains the widespread support for individual investment accounts. Younger workers, in particular, are skeptical that they will get anything like their money's worth for the Social Security taxes that they and their employers pay. They believe they would do much better if they could invest the money in their own 401(k)s or the equivalent.

But if that is so, why replace only *part* and not *all* of government benefits? The standard explanation is that this is not feasible because payroll taxes—or part of them—are needed to pay benefits already committed to present and future retirees. That is how they are now being used, but there is nothing in the nature of things that requires a particular tax to be linked to a particular expenditure.

The Myth of Transition Cost

The link between the payroll tax and benefit payments is part of a confidence game to convince the public that what the Social Security

Originally published in the New York Times, *January 11, 1999. Reprinted by permission as Cato Briefing Paper no. 46, April 12, 1999.*

Administration calls a social insurance program is equivalent to private insurance; that, in the administration's words, "the workers themselves contribute to their own future retirement benefit by making regular payments into a joint fund."

Balderdash. Taxes paid by today's workers are used to pay today's retirees. If money is left over, it finances other government spending—though, to maintain the insurance fiction, paper entries are created in a "trust fund" that is simultaneously an asset and a liability of the government. When the benefits that are due exceed the proceeds from payroll taxes, as they will in the not very distant future, the difference will have to be financed by raising taxes, borrowing, creating money, or reducing other government spending. And that is true no matter how large the "trust fund."

The assurance that workers will receive benefits when they retire does not depend on the particular tax used to finance the benefits or on any "trust fund." It depends solely on the expectation that future Congresses will honor the promise made by earlier Congresses—what supporters call "a compact between the generations" and opponents call a Ponzi scheme.

The present discounted value of the promises embedded in the Social Security law greatly exceeds the present discounted value of the expected proceeds from the payroll tax. The difference is an unfunded liability variously estimated at from $4 trillion to $11 trillion—or from slightly larger than the funded federal debt that is in the hands of the public to three times as large. For perspective, the market value of all domestic corporations in the United States at the end of 1997 was roughly $13 trillion.

To see the phoniness of "transition costs" (the supposed net cost of privatizing the current Social Security system), consider the following thought experiment: As of January 1, 2000, the current Social Security system is repealed. To meet current commitments, every participant in the system will receive a governmental obligation equal to his or her actuarial share of the unfunded liability.

For those already retired, that would be an obligation—a treasury bill or bond—with a market value equal to the present actuarial value of expected future benefits minus expected future payroll taxes, if any. For everyone else, it would be an obligation due when the individual would have been eligible to receive benefits under the current system. And the maturity value would equal the present value of the benefits the person would have been entitled to, less the present value of the person's future tax liability, both adjusted for mortality.

The result would be a complete transition to a strictly private system, with every participant receiving what current law promises. Yet, aside from the cost of distributing the new obligations, the total funded and unfunded debt of the United States would not change by a dollar. There are no "costs of transition." The unfunded liability would simply have become funded. The compact between the generations would have left as a legacy the newly funded debt.

How would that funded debt be paid when it came due? By taxing, borrowing, creating money, or reducing other government spending. There are no other ways. There is no more reason to finance the repayment of this part of the funded debt by a payroll tax than any other part. Yet that is the implicit assumption of those who argue that the "costs of transition" mean there can be only partial privatization. The payroll tax is a bad tax: a regressive tax on productive activity. It should long since have been repealed. Privatizing Social Security would be a good occasion to do so.

Should Social Security Be Mandatory?

Should a privatized system be mandatory? The present system is; it is therefore generally taken for granted that a privatized system must or should be as well.

The economist Martin Feldstein, in a 1995 article in the *Public Interest*, argued that contributions must be mandatory for two reasons. "First, some individuals are too shortsighted to provide for their own retirement," he wrote. "Second, the alternative of a means-tested program for the aged might encourage some lower-income individuals to make no provision for their old age deliberately, knowing that they would receive the means-tested amount."

The paternalism of the first reason and the reliance on the extreme cases of the second are equally unattractive. More important, Professor Feldstein does not even refer to the clear injustice of a mandatory plan.

The most obvious example is a person with AIDS who has a short life expectancy and limited financial means, yet would be required to use a significant fraction of his or her earnings to accumulate what is almost certain to prove a worthless asset.

311

More generally, the fraction of a person's income that it is reasonable for him or her to set aside for retirement depends on that person's circumstances and values. It makes no more sense to specify a minimum fraction for all people than to mandate a minimum fraction of income that must be spent on housing or transportation. Our general presumption is that individuals can best judge for themselves how to use their resources. Mr. Feldstein simply asserts that in this particular case the government knows better.

In 1964, Barry Goldwater was much reviled for suggesting that participation in Social Security be voluntary. I thought that was a good idea then; I still think it is.

I find it hard to justify requiring 100 percent of the people to adopt a government-prescribed straitjacket to avoid encouraging a few "lower-income individuals to make no provision for their old age deliberately, knowing that they would receive the means-tested amount." I suspect that, in a voluntary system, many fewer elderly people would qualify for the means-tested amount from imprudence or deliberation than from misfortune.

I have no illusions about the political feasibility of moving to a strictly voluntary system. The tyranny of the status quo, and the vested interests that have been created, are too strong. However, I believe that the ongoing discussion about privatizing Social Security would benefit from paying more attention to fundamentals, rather than dwelling simply on nuts and bolts of privatization.

15. Administration Costs and the Relative Efficiency of Public and Private Social Security Systems

Robert Genetski

A consensus has been reached on several issues in the debate over the merits of the present government-run Social Security system versus personal retirement accounts (PRAs). First, it is widely recognized that the current government-run pay-as-you-go system is in serious trouble and cannot pay promised retirement benefits within the present tax structure. Second, it is widely acknowledged that the returns of the present system will be zero to negative for most of today's younger workers. As a result, trying to solve the Social Security problem by raising payroll taxes or postponing the retirement age, or both, ends up further reducing returns to today's workers and turns a bad deal into something much worse. Third, it is widely recognized that market-based returns to PRAs would produce returns that are three to five times higher than those promised by the government system. Returns on PRAs would be so high that, even when adjusted for risk, they would be far superior to the returns promised by the government-run system.[1]

A remaining issue of concern involves the cost of administering a system of PRAs versus the cost of the current system. By several measures, the cost of administering the current Social Security system seems to be fairly low. Some observers have suggested that the cost of administering a system of PRAs would be far higher. A study by the Employee Benefit Research Institute (EBRI) suggests that various administrative issues relating to PRAs may make the accounts too complex to understand or too difficult for record keepers to administer.[2] EBRI's study is correct in raising many important

Originally published as Cato Institute Social Security Paper no. 15, March 9, 1999, and updated to reflect current information.

313

issues affecting the cost and complexity of PRAs. A careful examination of those issues, however, shows that PRAs can be administered efficiently and cost-effectively.

Some observers have suggested that in order to minimize cost, the government should continue to administer the program, but invest Social Security funds in stock or bond markets to achieve the superior returns of market-based investing. The idea of the government investing Social Security funds in private capital markets has serious drawbacks.[3] Perhaps the most serious is the shift in power and influence from individuals to government. The vast amount of funds involved would dramatically increase government's control and influence over the economy. That increase in power would come at the expense of private individuals and would represent the most significant shift in power from private individuals to government since the creation of the income tax.

When one compares the costs of administering the current Social Security system with the cost of administering a system of PRAs in an effort to determine the comparative efficiency with which each system might work to achieve those objectives, it is apparent that the present government-run system may cost slightly less to administer than a system of PRAs. However, the relative efficiency gains in administering the current system are overwhelmed by the relative inefficiency of the government-run system in achieving its key objectives. To say that the government-run system is relatively efficient based on administrative costs is similar to saying that a Trabant (a cheap East German car that never worked) is less expensive than a Taurus or a Mercedes. While true, the comparison is hardly appropriate. Most people prefer to pay more for a car that works than to pay less for one that is unlikely to get them to their destination.

The administrative cost of a system of PRAs can vary significantly depending upon how the system is set up, the size of the accounts, and various rules and regulations associated with them. The more elaborate the requirements, the more expensive it will be to administer a private system. Since even small gains in efficiency in terms of administering the system compound over a lifetime, it is crucial to minimize administration costs wherever possible. If wise decisions are made with respect to the administration of the PRAs, administrative costs will be close to or only modestly higher than those associated with the present government system. At the same time, workers will receive the benefit of safe, secure retirement incomes that are substantially greater than those promised under the current system.

The Objectives of Social Security

Traditionally, the government-run Social Security system has had two main objectives: first, to provide earnings replacement for retirees and, second, to provide welfare support for the elderly indigent.[4] Although they are seldom mentioned, there are other important objectives. The returns to the system in the form of benefits should be as great as possible in relation to the contributions to the program. That means that any supplemental retirement program should be run in the most efficient manner possible. Efficiency means not just running the program at the lowest possible administrative cost but also ensuring that the net returns to the worker are as large and secure as possible for any given level of contributions.

Administrative Functions of a Social Security System

Any retirement system has four important administrative functions: collection, transmission, record keeping, and money management. First, there must be a system to collect the retirement funds from the worker. Next, the funds must be transmitted to an administrator. The administrator is responsible for keeping records of each worker's contribution to the retirement program and the benefits that each worker will eventually receive. Finally, the money has to be invested and managed between the time it is received and the time it is disbursed.

The present government-run Social Security system may be considered highly efficient in the management of some administrative functions. It collects retirement funds through the Internal Revenue Service (IRS). Each employer calculates the total obligation for retirement funds for each of its workers and deposits the amount in a special IRS account at the employer's bank. No worker ever gets to see his or her retirement funds. In fact, the worker's payroll statement identifies only half of the amount that is collected. The other half comes in the form of a tax on the employer (effectively a tax on employing the worker) that is equal to the tax on the worker. Few workers realize that the full amount of funds they are contributing to the government-run retirement system is twice what appears on their pay stubs.

Once deposited with the IRS, retirement funds go into the general account funds of the U.S. Treasury, where they are indistinguishable from all other government revenues. The Treasury makes the appropriate accounting entries to the Social Security retirement account to allow for the total amount collected. When retirement benefits are paid, the account is debited. Whenever more money comes into the Social Security retirement account than goes out, the Treasury spends that money on other government programs. It recognizes the surplus in the Social Security account by issuing IOUs to the Social Security Administration (SSA). By law, those IOUs take the form of a special class of Treasury securities, which are credited to the SSA and are the only type of investment the Social Security Trust Fund is permitted to hold.

Throughout the year, each employer continues to calculate the wages and Social Security contributions for each employee. However, employers send only the *total* contributions for all their workers to the IRS. When the year is over, each employer notifies the SSA of the wages and salaries of its individual employees and the amount of retirement contributions for each employee. Hence, the SSA enters the information on the contributions of each worker once a year.

The SSA is also responsible for calculating benefits. The benefits formula is based on a number of factors, including earnings history, marital status, age, and anticipated wages and salaries for the coming calendar year.[5] To receive benefits, a worker must apply to the SSA prior to his or her expected retirement date. The worker is also responsible for estimating expected wages and salary for the upcoming year. Even though workers may be "retired" and receiving Social Security retirement benefits, any wages and salaries they receive continue to be subject to the same retirement contribution rates as the earnings of other workers.

Costs of Administering the Current Social Security System

In several important ways, the present Social Security Administration does a highly efficient job in administering the retirement program. Overall administration costs are currently close to $10 per worker. Those costs amount to 0.42 percent of contributions and 0.57 percent of benefits paid. As a percentage of assets, the administration costs are 0.39 percent. However, since the government system has only minimal assets, that figure is not comparable to the cost figures for private plans.[6]

In assessing the cost of the current system, it is important to note that the costs of administering retirement systems tend to be relatively high when the system is first put into place. Those costs fall over time as the fixed costs are spread over larger participant pools.[7] For example, in the early days of the program, SSA costs were roughly ten times their current levels.[8]

There are other reasons why the costs of administering the government-run system are so low: The collection function piggybacks off the IRS collection system, and, since there is no investment or money management function, there are few expenses in that category. The bulk of the administrative expense (93 percent) involves administering the benefit function. By all objective measures of timeliness and accuracy, the SSA does an excellent job in that area.[9]

The only area where the SSA administrative system does not perform particularly well is in terms of the timeliness of tracking earnings and contributions. For the 1991 calendar year, only 70 percent of earnings contributions were tracked within six months of the end of the year. But, since workers have no legal rights to their contributions, that is not a significant shortcoming.[10]

Overall, the SSA does a highly efficient job in administering the various functions of the current retirement program.

Administration Costs in a PRA System

Given the relatively low costs associated with many of the administrative functions of the present Social Security system, there is a natural assumption that a system of individual PRAs would be less efficient and cost much more than the present government-run system. However, the extent to which this may be true depends on the parameters of the private system. Consumers who choose to pay more for a Mercedes than for a Ford Taurus do so because they find greater value in the higher-priced alternative. Those who choose to pay for a Taurus instead of buying a Trabant realize that it is often necessary to pay a price to get where you want to go. Even so, it is true that "every dollar which is unnecessarily or uneconomically expended on administration is a dollar which could otherwise go to the plan participants."[11] Over a lifetime, the compound interest impact of even a relatively small boost in administrative costs leaves retirees worse off than they might have been. So, it is important to assess the likely costs associated with administering a system of PRAs.

General Parameters of a PRA System

While there are infinite combinations of parameters that might apply to PRAs, the following can be considered reasonably accepted principles in providing for secure earnings for retirees and welfare support for the elderly indigent:

1. All current workers should have a choice as to whether to stay with the current system or switch to a private account. Those who decide to switch should be given some compensation in their private accounts (such as a discounted government bond) to reflect some portion of their past contribution to the Social Security system.
2. No one should be worse off under a system of PRAs than under the current system.
3. There should be some minimum level of benefits comparable to that of the present system. Those reaching retirement age who have worked for a total of 40 quarters and do not have the minimal level of benefits should receive supplemental government payments sufficient to allow for a minimal level of monthly benefits.
4. The system should be regulated by a self-regulatory organization (SRO) that is responsible for certifying administrators and money managers, regulating the types of investments permitted in accounts, and determining other details necessary to provide maximum security for PRAs while minimizing administrative costs.
5. All new workers entering the labor force must be part of the new system.
6. Married couples should have joint ownership of their accounts.[12]

Factors Affecting Administrative Costs

Like the government-run system, a system of PRAs must deal with the basic administrative functions of collection, transmission, record keeping, and money management. A system of PRAs may be organized in a variety of ways to accomplish those administrative functions. The cost will depend on how the system is organized.

While there are many directions that a private system could take, the most efficient system would use the existing infrastructure to accomplish the administrative functions.[13] At the present time, there is an entire industry that is responsible for most of the various administrative functions associated with collection, transmission, record keeping, and money management of individual retirement accounts.

Collection and Transmission

In large firms (usually those with more than 50 employees), the payroll function is generally automated and performed by outside vendors that specialize in the field. As a result, there would be few, if any, costs associated with changing the individual's payroll deduction from a category that currently gets deposited in the IRS collection system to one where the money is sent directly to the plan administrator.

For small employers that handle their own payrolls, the collection problem becomes only slightly more involved. Instead of sending one check for employee retirement contributions to the IRS each month, the employer could choose to send the check to any certified PRA administrator. (The employer would still have to send a check to the IRS for the Medicaid and Medicare portion of Social Security.) Along with the check, the employer would have to send a form showing the wages and retirement contributions for each worker. Since each employer already calculates that information in order to determine the total Social Security contribution, only a relatively minor additional burden would be placed on small employers. First, they would have to choose a certified administrator. Second, they would have to send the administrator the name and Social Security number of each worker along with information about the worker's wages and contributions for the period.

To prevent discrimination against small businesses, each certified administrator could be required to provide its services to all businesses. To keep costs at a reasonable level, administrators might be required to charge the same basis point cost for all individual accounts. In that case, the relatively low cost of administering large business accounts would subsidize the accounts of smaller businesses. An alternative to the idea of cross-subsidies would be a "default pool" for businesses that are too small to attract an administrator. The system regulator could decide to bid out the function of administering small business accounts so that the costs to that group would be fully transparent.

To summarize, the above-described system for collecting funds for PRAs and transmitting them to an account administrator involves only a negligible additional burden for small businesses. Under this proposal, the owner of a small business would simply choose an account administrator and send the total contributions to the administrator instead of to the IRS. Along with the check (or electronic deposit), the business owner would have to send a list of individual workers and each worker's Social Security number, wages, and contributions. Every employer already has to perform those calculations. The only additional burden on owners of small businesses would be sending the information to the account administrator. Surveys of small businesses indicate that most do not believe it would pose a significant burden.[14]

However, a significantly greater burden would be placed on the administrator. The administrator is responsible for all record-keeping functions and for ensuring that the funds are sent to the appropriate money manager. Those functions do entail additional expense.

Record Keeping and Money Management

Under a system of PRAs, it would be the administrator's responsibility to make sure that the appropriate funds were credited to each worker's account and to send out statements to each worker reflecting reported wages and contributions. (To keep administrative expenses low, employees should be responsible for verifying the accuracy of their quarterly wage and contribution statements.) Discrepancies would be handled through procedures similar to those followed when an employee receives an incorrect paycheck. If a dispute could not be reconciled between employer and employee, the employee could file a complaint with either the Labor Department or the organization regulating PRAs.

The administrator would also be responsible for transferring funds to an appropriate money manager to ensure that the funds in each account were prudently invested. For most employees, there would be no delay at all between the employer's sending contributions to the administrator and the administrator's redirecting the funds to an appropriate money manager.

In addition, administrators would have to keep track of potential benefit levels, potential options for annuities, and notifying the government when retirement account balances were no longer sufficient to provide for minimal monthly retirement benefits. It is in those areas that costs would be incurred. However, a vast industry performing functions similar to these already exists. Over the past two decades, the development and growth of individual retirement accounts (IRAs), 401(k)s, 403(b)s, and countless other individual retirement programs has led to a substantial infrastructure to handle the types of administrative functions that would be associated with PRAs. As that infrastructure developed over the past two decades, it went through a normal process in which expenses were relatively high in the early part of programs but, as the number of accounts increased and the assets under management grew, administrative expenses declined.

Among the industries that have developed the existing infrastructure to perform such administrative functions are mutual funds, pension plans, insurance companies, banks, brokerage firms, and data and systems administrators. Discussions with representatives of those groups suggest that administrative expenses could be reduced substantially if the government reduced the reports and regulations associated with retirement funds.

Costs of Administering Existing Retirement Programs

Using existing retirement programs to gauge the cost of administration produces a wide range of estimates. At the low end of administrative expenses is the Federal Retirement Thrift Investment Fund, a fairly large civil service retirement plan with more than two million participants and $36 billion in assets. Its 1996 annual report indicates that administrative expense ratios total nine basis points or $16 per participant.[15] Next on the list is the College Retirement Equity Fund (CREF), the nation's largest defined-contribution pension plan, covering workers in higher education and research institutions. According to Mitchell, "The system is quite responsive to individual participating employers, permitting cross-employer differences in contribution levels, rules regarding lump sum versus annuity payouts, and asset allocation choices; these differences may drive up expenses."[16] Even so, administrative record-keeping expenses for 1994 averaged 24 basis points, or less than one-quarter of 1 percent of assets.

The costs associated with administering private pension plans vary significantly. For single-employer defined-contribution plans, the costs (excluding money management) came to 11 basis points of assets under management, or less than $22 per participant per year. For multi-employer defined-contribution plans, administrative costs amounted to 57 basis points, or $68 per participant. Mitchell's analysis of these costs suggests that the administrative costs for single-employer plans may be understated because the sponsoring companies absorb some of the expenses. On the other side, the administrative costs for the multi-employer plans are probably over-stated because such plans have a relatively smaller asset pool and are faced with substantial legal expenses.[17]

Based on existing pension plans, it appears reasonable to assume that the costs of administering a well-run system of PRAs might be anywhere from a low of roughly 15 basis points to a high of roughly 50 basis points. It is important to understand that those costs would vary significantly depending on such factors as the size of the retirement accounts, the regulations and reporting requirements placed on the administrators, and their legal liability for handling the accounts. As a percentage of assets, administrative costs would be larger in the early years, when the size of an average account is smaller, and would drop significantly as the size of the accounts grew. Thus, starting the system with workers placing a full 10 percent of their wages in PRAs would substantially reduce administrative costs as a percentage of assets.

If every worker participated in the program and a full 10 percent of wages and salaries went into PRAs, those accounts would amount to close to $400 billion in the first year. With 130 million workers, the average account size would be close to $3,000. Discussions with industry representatives suggest that there would be a minimum cost of $30–$50 to handle any account. If administrative costs (not including money management costs) amounted to $30–$50 per account, the average cost would be 1.0–1.7 percent of assets the first year. If money management costs were included it would add an additional cost of about $5 per account. Within five years, the average account would be close to $18,000. At that point, the same $30–$50

Table 1
EXPENSES ASSOCIATED WITH PERSONAL RETIREMENT ACCOUNTS
(ESTIMATES BASED ON EXISTING EXPERIENCE)

	Low	High
Expenses as a percentage of assets under management:		
Administration expenses without money mgmt.	0.15%	0.50%
Money mgmt. expense	0.15%	0.15%
Total	0.30%	0.65%

	Dollars per Account*	Percentage of Assets
First-year expense without money mgmt.	$30–$50	1.00%–1.67%
First-year expense with money mgmt.	$35–$55	1.17%–1.83%
Fifth-year expense with money mgmt.	$54–$117	0.30%–0.65%

* Dollar estimates are based on an average size of $3,000 for the first year and $18,000 for the fifth year.

per account administrative costs would average anywhere from 17 to 28 basis points. This is close to the 15–50 basis point range discussed earlier. Over time, as the average account size increased, administrative costs would become an insignificant percentage of total assets (Table 1). Although individual account plans are not prohibitively expensive, if less than 10 percent of wages and salaries were to go into PRAs, it could cause additional administrative problems. For example, at 2 percent of wages and salaries, low-wage workers would end up with very small amounts in their PRAs. Under a 2 percent plan, the main benefits of individual accounts would go mostly to higher-income individuals, since 2 percent of a higher income is proportionately greater. Because the administrative cost burden increases as a percentage of assets for smaller accounts, the cost of administering the accounts would take a significantly greater portion of the returns during the early years—another reason for large accounts, or at least most of a worker's contribution, instead of a mere 2 percent of income. If a program of PRAs will significantly benefit all workers, it is sensible to adopt it completely so that workers enjoy the full benefits rather than only a small portion of those benefits.

Money Management Expenses for PRAs

Research into the expenses associated with managing the money for PRAs points to management fees of anywhere from 15 basis points for passively managed indexed portfolios to close to 200 basis points for actively managed international portfolios.[18] That suggests that money management fees might be reduced substantially for workers who invest in passively managed index funds. In some markets, passively managed portfolios have provided returns that are competitive with those of actively managed portfolios. If the investment options provided to workers included passively managed products, workers would have an option that offers high returns with low administrative costs.

Total Expenses for Administration and Money Management of PRAs

Representatives of money management firms have stated that costs can easily be prorated on the basis of overall assets, which means that they could be included in the basis points associated with the fee for money management. If that approach were used, larger accounts would tend to subsidize the cost of administering smaller accounts. Thus, new, smaller accounts would not see their entire first year's return wiped out by a fixed administration fee. Industry officials also point out that the current experience with IRA accounts suggests that PRAs would be relatively inexpensive to administer and manage. They point out that the huge potential size of each personal account and current experience with the stability of IRAs (where transfers are relatively infrequent) suggest that competition for the accounts is likely to be intense. As a result, many believe that their firms would be willing to lose money on the accounts in the initial years in return for the opportunity to earn large profits as the accounts grew.

Based on existing plans and on discussions with industry representatives, it is likely that the range of administrative and money management expenses for PRAs could reasonably be expected to fall between 30 and 65 basis points of the assets under management. In the first year, if the PRAs were to total 10 percent of wages and salaries, total administrative and money management expenses would be likely to range between 1.17 percent and 1.83 percent of assets, or roughly $35–$55 per worker. As the size of the average

PRA grows over time and as technology improves, total administrative costs could be expected to decline. For example, after five years the average cost would be expected to be 30–65 basis points or $54–$117 per account. Eventually the size of the accounts would dwarf the cost of administration. Even so, it is likely that PRAs will cost at least $25–$45 more during the first year than the cost of the existing Social Security system. As the size of each worker's account increases, the dollar expense would rise, but this expense as a share of total assets would decline dramatically.

The range of expenses predicted by industry representatives is at the lower end of the 30–250 basis point range suggested by Mitchell's survey of current retirement plans. However, at the high end of the range are relatively high expenses associated with actively managed accounts and accounts that are relatively small in size. The lower end of the range is justified by two factors. First, the relatively large size of a system of PRAs that consisted of 10 percent of wages and salaries would create significant economies of scale. Second, if workers chose passively managed accounts, it would tilt the survey results closer to the range suggested by industry representatives.

Although costs would normally be expected to be larger in the early years when account sizes are smaller, many believe that the potential for higher profits as the accounts grow is so apparent that administrators and money managers would compete intensely for accounts. Competition could be expected to lower costs considerably in the early years.

The estimates above are based on extensive discussions with industry representatives as well as research into the cost of existing investment funds. But there are some factors—involving additional administrative requirements that may apply to the new accounts— that have the potential to raise the cost of the system substantially. In general, the more reporting and regulatory burdens that are placed on administrators, the greater will be the costs of administering the personal accounts. The following are examples of requirements that are likely to lead to a substantial increase in administrative costs:

1. Limiting the size of accounts by allowing only a small portion of Social Security taxes to be privately invested,
2. Requiring administrators to be responsible for educating individuals about prudent investment choices,

3. Subjecting administrators to extensive new reporting requirements,
4. Requiring administrators to produce monthly statements,
5. Permitting individuals to borrow from their accounts,
6. Allowing a wide range of actively managed accounts,
7. Permitting frequent changes in investment choices, and
8. Placing the burden for employer compliance on administrators.

In many instances, the dynamics of the industry with respect to administration are changing dramatically with changes in technology. For example, some industry officials suggest that limiting the choice of accounts to passively managed index accounts, limiting the frequency at which individuals could move their accounts, and limiting the number of investment choices would substantially reduce administrative expenses. Others suggest that computer systems are becoming so efficient that such additional expenses may soon become insignificant.

Rather than specifying a list of extensive requirements, administrative costs could be lowered, and the potential for higher administrative expenses reduced, by means of a system that limits regulations and requirements to the minimum amount necessary to ensure the safety and security of PRAs.[19] To ensure that the system offers appropriate protections for individuals, it would be wise to establish an independent self-regulatory board to certify investment managers and provide guidelines for prudent investments. The board could direct administrators to prorate administrative fees as suggested above. It could also initially suggest limiting investments to a narrow range of passive index funds and requiring that stocks make up no more than a certain percentage of an individual's portfolio as that individual approaches retirement. Or the regulatory authority could decide that once an individual's account exceeds an amount needed for adequate retirement income, the individual should be allowed greater discretion with respect to investing any amount above that level. Over time, as economic conditions and perceptions of risk change, the degree of control over the accounts exercised by this board could also change.

Can Government Invest More Efficiently Than Individuals?

Some have suggested that it would be far easier and more efficient to maintain the existing system for the collection, transmission, and record-keeping functions and to permit the government to invest in stocks. They have suggested that by allowing government to invest in stocks, we could enjoy the best of all worlds. Not only could we ensure that administrative costs are no more than $10 a year per worker, but they believe that the increased returns from market-based investing could be used to help solve the problems associated with the current system. This line of reasoning has several flaws, all of them related to the essential question of the nature of retirement funds and who owns them.

Under the present system, the government owns these retirement funds. Individuals have no legal claim to them. Congress has the right to eliminate benefits at any time. In fact, it does just that every time it postpones the retirement age. Most proposals for retaining the current government-run system include recommendations for further raising the retirement age. Since the government owns these funds, it is perfectly legal for Congress to decide not to pay full benefits to anyone at any time.

In addition, so long as the retirement funds belong to the government, they are available to be used for whatever purpose Congress decides. That is one of the root causes of the system's financial troubles. Political pressures to increase benefit levels and to use surplus funds for other government programs have simply been too strong to overcome, a point that was made again last year during the budget process. Both the administration and Congress have accepted the principle of not raiding the Social Security retirement funds. And yet that fund is running a surplus of just over $80 billion. Since the government counts the money as its own, it spent the surplus on other things and sent the Social Security Administration IOUs for $80 billion. Without access to those funds the government would have recorded not a $70 billion surplus but a $10 billion deficit.

In spite of pleas by both the administration and Congress that the entire surplus in Social Security retirement funds be used to help save the program, both parties recently chose to add to the federal budget funds for farmers, for peacekeeping operations, for anti-terrorism, and even for a bailout for Brazil. In effect, politicians concluded that all of those items were more important than Social Security.

There is a fundamental difference between the government's *trying* to save for retirement expenditures and individuals' *actually* saving. So long as government retains the property rights to the retirement funds, those funds belong to the government and can be used for any purpose that is deemed by legislators to be worthy at that moment. When each individual has property rights to the retirement funds, that temptation does not exist.

Another important reason why government cannot invest the Social Security Trust Fund is that the funds do not exist. The trust fund includes special Treasury securities, which are merely government IOUs. Some have argued that the interest rate on those securities provides the fund with an attractive return. However, since the government has no savings, whatever interest rate it pays simply represents a higher tax burden on the public. The interest rate the government pays to the trust fund (or, alternatively, that the government pays itself) has no economic significance. Every increase in the rate on the Treasury securities adds the same amount to taxpayer liabilities that it adds to the trust fund. It represents a classic case of taking money from one pocket and putting it into another.

Since there are no real assets in the Social Security Trust Fund, the government has to resort to some combination of borrowing from the private sector, raising taxes, and cutting spending in order to raise the money necessary to buy stocks. Of course, the government may have to resort to some of those options in making the transition to a system of PRAs, but such options would be far more palatable if individuals were to receive a direct benefit in the form of an increase in their personal assets. The most compelling argument against government investment of retirement money involves the extent to which it would increase government power at the expense of individuals. It is frightening to contemplate how government might abuse the power to invest nearly $400 billion per year, picking and choosing corporate winners and losers, interfering with corporate governance, and dispensing corporate welfare and political favors. Allowing the government to invest directly in private capital markets would amount to the largest shift in power from private individuals to government since the creation of the income tax.

Efficiently Fulfilling the Objectives of Social Security

The objectives of Social Security involve providing earnings replacement for retirees and providing welfare benefits for the elderly indigent. It is generally accepted that those objectives should be achieved as efficiently as possible so workers can achieve the maximum retirement benefits for their contributions. The current Social Security system is a low-cost system in terms of collecting, transferring, and paying benefits. The monthly benefit for low-income workers is close to $600, for the average-income worker the benefit is close to $900, and the maximum benefit is close to $1,300. In terms of costs, the current system delivers these benefits at an administrative cost of roughly $10 per year per worker. There are several reasons for the low costs associated with the government-run system. Because the money belongs to the government instead of the individual, the IRS system serves as the collection agent. More important, there is no money management function and no administrative cost of running personal accounts.[20] In return for that "efficiency," the returns promised to many of today's workers are either zero or negative.

Extrapolating from existing costs, one should reasonably expect that administrative and money management expenses for a system of PRAs would amount to anywhere from roughly 1.17 to 1.83 percent of assets or roughly $35–$55 per worker for the first year. After five years, as the size of the average account increases, the cost would be anywhere from roughly 30 to 65 basis points or approximately $54–$117 per year. For the great majority of businesses with outside payroll services, the collection function would entail little, if any, additional cost. For those businesses that do payroll without the aid of electronic technology, there would be some modest additional reporting requirements.

In the early stages of the process it may be necessary to require certified administrators and money managers to accept all applicants and charge similar fees based on a percentage of the assets under management. Such a requirement may be necessary to ensure that administrators and money managers will be available for small businesses with low-wage workers and high turnover. Because the amount of money administered and managed by the system would be so large, the cross-subsidizing of less attractive accounts is likely to be a relatively small price to pay for equal treatment.

Extensive research shows that the returns to PRAs are likely to be substantial. Historical analysis shows that had workers contributed to individual accounts in the past, retirees would have received three to five times the monthly income currently promised by the

329

existing Social Security system. This means that for the same amount of money paid in, the minimum monthly benefit for a low-income worker would be $1,800–$3,000 instead of $600. For the typical worker, the monthly benefit would be $2,700–$4,500. For those with the maximum benefit, the monthly benefit would be $3,900–$6,500 rather than $1,300.

Looking to the future, one could expect workers with PRAs to retire with a substantial nest egg. At the low end of the scale, a worker who spent his or her entire working life making the minimum wage (and working without interruption) would retire with more than $450,000 in terms of today's buying power,[21] and with an annuity paying well over $4,000 a month. Obviously, workers who earn more than the minimum wage would do even better.

Whereas administration costs under the current Social Security retirement system amount to close to $10 a year, the costs associated with PRAs would vary depending upon the nature of the system that is established and the rules and regulations imposed on the system. Most current retirement programs suggest that a system of PRAs is likely to cost from $30 to $50 more a year per worker at the start of the program. Costs are then likely to increase in dollar terms, but decline significantly as a percentage of assets as the size of the average account grows. In return for the possibility of a modest increase in expenses, the system would provide substantial, secure retirement income far in excess of that provided by the current system.

Returning to the analogy used earlier, a system of PRAs will enable the lowest-paid worker to purchase a Mercedes for the cost of a Trabant.

Notes

1. See Peter Ferrara and Michael Tanner, *A New Deal for Social Security* (Washington: Cato Institute, 1998); and Robert Genetski, *A Nation of Millionaires* (Lanham, Md.: Madison Books, 1997).

2. Kelly Olsen and Dallas Salisbury, "Individual Social Security Accounts: Issues in Assessing Administrative Feasibility and Costs," Employee Benefit Research Institute Special Report no. 34, November 1988.

3. See, for example, Michael Tanner, "The Perils of Government Investing," Cato Institute Briefing Paper no. 43, December 1, 1998; and Krzystof Ostaszewski, "Privatizing the Social Security Trust Fund? Don't Let the Government Invest," Cato Institute Social Security Paper no. 6, January 14, 1997.

4. Olivia Mitchell, "Administrative Costs in Public and Private Retirement Systems," in *Privatizing Social Security*, ed. Martin Feldstein (Chicago: University of Chicago Press, 1998), p. 404.

5. Benefits are *not* based on contributions, or on the compounded contributions invested in specific retirement accounts as in a PRA. Therefore, the Social Security Administration does not perform all the tasks of a PRA administrator.

6. Mitchell, p. 422.

7. Ibid., p. 414.

8. Robert Myers, "Can the Government Operate Programs Efficiently and Inexpensively?" *Contingencies* (March/April 1992): 15–17.

9. Mitchell, p. 415.

10. The U.S. Supreme Court held in the case of *Flemming v. Nestor* that workers have no right to Social Security benefits based on having paid Social Security taxes and that there is no direct link between Social Security taxes and benefits. *Flemming v. Nestor*, 36 U.S. (1960).

11. Elsie Hoextra, *Administrative Expenses of Welfare and Pension Plans*, U.S. Department of Labor, Labor Management Services Administration, Washington, 1970, p. 134.

12. Earnings sharing might be a better method of achieving this objective, but it would be more administratively complex. See Ekaterina Shirley and Peter Spiegler, "The Benefits of Social Security Privatization for Women," Cato Institute Social Security Paper no. 12, July 20, 1998.

13. It should be noted that there are a number of possible administrative benefits of combining existing 401(k) and other defined-contribution administrative functions with private administration of Social Security. Currently, more than 40 million working people participate in one defined-contribution plan or another. As noted elsewhere, for many of those plans, there are electronic links between the payroll systems and the record-keeping systems. Many workers participate in more than one plan. For example, a company might have both a 401(k) plan and a profit-sharing plan. Given the electronic links, the marginal administrative costs of keeping track of an additional account for the worker are low. For companies that have defined-contribution plans already in place, the marginal cost of adding a private Social Security account for each worker could be quite low. A combined (defined-contribution and Social Security) statement and record keeping would be viewed as a major positive by the workers. Since the number of workers already participating in defined-contribution plans is so substantial, the possibility of this administrative synergy would be significant.

14. See, for example, William Dennis Jr., "Small Business Assesses Social Security: Results of a Survey," National Federation of Independent Business, September 10, 1998.

15. Mitchell, p. 439.

16. Ibid., p. 440.

17. Ibid., pp. 432–34.

18. Ibid., p. 420.

19. The author does not necessarily endorse any of the regulatory requirements discussed. These are merely theoretical options available to lawmakers to address specific objections to individual accounts.

20. If the Social Security Administration were to try to invest money on behalf of individuals with different asset allocation choices, and keep track of specific performance of each account, its costs would be higher than those for the current system. It is misleading, therefore, to compare the cost of private accounts directly to current SSA costs. Rather, the comparison should be to the higher costs that SSA would incur if it were to try to do the same job as the private fund managers.

21. Genetski, p. 41 (updated for current minimum wage).

16. Personal Accounts in a Down Market: How Recent Stock Market Declines Affect the Social Security Reform Debate

Andrew G. Biggs

Imagine the following deal: You could invest part or all of your Social Security taxes in a personal retirement account. However, your account could hold nothing but stocks and you would retire during the biggest bear market since the Great Depression.

Would workers accept such a deal? I would. Even today, personal accounts would increase retirement benefits while giving workers greater ownership and control over their savings.

Slumping stock markets have opponents of personal accounts claiming vindication. A falling stock market, they argue, shows that only a traditional government-run, defined-benefit Social Security program can provide adequate retirement security. As Senate Majority Leader Tom Daschle (D-S.D.) put it on July 12, 2002:

> After what's happened in the stock market the last few weeks, we think it's a terrible idea. . . . Imagine if you were retiring this week, with most major stock indexes hitting five-year lows.[1]

Indeed, many Americans are sure to be concerned after hearing such comments.

But in judging the risks of long-term market investment on the basis of just a few months or years of returns, these opponents of personal accounts are victims of the so-called law of small numbers—the propensity to believe that a small sample is representative of the larger universe of outcomes.[2] Like those who took a few years

Originally published as Cato Institute Briefing Paper no. 74, September 10, 2002, and updated to reflect current information.

of double-digit stock returns in the 1990s to portend a future of limitless investment riches, opponents of personal accounts have failed to examine the historical facts regarding stock and bond returns over the long term.

Those facts show that, even today, personal accounts would increase benefits and help strengthen Social Security for the long term. However bad the market's recent performance, a worker retiring today would have begun investing in the late 1950s. The stock market has never once lost money over even 20-year periods. Even without diversification, a worker retiring today would have 40 years of investment behind him to make up for recent losses. A worker just entering the market would have 40 years to regain lost ground. There is simply no way recent events can credibly justify a disastrous scenario for personal accounts. Even a worker retiring in the Great Depression would have received a 4 percent annual return after inflation;[3] a worker retiring today would do substantially better.

Personal accounts give workers the opportunity to diversify their investments across hundreds or even thousands of stocks and bonds, reducing the risk that declines in a single company or asset class would severely harm a worker's retirement income. Moreover, long time horizons provide "time diversification" that smoothes out the short-term volatility of investments in the stock market.

Historically, in almost all cases workers with diversified market investments would have received substantially higher benefits if allowed to invest part or all of their payroll taxes in personal retirement accounts. Under Social Security reform proposals already on the table, practically all workers could expect to increase their total retirement incomes by opting to participate in personal accounts, even if they had to give up part of their traditional benefits to do so.

Stock market investment is indeed risky over the short term. But over the long term, stocks and bonds clearly can form the basis of stable and adequate retirement wealth accumulation for all workers.

Asset Diversification: Mixing Stocks and Bonds

Stocks are risky investments over the short run, varying greatly from year to year. Bonds and other fixed-income investments, while producing lower returns over the long term, provide the year-to-year stability that many investors demand (Figure 1).

Figure 1
STOCKS PRODUCE GREATER RETURNS THAN BONDS OVER THE
LONG RUN, BUT AT THE COST OF HIGHER SHORT-TERM
VOLATILITY

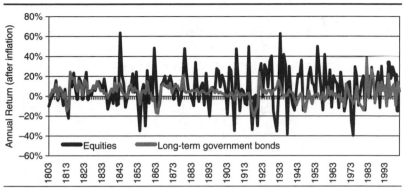

SOURCE: Global Financial Data.

For this reason, most financial advisers recommend that investors move from a predominantly stock-based portfolio when they are young to fixed-income investments such as bonds as they near retirement. Younger workers have more time to make up for market losses, and more future labor income with which to supplement their savings. A common rule of thumb is that the percentage of stocks in a worker's portfolio should equal "100 minus your age," such that a 20-year-old would begin his working life with 80 percent of his savings going into stocks and retire at 65 with just 35 percent in equities.

Statistics from 401(k) plans show that most workers stick reasonably close to these guidelines.[4] The average worker (Figure 2) aged 60–65 years keeps about 40 percent of his 401(k) assets invested in stocks and 60 percent invested in fixed-income assets such as bonds. A younger worker, by contrast, reverses the mix to 60-40 in favor of stocks.[5]

To illustrate the results of life-cycle investing, imagine a 65-year-old average-wage worker retiring today. One year ago he had $100,000 in his personal account, of which he had allocated 40 percent to the S&P 500 stock index and 60 percent to the Lehman Brothers aggregate bond index. What would his account be worth today, assuming he made no additional contributions in the last year?

Figure 2
WORKERS MOVE OUT OF EQUITIES AS THEY NEAR RETIREMENT,
LIMITING THEIR EXPOSURE TO STOCK MARKET RISK

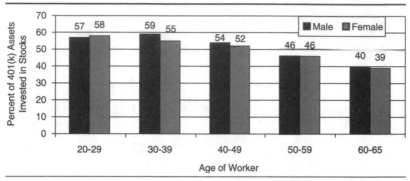

SOURCE: Robert L. Clark et al., "Making the Most of 401(k) Plans: Who's Choosing What and Why," in *Forecasting Retirement Needs and Retirement Wealth*, ed. Olivia S. Mitchell, P. Brett Hammond, and Anna M. Rappaport (Philadelphia: University of Pennsylvania Press, 2000).

Believe it or not, despite truly awful stock market returns in the past year, a typical worker's account balance would be virtually unchanged. The loss of 21.6 percent on the stock portion of his portfolio would be almost matched by the 9.9 percent gain on the larger bond portion, for a total year-end loss of just 3.25 percent (Figure 3).

In other words, if that worker had started the year with $100,000 in his account, he would have ended with $97,288. This loss would reduce his monthly retirement income by only around $15.[6]

Moreover, a typical low-income worker aged 60–65 has only 23 percent of his 401(k) invested in equities. This low-income worker would have made money in 2001, earning a return of 2.6 percent as gains from the bonds in his portfolio outweighed losses in the stock market.

Any investor would rather make money than lose it. But these results show that even the poor stock market results of the past year would have had only a small impact on a typical worker holding a personal retirement account. As Dallas Salisbury of the Employee Benefit Research Institute remarks, "There is no retirement crisis because of the stock market decline."[7] Workers' retirement accounts are sufficiently diversified that accounts lost only 5–10 percent on

Figure 3
TYPICAL WORKER AGED 60–65 WOULD HAVE LOST ONLY ABOUT 3 PERCENT ON HIS ACCOUNT LAST YEAR

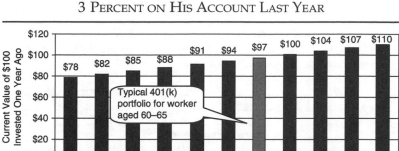

SOURCE: Author's calculations. Nonstock portion of account assumed to be invested in Lehman Brothers long-term bond index. Based on 21.6 percent loss on S&P 500 in prior year (net of dividends) and 9.9 percent gain on Lehman Brothers bond index.

average last year, according to the *Los Angeles Times,* with those nearing retirement presumably suffering even smaller declines.[8]

Time Diversification: Stocks for the Long Run

While relatively small portfolio declines despite recent stock market losses may reassure the nervous, what really matters for personal accounts isn't how they would have performed over the last year, or over any single year. For retirement investment, what matters is where you start and where you end up. What happens in between is much less important. Retirement investing is about the long run, and over the long run stocks have been remarkably safe investments.

As noted earlier, most workers diversify their investments between stocks and bonds, moving out of equities as they approach retirement. Opponents of personal accounts, however, often assume that workers have their entire accounts invested in stocks, maximizing their risk in the event of a market decline. Let's see what that would mean.

Figure 4 uses a male worker earning the average wage each year, currently $35,000, and retiring in 2002. It assumes that he deposited 3 percentage points[9] of his wages in a personal account invested only in the S&P 500 stock index. Compared to this amount is the

Figure 4
EVEN AFTER MARKET DROP, PERSONAL ACCOUNT WOULD PAY HIGHER RETURN THAN TRADITIONAL SYSTEM

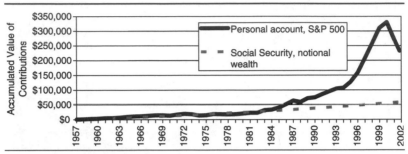

SOURCE: Author's calculations.

notional "wealth" he would have accumulated by putting the same amount of money into the current system.[10]

The return from Social Security is assumed to be 1.74 percent annually above inflation. This percentage is the return the Social Security Administration projects that a single male retiring today can expect from his Social Security payroll taxes. This estimate includes all retirement, survivors', and disability benefits.[11] Married couples, particularly those with only a single earner, could expect somewhat higher returns. Future retirees can generally expect lower returns than those retiring today.

As Figure 4 shows, even with the recent stock market decline, a worker investing only in stocks would receive benefits 2.8 times higher than he would had he "invested" the same amount of money in the current program.

Put another way, the recent decline in stock prices means the worker's personal account would be worth the same today as it was worth in 1997. But that worker's Social Security "savings" would be worth today only what the personal account was worth in the late 1980s. It would take a much larger decline than the one we have seen for a personal account to be a worse "deal" than the current program.

Personal account–based reform proposals, such as those from the President's Commission to Strengthen Social Security, establish an "offset interest rate" that governs the amount of traditional benefits an individual must give up in exchange for being allowed to invest

Figure 5

PERSONAL ACCOUNTS WOULD INCREASE BENEFITS FOR WORKERS
RETIRING TODAY, EVEN AFTER GIVING UP PART OF THEIR
TRADITIONAL BENEFITS AS ENVISIONED UNDER PLANS FROM THE
PRESIDENT'S COMMISSION TO STRENGTHEN SOCIAL SECURITY

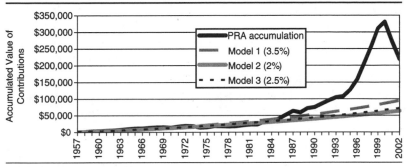

SOURCE: Author's calculations.

part of his payroll taxes in a personal account.[12] If the personal account's rate of return equals the offset interest rate, the amount deducted from the worker's traditional benefits would precisely equal the amount he would gain via the account. If the account's return exceeded the offset interest rate, the worker would receive higher total retirement benefits by virtue of opting for an account.[13]

In the commission's three reform proposals, the members established offset interest rates at 3.5 percent, 2 percent, and 2.5 percent, respectively. As Figure 5 shows, in all three cases a worker retiring today and holding a personal retirement account would have received an average return exceeding the offset interest rate and would therefore have received higher total benefits by holding a personal account.

Hence, even if the government must incur costs to move the system to a sustainable basis, which is the case regardless of whether personal accounts are incorporated into the program, at the margin a worker would have been wise to opt for an account.

Some observers might note that for a worker retiring today it was not until the mid-1980s that the balance of the personal account portfolios permanently exceeded the notional balance accumulated via the personal account offset. This is not to say, however, that an individual who retired before the mid-1980s would not have benefited by holding a personal retirement account. Figure 5 applies only to an individual retiring this year. A worker retiring in the mid-1980s would have begun investing in about 1940, benefiting from years of above-average growth during that period.

Others would argue that reform proposals make other changes to benefits in addition to introducing personal accounts. Two of the three reform models from the President's Commission would reduce the rate of future benefit growth in order to bring the system back to financial balance. Some might object that excluding these other changes gives an unrealistically optimistic picture of the benefits that personal accounts might provide.

But Social Security will require changes in the future to balance its finances whether or not personal accounts are introduced.[14] If these changes must take place even in the absence of personal accounts, it is not inappropriate to examine the effects of accounts as an individual element in overall reform. Moreover, if Social Security were in financial balance—as it is at present, even if not over the long term—personal accounts could be introduced without detriment to the traditional system's long-term financing.[15]

Simulating Personal Accounts through History

The Congressional Research Service took a more wide-ranging look at market risk and personal retirement accounts, using stock and bond returns dating back to 1927 to simulate how individuals with personal accounts would have fared had accounts been introduced in the past.[16]

It is true, as the CRS finds, that stock returns vary greatly from year to year. But that variation takes place at a level higher than that provided by Social Security. That is, while historical returns don't guarantee that a worker retiring today would receive higher benefits than a person retiring last year or next year, he could be reasonably sure of receiving more than if he had invested the same amount of money in the traditional pay-as-you-go program. Of the 35 different 41-year periods the CRS studied, there is not one in which a worker who had invested his payroll taxes in stocks would have been better off remaining in the current system. On average, a personal account invested only in stocks would produce benefits two and one-half times higher than the traditional pay-as-you-go program.

Figure 6
STOCK RETURNS VARY BUT CONSISTENTLY EXCEED THOSE OF THE TRADITIONAL PAY-AS-YOU-GO PROGRAM

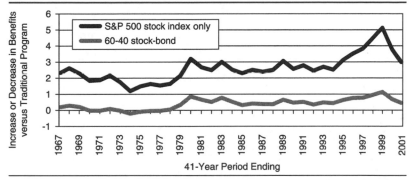

41-Year Period Ending

SOURCE: Congressional Research Service, "Social Security Reform: The Effect of Economic Variability on Individual Accounts and Their Annuities," February 28, 2002.

A mixed portfolio of stocks and bonds was not always better than Social Security, but nearly always so. Of the 35 different 41-year periods studied, in 7 of them a worker would have been better off investing his payroll taxes in Social Security than in a 60-40 stock-bond portfolio, though the difference is small, an average of just 6 percent (Figure 6).

The relative weakness of a mixed portfolio during the 1970s is attributable to two factors. First, investment returns were low by historical standards, with a slow economy reducing stock returns and high inflation making real bond returns negative from 1970 to 1979. Second, Social Security paid substantially higher returns during that period than it does today or will in the future. Workers retiring in the 1970s received real annual returns from Social Security averaging around 10 percent. Future retirees can expect to receive returns of approximately 2 percent, depending on their income and marital status.[17] While low market returns are possible in the future, the current Social Security program can never again pay returns similar to those received during the 1970s and before.

Overall, as Table 1 shows, a 60-40 stock-bond portfolio would have paid an average of 39 percent more than Social Security, even compared to the higher rates of return the current program paid in

341

Table 1
PERSONAL ACCOUNT BENEFIT AS MULTIPLE OF AVERAGE BENEFIT
FROM PAYGO PROGRAM

| | Portfolio | |
	Stocks Only	60 Percent Stocks/ 40 Percent Bonds
Average	2.6	1.39
Minimum	1.19	0.8
25th percentile	2.15	1.13
50th percentile	2.51	1.41
75th percentile	2.96	1.64
Maximum	5.12	2.13

SOURCE: Congressional Research Service, "Social Security Reform: The Effect of Economic Variability on Individual Accounts and Their Annuities," February 28, 2002.

the past. From the late 1970s onward, no individual—including individuals retiring today—would have been worse off with a personal account than he would have been had he remained in the current system. All workers would have received higher benefits by investing in personal accounts, even if their accounts contained a high proportion of bonds, and many workers would have received much higher benefits.

These results may understate somewhat the returns from personal account plans such as those from the President's Commission, because the CRS assumed administrative costs of 1 percent of assets managed versus an estimate of 0.3 percent of assets managed by Social Security's independent actuaries for the commission's account structure. Over a 41-year working lifetime, a 0.7 percent increase in the net investment return would increase the final asset accumulation by slightly more than 20 percent, further increasing the advantage of personal accounts over pay-as-you-go financing.

Long-Run Market Risk

Another way to consider stock market risk is to compare the variations in returns over various holding periods. Figure 7, adapted from *Stocks for the Long Run* by Wharton School finance professor Jeremy Siegel, shows the standard deviation of returns for stocks,

Figure 7
STOCKS HAVE BEEN VERY RISKY IN THE SHORT TERM BUT MORE
STABLE OVER THE LONG RUN

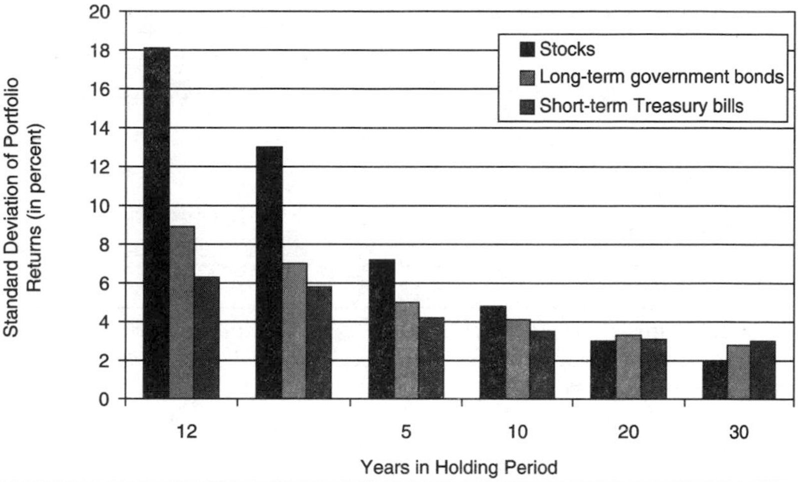

SOURCE: Jeremy J. Siegel, *Stocks for the Long Run* (New York: McGraw-Hill, 1998), p. 32.

bonds, and Treasury bills held for different periods of time. The standard deviation measures the dispersion of statistical data, showing how much individual instances tend to vary from the average for the group.[18]

In the short run, the standard deviation of stock returns is very high, such that the return in one year could be very different from that of another. Fixed income investments, by contrast, have lower standard deviations and hence lower risk.

Over the long term, however, the standard deviation of stock returns has fallen. That is to say, the return from holding stocks for, say, 20 years does not vary so much, regardless of which 20-year period of American history you chose. For 30-year periods, the standard deviation of returns is lower still.

Moreover, for long holding periods the standard deviation of stock returns is actually lower than for bonds or Treasury bills. That is to say, in a certain sense at least, stocks were less risky over the long term than bonds. It is this reduction of the variance of returns over the long term that forms the basis for the time diversification and

343

Figure 8
WORST CASE SCENARIOS: UNLIKE SUPPOSEDLY "SAFE" BONDS, STOCKS HAVE NEVER LOST MONEY OVER THE LONG TERM

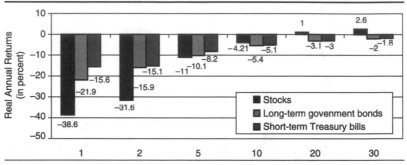

SOURCE: Jeremy J. Siegel, *Stocks for the Long Run*, p. 27.

for the common advice for younger individuals to hold riskier investments.

Worst-Case Scenarios

Opponents of personal accounts are quick to point out that, while stocks have high average returns,

> the promise of guaranteed protection against poverty cannot be "averaged out" if some people feast on the rewards of a rich stock account while others cannot afford to eat. Social Security is supposed to be there for everyone, regardless of whether they have good luck or know how to manage investments.[19]

Hence, opponents of reform are justified in demanding that we look not just at the average returns available from personal accounts but also at how people would fare if they experienced low returns over their lifetimes.

Another way to look at stock investment for personal accounts, then, is to look at the extremes. If you had had a personal account and received below-average returns on your investments, how badly would you have fared?[20]

As expected, stocks have often produced large losses in the short term. For instance, over single-year holding periods, the worst performance from stocks in American history was a loss of 38.6 percent, as shown in Figure 8. The worst case for bonds in a single year was a loss of 21.9 percent and for Treasury bills a loss of 15.6 percent.

Over the long term, however, annual gains and losses offset each other. When stocks were held for 10 years, the largest average annual loss was 4.2 percent after inflation. Over 20 years or more, however, stocks have never failed to produce positive returns, with the worst annual return being 1 percent. Over 30 years, the worst annual return from stocks was a gain of 2.6 percent after inflation.

Bonds actually produced lower worst-case returns over the long run than stocks. The worst 30-year return from bonds was an annual loss of 2 percent and for Treasury bills, a loss of 1.8 percent. In other words, the true worst-case scenarios would not have involved stock investment but holding supposedly "safe" government bonds.

Now, these figures assume that workers hold a diversified portfolio replicating the performance of the stock market as a whole.[21] A worker could lose his savings simply by investing his entire portfolio in one of the approximately 200 public corporations that declare bankruptcy in any given year.[22] It is precisely for this reason that all major personal account–based reform legislation mandates that workers not invest in single stocks or even in single corporate sectors. Workers with accounts could purchase only highly diversified mutual funds holding dozens, hundreds, or even thousands of stocks or bonds. Some reform plans base their account administration on the federal Thrift Savings Plan, which gives workers the option to invest in one or more of five stock or bond index funds, coupling simplicity and extremely low administrative costs with high levels of diversification. Hence, while opponents of personal accounts cite the amount a worker might have lost by investing in the NASDAQ index, there is no existing reform legislation that would allow such an investment to take place.

In practice it would be next to impossible for an individual to lose his money. To illustrate, imagine a worker who could invest in either the S&P 500 stock index or in a fund of AAA rated corporate bonds. Each year, he moved his entire portfolio to the investment that would reap the lowest returns for that year. Even after making the worst investment choices possible, he, if retiring today, would still have had positive net returns on his portfolio as a whole.[23]

Outstanding Issues

Despite the evidence of historical market returns, policymakers and the public should not treat equity investment for Social Security

Table 2
SINCE WORLD WAR II, THE RISK PREMIUM PAID TO STOCKS
HAS RISEN SHARPLY

Period	Premium vs. Long-Term Government Bonds	Premium vs. Short-Term Treasury Bills
1802–1997	3.5	4.1
1802–1870	2.2	1.9
1871–1925	2.9	3.4
1926–1997	5.2	6.6
1946–1997	6.4	7.0

SOURCE: Jeremy J. Siegel, *Stocks for the Long Run* (New York: McGraw-Hill, 1998), pp. 13, 15.

or other purposes as if it constituted "free money." Actuarial analysis of reform legislation can sometimes encourage this viewpoint: although the text rightly highlights issues of risk, the numbers that receive greater public attention often appear to treat stocks as if they were bonds with higher-than-average returns. Whether equity investment is envisioned through personal accounts or through a central government-managed fund, the market rewards people who are willing to take risk, even if diversification and long time horizons have historically ironed out the short-term fluctuations of the stock market.

Moreover, some observers believe that the equity premium—that is, the extra reward paid to holders of risky investments like stocks over safer investments like short-term bonds—could be smaller in the future than in the past. Historically, stocks have paid a "risk premium" of 6–7 percentage points over safer investments like short-term government bonds.[24] Longer-term bonds, such as those held by the Social Security Trust Fund, also receive a premium of about 1 percentage point over shorter-term bonds, primarily because of the increased risk of inflation eating away the real returns.[25]

Some analysts believe that the relative increase in stock returns in recent decades (Table 2) reflects a reduction in the equity risk premium demanded by investors. Such a change in investor attitudes would increase returns in the near term, because the price of an asset will rise if investors perceive it to be less risky. Once the price had adjusted, however, the risk premium would be smaller than in the past.[26] While there is merit to this argument, it remains the case that stocks are far riskier than bonds in the short run and that the average share on the New York Stock Exchange today is held for less than one year.[27] For shorter-term investors, a substantial risk premium continues to make sense.

A second current debate within the finance community regards the question of time diversification, the degree to which long holding periods reduce the risk of stock ownership. Zvi Bodie of Boston College argues that, contrary to accepted wisdom, the risk of owning stocks increases rather than decreases with time.[28] Bodie contends that the proper measure of the risk of a stock investment is the cost of a "put" option contract allowing the holder to sell the stock in the future at a price sufficient to guarantee a return no less than that paid by short-term government bonds.[29] Bodie applies the Black-Scholes formula used in pricing financial options, which give the holder the right to buy or sell an asset at a designated price in the future. Since under the Black-Scholes formula the cost of a put option increases over time, Bodie concludes that the cost of insuring against stock losses—and hence, the risk of stocks—increases the longer you hold them.[30]

One difficulty with Bodie's thesis is that the Black-Scholes formula assumes that stock prices follow a "random walk," that is, that a gain or loss in one period does not influence whether there will be gains or losses in the following period. While that is true over the short time periods during which options are ordinarily issued, over long periods stock returns deviate substantially less from the average than a random walk would predict (Figure 9). Adjusting Bodie's model to include the declining standard deviation of stock returns over time confirms conventional wisdom that time diversification can reduce the risk of holding equities.[31]

While this debate continues, financial advisers continue to recommend that equity investment increase along with time horizons, indicating continued belief that time diversification will smooth the short-term volatility of the stock market.

Public Opinion on Personal Accounts: Have Americans Lost Faith?

Even workers retiring today, with the markets in turmoil, would have received high total retirement incomes by virtue of holding a

Figure 9
Over 45-Year Holding Periods, the Average Returns from Stocks Are More Constant Than a "Random Walk" Would Predict

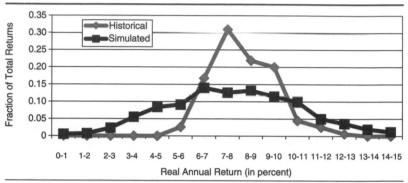

Note: Historical returns based on arithmetic mean return for 45-year holding periods, 1802–2001. Simulated returns are based on 1,000 instance random number generation with identical single-year mean return and standard deviations.

personal retirement account. But does the public still believe in personal accounts, or has negative publicity associated with the market decline caused Americans to lose faith in Social Security reform?

By coincidence, the Cato Institute commissioned a survey of public opinion on personal accounts for the period July 8–12, 2002, during which the Dow Jones Industrial Average fell almost 700 points and executives at WorldCom pleaded the Fifth Amendment in congressional hearings that were investigating corrupt corporate accounting methods. The survey, undertaken by the respected polling firm of Zogby International, would show the effect of these factors on public support for accounts.[32]

Despite all expectations, support for accounts remained strong: fully 68 percent of likely voters support the addition of voluntary personal accounts to Social Security. For perspective, in July 1999, when the Dow was almost 25 percent higher than it was in the fall of 2002, only 54 percent of likely voters supported accounts.[33]

Despite the current market fluctuations, 55 percent of working-age voters today think personal accounts are less risky than the current system, which can remain solvent only with substantial tax increases or benefit reductions. By a two-to-one margin, likely voters think the lesson of the Enron scandal is that workers need more control over their retirement savings, including personal accounts for Social Security, not that markets are dangerous and that accounts shouldn't be allowed. By 62 to 22 percent, likely voters believe that if Social Security funds are to be invested privately, individuals rather than government should undertake and control that investment.

Individual control is a recurring theme: voters cited it as the main reason for favoring personal accounts, even over higher benefits and the ability to pass on the account to their heirs. (Not surprisingly, risk was the most cited reason for opposing personal accounts.)

Although politicians may have grown nervous as an election-year bear market gave their opponents ammunition for attack, the public appears to have remained strong and steady in its support of Social Security reform incorporating personal retirement accounts.

Conclusion

Short-term investors are right to be concerned about short-term stock market volatility. Long-term investors, such as those saving for retirement, should focus more on long-term returns and long-term volatility. And over the time frames in which individuals would accumulate funds in their personal accounts, diversified investments in stocks and bonds remain a perfectly adequate means to prepare for retirement.

Indeed, a review of the evidence shows the hysterical reactions of personal account opponents to recent stock market declines to be wholly overblown. Most workers nearing retirement would have had relatively little exposure to stock market risk and thus would have experienced only small declines in their account values. Most workers who would have had large proportions of their accounts invested in stocks would be young, with many years to make up for today's losses. Even workers who had invested entirely in stocks and who were retiring precisely when the market had fallen would still have received higher returns than the current Social Security program can produce. Historical evidence shows that even a worker retiring in 1933, when the Great Depression had dragged the stock market to its low, would still have received a 4 percent average annual return, twice what today's average worker can expect from Social Security.

Moreover, experience shows that workers can invest their assets wisely, taking into account stock market risk. In the 1980s and 1990s, millions of new investors entered the market as employers shifted from traditional defined-benefit pensions to employee-controlled defined-contribution accounts. Many of those new investors had little experience with stocks or bonds, but data show that generally they have made reasonable decisions about how to allocate their assets as they aged. Personal accounts would be designed with new investors in mind, ensuring low costs and adequate diversification so that inexperienced investors did not lose money because of high administrative fees or inappropriate reliance on just a few stocks.

Just as important, personal accounts give workers the opportunity to stay out of the stock market entirely if they so choose. They could invest only in corporate or government bonds and still receive higher benefits than by staying in the current program. This feature stands in contrast to plans in which the government itself would invest the Social Security trust fund in the stock market. Not only would such investment open the fund to political manipulation, but it would also make workers and retirees subject to stock market risk, whether they desired it or not.

Personal accounts are voluntary: no worker would be forced to choose one. Moreover, no worker with a personal account would be forced to invest even a penny in the stock market. Given the relative safety of long-run diversified market investment, there is little reason that individual workers should not be allowed to choose.

Yes, the stock market is risky, and individuals should bear this risk in mind when making investment decisions. But while opponents of personal accounts trumpet the amount that accounts might have lost in the past 5 years, they decline to discuss how much workers would have gained over the past 40—not just in dollars, but in the security and dignity that come from ownership and control of one's own retirement wealth.

Notes

1. Sen. Tom Daschle (D-S.D.), Press conference with House Minority Leader Richard Gephardt (D-Mo.), Sen. Jon Corzine (D-N.J.), Rep. Robert Matsui (D-Calif.), and Rep. Charles Rangel (D-N.Y.) on Corporate Accountability and Social Security Privatization, July 12, 2002.

2. See, for instance, Matthew Rabin, "Inference by Believers in the Law of Small Numbers," Economics Department, University of California–Berkeley, Working Paper E00-282. June 4, 2002, www.repositories.cdlib.org/iber/econ/E00-282

3. Gary Burtless, "Social Security Privatization and Financial Market Risk," Center on Social and Economic Dynamics Working Paper no. 10, February 2000, Figure 4, p. 28.

4. Workers generally have a number of different retirement assets; asset allocations for 401(k) accounts do not necessarily represent their total risk exposure, which could be higher or lower depending on the individual.

5. Robert L. Clark et al., "Making the Most of 401(k) Plans: Who's Choosing What and Why," in *Forecasting Retirement Needs and Retirement Wealth*, ed. Olivia S. Mitchell, P. Brett Hammond, and Anna M. Rappaport (Philadelphia: University of Pennsylvania Press, 2000), pp. 95–138.

6. Assuming it was annuitized at the government bond rate of return.

7. James Flanigan, "Nest Eggs Cushioned from Market's Drop: Retirement, Diversified Investments Have Kept Pensions from Falling As Far As Key Stock Indexes," *Los Angeles Times*, July 26, 2002, p. A1.

8. Ibid.

9. Two of the three proposals from the president's commission, which are analyzed in Figure 5, advocate personal accounts investing roughly 3 percent of wages. For uniformity of analysis, 3 percent accounts are used in this chart as well, though there would be no qualitative difference in analyzing an account investing a larger portion of the payroll tax.

10. This idea of Social Security wealth is helpful in comparing the monthly retirement benefits that the current system could produce relative to personal accounts. However, contributions to Social Security do not produce wealth in a conventional sense. Unlike money in a personal account, a worker cannot pass on the money paid into Social Security, nor does he have legal ownership or control over it.

11. Orlo R. Nichols, Michael D. Clingman, and Milton P. Glanz, "Internal Real Rates of Return under the OASDI Program for Hypothetical Workers," Social Security Administration, Office of the Chief Actuary, Actuarial Note no. 144, June 2001.

12. For more information on proposals from the President's Commission, see Andrew G. Biggs, "Perspectives on the President's Commission to Strengthen Social Security," Cato Institute Social Security Paper no. 27, August 22, 2002.

13. This point is worth noting, because some people argue that straightforward comparisons between the return paid by a pay-as-you-go system like Social Security and the return from a funded system are not always appropriate, in that the first generation entering the funded system must honor the benefit obligations amassed under the pay-as-you-go program. See John Geanakoplos, Olivia S. Mitchell, and Stephen P. Zeldes, "Would a Privatized Social Security System Really Pay a Higher Rate of Return?" National Bureau of Economic Research Working Paper no. 6713, August 1998. Nevertheless, this fact does not render meaningless the comparisons that are based on market returns. The change in the average return under a reformed system depends in large part on how the transition to personal accounts is financed— doing so by increasing taxes would likely lower net returns, by reducing other government spending would likely increase returns, and by issuing debt would leave returns unchanged. Nevertheless, comparison of market returns to the offset interest rates incorporated in reform proposals shows that at the margin returns would increase. Hence, individuals faced with the option of investing part of their payroll

taxes in an account could be reasonably assured of increasing their returns from Social Security as a whole by doing so.

14. See, for instance, Bob Kerrey and Warren Rudman, "Social Security Shell Game," *Washington Post*, August 12, 2002, p. A15.

15. Assuming that the offset interest rate, as used in the commission proposals, equaled the interest rate earned by the Social Security trust fund (assumed to be 3 percent annually after inflation). Two commission plans have offset interest rates below the trust fund rate, which can be accomplished as other measures in the plan bring the traditional system to solvency. The commission's Model 1 has an offset interest rate above the trust fund rate, which means that account holders are effectively subsidizing the traditional system (even if account holders themselves would also receive higher benefits by virtue of choosing an account).

16. Congressional Research Service, "Social Security Reform: The Effect of Economic Variability on Individual Accounts and Their Annuities," February 28, 2002.

17. U.S. General Accounting Office, "Social Security: Issues in Evaluating Rates of Return with Market Investments," August 1999, p. 6.

18. Assume that for a set of values $a1, a2, a3, \ldots an$, the mean (or average) value is designated m. The deviation of each value from the mean is $|m - a1|$, $|m - a2|$, etc. The standard deviation of the set is the square root of the mean of the squares of these deviations, i.e., $[(|m - a1|2 + \ldots |m - an|2)/n]1/2$. When a set of values is normally distributed in a bell-shaped curve, 68 percent of the data points will rest within one standard deviation of the mean, 95 percent within two standard deviations, and 99.7 percent within three standard deviations. Hence, if the standard deviation of stock returns over 30-year holding periods is 2 percentage points with a mean return of 7 percent after inflation, we can assume that roughly two-thirds of the returns are between 5 and 9 percent and only 1 in 20 is either less than 3 or greater than 11 percent.

19. Hans Riemer, Campaign for America's Future/2030 Center, Testimony before the President's Commission to Strengthen Social Security, October 18, 2001.

20. More detailed analysis is contained in Melissa Hieger and William Shipman, "Common Objections to a Market-Based Social Security System: A Response," Cato Institute Social Security Paper no. 10, July 22, 1997.

21. Individuals can purchase such a diversified portfolio at low cost via funds tracking the Wilshire 5000 index, which tracks the prices of all U.S.-headquartered equity securities with readily available price data (now numbered at slightly more than 6,300, though the "5000" moniker remains).

22. BankruptcyData.com.

23. The arithmetic mean return would equal approximately 0.7 percent annually.

24. 1999 Technical Panel on Assumptions and Methods, "Report to the Social Security Advisory Board," November 1999, p. 27, www.ssab.org. Since World War II, the equity premium has increased. Several factors may account for this rise. First, following the Great Depression investors demanded a higher premium for stocks in compensation for the higher perceived risks they were undertaking. Hence, stock returns from 1946 to 1997 averaged 7.5 percent after inflation, 0.5 percentage points higher than the average since 1802.

25. At the same time, rising inflation reduced the real returns from fixed income investments such as bonds. The consumer price index rose at an annual rate of 4.3 percent from 1946 to 1997, versus a 1.3 percent annual rise throughout American

history. The effect of inflation was to reduce the real return from short- and long-term bonds to 0.5 and 1.1 percent annually, versus their historical returns of 2.9 and 3.5 percent after inflation. Jeremy J. Siegel, *Stocks for the Long Run* (New York: McGraw-Hill, 1998), p. 15. In the absence of historical events such as the depression and postwar inflation, one could expect that the equity premium would return to something closer to its historical average.

26. A 2000 survey of 226 financial economists found an average forecast for the equity risk premium over the next 30 years of roughly 5 percent, with pessimistic- and optimistic-case forecasts at 2–3 percent and 12–13 percent, respectively. Ivo Welch, "Views of Financial Economists on the Equity Premium and Other Issues," *Journal of Business* 73, no. 4 (October 2000): 501–37. The average of the economists' forecasts was an arithmetic mean equity premium of 7 percent; given historical volatility, this number translates to a geometric mean equity premium of roughly 5 percent. The Technical Panel to the independent Social Security Advisory Board recommended an equity premium of 3 percent over the 3 percent real return assumed for the bonds in Social Security's trust fund, thus implying 6 percent real annual returns from equities in the future. 1999 Technical Panel on Assumptions and Methods, p. 27. Social Security's own independent actuaries assume a 6.5 percent real annual return from equities over the long run. For details, see Stephen C. Goss, "Equity Yield Assumptions Used by the Office of the Chief Actuary, Social Security Administration, to Develop Estimates for Proposals with Trust Fund and/or Individual Account Investments," in "Estimating the Real Rate of Return on Stocks over the Long Term," report to the Social Security Advisory Board, August 2001.

27. The *Dow 36,000* thesis takes this widely accepted premise to its extremes. Authors Glassman and Hassett argue that because stocks are no more risky over the long run than bonds, rational investors should be willing to pay the same for stocks as they would for bonds producing a similar cash flow. Once the correct price had been reached—36,000 for the Dow Jones Industrials Index, the authors speculate—stocks would produce long-term returns similar to those of bonds. Hence, a larger equity premium (and higher returns) in the short term followed by a smaller premium (and lower returns) in the long term. See James K. Glassman and Kevin A. Hassett, *Dow 36,000: The New Strategy for Profiting from the Coming Rise in the Stock Market*, 1st ed. (New York: Times Business, 1999). An abridged version of the argument is available at www.theatlantic.com/issues/99sep/9909dow.htm.

28. Source: New York Stock Exchange statistics archive.

29. See Zvi Bodie, "On the Risk of Stocks in the Long Run," *Financial Analysts Journal* 51, no. 3 (May–June 1995): 18–22.

30. A "put" option allows the holder to sell an asset at a designated price at a designated time in the future. A "call" option allows the holder to purchase an asset at a designated price at a designated time. So-called European puts and calls allow the sale only at the precise time designated; American puts and calls allow the sale at any time prior to the designated date. Bodie's analysis assumes the use of European options.

31. Bodie is clearly correct that, on the one hand, the degree of *possible* losses increases over the long term, if we assume that repeated annual losses compound year after year. On the other hand, if the standard deviation of stock returns declines over time, then longer holding periods should tend to average out gains and losses. Hence, while a longer holding period increases the likelihood of a single disastrous year of stock returns, it also increases the time available for recovery.

Taylor and Brown argue that Bodie inappropriately "assumes that the annualized standard deviation of 20 percent is appropriate for all holding periods. This assumption of a constant annualized standard deviation of returns across all time horizons ensures that he will get the answer he desires." Richard Taylor and Donald J. Brown, "On the Risk of Stocks in the Long Run: A Note," *Financial Analysts Journal* 52, no. 2 (March–April 1996): 69–71. Ferguson and Leistikow counter Bodie's argument in a somewhat different way. Bodie imagines a put option allowing the holder to sell a stock at a future date for the same price at which he could sell a short-term bond, thus assuring the holder of at least the risk-free rate of return. Because Bodie's formula showed the price of this option rising over time, he concluded that the risks of holding equities similarly rose with time. Ferguson and Leistikow imagine a similar but opposite option: a call option that allowed the holder of a risk-free asset to sell it at a future date for the same price as a stock. If an option enabling one to sell the stock at the bond price rose in price over time, one would assume that an option enabling one to sell a bond at the stock price would fall over time. But under Bodie's methodology, the bond-for-stock call option would rise in price over time, just as the stock-for-bond put option did. This counterintuitive result, Ferguson and Leistikow argue, "justifies a reexamination of Bodie's methodology and conclusions." Robert Ferguson and Dean Leistikow, "On the Risk of Stocks in the Long Run: A Comment," *Financial Analysts Journal* 52, no. 2 (March–April 1996): 67–68. See also, Mike Dempsey et al., "On the Risk of Stocks in the Long Run: A Resolution to the Debate?" *Financial Analysts Journal* 52, no. 5 (September–October 1996): 57–62.

32. Cato Institute/Zogby International, conducted July 8–12, 2002. Sample size: 1109, margin of error: ±3.1 percent, www.socialsecurity.org/zogby/zogby-2001.pdf.

33. Cato Institute/Zogby International, conducted July 29–August 2, 1999. Sample size: 1,250, margin of error: ±3 percent, www.socialsecurity.org/zogby/fullreport.pdf.

PART V

THE PUBLIC

17. Public Opinion and Private Accounts: Measuring Risk and Confidence in Rethinking Social Security

John Zogby

The results of the 2002 congressional elections surprised many people. In the 20 years since the late house speaker Tip O'Neill termed Social Security the "third rail of American politics," you were more likely to find politicians attacking mom or apple pie than talking seriously about Social Security reform. As the national retirement program slipped closer to financial insolvency and the rate of return for young workers threatened to turn negative, politicians in Washington alternately turned a blind eye to the program's plight or mindlessly demagogued any whiff of reform.

For the 2002 elections, Democrats certainly tried to keep the rail charged. In race after race across the country, Democratic candidates attacked their Republican opponents for having "a secret plan to privatize Social Security." Advertisements equated proposals to allow younger workers to privately invest a portion of their Social Security taxes through individual accounts to Enron or a "Las Vegas gamble," designed to help the candidate's "wealthy Wall Street backers." Allies from anti-reform groups, like the labor-backed Campaign for America's Future, added millions of dollars of their own commercials, as well as ground troops.

Democratic Party spokesmen called the campaign "a referendum on the future of Social Security." The Democratic National Convention Web site even featured a cartoon of President Bush pushing senior citizens off a cliff to their deaths. But in the end, in every race where Social Security was a major issue, the pro-account candidate won.

Originally published as Cato Institute Social Security Paper no. 29, January 6, 2003, and updated to reflect current information.

Figure 1
SUPPORT FOR AND OPPOSITION TO INDIVIDUAL ACCOUNTS

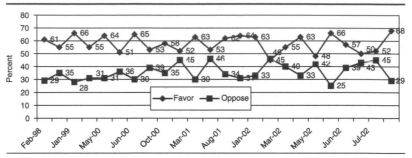

NOTE: Questions included do not mention either the risk that Social Security will collapse or that private investments will lose money.

Perhaps the election outcome should not have been so surprising. A growing body of evidence from public opinion polls shows that, in recent years, public confidence in Social Security has begun to decline, especially among younger Americans. This is entirely reasonable given Social Security's looming financial crisis and the likelihood that it will not be able to pay promised levels of benefits (see Figure 1).

Moreover, a growing number of Americans have been willing to consider alternatives to traditional Social Security. In particular, a majority of Americans have been willing to support the concept of using a portion of Social Security contributions to create private retirement accounts. Under that proposal, younger workers would be able to privately invest some or all of their Social Security taxes in individual accounts, similar to IRAs or 401(k) plans.

The largest single reason for this shift in public opinion is the growth of the investor class over the last 25 years, sparked in no small measure by the advent of defined contribution retirement planning in the form of IRA, 401(k), and Keogh accounts (see Figure 2).

Those retirement accounts have dramatically improved the economic outlook of retirees and have grown significantly as a proportion of elderly income. Compared with Social Security, private retirement accounts offer these key advantages: ownership of funds invested, the freedom to direct investments, and the opportunity to participate in the historically solid growth of the U.S. stock market.

Figure 2
Sources of Retirement Income

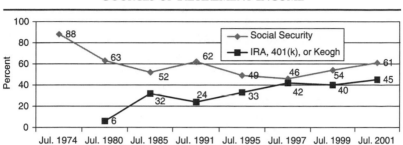

SOURCE: ASW Roper. Respondents were asked: "Are there any of these things that you feel fairly sure you can count on as a source of income during your retirements years? Which ones? Social Security, IRA, 401(k), or Keogh account?"

When told that Social Security could offer similar aspects of owner-ship freedom and opportunity while retaining its original mission as a buffer of economic stability, it is no surprise to find that Americans support proposals to allow workers to invest at least a portion of their Social Security taxes through individual accounts.

That said, differences in the language used in survey instruments yield different polling results. This paper will address and clarify the record of public opinion research with respect to Social Security and support for plans to allow private retirement accounts.

Analysis of Support Questions

A number of different questions are used to measure support for Social Security. Among those that describe a plan for private investment of Social Security taxes, the two most common types are differentiated by the mention of investor risk.

As might be expected, support levels are generally lower when respondents are told that private investments may risk significantly lower Social Security returns (see Table 1).

The problem with questions like the latter is an imbalance in the statement of risk. Although there is risk in private investments, polling results have consistently shown that Americans also perceive risk in Social Security and are not confident that they will realize an adequate return for the taxes they have paid.

Table 1
TWO TYPES OF INDIVIDUAL ACCOUNT QUESTIONS

2002	Source	Question	Support	Oppose
		No Risk Mentioned		
July 2002	Zogby International	There are some in government who advocate changing the Social Security system to give younger workers the choice to invest a portion of their Social Security taxes through individual accounts similar to IRAs or 401(k) plans. Would you strongly support, somewhat support, somewhat oppose or strongly oppose this plan?	68	29
		Risk Mentioned		
July 2002	Hart-Teeter/ NBC/*Wall Street Journal*	One proposal would allow people to put a portion of their Social Security payroll taxes into personal retirement accounts that would be invested in stocks and bonds. Some people think that individuals would have more money for retirement if they were allowed to invest and manage some of their Social Security payroll taxes themselves. Others think that it is too risky and could leave some people without adequate money for retirement if the stock market were to decline in value significantly. Do you favor or oppose this proposal?	41	55

Critics who dismiss support for personal accounts take the financial stability of Social Security for granted. In one example Bernard Roshco, former editor of *Public Opinion Quarterly*, described support for accounts as "soft," based on the response to the following question quoted from an August 1998 poll conducted by Princeton Survey Research Associates:

360

> We'd like your opinion on what policy makers' priorities
> should be when they are making decisions about Social Secu-
> rity's future: keeping Social Security as a program with a
> guaranteed monthly benefit based on a person's earnings,
> [or] letting workers invest some of their own Social Security
> contributions themselves even though an exact benefit would
> not be guaranteed? (61 percent to 31 percent in favor of the
> "guaranteed" benefit).[1]

The problem is, Social Security benefits are not guaranteed. This is a matter of long established Supreme Court precedent (*Flemming v. Nestor*, 1960; *Helvering v. Davis*, 1936).[2] The Court has been consistent in considering Social Security contributions as taxes, which convey no contractual or property rights to recipients and are subject to change or revocation.[3]

Moreover, future Social Security benefits are far from guaranteed in a financial sense, as the program faces significant financing problems. Quite simply, the program cannot pay the promised level of future benefits given the current level of tax revenue. In the future, benefits will have to be cut or taxes raised.[4]

Notwithstanding its falsity, the "guaranteed benefit" rhetoric is used as a club to move opinion against private accounts. The 1983 amendments' retirement age increase provisions question any meaningful notion of a guarantee and imply a slippery slope of difficult choices that can seriously erode the terms of the guarantee.

A more balanced measurement of risk includes both the market risk of private investments and the risk that Social Security will be unable to pay promised benefits. When asked to choose between risk statements, recent results show that similar percentages of Americans perceive Social Security to be too risky as perceive private accounts to be too risky (see Table 2).

It is worth noting that the perception of risk in private investments did not grow in 2002, even in the wake of severe market declines amid a constant barrage of headlines decrying corporate corruption.

When asked whether the Enron collapse showed that the market was too risky and that Social Security should remain as it is, only 29 percent agreed. In contrast, 64 percent chose the statement, "The Enron scandal shows that people need more choice and more control over their retirement savings, including allowing workers the option

Table 2
PERCEPTION OF RISK

Date	Dow Jones Industrial Average	Percentage of Respondents in Agreement
July 2002	9,239 (7/2/02)	
Statement A:	Allowing workers to invest a portion of their Social Security taxes would be too risky because individuals might lose their money if the market performs poorly.	45
Statement B:	The current Social Security system is more risky because the government cannot pay all the benefits that it has promised.	44
January 2001	10,790 (10/2/01)	
Statement A:	A privatized Social Security system would be too risky because individuals might lose their money if their investments performed poorly.	45
Statement B:	The current Social Security system is more risky because the government cannot pay all the benefits that it has promised.	39
August 1999	10,654 (8/2/99)	
Statement A:	A privatized Social Security system would be too risky because individuals might lose their money if their investments performed poorly.	33
Statement B:	The current Social Security system is more risky because the government cannot pay all the benefits that it has promised.	43

SOURCE: Zogby International, July 9–15, 2002, 1,109 likely voters, margin of error +/−3.2 percent. January 14–22, 2001; 1,070 likely voters; margin of error +/−3.2 percent. July 29–August 2, 1999; 1,205 likely voters; margin of error 3 percent.

Table 3
PERCEPTIONS OF INVESTMENT RETURNS

Which would yield higher returns?	March 2000	April 1994
Investing for yourself	80	74
The current Social Security system	7	21
Not sure	13	5

SOURCES: Rasmussen Research, March 30, 2000, 1,000 adults. The question was, "Would you have more money to live on in retirement if you invested that money [Social Security taxes], or would you have more if you relied on the government Social Security program?" Gallup, March 1994, 1,000 adults. The question was, "Do you agree or disagree: Most people could make more money by investing their retirement funds in the private sector than they could with Social Security."

to invest part of their Social Security taxes in a personal retirement account."[5]

When asked which would pay more, Social Security or private investments, polling data show that Americans are much more likely to think private investments would provide higher benefits to retirees than taxes paid into the current system. In July 2002, 48 percent of likely voters said "voluntary personal retirement accounts" would pay more compared to 30 percent who said Social Security would pay more.[6] When the question is phrased differently, Americans are even more likely to say that private investments would pay more (see Table 3).

When elements of individual account proposals other than investor risk are mentioned, support varies widely—which is not a surprise given the complexities a transition to private accounts would involve.

For example, in 1997 Hart–Teeter asked whether Americans favored or supported individual accounts after hearing that new payroll taxes and a higher federal deficit would result.[7] Not surprisingly, only 22 percent favor individual accounts in that scenario, compared to 61 percent opposed. (It is worth noting, as well, that the premise of the question is wrong. Under proposals by the President's Commission to Strengthen Social Security, for example, neither higher payroll taxes nor higher deficits would result. Moreover, because Social Security is currently unfunded by nearly $25 trillion,

Table 4
RESPONSE TO PUSH QUESTIONS

Issue	More Likely	Less Likely	No Difference	Not Sure
Economy will benefit	67	9	19	5
Social Security revenues will not cover benefits by 2014	59	12	23	5
No right to benefits under current law	57	12	16	5

SOURCE: Zogby International, July 29–August 2, 1999, 1,205 likely voters, margin of error +/−3 percent.

higher taxes or increased deficits would be required to fund promised benefits.)[8]

On the other hand, data show that Americans also respond to the benefits of individual accounts, including investment flexibility. In July 2002, 42 percent of likely voters said they would be more likely to support individual accounts when told that investment choices would include low-risk options including money market funds and bank accounts.[9] In earlier polling, suggestions that the economy would benefit from higher savings rates moved two-thirds of Americans to favor individual accounts, while the concern that there will be no benefits by 2014 and that individuals have no right to benefits under the law also encouraged support for such accounts (see Table 4).

It is also important to note that support for private investment declines dramatically when questions are worded to suggest that the government, not individuals, would be responsible for investing Social Security funds, or approving private investment of Social Security funds.

In a typical result, 62 percent of Americans said that if Social Security funds were invested in stocks and bonds, individuals should invest. Just 22 percent preferred that the government do the investing.[10]

Results of this kind occur in the overwhelming majority of public opinion polls and demonstrate that support for individual accounts is strongly connected to values of autonomy and personal choice.

Table 5
REASONS GIVEN FOR SUPPORTING INDIVIDUAL ACCOUNTS

Reason	Percentage
I, not the politicians in Washington, could control the money in my account.	39
People should be allowed to invest privately in case the Social Security system can't pay benefits as promised	26
Higher retirement benefits would result from private investment	16
Money in private accounts could be passed on to children and heirs.	14
Other	4
Not sure	1

A Matter of Values

Proponents of individual accounts have advanced many reasons for their position, including higher rates of return, better retirement benefits, fixing the program's insolvency, the inheritability of money in accounts, and the current program's unfairness to women and minorities.[11] But voter support for individual accounts may not be based on any of these reasons.

In a July 2002 poll, supporters of individual accounts were asked the reason for their support.[12] Two in five (39 percent) said they support individual accounts because such accounts would allow them to control their own money, and one-fourth (26 percent) believe that people should have the option of investing privately in case Social Security cannot pay promised benefits. Sixteen percent agreed that private accounts would yield higher retirement benefits, while 14 percent thought money invested in private accounts could be passed on to heirs (see Table 5).

Support for individual accounts may, therefore, be more a matter of basic values than of specific claims about the benefits of a system of individual accounts. Americans have internalized the issue of individual accounts as a question of controlling their own money and their own retirement. This may, in part, explain why support for individual accounts has remained strong in the face of a declining stock market. Even though people believe that there is increased

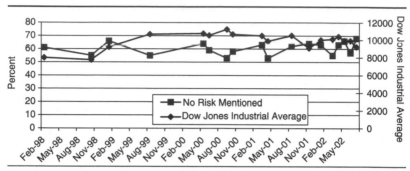

Figure 3
SUPPORT FOR INDIVIDUAL ACCOUNTS VS. DOW JONES
INDUSTRIAL AVERAGE

NOTE: In months when a support question was asked more than once, the highest measure of support is used.

risk in private investment, their basic desire to control their own money remains unchanged. In short, Americans seem willing to accept some risk, if they are able to make that choice for themselves.

Some opponents of individual accounts have suggested that support for the idea is largely a result of the 1990s stock market boom. They suggest that current declines in the market will cause Americans to reject proposals for private investment. However, it does not appear that support for individual accounts is, in fact, related to movement of the Dow Jones Industrial Average (see Figure 3).

On 9 of 17 occasions shown in Figure 3, changes to support for Social Security have not followed the Dow up or down. Of the 9 occasions when the Dow fell, on only 3 occasions was there a corresponding drop in support for Social Security. It is notable that during 3 periods of steep decline—between June and July of this year, between August and November of 2001, and between September and October of 2000—support levels rose.

Therefore, support for individual accounts is likely to remain strong. As a matter of fundamental values, outside events such as stock market fluctuations will not erode support. Therefore, politicians supporting individual accounts can count on continued public backing.

Table 6

AMERICANS' RELIANCE ON SOCIAL SECURITY VS. 401(k) PLANS

Proportion of Retirement Income	Social Security	401(k) Plan
Half or more	40	45
	14	20
Half	17	18
Less than half	30	13
Almost no part	19	23
Don't know	11	19

SOURCE: National Public Radio, Greenberg Quinlan Rosner Research (D), March 4–7, 2002, and Public Opinion Strategies (R), March 19–25, 2002; 1,510 likely voters; margin of error + / − 3.6 percent.

Conclusion: Communicating Private Accounts

The message of reforming Social Security through individual accounts is the same message that has attracted an ever-larger investing public: the American economy is a remarkable story of growth. Since the Great Depression, its recessions have been shallow and short-lived. A sensible plan to allow younger workers to privately invest a portion of their Social Security taxes can retain the aspect of a safety net while affording millions more Americans the opportunity to own a piece of the nations' success.

The shift in retirement planning away from traditional employer-provided defined benefit pensions toward dynamic opportunities to invest in markets through 401(k) and IRA accounts has offered Americans a standard against which Social Security can be judged. Table 6 shows that Americans are more likely to count on 401(k) plans than on Social Security for the bulk of their retirement income.

This does not diminish the importance of Social Security. The program remains an essential ingredient in Americans' retirement income. In fact, Americans in 2001 were more likely to say that Social Security was their most important source of retirement income than they were in 1969 (see Table 7).

It is because Social Security remains such an important piece of the retirement pie that the idea of private accounts has won solid support. In a recent poll, 41 percent said private accounts would increase benefits, while 31 percent said they would have no impact and 16 percent said benefits would decrease.[13]

Table 7
MOST IMPORTANT SOURCE OF RETIREMENT INCOME

Date	Individual Savings (%)	Employer/Union Pension (%)	Government (Social Security) (%)
1969	50	28	23
1971	42	34	22
1973	39	38	22
1975	39	35	24
1977	35	43	21
1978	36	34	28
1979	27	31	37
1981	45	31	22
1984	48	33	18
1995	53	23	20
1997	54	16	28
2001	42	27	28

In communicating private accounts, it is clear that younger voters, Republicans, and Independents offer the strongest support base, while older voters and Democrats are beginning to respond favorably to the idea.

Age is the most crucial factor in determining support for private accounts, given the impact that private accounts will have on the future of younger workers' retirement income. The data show that support has remained consistently high among younger earners between 18 and 49 years old. In recent years, support among Americans 50 and older has risen more than 50 percent (see Figure 4).

Considering party ideology and the stated positions of party leaders, it is no surprise that Republicans have been consistently more likely to support individual accounts than Democrats. Independents, meanwhile, tend to break in favor of giving workers the opportunity to invest their Social Security taxes. However, support for individual accounts still cuts across party lines (see Figure 5).

Although Americans recognize that Social Security has done much to help current seniors, they understand that the system will not be sustainable in the future. Confidence in the system is declining, and they clearly understand that reform of the system will be necessary

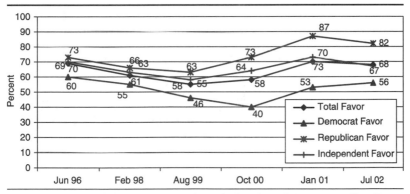

Figure 4
SUPPORT FOR INDIVIDUAL ACCOUNTS, BY AGE

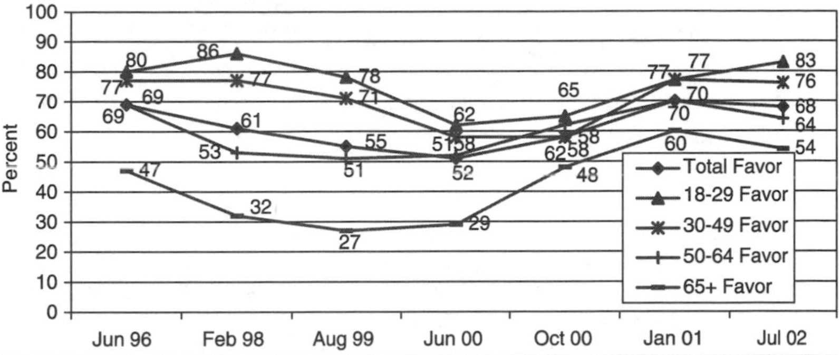

NOTE: Questions did not mention the risk that Social Security will collapse or that private investments will loose money.

Figure 5
SUPPORT FOR INDIVIDUAL ACCOUNTS, BY PARTY

NOTE: Questions did not mention the risk that Social Security will collapse or that private investments will loose money.

to ensure that younger workers will also be able to have a secure and dignified retirement.

A substantial majority of the American public supports proposals to invest a portion of their Social Security taxes through individual accounts. This public support is consistent over time and in a broad range of public opinion surveys taken by various organizations. It is driven, not by temporary fluctuations in the stock market, but by a basic American value—the desire of Americans to control their own money and their own futures.

The 2002 elections may have been the beginning of a trend. As public support emerges into the political process, politicians will no longer be able to avoid discussing the issue. The days in which campaigns were marked by demagoguery and cowardice on Social Security may have come to an end.

Notes

1. Bernard Roshco, "The Devil's Tune and the Siren's Song: Privatizing Social Security," *Public Perspective* (October/November 1999).

2. *Flemming v. Nestor*, 363 U.S. 603 (1960); *Helvering v. Davis*, 301 U.S. 619 (1937).

3. See Charles Rounds, "Property Rights: The Hidden Issue of Social Security Reform," Cato Institute Social Security Paper no. 19, April 19, 2000.

4. See Michael Tanner, "No Second Best: The Unappetizing Alternatives to Individual Accounts," Cato Institute Social Security Paper no. 24, January 29, 2002.

5. Zogby International, July 9–15, 2002, 1,109 likely voters, margin of error +/−3.1 percent.

6. Zogby International, July 19–21, 2002, 1,109 likely voters, margin of error +/−3.1 percent.

7. Hart and Teeter Research Companies, January 25–27, 1997, N = 1,002. The question was: "This proposal to allow people to invest Social Security contributions in the stock market also includes an increase in the payroll tax for current employees, as well as an increase in the federal deficit, so that benefits to current retirees also can be maintained. Do you think the benefits of allowing people to invest Social Security contributions in the stock market outweigh these costs of higher payroll taxes and deficits, or do you think the costs outweigh the benefits?"

8. See Andrew Biggs, "Perspectives on the President's Commission to Strengthen Social Security," Cato Institute Social Security Paper no. 27, August 22, 2002.

9. Zogby International, July 30–August 2, 2002, 1,008 likely voters; margin of error +/−3.2 percent.

10. Zogby International, July 9–15, 2002; 1,109 likely voters, margin of error +/−3.1 percent. "More likely" includes much more likely and somewhat more likely. "Less likely" includes much less likely and somewhat less likely.

11. See, for example, Michael Tanner, "Saving Social Security Is Not Enough," Cato Institute Social Security Paper no. 20, May 25, 2000.

12. Zogby International, July 9–15, 2002; 1,109 likely voters; margin of error +/−3.1 percent.

13. Bloomberg, April 30–May 5, 2002; 1,200 adults nationwide; margin of error +/−3 percent. The question was, "If Social Security changes into a system where individuals could choose to invest some of their own payroll tax contributions themselves, do you think this change would increase, decrease or have no impact on your retirement savings benefits?"

Contributors

Leanne Abdnor is national chairman of For Our Grandchildren, a grassroots organization promoting Social Security reform. A former vice president of the Cato Institute, she served as a member of President Bush's bipartisan Commission to Strengthen Social Security.

Andrew G. Biggs served as assistant director of the Cato Project on Social Security Choice from 1999 to 2003 and as a staff member of President Bush's bipartisan Commission to Strengthen Social Security. He is currently associate commissioner of social security for retirement policy.

Martin Feldstein is a professor of economics at Harvard University and president of the National Bureau of Economic Research.

Milton Friedman is a senior fellow at the Hoover Institution. He is the recipient of the 1976 Nobel Prize in Economics.

Robert Genetski is senior managing director of Chicago Capital and former chief economist at Chicago's Harris Bank.

Jagadeesh Gokhale is a senior fellow with the Cato Institute and a former chief economic adviser to the Federal Reserve Bank of Cleveland.

June O'Neill is Wolman Professor of Economics at the Zicklin School of Business and director of the Center for the Study of Business and Government at Baruch College, City University of New York. She was director of the Congressional Budget Office from 1995 to 1999.

José Piñera is president of the International Center for Pension Reform in Santiago, Chile, and co-chair of the Cato Project on Social

Security Choice. As Chile's minister of labor, he was largely responsible for successfully reforming that country's pension system.

Charles E. Rounds Jr. is a professor of law at Suffolk University.

Daniel Shapiro is associate professor of philosophy at West Virginia University.

Thomas F. Siems is a senior economist and policy adviser to the Federal Reserve Bank of Dallas.

Michael Tanner is director of health and welfare studies at the Cato Institute and director of Cato's Project on Social Security Choice. He is the coauthor of *A New Deal for Social Security* (1998).

John Zogby is president and CEO of Zogby International, a public opinion research firm.

Index

retirement, financial wealth at, 134
saving by, 138
shortfall of system, 133
Social Security benefit features, investing, 134
tax increases, 134–38
Lynch v. Household Finance Corp. (1972), 78

Maatz, Lisa, 167
MacBride Principles, 179
Market-based portfolios, performance of, 26–28
Marriage later in life, effect of, 113, 116–17
Massachusetts Institute of Technology, 30
Matsui, Robert, 210, 217–18, 252, 261, 262
Maximum earnings ceiling, raising of, 13–32
McCain, John, 294
Means-tested program threat of, 96–98
Median financial assets, relation to replacement rate, 85
Medicaid, rise in benefits, 42
Medical advances, effect on government-run Social Security systems, 189
Medicare
establishment of, 17
rise in benefits, 42
Meinhard v. Salmon (1928), 79
Minimum pension guarantee, politicization around, 101–2
Minorities, 147–62
alternatives to individual accounts, effect on, 181–82
bonds, ownership by, 152
business bankruptcy rates, effect of scarcity of, 153
certificates of deposit, ownership by, 152
civil rights issue, Social Security reform, 159
crime rates, effect of scarcity of, 153
deficit, 154–55
dependence on Social Security, 147
education, wealth gap and, 151
effect of current law on, 165
entrance into workforce, age, 150
family structure, wealth gap and, 151
financial crisis, effect of, 147
gifts, taxation of, 155

households owning financial assets, 152
income, minorities, whites contrasted, 152
individual accounts, benefits to, 155–58
inheritances, taxation of, 155
inner-city neighborhoods, 153
insolvency, Social Security, 154–55
interest, taxation of, 155
investment patterns, 151–52
life expectancy, 147, 148–49, 150
lower return due to, 149
life insurance, ownership, 152
males, payroll tax returns, 149
mortality, 147–49, 150
mutual funds, ownership by, 152
private pension coverage, 151–52
profits, taxation of, 155
replacement rate, Social Security, 154
retirement accounts, ownership by, 152
retirement age, effect on, 155
scarcity of investment capital, effect of, 153
shortfall, 154–55
single black man, inequity in payroll tax returns, 149
stock, ownership by, 152
transaction accounts, ownership by, 152
unemployment, periods of, 150
wealth gap, 147, 151–53
Mitchell, Olivia, 203, 322, 325, 336
Modigliani, Franco, 30
Money, control of, public desire for, 365–70
Money management expenses, per worker, individual accounts, 329–80
Moon, J. Donald, 96
Moral pluralism, celebration of, 89
Mortality, minorities, impact of Social Security, 147–49, 150
Mothers with infants, in workforce, 114
Moynihan, Daniel Patrick, 203
Munnell, Alicia, 39, 177, 178, 210, 213, 216, 219–22
Muralidhar, Arun, 30
Mutual funds, ownership by minorities, 152
Myers, Robert, 168, 177

Nadler, Jerrold, 180

381

Cato Institute

Founded in 1977, the Cato Institute is a public policy research foundation dedicated to broadening the parameters of policy debate to allow consideration of more options that are consistent with the traditional American principles of limited government, individual liberty, and peace. To that end, the Institute strives to achieve greater involvement of the intelligent, concerned lay public in questions of policy and the proper role of government.

The Institute is named for *Cato's Letters*, libertarian pamphlets that were widely read in the American Colonies in the early 18th century and played a major role in laying the philosophical foundation for the American Revolution.

Despite the achievement of the nation's Founders, today virtually no aspect of life is free from government encroachment. A pervasive intolerance for individual rights is shown by government's arbitrary intrusions into private economic transactions and its disregard for civil liberties.

To counter that trend, the Cato Institute undertakes an extensive publications program that addresses the complete spectrum of policy issues. Books, monographs, and shorter studies are commissioned to examine federal budget, Social Security, regulation, military spending, international trade, and myriad other issues. Major policy conferences are held throughout the year, from which papers are published thrice yearly in the *Cato Journal*. The Institute also publishes the quarterly magazine *Regulation*.

In order to maintain its independence, the Cato Institute accepts no government funding. Contributions are received from foundations, corporations, and individuals, and other revenue is generated from the sale of publications. The Institute is a nonprofit, tax-exempt, educational foundation under Section 501(c)3 of the Internal Revenue Code.

CATO INSTITUTE
1000 Massachusetts Ave., N.W.
Washington, D.C. 20001
www.cato.org